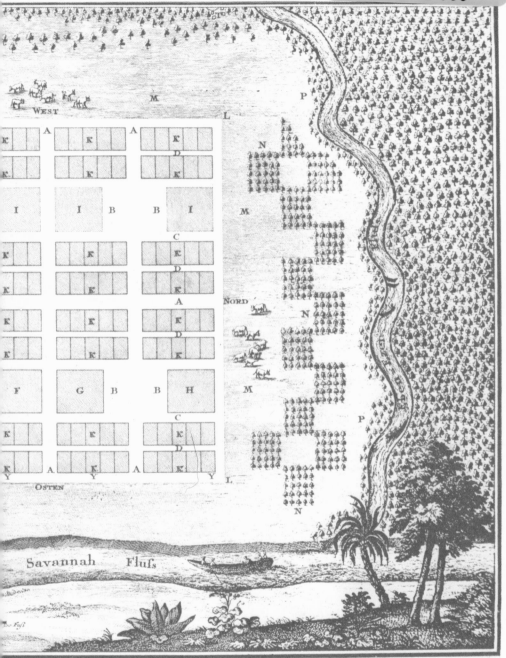

...achrichten, *13te Continuation, Erster Theil* (Halle and Augsburg, 1747).

...ollection, University of Georgia Library.

Detailed Reports on the

Salzburger Emigrants Who

Settled in America . . .

Edited by Samuel Urlsperger

TOMOCHICHI, MICO OF THE YAMACRAWS
AND HIS NEPHEW TOONAHOWI

Detailed Reports on the Salzburger Emigrants Who Settled in America . . . Edited by Samuel Urlsperger

VOLUME SIX, 1739

Translated and Edited by
GEORGE FENWICK JONES
and
RENATE WILSON

THE UNIVERSITY OF GEORGIA PRESS
ATHENS

Set in 11 on 13 point Mergenthaler Baskerville type
Printed in the United States of America

Library of Congress Cataloging in Publication Data (Revised)

Urlsperger, Samuel, 1685–1772, comp.
    Detailed reports on the Salzburger emigrants who set-
tled in America.

    (Wormsloe Foundation. Publications, no. 9–   )
    Translation of Ausführliche Nachricht von den saltz-
burgischen Emigranten, die sich in America niedergelassen haben.
    Beginning with v. 6, translated and edited by G. F.
Jones and R. Wilson, no longer published in series.
    Includes bibliographical references and indexes.
    CONTENTS: V. 1. 1733–1734.—V. 2. 1734–1735.—
[etc.]—v. 6. 1739.
    1. Salzburgers. 2. Indians of North America—
Missions. 3. Georgia—History—Colonial period, ca.
1600–1775—Sources. 4. South Carolina—Description
and travel. 5. Augsburg. Evangelisches Armenhaus.
I. Jones, George Fenwick, 1916– II. Wilson, Renate,
1930– III. Title. IV. Series.
F295.S1U813   284.1'758724   67–27137
        ISBN 0–8203–0512–x (v. 6)

Volumes 1–5 of *Detailed Reports on the Salzburger Emigrants Who Settled in America* were published as part of the
Wormsloe Foundation Publications series. The publication of volume 6 has been made possible by a grant from
the University of Maryland. The preparation of this volume was supported in part by a grant from the Program
for Translations of the National Endowment for the Humanities, an independent federal agency.

Contents

Sechste
CONTINVATION
der ausführlichen Nachricht
von den

Saltzburgischen
Emigranten,
die sich in America niedergelassen haben.

Worin enthalten sind:

I. Das Tage-Register der beyden Prediger zu Eben-Ezer in Georgien vom Jahr 1739.

II. Gedachter Prediger, wie auch anderer Briefe vom Jahr 1740.

herausgegeben
von
Samuel Urlsperger,
Des Evangelischen Ministerii in Augspurg Seniore und Pastore
der Haupt-Kirche zu St. Annen.

HALLE,
In Verlegung des Wäysenhauses, M DCC XXXXI.

Sixth

CONTINUATION

of the Detailed Reports

of the

SALZBURG

EMIGRANTS

who have settled in America

in which are contained

I. The Diary of the two ministers at Ebenezer in Georgia from the year 1739.

II. Letters from the above-mentioned ministers and other letters from the year 1740.

edited
by

SAMUEL URLSPERGER

Senior of the Evangelical Lutheran Ministry of the city of Augsburg and pastor of St. Anne's Church

---

HALLE

Published by the Orphanage Press, MDCCXXXXI

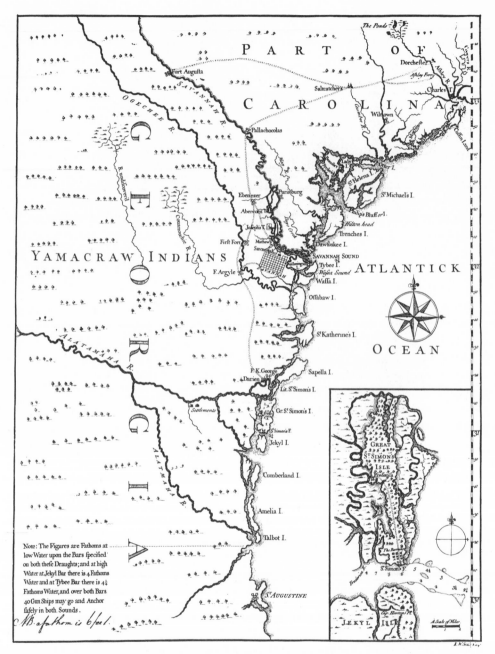

From an original in the De Renne Collection, University of Georgia Library. It is supposed to have been drawn during the period 1741–1743. It has been reproduced in several publications, including Urlsperger's *Ausführliche Nachrichten, 13te Continuation, Erster Theil* (Halle and Augsburg, 1747).

 *Introduction*

THE following reports, which cover the year 1739, were written by Johann Martin Boltzius and, during his absence or sickness, by his assistant, Israel Christian Gronau, the Lutheran ministers assigned to the Salzburger exiles at Ebenezer in the colony of Georgia. For information about the expulsion of the Protestants from Salzburg in 1731 and the reception and settlement of some two hundred of them in Georgia the reader is directed to the introductions of the previous volumes of this series and to that of Henry Newman's *Salzburger Letterbooks*.[1]

The reports for the year 1738 indicate that, having moved from the sterile and isolated spot where they first settled to the more fertile and accessible Red Bluff on the Savannah River, the Georgia Salzburgers were at last self-sustaining. The health conditions at New Ebenezer were still just as bad, however; and the mortality rate remained high. Nevertheless, those who had survived years of malaria, dysentery, and other illnesses had enough antibodies to resist them further; and they continued to function despite constant sickness. It was the new arrivals who now suffered the high mortality previously suffered by the first settlers. The population of New Ebenezer (or Ebenezer, as the new town began to be called, as the older settlement disappeared from map and memory) gradually increased through the addition of other Salzburgers, who had found refuge in Protestant cities of South Germany, and of indentured "Palatines" from Savannah.

This volume continues in the same style as the earlier ones with only minor changes. For the sake of simplicity, footnotes are now numbered according to the month rather than numbered throughout. The old, mostly Latin, names of the days of the church calendar are increasingly modernized: for example, *Dominica Oculi* is rendered as the 3rd Sunday in Lent and *Dominica Laetare* is rendered as the 4th Sunday in Lent. Since hymns usually have no true title but are identified by their opening line, however meaningless it may be out of context (especially when translated), the titles (i.e. opening lines) of hymns are given in German, and an alphabetical list is provided in Appendix I. Because the surname of the Jewish convert Johann Gottlieb Christ causes confusion in certain contexts, his Christian name is inserted to distinguish him from Jesus Christ (whose epithet in German is Christus, and therefore not in danger of being confused with the surname Christ).

As in the previous volumes, the word "Fathers" is capitalized when referring to the Salzburgers' spiritual sponsors or "Reverend Fathers": Gotthilf August Francke, Samuel Urlsperger, and Friedrich Michael Ziegenhagen. It will be noticed that Boltzius never uses the Salzburgers' Christian names except to distinguish between two of them bearing the same surname, and even then he prefers to call them "the older" or "the younger," when that is applicable. New readers are advised that, to economize on footnotes, all proper names are identified in the index.

Boltzius uses pronouns peculiarly: for example, he says he loves Kalcher and receives much good from him and her (*her* being Mrs. Kalcher, of course!). Incidentally, Boltzius never designates the Salzburger women as "Mrs." (*Frau*), that title being reserved for women of quality. Instead, he uses the feminine ending *in* (e.g., die Schweigerin, die Spielbieglerin), a suffix which has confused many historians and genealogists, who mistake it for a part of the family name. Since English has no feminine ending for this purpose, this translation uses the titles "Mrs." and "Miss," as modern usage would require. Boltzius also says that, while he was talking to a certain man, another woman came into the room; and he also speaks consistently of the "oldest" of two people. Like the good preacher that he was, he loved redundancy, since a thing repeated twice is easier to understand and comprehend and also easier to remember and recollect. Consequently, we find tautologies like "slothful and lazy" (*lass und träge*), "guide and lead" (*leiten und führen*), and "absence and short separation" (*Abwesenheit und kurtze Entfernung*). Like other preachers, Boltzius was fond of using triads of words: for example, in the short entry for 22 April we find four of them: "faith, love, and joy," "instruction, edification, and imitation," "acquaintance, company, and instruction," and "thoughts, wishes, and resolutions."

A reader unfamiliar with the technical jargon of the Pietists must pay close attention to terms like "external" (*äusserlich*), "external respectability" (*äusserliche Ehrbarkeit*), "legalistic" (*gesetzlich*), "legalistic anxiety" (*gesetzliche Unruhe*), "temptation" (*Anfechtung*), "honest" (*ehrlich*), "miserable" (*elend*), and "civil righteousness" (*bürgerliche Gerechtigkeit*), many of which will be explained a few paragraphs below or else in the notes.

As mentioned in previous volumes, Samuel Urlsperger took great liberties in editing Boltzius' reports, as editors often did in the eighteenth century; and his *Ausführliche Nachricht*[2] expunged everything that might reflect unfavorably upon the Salzburgers or the decision to settle them in Georgia. These unhappy, but usually most interesting, omissions have been restored to the previous volumes in this series through the kindness of the authorities of the Francke Foundation in Halle, who have permitted me (GFJ) to search their archives on three occasions to find and photograph the unexpurgated versions of Boltzius' reports, which had been copied into the Foundation's records.[3]

Unfortunately, these unexpurgated copies are now beginning to run out. For the year 1739 we have only part of those for July and August and for the year 1740 none survive. We do have the entire unexpurgated report for the year 1741, after which there are no more. From then on we will have to resign ourselves to the suppression of the most interesting and sensational passages, as well as the most wicked and therefore interesting people. Whenever we find a gap in the expurgated reports, such as the missing entries from 29 through 31 January in this volume, we can safely assume that Urlsperger deleted them, since Boltzius tried to make some entry, no matter how trivial, every day. This tampering with the text probably explains such discrepancies as the fact that Boltzius mentions Muggitzer's return on 10 February even though he has not mentioned his departure; Urlsperger did not wish the benefactors or potential emigrants to know that some people were displeased with Ebenezer, nor would he wish anyone to know that a Salzburger had become a slave-driver. Urlsperger is quite inconsistent with his deletions: sometimes he deletes the name Zuebli for no reason, and at other times he does not (14, 16 June); sometimes he suppresses the name Schweighofer even when the description clearly reveals the widow's identity (24 March).

It is a rare event for Boltzius to show a sense of humor, as he does in his comment of 19 March that, if it is true that all the Salzburgers do is eat and pray, then to judge by their bountiful harvest God certainly must be answering their prayers. Since man's only purpose in this vale of tears is to prepare for a happy death, frivolity is not only a vanity but also a sin. Boltzius reveals his sense of values on 20 October when he quotes the long-winded letter from Samuel Lau, the court chaplain at Wernigerode who ordained him and Gronau on their journey from Halle to Rotterdam. The pious behavior demanded by Boltzius explains why certain frivolous people like the shoemaker Reck, the schoolmaster's wife Juliana Ortmann, and the widow Rheinlaender were not happy in his celestial city. An English inhabitant of Georgia at that time exclaimed, "Oh that we had a prudent Zealous & painful Minister," a description which would have well fitted Boltzius, even if "painful" were taken in its modern meaning.

Whenever we read that a certain Mrs. N., a pious widow, has been regurgitating pious platitudes, we may be sure that it is the tedious Mrs. Schweighofer, a moral hypochondriac who was chronically concerned with her own and her children's salvation. Even though Boltzius was always refreshed by her edifying expressions, most of our worldly generation would have liked to report her to the Mikado, at whose court "All prosy, dull, society sinners Who chatter and bleat and bore, are sent to hear sermons By mystical Germans Who preach from ten to four." But alas, the good widow would have enjoyed such mystical sermons even if they lasted until five or six, provided they did not conflict with prayer meeting, repetition hour, or house devotions. In marvelling at this excess of religious fervor at Ebenezer and the time spent in devotions, we must remember that it was largely the same people who participated in prayer meetings and that they represented only a fraction of the entire populace, since Boltzius' house would not hold many people. Many families remain almost entirely out of our view for long periods and emerge only in case of sickness or as signers of petitions or as harvesters of crops.

Although Boltzius was a Pietist, his Christianity was strictly orthodox Lutheran; and nearly all the dogma he acquired from his mentors at the University of Halle can be traced back to Martin Luther himself. During the year 1739 Boltzius' chief concern seems to have been to persuade his parishioners that salvation can be achieved only through faith and not through good works. To understand his use of the terms "faith," "justification," "work-righteousness," etc., we need only consult the opening paragraphs of Luther's preface to the book of Galatians, which he wrote in Latin in the year 1535 and in which he presents his interpretation of St. Paul's argument in this epistle. Those readers averse to theology are free to skip the next four paragraphs.

"First of all, we must speak of the argument, that is, of the issue with which Paul deals in this epistle. The argument is this: Paul wants to establish the doctrine of faith, grace, the forgiveness of sins or Christian righteousness, so that we may have a perfect knowledge and know the difference between Christian righteousness and all other kinds of righteousness. For righteousness is of many kinds. There is a political righteousness, which the emperor, the princes of the world, philosophers, and lawyers consider. There is also a ceremonial righteousness, which human traditions teach, as, for example, the traditions of the pope and other traditions. Parents and teachers may teach this righteousness without danger, because they do not attribute to it any power to make satisfaction for sin, to placate God, and to earn grace; but they teach that these ceremonies are necessary only for moral discipline and for certain observances. There is, in addition to these, yet another righteousness, the righteousness of the Law or of the Decalog, which Moses teaches. We, too, teach this, but after the doctrine of faith.

"Over and above all these there is the righteousness of faith or Christian righteousness, which is to be distinguished most carefully from all the others. For they are all contrary to this righteousness, both because they proceed from the laws of emperors, the traditions of the pope, and the commandments of

God, and because they consist in our works and can be achieved by us with 'purely natural endowments,' as the scholastics teach, or from a gift of God. For these kinds of the righteousness of works, too, are gifts of God, as are all the things we have. But this most excellent righteousness, the righteousness of faith, which God imputes to us through Christ without works, is neither political nor ceremonial nor legal nor work-righteousness but is quite the opposite; it is a merely passive righteousness, while all the others, listed above, are active. For here we work nothing, render nothing to God; we only receive and permit someone else to work in us, namely, God. Therefore it is appropriate to call the righteousness of faith or Christian righteousness 'passive.' This is a righteousness hidden in a mystery, which the world does not understand. In fact, Christians themselves do not adequately understand it or grasp it in the midst of their temptations. Therefore it must always be taught and continually exercised. And anyone who does not grasp or take hold of it in afflictions and terrors of conscience cannot stand. For there is no comfort of conscience so solid and certain as is this passive righteousness.

"But such is human weakness and misery that in the terrors of conscience and in the danger of death we look at nothing except our own works, our worthiness, and the Law. When the Law shows us our sin, our past life immediately comes to our mind. Then the sinner, in his great anguish of mind, groans and says to himself: 'Oh, how damnably I have lived! If only I could live longer! Then I would amend my life.' Thus human reason cannot refrain from looking at active righteousness, that is, its own righteousness; nor can it shift its gaze to passive, that is, Christian righteousness, but it simply rests in the active righteousness. So deeply is this evil rooted in us, and so completely have we acquired this unhappy habit! Taking advantage of the weakness of our nature, Satan increases and aggravates these thoughts in us. Then it is impossible for the conscience to avoid being more seriously troubled, confounded, and frightened. For it is impossible for the human mind to conceive any comfort of itself, or to look only at grace amid its consciousness and terror of sin, or consistently to reject all discussion of works. To do this is beyond human power and thought. Indeed, it is even

beyond the Law of God. For although the Law is the best of all
things in the world, it still cannot bring peace to a terrified conscience but makes it even sadder and drives it to despair. For by
the Law sin becomes exceedingly sinful (Rom. 7 : 13).

"Therefore the afflicted conscience has no remedy against despair and eternal death except to take hold of the promise of
grace offered in Christ, that is, this righteousness of faith, this
passive or Christian righteousness, which says with confidence:
'I do not seek active righteousness. I ought to have and perform
it; but I declare that even if I did have it and perform it, I cannot trust in it or stand up before the judgment of God on the
basis of it. Thus I put myself beyond all active righteousness, all
righteousness of my own or of the divine Law, and I embrace
only that passive righteousness which is the righteousness of
grace, mercy, and the forgiveness of sins.' In other words, this is
the righteousness of Christ and of the Holy Spirit, which we do
not perform but receive, which we do not have but accept, when
God the Father grants it to us through Jesus Christ." [4]

Again and again we see members of Boltzius' congregation
who do not understand this "passive righteousness" or "justification by faith" and therefore fear damnation under the Law
because of their sins; and we see Boltzius constantly reassuring
them of the comfort of conscience afforded by passive righteousness and promising them the grace offered in Christ. It is
to this end that he stirs up their memories of past sins committed in Salzburg or Germany, as in the case of the woman
mentioned on 22 January who restored a portion of what she
had stolen years before while in service. Once the sinners have
confessed and attempted restitution, Boltzius tries to free them
from their "legalistic fears," or their fear of punishment under
the Law.

Boltzius is particularly severe towards those misguided souls
who put their faith in good works and hope to achieve salvation
on their own merits. Of course Boltzius, like Luther, was not
opposed to good works, as we see in the entry for 28 March,
when he tells a woman that Luther "considered a faithful and
patient execution of one's work to be a prayer and God-pleasing
service." However, good works must be the result of faith, not a
means to an end. The righteousness of the Law applies to the

Old Adam, whereas Christian righteousness or justification by faith belongs to the New Man who has been reborn in the wounds of Jesus. Before Held's wife died (17 August), Boltzius had feared she was not yet truly converted but comforted herself in her previous good behavior, and therefore he had preached eloquently against self-justification (*eigene Gerechtigkeit*), false comfort (*falschen Trost*), and self-made comfort (*selbstgemachten Trost*).

Despite all the sorrow and suffering he had witnessed during his five years in Georgia, Boltzius had lost none of his optimism, an attitude inevitable in one who believes in God's omniscience, omnipotence, and loving kindness. He often taught, as he did on 9 May, that "even the cross, physical want, and trials are benefits bestowed by the Lord," so it is not surprising that his parishioners also realized that what appears to be evil is often a blessing in disguise, as was the case on 16 January when a woman recognized that her protracted illness was sent by God for her own good. Regardless of his faith in the Lord, Boltzius knew that God helps those who keep their powder dry: on 12 May, while assuring a cowherd of God's help against snakebite, he nonetheless had a pair of leather leggings made for him.

Although God is a loving God, He is also a just God; therefore a person who is punished must be guilty (unless, of course, it is merely a loving chastisement for his own good). When Boltzius learned on 1 February that a French doctor from Purysburg had been drowned with his entire family, it was clearly a judgment of God, because they were all atheists. Likewise, when Boltzius learned two weeks later that his former pupil Johann Jacob Metzscher had drowned along with his younger brother and sister in the same disaster, it was a judgment against their father for keeping his house in disorder; besides that, the boy had begun using blasphemous language since leaving Ebenezer (21 February). The smaller children were, it would seem, victims of collective guilt. When some Scots drowned in an accident somewhat later, Boltzius mentioned in his entry for 22 March that they must have been drunk on St. Patrick's Day. Perhaps Boltzius did not distinguish between St. Patrick and St. Andrew, but undoubtedly he was right about the Highlanders' propensity to drink.

These reports reveal not only Boltzius' theology, but also the way he conducted his church services; church historians should be pleased with his accounts of catechism lessons (18 October), church penance (16 December), and confirmation (23 December). Also of interest is the account of musical life at Ebenezer, still entirely in the service of God. Unlike the Quakers, the Pietists were not averse to good music, provided it was for religious purposes. Before allowing the children to join the singing hour on 21 December, Boltzius had to assure himself that they would bring not only their mouths but also their hearts full of praise. His description of polyphonic music on 25 December is surely the oldest such account in Georgia; the introduction of polyphonic music possibly helps explain why most of the hymns mentioned in 1739 were new to the congregation. Also of interest, and pointing toward the future, were the "adult education courses" provided for those like Simon Reiter and Margaretha Berenberger who had not had an opportunity to learn to read in their youth (22 June, 18 July). Young Theobald Kieffer had an even more difficult task to perform in teaching his father's slaves to read, since they had to learn German first (14 May).

In reading these reports, the reader may wonder whether the good pastor was not sometimes duped by his parishioners. When he finds a married couple praying in the forest on 11 October, we ask ourselves whether or not they might have fallen on their knees only after seeing him approach. When he finds two women walking together on 4 May, we suspect that possibly they had been talking about something other than salvation. We may also question whether tears really flowed as copiously as reported; if we are to believe their pastor, the Salzburgers of Ebenezer must have dampened many a handkerchief. The tearful emotionalism of the Pietists stemmed from the Biblical idea of tears as an indication of remorse, and this Pietist emotionalism may have been the source of the many tears shed by the heroes of the Romantic Movement, a literary trend that arose in the part of Germany inhabited by the Pietists.

Although Boltzius was primarily interested in the salvation of his parishioners' souls, he was responsible for the survival of their bodies as well, a responsibility he had inflicted upon himself by expelling the two secular commissioners, Baron von

Reck and Jean Vat. His method of exhausting his financial re-
sources and even going into debt for the orphanage and church
was very astute; he knew that God would bail him out through
some human agency (2 January).

It should be noted that, as is the case in all undeveloped lands,
nearly all enterprise in the American colonies was based on
debt. Most settlers arrived in South Carolina and Georgia in
debt to the ship's captain or to the planter who bought their
indenture. When redeemed, they were usually still penniless
and had to contract debts to acquire their tools and cattle. Interest was at usurious rates, since the high mortality made lending
a risky business. In South Carolina, and later in Georgia, the
planters received free land, which was worthless in its natural
state but had enough value when cleared and cultivated to stand
as collateral for further loans so that the planter could purchase
more land and perhaps a slave or two, which were then mort-
gaged in order to buy more land and slaves. As a result, wealth
and power did not lie in the hands of the planters, as our Ante-
bellum literature would have us believe, but in the hands of
merchant-moneylenders, who sometimes maintained plantations on the side, as Samuel Montagut did (23 May). Since
nearly all transactions were made on credit, a merchant had to
be a moneylender and charge high enough interest to cover
losses. It will be noted that most of the wealthy Englishmen whom Boltzius met and mentioned were moneylending
merchants.

In view of the deficit economy of the area, the people of
Purysburg and Savannah were amazed that the Salzburgers
paid cash and did not ask for credit (9 June); these frugal
mountain folk wished to keep their economic freedom. It will
be noticed that they pinched their pennies to buy cattle, that
being their chief source of income and status, and that by 27
July 1739 they had 250 head. Boltzius' strong sense of business
ethics is shown by his concern for the debt owed to the Swiss
merchant Schlatter, who had sent a benefaction some years earlier along with an unsolicited shipment of linen for sale.[5] This
linen had been sold at the storehouse in Savannah by Thomas
Causton, who then failed to compensate the sender.

Perhaps the most important event in Ebenezer during the

year 1739 was the arrival of Georg Sanftleben, the Silesian carpenter who had returned from Ebenezer to Germany to fetch his sister, some tradesmen, and some unmarried women. Sanftleben wrote a travelogue, as Boltzius urged him to do (2 July); and we can also follow his journey through a voluminous correspondence maintained by Urlsperger and the Trustees.[6] Sanftleben's party had sailed from England on 29 March on board the *Charles*, with Captain Haeramond,[7] just two weeks after the Salzburgers had sent a long letter petitioning Oglethorpe to have more Salzburgers sent over.[8] The captain treated them well and they arrived safely in Charleston; but the journey from there to Ebenezer in an open boat in bad weather caused illness, and they were all sick upon arrival, as Boltzius observed on 25 July.

Despite his sickness, the saintly shoemaker Johann Caspar Ulich married one of his travelling companions, Margaretha Egger, two weeks after arriving but then died three weeks later. Gertrud Lackner, the sister of Martin Lackner of Ebenezer, never recovered from her sickness and slowly wasted away. The three other surviving women eventually married or were otherwise provided for; the widow Ulich soon married Martin Lackner, as her friend Gertrud had urged on her deathbed. With everyone sick, two fatally, this group closely matched the performance of the first settlers. We do not know why Elisabeth Sanftleben had difficulty in adapting, unless perhaps she could not find a husband even in that favorable matrimonial market (18 October).

The next most important events of 1739 were the construction of Boltzius' house, which was begun the second day of the year, and of the church, which was begun shortly thereafter. Although Boltzius was delighted with his house and thought it would last a century, the great Lutheran patriarch Heinrich Melchior Mühlenberg was greatly disappointed in it when he visited Ebenezer some thirty-five years later.[9]

Like the Germans of Germantown in Pennsylvania, those of Ebenezer were outspoken opponents of slavery, on both moral and practical grounds. It is impossible to know whether Boltzius' views were innate or whether they had been influenced by those of Oglethorpe, with which they largely agreed; but in any case they were forcefully expressed, as we see in his and his parishioners' letters. His views regarding Negroes were ambivalent: he considered them innately vicious, yet he realized that they were brutally treated (13 March). The "Moors" who had been lent to the Salzburgers as sawyers upon their arrival had been very savage, and one had injured another seriously with a knife, after which the Salzburgers stood in dread of them. On the other hand, on his trip to Charleston in May 1735, Boltzius had found that they were poor benighted heathens who thirsted for knowledge of Jesus.[10]

In addition to information about the Salzburgers themselves, these reports also give us insights into life in Georgia in general, much of which is not recorded elsewhere. We see the nebulous character Falk, a Swede who claimed to be an ordained Lutheran minister and wished to preach to the Germans, even though he had no credentials and could hardly speak German (3 January); and we see the sinister Spanish spy who called himself Anton Masig and claimed to be a German from Cologne (31 July). We also hear the murmurings of Malcontents in Savannah, who wished to cast off all the restrictions of the Trustees (18 February), and we find an amusing description of the Indians who visited Savannah on 6 March.

Previous volumes in this series have made occasional reference to the "Palatines," the indentured servants in Savannah, who had come not only from the Rhenish Palatinate but also from other parts of Germany. Boltzius, who looked out for their spiritual needs once a month and gave Holy Communion to the few who merited it, generally spoke negatively of them, because they were not so docile as his captive congregation at Ebenezer. Besides that, many were Reformed and preferred to wait for the occasional visits of the lazy and profligate Reformed minister Chifelle of Purysburg, even though he could hardly speak German.[11] Boltzius' attitude toward these so-called "Dutch" servants was as ambivalent as it was towards the Negroes: he accused them of sloth and disloyalty, yet at the same time he realized that they were being shamefully mistreated. In general he took the side of the English authorities when the Dutch came to him with their grievances, and he resented their accepting his spiritual ministry merely as an excuse to win him as their advocate.

In one case Boltzius' action brought him little credit among the Dutch in Savannah, namely when he was summoned to endorse a coroner's report exonerating the bailiff John Fallowfield[12] for having struck and killed a servant who resisted arrest (7 March). It was at this time that Boltzius received thirty pounds for Gronau's house[13]; we hope no one is reminded of another payment of thirty pieces of silver.

The British authorities were as ambivalent about the Dutch servants as was Boltzius: they constantly complained of their sloth and disloyalty, yet they had to admit that they were the best servants that could be had.[14] On 21 November 1739 Colonel William Stephens, the Trustees' representative in Georgia, wrote that "the Palatine servants sent over from Holland on board Cap.ᵗ Hewet are the most lazy of all, but those which went with Cap.ᵗ Thomson are good, and would have done well, if immediately on their arrival they had been made free, a little land given them, and a tolerable support in the beginning."[15] Here we have the crux of the matter: human beings, white or black, seldom work well if they are not to share in the proceeds of their work.

The entry for 7 May begins a melodrama that might well serve as the basis of a romantic novel. Boltzius learns that two German servants are living in sin and thus reflecting badly on the Germans and, indirectly, on the Salzburgers. The man, having been impoverished by his spendthrift wife and her relatives in Germany, had fled with his serving girl and had married her, assuming that his previous marriage was terminated. With much persuasion, and a bit of help from the authorities, Boltzius was able to break up this common-law marriage; but the end of this soap opera belongs better to the following year, when the woman becomes part of Ebenezer history. The same entry relates another scandal, namely that of a Roman Catholic girl who fled to St. Augustine after leaving her baby on a Jew's doorstep. Boltzius did not doubt that the Jew was the father. It seems probable, however, that the mother had selected him as the only German in Savannah with sufficient means to support the child, for it is quite apparent that the man in question was the righteous Benjamin Sheftal, the advocate of the Germans in Savannah. The Christian authorities, obviously pleased by the embarrassment of this pious man, held him responsible but did help support the child. Yet an even more sensational event occurred during 1739: the Anglican minister raped a German girl. This sordid affair will be reserved for the reports of the year 1741, at which time it came to the attention of the harried Ebenezer minister.

Because so many of the Savannah Germans eventually found their way to Ebenezer, their story will begin to play a larger role in these reports. For this reason Appendix IV of the present volume includes a list of the "good" Palatines mentioned by Stephens and the Trustees on 20 June 1739 when they "read a memorial from the said Cap.ᵗ (William Thomson) alledging that he had carry'd over 116 heads of German servants at his own risk: which servants Col. Oglethorpe received, wherefore he pray'd payment for the charges of freight &c of said servants amounting to 826.2.11¼."[16]

We take this opportunity to thank the American Philosophical Society for supporting another visit by Dr. Jones to the archives of the Francke Foundation in Halle; and we also wish to express our appreciation to the authorities of the University and State Library of Sachsen-Anhalt for kindly furnishing microfilms of Boltzius' unexpurgated reports, from which those passages deleted by Urlsperger have been restored. We are likewise indebted to the General Research Board of the University of Maryland for defraying typing charges and to the National Endowment for the Humanities for a generous grant which supported Dr. Jones as scholar in residence at the Georgia Historical Society in Savannah during his sabbatical leave in 1977 and also covered other related costs.

GEORGE FENWICK JONES
University of Maryland

RENATE WILSON
The Johns Hopkins University

Daily Register

Of the two pastors, Mr. Boltzius and Mr. Gronau
From January 1st to the end of the year 1739

JANUARY

Monday was the first day of the New Year. Our always generous and gentle Lord God has continued to help us and has bestowed much mercy on us during the past year in giving us strength not only of body and spirit but also in the conduct of our office for both old and young alike. For this we have right fully offered Him our thanks and praise in the name of the Lord Jesus Christ on several occasions. Last year our community saw the birth of ten children; and four persons, i.e. three children and one woman, have died and four couples have been given in matrimony.

Tuesday, the 2nd of January. This morning our carpenters and others who have volunteered their help have started to cut the wood for my house. I and my dear colleague visited them toward evening and, at their request, prayed with them at the conclusion of their day's work. It is true that I still have no funds in hand for the completion of this house, which is destined to be the regular parsonage in our town; but, relying on God's blessing (which is always safest in the Father's hands), I have chosen to start this building which has become ever more indispensable because of the circumstances of my office, the health of myself and my family, and the poor state of our previous hut. The workmen have embarked upon this enterprise not only with much joy, but certainly also in the name of Jesus, as they were instructed yesterday in Colossians 3:17. I was strongly impressed by this in my prayer with them, when I reminded myself and them of the fact that, in yesterday's gospel, the Lord Jesus offered us His first drops of blood, which speak on our behalf, and His previous name as a gift for the new year.

Will He not be all the more ready to offer us the much lesser gift, i.e. the funds for this new house, and to strengthen the workmen in their effort, who are ready to do all they can to help me obtain proper lodgings, as my dear colleague has done.

Today it has again been my dearest resolution, if God grants me the joy of moving into this house, to seek to step before the throne of our dear Father together with our listeners and, by the strength of this blood of reconciliation and the most precious name of Jesus, to pray for them and all people and among them in particular those dear benefactors who will contribute something to this dwelling. Yesterday as an exordium we heard Esther 5:6, wherein we were told of the advantage we have over Esther: she came to a proud, lascivious heathen king, without being called, and was faced by a strict interdiction, nor did she have any friend to lead her to the king or present her word to him. We, on the other hand, are instructed in the gospels to come to a reconciled Father, to the Lord of all love and mercy; we are called by Him, urged by Him, prompted by Him, and have the most certain promises to us, as well as the Holy Ghost as an aid and Jesus as mediator of the New Testament, for our advocate. That can encourage us to prayer, etc.

Wednesday, the 3rd of January. Kieffer of Purysburg brought Mr. Falk to our town yesterday, of whom we spoke the other day in our diary.[1] This man will continue via Old Ebenezer and Palachocolas to Savannah-Town, where he wishes to act as a preacher to the crude people there, since he was told in Savannah that such a man was needed there. He feels he has been convinced by divine will to do so; and we will hear and see what he can accomplish there and whether this is in truth the only reason for his journey. He stayed with us till this morning and attended the evening prayer meeting with us last night, by which he claimed to be quite edified. I cannot make much of him, nor fully accept him. He claims to have been ordained and sent to this country without a specific destination. He has spent much time in Pennsylvania and himself acknowledges that evangelical preachers are very necessary there; but nonetheless he comes here without having been summoned, where he will probably be even less able to accomplish anything. Also, there are three Swedish communities there, where they surely need some help with the young people. In Purysburg they asked him to help instruct the children, for which they would take care of his subsistence; this, however, he did not wish to accept. On the other hand the Reformed people in Savannah, where he has offered to become the preacher, do not want him. He does not really master the German language and speaks more Dutch than German.[2] He asked to be shown our orphanage and showed himself to be both modest and orderly.

I learned today from several people in the community that our dear God has blessed the gospels of His Son in them so much that they are prepared even more seriously than ever before to embark on their salvation in this new year. A man who is almost always sickly called on me and recognized quite well the salutary purpose which God has in burdening him with such a lingering disease. Our heavenly Father has relieved him of the worry of how he and his family will support themselves, since he can barely work; and He had also given him a light heart and a good conscience through the prayerful recognition of His dear Son, the Conciliator and Savior of this world. Thus, he did not fear death. He had long tortured himself with his own thoughts and the legalistic attempt to force himself to repentance and sorrow for his sins. However, the Lord has given him a better insight than that. Since this man is poor and now incapable of working in the fields, I have assigned him to bringing in the boards for my house with cart and horse, so that he may earn some money. We have only one horse that is at all serviceable, and it is being used and fed by the whole community. However, I have been given hope that I may receive another serviceable horse for bringing in the wood for the building.

Thursday, the 4th of January. I visited the workmen at my house before quitting time so as to conclude their work with a prayer, which they much like. I was told that one of the workmen had been in danger of losing his life, in that a dead tree had been toppled by another and had fallen toward him. But God had saved him. I reminded the man of these words: "We have a God who helps, and a Lord, who saves us from death."[3] We praised the Lord for His help and admonished each other to commence, continue, and complete all our work in the name of Christ so that we may work and achieve a blessing not only as natural humans but as Christians, anointed and protected by divine providence. Today was a very cold day, such as we have not had this year. Last night the wind was strong and cold. The ice froze thicker than ever before.

Friday, the 5th of January. As it was too cold both yesterday and today, we have had to cancel school, since we still lack a good house in which to hold classes. The cold is most uncomfortable during the writing classes, and little can be accomplished in them during the winter months. For this reason we have seen fit to suspend writing classes for a while so that the children may help in the house and stables, both in the orphanage and at home. They are much needed everywhere. Since my dear colleague now has time during this hour, he will take charge of the larger children who cannot yet read sufficiently; and the schoolmaster will continue to help the little ones who must learn the alphabet and the fundamentals of reading. The Salzburgers also send those girls to school who have recently been taken into service from Savannah,[4] and in this manner they will be brought to reading all the sooner so that, once they have learned the catechism too, they can do their work properly at home.

Saturday, the 6th of January. The dear Lord has again revived us today, both from the example of the Three Kings and from other fortifying verses that have been offered to us from His word, and encouraged us to seek His dear Son, our dearest Savior, as the most precious pearl. I have also learned from some people that they have now arrived at a new seriousness and wish to sell everything, as it were, so as to be able to obtain in truth this jewel, which surpasseth all things, especially since it is being offered to them for nothing and as a gift.[5] By the grace of God, we hear and see in many of our dear souls that they are not content in seeking satisfaction in external exercises and practices, however well they may use them, but will fight their way to the Lord Christ, the Son in whom God is well pleased.

Sunday, the 7th of January. This afternoon we again started on the catechism, after my dear colleague had used a number of Christmas verses as the basis of catechization. In the repetition hour I conducted an examination of both children and adults as to the manner in which each had applied and used the holy days, during which the dear Lord had had His gospel preached in circumstances of external peace and good order. At the end we read the two verses from 2 Corinthians 8:9 and Malchi 4:2, wherein it is clearly stated how far each of us must and can go if the word of God's grace in Christ shall achieve its purpose. The severe cold had already ceased yesterday; and we have thus been less inconvenienced during the public divine service. All this is a gift of the Lord and attests how well He means to treat us in His fatherly heart.

Monday, the 8th of January. God be praised there is no lack of people among us who provide us much comfort and joy when we witness how they walk in truth and seek nothing but to please the Lord Jesus both inwardly and outwardly. During the last days a few among them have truly penetrated into God's mercy and have found Him who loves their souls, which grace they hold in higher esteem than all the world's treasures, and for which they praise the Lord from their hearts. Others tell us how they have lost their previous joy and must bear a new tribulation, in that God has revealed to them their false heart, their arrogance, and self-righteousness; and therefore they must fight anew for the crown. May God give us the wisdom to accommodate ourselves to all circumstances and to deal with each according to the condition of his soul. May He make us ever more obedient to His word, and then He will richly fulfill in us that which He said to Joshua (Joshua 1), so that we may act prudently and succeed in everything we do.

Tuesday, the 9th of January. There are some very poor people in the community who lack both clothing and other necessities. Although our poorbox is empty, we must not fail to see what we can do in the greatest need. I will have some of the clothes distributed that God has presented to the orphanage. It is nothing for the Lord to grant us a new gift so that we can discharge the debts we have been forced by necessity to incur for the orphanage. We shall humbly praise Him for such munificence.

The sins of her youth arose in one woman and caused her much anxiety, and she believes she would gain greater peace if she were to confess her sins to the people whom she has insulted and thus atone for them. One single word that once penetrated her conscience causes her uncommon grief and many tears of fear. I sought to direct her to Christ, the eternal Peace of tired and burdened sinners, to which end I read her the passage from Luke 7 about the sinful woman and showed how Jesus has a heart for even the most grievous sinners: He has paid for the sins of all men and thus also the most grievous sinners fully by His death on the cross and cried out in witness thereof: "It is finished." Now He asks nothing but that a fearful conscience come to him in humility and faith; and He wished to fulfill for all these sinners His words from Matthew 11:28, just as He fulfilled them for the sinning woman.

Wednesday, the 10th of January. During yesterday evening's prayer meeting we read the last part of the first chapter of Joshua, which gave me an occasion to speak to the congregation of some things which I believed necessary in our present circumstances. There it is told how the people had agreed among themselves on a rule under which those should die who proved disobedient and recalcitrant to Joshua; and in this manner I reminded them how good it would be if we adopted a similar rule to pursue those disorderly people who resist the teaching and beneficial order of our Jesus and even cause annoyance among us, although we would not persecute such souls but treat them in a manner demanded by the Apostle Paul, 2 Thessalonians 3:6–15, whose words I read and explained.

Thursday, the 11th of January. Since yesterday we have had a steady rain, and the air has been warm and pleasant. Some people have again been attacked by the cold fever; and in our house, for instance, three persons were affected at once, although God soon showed us help. A good portion of our dear people have started some work on their new plantations on Abercorn Creek, although they are forced to suffer much inconvenience because of the inconstant weather. They first build small huts in which to sleep and be protected from the rain. However, since it is their main goal to prepare some land for planting, these huts are but very poor structures that will have to do until they can erect better ones. The women and children will stay in town and conduct their affairs and work here until the men have made better preparations for moving out there. The Salzburgers shy away from nothing and work quite hard to gain

their bread according to divine order, and we trust in the goodness of the Lord that He may crown their work, which most of
them undertake in true faith, with His blessing, strengthen their
health, and slowly but surely permit them to earn their livelihood. At present they still need the support of their dear benefactors. For a long time we have received no help from the
storehouse in Savannah, and there is now even less hope that
Mr. Oglethorpe has changed the administration and conduct of
the storehouse.[6]

Friday, the 12th of January. Zettler,[7] who was brought to us
by Michael Rieser with the third transport, will enter into shoemaker Adde's service so as to learn his trade, an undertaking
for which he has both the necessary strength and much desire.
This trade will suit him better than work in the fields; and, since
he has been quite orderly until now and has accepted instruction, for which reasons the Salzburgers love him well, he will be
of much use to the community once he has finished his apprenticeship. One shoemaker is not enough for us, and as he has too
much work, he will occasionally make bad shoes. On the other
hand, where there are two shoemakers in the community, he
will have the biggest business who best serves the people. He will
have to learn for two years, and for his apprentice money,
provisions, laundry, and mending he will only have to pay £2
10s sterling.

The Rheinlaender boy is going to Purysburg and will also
learn the shoemaker's trade;[8] he is intending to return to us
after he has learned the trade and establish himself here. I
called him to my house today and told him that I had learned
that his mother intended to let her house lot and plantation lie
uncultivated and rent it out so that he might find it for his use
on his return. However, I told him that, as this was against the
intent of the Trustees as well as disadvantageous to the community if he were to let trees stand on her land that would cause
shade for the neighbors and harbor harmful insects and vermin, I could not consent to this but would request Mr. Oglethorpe to free us from this obligation. He returned after a while
and said that his mother would let go of the plantation on the
condition that he might in the future be assigned another piece
of land, such as had been promised to Zettler. However, I pre-

fer to speak to the congregation and to Mr. Oglethorpe on this matter.

Saturday, the 13th of January. My dear colleague has again assumed the burden of preaching to the Germans in Savannah tomorrow, for which reason he departed today. I am somewhat weak because of the fever suffered a few days ago; but I hope that, since it has not returned for one day, I shall be strong enough to conduct the public service here tomorrow. We do not like to miss the fourth Sunday, inasmuch as that is the day when the people come to Savannah from the plantations to hear God's word, and we do not wish to disappoint them and let them come in vain.

Monday, the 15th of January. After dinner we had a meeting in my dear colleague's house, during which I advised the assembled men of a matter that shall not be mentioned here and asked for their opinion. May the Lord grant us wisdom in all things so that we may not err to the extreme right or left, but keep to the middle path in all things, however insignificant they may appear on the outside. We have had rain last night and all day today, which has caused some inconvenience to my dear colleague on his return from Savannah. Mr. Oglethorpe is still being expected there, and Mr. Jones will advise me of his arrival as soon as he can, as he well knows the urgent business that I have with him.

Tuesday, the 16th of January. As often as we have an opportunity to speak to N.N.'s wife, she praises our merciful and loving Lord for having had mercy upon her and having brought her to the recognition of her sinful misery. As she and her husband are preparing this week to take Holy Communion next Sunday, her most urgent concern seems to be to go there with a sincere heart and thus to the benefit of her soul. She is much pained by the fact that, in the years of her ignorance, she went to this Holy Table only from custom. She also is quite worried that she might fall back into her former ways, since her wicked heart is becoming ever more clearly recognized by her; and she cannot trust herself to do any good. But she does trust in the Lord that He shall continue in her the work He has started. She marvels at the divine goodness that protects her otherwise weak infant child, although she has very violent fever. Whenever she has had no food for the child, God has provided it and the child has lacked for nothing. She is well equipped to accept her protracted illness because she accepts everything that occurs from God's hand and believes that all is happening for her good. Previously, she says, God could do nothing right by her.

Thursday, the 18th of January. N.N. visited me and told me something of the state of his soul, which gives me much hope that he will save his soul and participate in the mercy of the Lord in Jesus Christ. Afterwards, I visited him and his family in his hut; and our dear God gave me the strength to speak much that is good for their and other people's edification and to pray with them. In particular I addressed the children, and the parents told me what each of them left to be desired. It seemed as if my admonitions had struck their heart, and the parents also admonished their children with many tears.

Friday, the 19th of January. N. asked me in the street to accompany him to his hut and give him a word of admonition. Our dear Lord is awakened in him strongly by His word and has lit a light by which he can recognize the state of his soul and how dangerous that state is, in that until now he has lived only in hypocrisy and has not experienced anything of the true conversion to the Lord. He finds much difficulty in taking upon himself the cross of Christ and truly renouncing the world by deserting old companionships, chastising evil in word and deed, and associating closely with converted people, of whom he knows several. I seriously admonished him to apply faithfully all that he has learned by way of convictions and the effects of the Lord's word, and then prayed with him.

Because of her children, N. has again caused herself unnecessary grief, which delays her in her Christianity and weakens her body. Since she is of a frail constitution, as well as somewhat deficient in her mind and understanding of some external things that have happened to her, we have to yield to her, although it would alleviate her mind and lead her to greater calmness of spirit if she were to accept our advice in a particular matter.

N. and his wife will have things their way and have to bear the judgment of others, even from those of a kindly disposition; there is nothing that can be done, and it must be borne with patience. May the dear Lord grant them and us the spirit of wisdom, love, strength, and discipline so that we shall be all the more capable and sanctified to do His work.

Saturday, the 20th of January. The dear Lord in His mercy has made it possible for us to be more content with the N. woman after some troubles, since she has changed her mind in a number of matters that caused us grief and is trying to be closer to us than before. This morning she revealed a matter to me that means a lot to me because it leads me to recognize the divine wisdom and goodness that is governing us; and this strengthens and comforts me to perform my office without bothering about the judgment of others. Everything is finally becoming clear. She is quite poor, and we will gladly do all that is possible for her and her children, provided everything can be done in a proper way.

So far N. has lived in discord with his wife, and each blames the other. Before the prayer meeting I talked with them in moving terms and showed them the true foundation that must be laid in our hearts if a marital and Christian union is to be effected even in external matters. After this and renewed admonitions, I shall watch how they have made room for my words, and in the absence of true improvement I shall more seriously exercise my office toward them, so that this rough man, who is chiefly to blame for this sad state of affairs, may see that we insist on discipline among us and do not take such sins lightly.

Sunday, the 21st of January. On this day fifty persons came to Holy Communion.

Monday, the 22nd of January. Despite her poverty a woman has restored a portion of what she stole some years ago during her service, and she has promised to restore the rest at a later time. She told me with much emotion what the dear Lord had done to her soul from the mercy of His heart in the last and other prayer and repetition meetings by showing her much more clearly and strongly what she had heard in the morning service; and this I also heard from several others. May God be praised for such tangible encouragement in my work, which is so pleasant to my heart. She brought me her Bible so that I might underline for her the strength-giving verses that are particularly found in the exordia.

Tuesday, the 23rd of January. For some days now it has been as lovely as spring, and the blossoms have started to appear on the peach trees; this is much too early, however, because we will have to expect many and long frosts throughout February. There was an unusually violent storm in the evening, which lasted only for a few minutes but which blew down many of our fences. I was much surprised that in our large garden the thick oaken fence posts have already rotted through and been toppled by this wind, although they are less than two years old. The posts which support my hut have now been in the ground for three years and are quite rotten too. It is thus almost dangerous to stay in this dwelling much longer. The carpenters are still cutting wood for my house and will probably be finished this week. How I shall praise the dear Lord in heaven when I, like many other Salzburgers, finally have proper quarters wherein I can protect myself from the unpleasant and inconstant weather.

Wednesday, the 24th of January. Many of the people in this colony long for the return of Mr. Oglethorpe from Frederica, and our listeners much desire him to come to our town. I am aware of their desire to ask him for the removal of some of the disorderly among us. I believe that, when the measure of these is full and they are ready for God's judgment, they will be taken care of by His intercession; I myself will not remove them unless their excesses are too offensive, for this might cause much offence and calumny among those not well acquainted with the true circumstances.

Thursday, the 25th of January. It has been a great service to the community that they have been provided with two families of German people who work here as herdsmen.[9] They have to support them only with such provisions as they grow themselves, and the clothing is provided from the poor box and the orphanage. If these Germans remain as reliable as they have shown themselves until now, the community will do for them whatever is within their power, for they are much concerned that their cattle be well guarded. We hope that the Lord Trustees will leave these herdsmen not only for one year, but for the term of their indentured service.

Friday, the 26th of January. Those in the community who have a chance to earn something for their support in helping in the construction of my house are very glad of it and almost consider their well-earned wages as a gift, thanking God for the opportunity and the strength that He has given them for this service. There are many who need food and clothing and who are barely making out in this respect; these would be only too glad if they were needed for some weeks to help in the work. However, it is not possible to employ everyone, seeing that we have to be as parsimonious as possible so that the house will not cost too much. And I would never have thought that a simple house of one storey, with two living rooms and two small bedrooms, would cost as much as I now already realize that it will cost, when not even all the wood has been cut. However, the Salzburgers are rendering most loyal work and earn their money by the sweat of their brows, and such a house would easily cost three times as much if it were to be built by others. The wood is very tough and much more difficult to work than in Germany, as our carpenters have told us several times. All the more surprising is the fact that it rots much more quickly than in Germany.

I have long shied away from this construction and would not have started it now had not dire necessity dictated it. The best timber is being cut away month by month; and, if we had waited another year, we would have had to travel far in order to find good trees, and this would have increased the costs. Nor will our people be able to continue working forever for their present wage of eighteen pence and two shillings, since the carpenters in Savannah and elsewhere ask for four shillings. May the dear Lord look upon my and our listeners' prayers with grace and grant as much as will be necessary for this construction, for I have nothing to this end. We will have to see what Mr. Oglethorpe will contribute.

Saturday, the 27th of January. My physical weakness and all sorts of business have prevented me from going into the Salzburgers' huts as much as I would have liked to this week. Even if we talk to our listeners only about external matters, we are much edified by their honesty and serious and humble nature; and this is even more true when we take the occasion, or are asked by them, to talk of Christian matters. In the course of this week our dear Lord has richly edified my soul from that which has been treated in the prayer meetings from the word of the Lord, although I have not learned very much.[10] I have been incommodated by the fever, which has prevented some of my work; but it has not been strong enough to confine me to bed.

Sunday, the 28th of January. The dear Lord has again given us much edification from his holy word, and we have had cause to praise His name in this regard. In the morning we treated the regular gospel for the 4th Sunday after Epiphany, namely, the imitation of Christ, what it is, and what good it brings us. In the afternoon, my colleague treated of the Third Commandment.[11] Several people in the community work on their plantations during the week but come here on Saturdays for the prayer meeting and stay over Sunday.

Regarding the cowherd who is guarding our cattle in the woods several miles from here,[12] we have made a good arrangement that every Saturday he is relieved by two men from the community, so that he and his family may come to church. However, he is not quite as industrious in this respect as others. After the repetition hour, a fairly large group of people of both sexes met in the orphanage for prayer. I had promised to repeat the other part of the sermon on this occasion, an exercise which is both necessary and most beneficial and edifying by God's grace. However, I was so tired from prior talking that we only summarized what had been heard in our prayer, after having sung a hymn. We have had mild weather these days, and thus everything was very convenient.

FEBRUARY

Thursday, the 1st of February. At noon I returned in good health to Ebenezer from my voyage. Mr. Oglethorpe had not yet returned to Savannah. It had been assumed that he might come yesterday, but we received news that he might leave Frederica as late as next week. Since some of the English did not pay for their recently obtained male and female servants and cannot even support them with food and clothing, Captain Thomson says that Mr. Oglethorpe may be willing to send another few families to our town, since he knows the treatment that such poor people can expect here.[1] However, I did not wish to say much on this matter prior to talking to the congregation about it; for neither I nor my colleague are able to take any of them into our own service, although I would dearly have liked, out of compassion, to have accepted a family of four who had very good references and who movingly asked me to take them. Captain Thomson was in Savannah; and, since he will go back to England shortly via Charleston, I hurriedly wrote a brief letter to Court Preacher Ziegenhagen and enclosed the last part of the diary. I had left a fairly large packet of letters and our enclosed diary in Savannah as early as December, so that it might be given to the said Captain for delivery, he being in Frederica at the time. However, I learned that it had already been forwarded to Charleston, and I hope that it may be properly delivered.

In Savannah, I learned that a boat carrying people from Purysburg had capsized between Port Royal and Savannah and that all on board had perished in the water. The body of a maidservant was found, as well as a little box with papers from which the identity of those who died could be inferred, i.e. a French doctor from Purysburg and his wife and children, as well as some Frenchmen who had accompanied these people from Charleston to Purysburg.[2] We well knew the entire family, and those who knew their offensive, almost atheist views, must look upon their fate as a special judgment of the Lord.

Friday, the 2nd of February. A man told me that his conscience forced him to reveal to me that he had heard an ignorant man utter harsh words against his wife in anger; I shall reproach that man for his sinful conduct and shall examine him myself shortly. Some people become angry if they cannot have their way, and then they betray the wicked bottom of their heart. This, however, enables us to convince them all the more strongly of their unchanged heart and to admonish them seriously to earn their salvation.

Tuesday, the 6th of February. As a result of the recent and

pleasant spring weather the trees have started to show buds, and some of them are in full bloom; however, there are signs of more rough weather to come, and in other years this month has brought us some harsh night frosts. Now that we have become accustomed to this land, the Salzburgers like it better than their former homeland. They can work all winter in their fields, and it is particularly convenient that they can use the river to transport their things by boat to and from our place, whereas in other countries, as for example in Pennsylvania, everything has to be transported by horse and cart from one place to the other. Also, the river is navigable both summer and winter.

Wednesday, the 7th of February. The potter from Savannah[3] has been looking for lime and clay in our vicinity for his trade, but then he found a whole mound of stones[4] of which he took as many as his boat would carry and transported them to Savannah. He hopes to fire lime from the white kind he found; and he promised to let me know as best he could through our people whether that is possible or not. I do not think that these stones are strong enough to withstand a hot fire, but they might well serve to line a cellar or well. This man could hardly find words enough to praise the opportunity that we have, in contrast to others in this colony, to fire bricks,[5] and he has offered to show our people or those among them who are interested in this trade, how to fire them without kilns. I have made similar suggestions on several occasions, but no one among our people wants to engage in this, although there are some among the men who have worked in bricksheds in Germany.

In one woman, the sins of her youth relating to the Fourth Commandment[6] have stirred her conscience so that she wishes she could spend only a few hours in Germany so as to speak to those whom she has offended. I told her that that was not what she needed, for it would give her as little peace as was true for the dove that flew back and forth over the earth and found its peace only in Noah's ark. The well of grace is still flowing, and everyone may drink of it. Another complained that the struggle against the sins in her was so heavy on her heart that she felt she would not overcome; she cried much when telling me this. I comforted her with the words: "Therefore endure hardness as a good soldier of Jesus Christ," etc., and showed her from this that true Christians as spiritual soldiers do not only do battle, but suffer much in such battles, and overcome through their suffering. For, if it is a bitter pain to them that they still feel their sin within them and they pray and fight against it, then this will please the Lord. God will also permit the enemies to become strong and thus make the soldier feel his incompetence and weakness, as if he could not succeed, was bound to remain in one place, and had to succumb. Such humiliation, however, is most beneficial to our souls, I said, so that they may despair more and more of themselves and their strength and thus be forced to raise their eyes all the more to the mountain from which cometh our help, etc.

It is essential, I said, to despair more and more of oneself, but not of the help of the Lord. We shall shortly have an illustration of this in the story of Joshua, chapter 7, concerning the Israelites, whom God permitted to be beaten by their enemies for their humiliation and the recognition of their worthlessness.

The same woman complained bitterly of her useless, feeble prayer. If she could find no pleasure in it, she asked, how then could the Lord? I told her that, once she began to find pleasure in her prayer, this would but start a new struggle in her. Such prayer as arises from the recognition of our misery and the poverty of the spirit and is said in the name of Christ pleases the Lord, however pitiful and skimpy it might sound. I pointed out to her the prayer of Joshua in the aforementioned chapter 7. Reason might find much fault with it, and Joshua himself might not have found it to be free of fault; yet he brought it to the Ark of the Covenant, and thus through the seat of grace to God, and He accepted it, and its faults were covered and overlooked.

Thursday, the 8th of February. A certain person is much annoyed with me for having cited, in a recent prayer meeting and in connection with Joshua 7, the 5th chapter of the Corinthians, as if I wished to arouse the congregation thereby to expel another person, although in fact I did not say a single word about that woman and her most recent misbehavior, nor was I in need of doing so, as she is still under church discipline because of her previous vexations. The implication of the chapter referred to is as follows:

We learned from Joshua 7 that the Children of Israel, having ordered only 3,000 men for the taking of the city of Ai because of the frivolous and overly confident advice of their spies, had been driven to flight and had lost 36 men, the causes for which were stated as follows: (1) It had happened for their humiliation, so that they might recognize that without the Lord they could do nothing; for, if they were to conquer the entire land, they should not attribute this to their own strength, etc. The application of this is that in Christianity, too, God often chooses such paths for His people for their humiliation.

(2) It had happened because there was an accursed thing among them and God had to arouse them through this rod of chastisement to seek out this accursed thing and remove it. Also, we see in the following passage that God did not name the evil-doer but commanded Joshua to seek him out himself. And thus He approves if those who are in positions of authority seek out malice and malicious persons and try to expose godless behavior; for, if they are slack and negligent and fail to expel the rotten members, to their own shame and as a warning to others, then they will be participating in the sins of others[7] and God will charge them with the sins of one or several others, as in verses 1, 11, and 12. He has put each of us in charge of his neighbor.

In this connection I also compared the verse Hebrews 12:15, where it is clearly stated that they should look diligently, lest, etc. Moreover, when superiors and other honest members are careless, lackadaisical, and negligent in matters of offense, God must awake them by judgment and chastisement. We have not only the example in 1 Corinthians 5, where Paul was much dissatisfied with them because of their negligence and conceit, but I also, and expressly, cited 1 Corinthians 11:30 and 32, which was well suited as an illustration of my intent. It is not only this person who causes offense; there are several others in this class, and like Eli it would ill behoove us if we were to sit still in the presence of such occurrences and fail to use serious words openly and specifically. Thus I have clearly stated my mind as required on the occasion of this 7th chapter of Joshua.

I assume that N. has also resented what I had said last Sunday concerning the regular gospel Matthew 13:24 ff. I showed that it would be an ill use of the words of Christ, "Let both grow together," if we were to conclude therefrom that we should let wickedness and wicked malicious people act as they wish and leave them to their judgment. Such an interpretation would be contrary to what Christ Himself said in Matthew 18 and to what Paul said through the Holy Ghost in 1 Corinthians 5:13, and to other verses. Rather, this should be our view: The true members of the church should not weed out those who are like a tare in their understanding and their way of living, that is to say, they should not use physical force, persecute, and expunge them because they are not good wheat but tares and do not want to be converted. For this I cited Matthew 26:51 and Luke 9:54. On the other hand, church discipline and exclusion from the community of the church and its privileges are not contrary to the will of Christ and His kingdom, but instead most necessary for the sake of such offensive people and others. In this respect, I showed them that every man in Christendom should be considered *duplici respectu*:[8] (1) as a member of the Christian community, and (2) as a member of the polity and external human society, in which respect he is under the authority of the powers that be. If he sins against the order of Christ and His church by serious offenses, he will fall under the discipline of the church for his good and that of others; if he sins against the secular law and disturbs the external peace, he will fall into the hands of the authorities. Inasmuch as the wicked among us do not wish to see this distinction, they speak ill of the harshness and cruelty which is used when their godless ways are countered with serious measures.

In the repetition hour I talked again about the material presented in the morning concerning the children of the wicked one and showed them that they act like their father the evil one: he sows the seed of malice and false teachings, and then he leaves and will not acknowledge that he has committed evil. It is the manner of many wicked men that they commit evil as often as they have occasion to, but afterwards they act just as is written of a kind of godless people in Proverbs 30:10,[9] "Such is the way of an adulterous woman; she eateth and wipeth her mouth, and saith, I have done no wickedness."

I wished to state the relevance of my preachings in such detail so that, if N. should gather up all sorts of things and send them to London, our impartial friends and Fathers may recognize

how the truth will always offend the wicked. The worthy Senior
Preu in Augsburg once wrote us a most instructive and comforting letter; and, among other beneficial instructions on our
office, he quoted this: "Above all, prevent all troubles as soon as
they start; for, once these grow and become strong as a river,
they will tear down much, if not all, in their path and then almost nothing will help."

Friday, the 9th of February. Today the carpenters finished
cutting the wood for my house, after having spent thirty-one
days on this task. Because they had sent me news of the completion of this work, I went to visit them in the woods toward evening so as to praise the Lord with them for His assistance, His
removal of all danger from their heads, and for all the good of
which He has let them partake. We also implored Him for further blessing on the building and completion of our house. May
He give us from His large inexhaustible treasure the means to
defray our expenses! Nobody would have thought that the
preparation of the wood would take so much time; instead, the
estimate had been for 20 days. But our Father knows what we
need.

Saturday, the 10th of February. My dear colleague travelled
to Savannah this morning in order to preach the word of the
Lord there to the German people, if God be willing. May He
give him His merciful blessing and assistance for this task. The
weather has changed and we have strong winds and rains.

Muggitzer is back again to collect the money for the things he
has sold.[10] He has engaged himself as a overseer of black slaves
in Carolina, which is a very evil profession. Ordinarily, only
such people are used for this task as can be quite merciless with
these poor slaves. It may be assumed that Riedelsperger, who
left our place some time ago by very crooked paths, has also
taken on this type of work. In this manner both he and Muggitzer will fare very badly with respect to their souls. It is common knowledge that life on the plantations of the wealthy people in Carolina is both offensive and atheistic.

Sunday, the 11th of February. It has rained almost all day;
and both last night and yesterday afternoon, especially toward
evening, we had a penetrating rain. For this reason, yesterday's
prayer meeting had to be called off, and I therefore took over

the conclusion of the story from the 7th chapter of Joshua this afternoon instead of the catechism, which my dear colleague wishes to take himself in the proper order. The morning sermon on Matthew 17 ff. was repeated in the evening at the orphanage for the assembled children and others. God blessed this in me; and may He also bless this in the community, the adults and the children.

Monday, the 12th of February. A woman of the congregation told me this morning that her conscience had been full of disquiet and fear on the occasion of the story we have read so far from the 7th chapter of Joshua, so that she could not find rest day or night. She carried an accursed thing on her conscience: in her homeland a man had passed by on horseback and his purse, which he had carried on his belt, had opened and he had lost much money from it. She had seen it and picked up a handful and kept a guilder for herself. When the man had noticed his loss and saw her behind him, he accepted the money she held in her hand and returned to him, but she denied keeping the guilder. Her own people had told her she had been foolish not to keep the other money she had found, and therefore she had believed she was right in keeping the one guilder. Now, however, she realized full well why she could not make headway in her struggle, could not overcome and reach the true spirit of Christianity, for that was the accursed thing on her from which she would like to free herself. She had no money, but she would like to restore the theft from the crop that God would grant her.

A Salzburger man told me with great joy that, during the repetition in the orphanage, God had given him a beautiful blessing from the introductory words of John 17:24, "Father, I will . . . ," etc. This report from this man was all the more pleasant, since I knew that he had suffered much disquiet and worry on Saturday because of some external affairs; but he had not let this deter him from properly celebrating Sunday. Even among the good souls, there often occur outward circumstances that are quite unpleasant and upsetting; but our dear and faithful Lord helps in all these cases and also teaches us this: "For those who love God, all things will turn out for the best."

I found a few men discussing external business together; and, in accordance with the example of Joshua, who was much concerned with removing the accursed thing from Israel and with reconciling the Israelites with God (cf. 7:16), I sought to awaken them to seriousness and industriousness in achieving their salvation (cf. 2 Corinthians 11:2–3). They urged me to come into their quarters so as to pray with them, and on this prayer the dear Lord bestowed His blessing in such a manner that one of the men later took me to his hut so that I could speak with him and his wife for their edification in accordance with their circumstances. They had run into some discord with each other, for which the wife was entirely at fault because of her carelessness. She pays too little attention to her household and its economy, and this causes much loss and places a double burden on the husband. I read to her in particular the 31st chapter of Proverbs, verses 10 ff., through which I could give her many good admonitions. May God bless all this for the sake of His Son.

Tuesday, the 13th of February. Yesterday afternoon my dear colleague returned home safely and brought the news that Mr. Oglethorpe had written to the storekeeper in Savannah with the order to send all those Germans for whom the English could not pay to our place, where they shall be employed as we see fit, on the same conditions and in the same manner as applied to those whom he had sent before. It is to be hoped that this means that the people who take in the new servants shall be obliged to pay a yearly interest to the orphanage, as was Mr. Oglethorpe's instruction when he let us have the six young girls. It would indeed be of great benefit for the orphanage if the Salzburgers were in a position to pay such interest, which runs to 13 shillings sterling per year for each person. However, they would rather not accept anybody than to enter such an agreement, which it is not in their power to observe. The food and clothing which they must give to such servants are very expensive in this country, and they would have to work hard to accumulate such a sum. On the other hand, inasmuch as the poor and tormented Germans in Savannah would receive a great benefit by being accepted here, and since our people would also eventually have some profit and help from such servants, the latter shall be accepted here without obliging our people to pay anything to the orphanage for their services. If God will bless them and if they wish to be grateful, they will always find a way to show their gratitude to the orphanage.

Last night I talked to the men in the village regarding these new servants, and some soon declared their willingness to accept them. This time there will be about ten of them, for whom the boat has been sent this morning. One family, which is of good repute, will be kept by the manager of the orphanage and will be maintained by the orphanage.[11] He will place them on his own plantation, and the harvest from this land is for the benefit of the orphanage. In this manner, the orphanage will also be protected against any complaints which would be made if the trees were left standing on that plantation and if the manager were not willing or able to participate in the joint preparation of fences. I hope that the Lord, who knows of our shortages in regard to the orphanage, will soon let us see His blessing. The acceptance of these poor, well-meaning people is to be considered as a great charity on the part of our community, for which they will doubtless show their gratitude to the Lord and seek to avail themselves of this opportunity for their salvation.

N. N.[12] also has taken in his service two of these German people, a man and his wife, who will be rather poorly off in regard to food and clothing in this position; but they are prepared to suffer this provided that they may stay at our place and avail themselves of God's word. The woman, whom I visited while she was ill with the fever, told me that she thanks God for being here; she is calling to Him and hopes that He will let them see better times with respect to their physical needs. It is her resolution, she said, to become a true Christian with His help. She had always liked to go to church, and preachers in her town had preached well; nonetheless, she had never understood so clearly what was necessary for her salvation as here.

A few men who have also shown themselves frivolous in other matters have caused some dispute because of a whetstone on their plantations, and the wicked N. was the prime mover in this affair. I learned of this; and, since I feared discord, anger, and further disturbance among these people, I went out after the morning classes so as to inform myself fully of the matter and prevent an even worse dispute. I also used the occasion to visit some other plantations, where I talked to some of the workers for the benefit of their souls; in two newly erected huts I prayed with several people who had gathered there and consecrated the huts, which much pleased everyone.

Wednesday, the 14th of February. A Salzburger woman was much pleased that I told her little six-month-old some good things about the Lord Jesus. She does the same and, in repeating to the child some edifying words or prayers, she feels that the Holy Ghost will do His work in the child's heart, even if we cannot understand it. I also learned from the woman that keeping her daughter away from the last Communion had been of good effect, for she is now much better, more orderly, more obedient, and more industrious than before and prays with greater seriousness.

Thursday, the 15th of February. Since yesterday Mrs. Herrnberger has been in hard labor, and her condition is worse than that of any woman we have seen here before. Since nobody knew in what way to help her, the wife of a Frenchman who owns a plantation in Carolina not far away from here offered her services and God blessed her in this. As we have been told, the child had died several days before in the mother's womb and therefore did not emerge in the right position. The circumstances of the woman's delivery are said to have been extremely painful and traumatic. But God has let the mother escape with her life from this trial. Experienced women who assisted in the delivery much praised the French woman's skill. This case has led many to prayer.

I have learned that the tailor, Metzscher of Purysburg, who some time ago had placed two of his children in our orphanage and school, has also been affected by the recent disaster in which a boat from Purysburg capsized near the sea, with all the people in it killed. He lost three children on this occasion, a grown son of about 19 years, one of 13, and a girl of 10. His wife had left him again during the harvest and had taken two of the children.[13] When the man learned that she lived by begging in Charleston, he sent his grown son after her to bring back the children with the help of the authorities, and all three took passage on the boat that was destined for Purysburg. All three drowned together with eleven others. The man should not consider this judgment to have come for naught; for his house has been in great disorder at all times, and it is to be hoped that he may use these sad circumstances for his true conversion.

The German people who were brought here yesterday[14] show themselves very glad to have been saved, as they say it, from barbarism and slavery and thus brought to freedom. They hardly can say enough to describe their previous treatment. The woman met me in the street this morning and searched for words to wish upon me all the blessing of the Lord for having contributed to her acceptance in our community.

Saturday, the 17th of February. An Englishman told me the contents of the petition which the citizens of Savannah, from the highest to the lowest, have addressed to the Lord Trustees and of which a copy was sent to Mr. Oglethorpe in Frederica.[15] They ask: (1) For full power to dispose of their land as they wish, i.e. to sell it or to give it away to whomever they wish. (2) For free and full commerce with the West Indies, so that they may import from there not only a few restricted goods but all that can be bought, including rum, for their own trade here. For, unless they also buy rum from the merchants there, they are refused sugar, molasses or syrup, and other goods. If, however, such free trade were permitted, they hope that many ships will come from the West Indies to Savannah to deliver their cargo and load up with cut and sawed wood, boards, etc., of which there is said to be a great shortage down there, to the benefit of the inhabitants here, for otherwise no one can subsist in Savannah. (3) For a limited number of Negroes or Moorish slaves, without whom no Englishman here can exist. They cannot get anywhere with the whites, whom they cannot treat as they would the Negroes, the fault for which condition, however, is to be blamed more on the masters than on the servants.

It is said that many copies of this petition, which is a special document that is most obnoxious to Mr. Oglethorpe, have reached friends of high rank and members of Parliament in England and Scotland. It was drafted and sent, it is said, because the people in Savannah had learned that the citizens of Frederica had likewise drafted and sent a petition to the Trustees in London, wherein they requested the very opposite of the previous three articles, viz, to refuse permission for free disposition over the land, free commerce with the West Indies, and the introduction of Negro slaves. The original of the Savannah petition will be presented to the Lord Trustees themselves by a gentleman merchant from Savannah, a Captain Williams, who may well be the author of this document.[16] He is intending to travel to England shortly on his vessel via St. Christopher. If he should not succeed with the Trustees, he is empowered to present it to the King's Privy Council and to Parliament.

Monday, the 19th of February. This morning, after joint prayer, we started the workers on the construction of our house. Shortly before I had read the 3rd chapter of St. Luke with my family and had been much impressed with the words: "When Jesus prayed, the heavens were opened unto him." Since we have been promised by our dear Savior, in Matthew 7:7–8, that to him who knocketh it shall be opened, the connection between these two passages so strengthened me that I shall trust in our almighty heavenly Father in Christ to open His heaven and His good treasure also in response to our poor prayer (Deuteronomy 28:12) and to provide as many physical gifts as shall be required for the payment of the workers.

Tuesday, the 20th of February. Yesterday afternoon we both visited N. N.[17] on their plantation and prayed with them in their newly erected hut. Both are very industrious, but probably cannot obtain as much from their land for themselves as those who have been accustomed to field work from childhood on. They have cleaned about an acre and a half from trees and underbrush and hope to have three acres prepared by planting time, their health permitting. Their food and other means of sustenance are very poor, which does not leave them much strength for work; but they are patient and await the help of the Lord. They came to us in great poverty, and we have tried to help them get started, partly with money and some goods, and partly with intercessions on their behalf. However, since they have been quite abandoned by N. N.[18] and do not receive the least support from home and, finally, since they have had about the worst harvest among all the people, they are truly very poorly off.

Wednesday, the 21st of February. As I talked today to the children in the orphanage, as is my habit on Wednesdays and

Saturdays, the wife of the manager reminded me of the sad accident that killed the three children of the Purysburg tailor when their boat capsized. I remembered that all three had been for some time in our school and had heard much good for the salvation of their souls. The oldest, who had been prepared for the Lord's table by us, had made a good start and gave us much hope for his conversion. However, he was said to have learned the bad and disorderly life again after he left us and even to have become a curser and a blasphemer of God's name.[19]

Using this example, I impressed upon the children how necessary and blessed it is to accept the Lord's mercy for our conversion and to learn to fear Him, early in life, yea, even from childhood on, as is written of Obadiah in 1 Kings 18:12, "I thy servant fear the Lord from my youth." In last night's prayer meeting we discussed the example of the Gibeonites who had been much concerned for the safety of their lives even in the times before they were made subject to the courts. Not only did they abstain from uniting with the other Canaanites against Joshua and Israel, but they did not leave it to chance whether or not they would stay alive, but earnestly sought to emerge with their lives as their booty.[20] In this prudent and careful manner they put to shame many Christians, who gamble with eternity and comfort themselves that they will fare as others have fared. They hope that God will not be too strict with them because he is merciful. All of this is a pitiful and dangerous delusion of safety, from which may our pious Savior protect us and our children!

Thursday, the 22nd of February. Because of his physical weakness, Eischberger is still incapable of working in the fields, as much as he needs to do so and as much as he is willing. His right arm seems to be withering, and he is suffering from pain and discomfort in almost all members. He would gladly and carefully follow our doctor's cure, if he could but obtain one. Whenever I visit him, I find him in good spiritual state, and it is clear that he wishes to become certain of the state of his salvation and his soul. He knows how to retain and recite many good verses and evangelical truths, which serve him as a lesson, warning, and comfort so that we ourselves are edified and delighted.

We should gladly do everything toward improving his health if it were within our power.

Friday, the 23rd of February. Until now we have experienced pleasant spring weather; it has been a warm day and night, and some rain has fallen now and then. Our people have started planting their potatoes[21] as if no frost were to be expected. They do it with such industriousness at this stage for the sake of the greens from which the potatoes will grow, which are better if planted in the ground as early as possible. The tertian and quartan fevers will not cease among us, and there are still many among us who suffer from the attacks, although they are no longer as violent as in the first and second year. This year, the quartan fever is the more common; and some of the people drag themselves around with it for a long time yet keep doing some work. A new group of Indians has come to Savannah, and it is being said that they seek Mr. Oglethorpe's friendship and will receive some gifts, for which reason Mr. Oglethorpe is being expected with certainty any day now. These Indians are said to have suffered much from the French and are therefore seeking the protection of the English.

Saturday, the 24th of February. N.'s wife is not only an industrious listener but also a doer of God's word, and I am delighted at the mercy she has received for her earnest conduct in Christian ways and which she treasures with great poverty of the spirit. God is blessing her words and her example in others; she will not believe it, however, but considers herself the most useless and despicable creature. Her greatest complaint is about the sluggishness and weakness of her prayer, and she would not be surprised if God were to reject her because of her great unrighteousness. My council for her and her kind is mostly to the effect that such persons should not let themselves be kept away from the Lord Jesus by the recognition of their unworthiness and their lack of faith and righteousness, but rather they should let this feeling of their lack drive them to Him all the more, and all the more quickly and constantly, for He calls to Himself those who labor and are heavy laden and will strengthen them with righteousness and strength.

During last evening's prayer meeting, we learned from

Joshua 10 ff. that, when the Gibeonites were attacked and be-sieged by the Canaanite kings, they had implored Joshua for his help and had comforted themselves with his succor, (1) because they were his servants and (2) because they were suffering and persecuted for a good cause. They may well have remembered the canny and fraudulent means by which they had tried to in-sinuate themselves with Joshua, but this did not prevent them from seeking help and salvation earnestly, and they did in fact receive it.

Sunday, the 25th of February. The pleasant weather is con-tinuing, and the dear Lord has also let the sun of His mercy shine on us from the gospel, so that on this day we have had much edification among ourselves from His blessing.

The old carpenter from Purysburg,[22] who is helping to build my house, visited me; and I learned from his discourse on the inner nature of Christendom that he has not only a fine recog-nition, but also experience in matters spiritual. He leads a quiet Christian life among us and does his work faithfully according to his strength, although he is a bit slow. He attends our prayer meetings and services as regularly as anyone else in the commu-nity, and I hear from others that attending them gives him edification and pleasure.

Monday, the 26th of February. Since my dear colleague left for Savannah this morning, I conducted the prayer meeting tonight, beginning with the Sermon on the Mount of our dear Lord Christ, which came up in the sequence of the stories from the New Testament. It is noteworthy here, as it says in Luke, that Jesus lifted His eyes upon His disciples. True, He saw all the multitude around Him, but in particular He looked upon His disciples, who were the poor in spirit, whom He so praises as blessed and of whom it is said in Isaiah 66, "I shall look at the miserable," etc. This should be a comfort for all those among us who are miserable. May the Lord let them recognize this through His spirit.

Tuesday, the 27th of February. Today a couple of women from the orphanage visited my helpmeet while I was in the school for the afternoon; and upon my return I found them in prayer. When the prayer ended, they joined me in my room where one of them in particular spoke to me about the condition of her soul; and finally we prayed together.

MARCH

Thursday, the 1st of March. Last night we had thunderstorms and much rain, which will be of great benefit for the land. For several weeks now we have had wonderful growing weather; and it now remains to be seen whether we shall have more frost, as has occurred at this time and even later in previous years.

I met a man in the street who complained of his offense against a neighboring woman, to whom he had uttered angry words about another man. He knows, he said, that anger is wicked, but that it is worse to remain angry; and he therefore wished to be reconciled with those whom he offended. It was also to this end that I admonished him and made some suggestions.

On the occasion of the previous prayer meetings and our recent examination of the Sixth Commandment,[1] a woman has experienced a renewed disquiet in her heart, and she feels that she cannot be content until she has unloaded everything from her heart and been disgraced before other people. She would gladly bear this, if she could only find mercy and forgiveness before the Lord and gain certainty of her state of grace. She therefore wished that my house would soon be finished, so that she could confess all the better. I told her that, although the confession of certain serious sins is both necessary and useful in some circumstances, she should seek rest for her grieving soul not in that course, but solely in Christ's blood and wounds. Since God made her feel her sins so strongly and painfully, this was a move from the Father to the Son, whom He had sent into the world as the Savior of all sinners, and who wished to have all sinners close to Him so that He might save and deliver them. She should truly learn that the Savior had atoned in full for all her sins and paid for them; if she could take this in as part of her faith and make it her own (which is, of course, the Father's will), she would gain her peace. I guided her to 1 Corinthians 6:11, and read her the song, *Wenn dein hertzliebster Sohn, o Gott, nicht wär*, etc., and left her another for her own use, namely, *Kein grösser Trost kan seyn im Schmertz, als*, etc.[2]

Recently, N.N. has sinned by cursing offensively while in anger; and for this reason he has been kept from Holy Communion until he repents and recognizes his sin and asks for forgiveness. He is now ready to accept the deserved discipline and thus remove the offense; but I shall give him more time so that we, his wife, and others may work on him for his true improvement. Apart from this, he is still quite stupid and ignorant.

Friday, the 2nd of March. I met N. while she was singing the song *Mein Jesu, dem die Seraphinen*, etc.; and, since she had just sung the words, "I know you cannot reject me, how could you be so merciless," etc., I hoped the Holy Ghost would give her power to incorporate these dear final evangelical words into her faith so that she could hold them up to her faithful Savior even during her hours of temptation.[3] She told me how things had gone with her a short while ago; she had fallen into the most oppressive spiritual condition, in which she had only been able to crawl from one corner to the other as an impotent worm before the face of the Lord, unable to pray a single word or even to present the misery of her soul in her own thought and heart by sighing. But when she had thus whimpered for some time, she said, it had become lighter in her heart and it appeared to her as if her spirit had heard the call: "Fear not, for I am with thee," etc.; and from that time on things had gone better for her. She also said that she asked nothing more of the Lord than that He not reject her, although she well merited that; for all else, He should treat her as He wished. She was looking forward to our feast of remembrance and thanksgiving,[4] and she was resolved to thank the Lord for all His mercy and charity which He had shown to her, her late husband, and her children, particularly for having brought her to the gospel and to the recognition of the right path of salvation. She trusts more and more that the dear Lord will finally draw her children to Himself, since He had shown her so much mercy and has brought her to this country.

Because we intend to celebrate our remembrance and thanksgiving feast tomorrow, tonight's prayer meeting was largely directed to this end, as much as the Bible stories would permit, so as to prepare our minds for its proper celebration. In particular, in concluding the 11th chapter of Joshua, we learned, among other things, something about the constancy of the Israelites in the battles of the Lord; for, as it is believed, it took a full seven years until they had subdued the largest part of the Canaanites and rendered them incapable of taking back their land, and had themselves taken possession of their long promised heritage. During this time they had, it is true, experienced many trials and exercises in patience and in obedience to the Lord's will; but they had also seen much proof of the Lord's goodness, forbearance, and providence. I left it to the audience's own reflections and consideration to judge how they would have felt in their hearts if they had been among the Israelites, had been led along similar paths, and had been forced to bide their time, all the while waiting to take possession of their land, in huts, without any proper means of housekeeping, and subject to such hardships as war brings with it. Each of us would know in his heart whether he had been content with God's guidance when we incurred some delays in taking possession of our land and had to undergo much inconvenience.

Inasmuch as the Lord now had provided help and let us take possession of our land and provided other beneficial arrangements, it was our duty to thank Him all the more from the bottom of our hearts. I also asked my listeners to retain carefully in their hearts that which is noted in this chapter, both in regard to the meticulous fulfillment of the Lord's promises which He had given through Moses to the children of Israel regarding the land Canaan, and also concerning the obedience of Joshua and the children of Israel to the Lord's commandments. They would soon find, I said, that the Lord has richly fulfilled in us too all His promises, both spiritually and materially, for which we owe Him both praise and honor. But they would likewise soon realize that, in the matter of obedience to His commandments, much is still lacking, and that they should thus observe our day of thanksgiving also as a day of repentance.

Saturday, the 3rd of March. In grateful memory of God's great mercy, which He has shown to us at sea and now for some years in this country, we have celebrated again today a day of thanksgiving and remembrance, and our dear listeners have assembled several times to hear the Lord's word, to sing, and to pray; and I had heard from some among them even earlier this week that they had looked forward to this day with great joy. In the morning I spoke to the text of Acts 9:31, "Then had the churches rest," etc. In the afternoon, my dear colleague spoke to 1 Corinthians 3:6–7, "I have planted," etc. As usual, the children had memorized two Psalms for this day, namely, the 121st and the 127th; and they recited them publicly.

The morning text gave us the opportunity not only to recall the present physical and spiritual blessings provided by the Lord, in that He has kept us in peace and lets us live in a place where we can assemble quietly and without persecution, so as to edify ourselves both publicly and privately. I also reminded my listeners of how much good He had accomplished by the persecutions in their homeland, in the souls of many thousands of their countrymen, toward the extension of His kingdom; for He had chased them and driven them ever more closely to the free exercise of their religion and to the true recognition of Christ and the path to salvation by using as His tools the successors to the high priests and leaders of the Jewish people, that is, the Pope and his followers. For, if they had not been thus driven from their lands, one or the other soul might well have acquiesced and contented themselves with this or that version of the truth. And, since many had not wished to emigrate, they would probably have entangled themselves again, and more deeply, if they had not been driven out by force as suspicious people who were infected with the Protestant belief. And, since God has now brought them to peace and rest and saved them from persecution by others, it is incumbent upon them to follow in the steps of the first faithful expelled from Jerusalem and to confess Christ with heart and mouth before everyone so as to awaken others. See Acts 8:4, and 1 Thessalonians 5:11.

Sunday, the 4th of March. Today we celebrated Holy Communion with forty-four communicants. N.N., an otherwise ignorant and frivolous man, assured me that God had begun to bless in him, for the benefit of his soul, an accident by which a large branch from a tree had almost killed him and seriously injured his arm.

Right after the afternoon service my dear colleague, Mr. Boltzius, received a letter by express messenger from Savannah requesting him to go down there. He himself will report the reason for this message when the dear Lord has returned him safely to us. Because the time when we deal especially with the story of the Lord's passion is now beginning, my dear colleague had chosen to introduce the sermon on Luke 18:31 ff. with the words from John 1:29: "Behold the lamb of God, which taketh away the sin of the world." May the dear Lord fill our hearts with the beautiful matter that is contained in this verse, just as John's heart was filled with it, and teach us the right way of seeing.

Monday, the 5th of March. A little while ago an honest woman, who, like her husband, cannot read, came to me and told me, among other things, that she had to tell me something in praise of the Lord. God had listened to her prayer and united her husband with her in the spirit so that, whereas formerly each had prayed alone, they now prayed jointly in the morning and at night and took great pleasure in talking about the Lord Jesus. She had directed her husband to the example of N. and his wife, where the wife prayed first and was followed by her husband; but now that he has learned the prayer, he prays first and his wife prays after him. They should do likewise at first, she said, and afterwards he, as his wife's head, should lead the prayer, and she would follow him. The dear Lord would certainly assist them in this. She was much pleased by this; for, she said, she had heard that no one should take care of himself alone, but should also take care of others. Thus it was only proper for a married couple, who were joined in the flesh, to take care of each other's soul and thus be bound to each other in spirit.

Tuesday, the 6th of March. Last night in the prayer meeting I treated that part of the Sermon on the Mount wherein the Lord Jesus explains particularly the Fifth, Sixth, and Second Commandments.[5] When I visited a married couple today, they told me how much they cherished hearing this; and the husband said that he wished the entire congregation had been there and had heard it. This evening we will have the last part of Matthew 5, wherein again something is demanded that is quite impossible for merely natural people, but which is in fact possible for true Christians who are anointed with the Holy Ghost and full of the love of the Lord. May the Lord Jesus, who suffered for us and left us His example, fill us with the power of the Holy Ghost so that we may follow in His path and think as He, Jesus Christ, thought.

Wednesday, the 7th of March. A sudden death occurred in Savannah, for which reason Mr. Thilo and I were summoned in haste by letter to travel there and help investigate the matter.[6] We therefore departed last Sunday toward evening, running into dangerous situations twice while on the river during the night, but being delivered from any serious injury by the Lord's providence. It is dangerous to travel by water during the night because of the many floating tree stumps and other wood, particularly as the boat is carried with the greatest speed by the current.

The aforementioned death occurred as follows: A man from among the German indentured servants of the first transport[7] had received orders from the authorities to yield his musket to the constable or officer sent after him so that he, like the others, might be prevented from further shooting. However, he resisted, whereupon the constable, overcome with anger, hit him several times on the head with a leather riding crop. Finally, the man was overpowered and put in jail for resisting arrest. Upon entering the jail, he complained of a serious ache in his head, on which he had suffered many blows; and, when the prisoners were visited on Friday morning, he was found dead, having vomited all hard food he had eaten on the previous day. On the same morning the authorities set about to inspect the body, for which, according to English custom, twelve jurors or sworn honest men have been elected; in addition, the most renowned surgeon in the city as well as the storekeeper, Mr. Jones, have been summoned. Inasmuch as they cannot find any whip marks or other signs of injury, they did not consider it necessary to conduct an autopsy on the body, in particular on the head, although the widow insisted that they do so and caused witnesses to be heard under oath who testified, although with some contradictions, that he had received many blows on his head.

After Mr. Thilo discussed the matter with the city surgeon, he agreed that it was unnecessary, and might even be dangerous, to open the body, in that it had been dead for too long and the interior vessels might well have started to be affected by decomposition. At about this time Mr. Oglethorpe arrived from Savannah; and, because the German people were not content with the judgment of the jurors and of the two physicians, but demanded retribution, the widow addressed Mr. Oglethorpe, who then called me so that I would speak on his behalf; when she did not appear satisfied with his judgment either, he promised that he would make further inquiry into the circumstances of the death. This he did after dinner, at night, and asked me to be present.

These poor people see only the tragic happening, but not the judgment and the heavy hand of the Lord. The deceased was a wild man, spiteful and obstreperous during his life, and once would rather have me refuse him Holy Communion than promise his masters to improve and to hold his wife to her work. And thus it is with most of the servants from the first transport—they are disobedient loiterers, violators of the Sabbath, and drunkards, and they live in all sorts of disorder; and the only thing that surprises me is that they have been forgiven so much and not been punished with anything more severe than the withholding of their provisions. As a result, they go out to hunt and fish and even, as is being said, to steal. Some of these who belong to our church stated their desire to partake of Holy Communion next Sunday, but I refused this request pending their true improvement. There was a child to be baptized, whom I had fetched from the plantation.

Mr. Oglethorpe again showed great kindness to me; and, when he learned that the Salzburgers were requesting a new transport of their countrymen, he promised to do all he could to help and to give them their allowance in money rather than in provisions, so that each could buy what he needed for his sustenance. He has also given me good reason to hope that he will lend me such money as I might require for my house.[8] But first he will travel to Charleston, and after his return I shall take the matter up again through the offices of his storekeeper and administrator. Our poor people urgently need the wages that can be earned in building, and I do not wish to make them wait too long.

Mr. Oglethorpe was not at all pleased to learn that a warrant was recently brought to Ebenezer and that the authorities interfered in our business.[9] He is prepared to swear with hand and seal that I and my dear colleague have the power to settle any differences of opinion here and to send the disobedient who refuse to obey the rules to Savannah.

Yesterday afternoon Mr. Oglethorpe had all sorts of presents distributed among the foreign Indians,[10] of which there were about forty. For this purpose the citizens led them through the town in a procession to the town hall (which also serves as the church). They came accompanied by the music common among them, marching down the street in a rather confused fashion, and one of them had an iron pot with a hide stretched over it carried before him, on which he beat with a stick in an even rhythm, as if it were a drum. To this constant sound the Indians shouted some things with loud voices, but all on one beat and note, and they each carried a white staff bound with colored feathers in one hand, as a sign of peace, and in the other hand they carried a certain hollow dried fruit like a gourd, in which had been placed a few dried kernels, which made a rattling sound. All this, the drum as well as the chanting and the noise of the aforementioned kernels, was at one constant beat and was well coordinated: they all ceased at one time and recommenced at one time. With this music they arrived before Mr. Oglethorpe at the town hall and inclined their heads and their staffs of peace before him. Then eight of them, who are said to be their chiefs, stepped out before him, placed, one after the other, an animal skin at his feet as a gift, offered Mr. Oglethorpe their hand, and then talked to him one after the other through a French interpreter, who speaks their language.

In their speeches, they mainly sought presents from the English. Among other things they asked for horses, pistols, and money, with which they would seek to convince the French in their territory that they had not been made slaves by the English but had been treated as friends. However, nothing else was offered but the presents already prepared, in that each man received a new light musket, a piece of cloth for Indian leggings, a large white rug for a blanket and poncho, a mirror, knife, musket cleaner, shirt, and colored box, as well as powder and lead. The four women among them received such presents as befitted them.

The eight chiefs of the Indians wore old coats and had received old ugly wigs and hats, which they took off along with their hats. Some among them had long black hair into which had been braided old tobacco pipes and other strange things, and they carried whole dead birds tied to the tops of their heads. Most of the men were quite naked, apart from a small cloth in front and behind; but they were decorated in all sorts of ways from head to toe. They had painted themselves white all over with a thin paste of chalk or clay through which they had then made deep imprints or stripes with their four fingers so that their brown-black skin could be seen again. Their faces looked so terrible that one would have wished to run away upon seeing them: black, red, and white paint was painted on in a wild mixture, and with gun powder they had etched long thin stripes on their skin, both on their faces and their bodies. Most had partly dyed their hair red. Among the presents for each was also a little bag of vermillion which they use to paint and decorate themselves.

Their presentations to Mr. Oglethorpe, including the subsequent giving of presents, took from 12 noon to 4 in the afternoon, which was a great exercise in patience for him. During that time wine was poured for them and they smoked so much tobacco that the room was full of smoke. Before lighting their own pipes, they passed around one with a tin bowl filled with tobacco; it was lighted and each one inhaled a whole throat full of smoke and steam and exhaled that through both nose and mouth at once, which was a horrible sight to see. The ceremony was carried out by everyone in the room, and it is supposed to be a sign of familiarity and harmony. Finally, the citizens led them back to their quarters. For the duration of their stay in Savannah they have been maintained at the expense of the Trustees; and thus they were supplied daily with meat, fresh bread, beer, corn and other foods, which will be continued until they return to their own places. It is said that their customs are even worse than those of the Indians in our parts: they have subjected the white people to abominable things and secretly taken from their houses whatever they could lay hands on. Their drinking, shouting, and idleness they have in common with our Indians here.

Friday, the 9th of March. A married couple from among the German servants in Savannah was placed with somebody in our congregation; but, since they cannot get sufficient and properly prepared food in their place, they have asked me to take them in as servants in the orphanage.[11] They are both honest, if old, and not as suited for hard work as others; but they work faithfully with all their strength as if they were working for themselves. The man has a fine understanding and has held the prayer meeting for the people during their sea voyage. Since people are needed for the housekeeping, work in the fields, and for the children in the orphanage, and since Johann Christ has left, I have taken them in. They promised to be content with everything God may offer; and I have assured them that, if they are willing to suffer with us throughout the time of trial and beg God sincerely for His blessing, they shall participate in the blessing that will come to us in its time and praise the Lord with us. These people have left a grown son in Germany and asked me to write him in their name to join them here, as in Germany he is living among many worldly desires, as is true for most journeymen, and thus will lose the salvation of his soul. God is revealing to these people their perdition and the sins of their youth through His word; and therefore they have started to recognize those abominations, which have become almost accepted and a matter of custom in their home town, as the truly pernicious things they are, and to be horrified by them.

Saturday, the 10th of March. Today I talked to N. and N., each in his hut, and implored them to deliver themselves by means of a true conversion from the excommunication which is still binding and thus make it possible for the true purpose of this church discipline to be fulfilled in them. They promised much good, and N. requested me to include him in my prayers. These people can speak so kindly and give such good appearances that one would be tempted to think them better than they are if they had not revealed themselves by all sorts of serious outbreaks of sin.

The proverb Hebrews 2:18, "For in that he himself hath suffered being tempted," etc., which I plan to present as an exordium tomorrow, served me well today when I visited several who have borne their cross long and heavily. What could be more comforting to a grieving Christian who suffers both inwardly and outwardly than the knowledge that his Savior is a most merciful High Priest who has not only taken away both sin and its punishment through Himself but also takes into His heart the suffering of His members as if it were His own. His true help, which comes in His own time, will always reveal Him as a merciful High Priest.

A boy had sinned against his mother by disobedient and rude behavior, about which I talked to him before the others in a most serious manner, showing him that this sin was a violation of the Fourth Commandment.[12] Contrary to his usual custom, he cried bitterly on this occasion; and, when I asked him for the reason, he said that he was crying for his sin, etc.; and then he went like the prodigal son to his mother and asked her forgiveness. I thereupon asked him to come to me and admonished him to kneel together with his mother and implore our dear Savior for forgiveness for this and other sins.

Sunday, the 11th of March. Around midday an extremely strong wind rose, which blew down the fences and shook the huts to their foundations. As our church-hut is also quite decrepit, I could not hold the service there, but instead we met in the orphanage. In fact, part of that hut has been blown down by the wind. The wind continued all night so strongly that it was quite frightening to hear. I shall thank the dear Lord when I finally have a sturdier home. Not only were we much incommodated by all the dust that blew into our dwelling, but we feared that it might fall down on our heads. During this wind, the flames from a burning tree in the woods are said to have reached some of the fences outside the town and caused much damage. They would ordinarily have taken precautions; but, since the wind blew the flames about, the fire started in several places where they had not expected it.

Monday, the 12th of March. The wind has continued strongly throughout the day and has turned quite cold, so that we must fear a heavy frost tonight. A year ago we also had some very cold wind and a few night frosts, as a result of which the peaches as well as the oaks and walnuts were damaged. In our area, no acorns or nuts could be found anywhere, although they usually abound; but because of their thick shells and small kernels, there is not much to these nuts[13] anyway.

At tonight's prayer meeting, we took up the 13th chapter of Joshua, in which we find among other matters that (1) God initially gave His people only as much land as they needed for themselves and their families at that time, but promised them that He would enlarge their heritage when they had multiplied and thus required more land. At the same time we thought of the Lord's promise that He would expel the enemy not all at once but one by one, so that the animals in the woods should not have a chance to multiply and harm them. We often experience how inconvenient it is that other areas in our neighborhood are uninhabited, because the wolves and bears and other vermin have caused much damage. Therefore it is a blessing from the Lord that the Lord Trustees have ordered for each family to be given not too much and not too little land: for else we would fare like the people in Purysburg, who do not live close together as neighbors but are spread far apart because of the wide tracts of land that each of them owns, particularly the so-called squires among them. If anyone here in this land is capable of cultivating more than 50 acres with his family, he is free to sell these and is given a grant or allocation of 500 acres.

(2) We also find in this chapter that God did not mean for the Israelites to live and work together permanently, as had been necessary at the beginning when occupying the land, but that He ordered Joshua to distribute the land among them by lot and clearly define the boundaries, so that each might have his own. How good it has been for us both spiritually and materially that we should have lived for close to five years now in a close community. Now, however, the Lord has ordained that each should have his own land, on which each family should work and await the Lord's blessing. And, just as our wonderful and merciful Lord not only provided His world and divine service to

the Israelites while they lived together but also took charge of their salvation and edification by means of scattered priests and levites, so too He has instilled in our minds even in advance how we can edify both the people in the town and the people on the plantations.

Tuesday, the 13th of March. Last night we had a severe frost which has completely spoiled some things that had progressed beautifully during the preceding temperate weather. Our vines had sprouted by more than a hand, and some had new grapes; these are now completely shrivelled and ruined. It is too early to say whether the peaches have suffered.

My dear colleague returned today from Savannah to where he had travelled on business to the German people there last Saturday morning. Mr. Oglethorpe gave him £10 sterling for me to pay for some of the work on my house; and he is giving me hope that he will lend me more, as I requested in a recent letter. He also intends to return to me the money that was advanced for the surveyor and his men when they surveyed our land, which money will be used for the benefit of the congregation, in particular their herdsmen.

Mr. Oglethorpe has now gone to Charleston, where he has long since been expected. He is willing to accept a new transport of Salzburgers and to provide them with food for the initial period. But, since the inhabitants of Savannah have ganged together and made a written presentation to the Trustees that it is impossible for white people or Europeans to work here during summer time, in particular in the planting of rice, and generally as far as all fieldwork for gaining their sustenance is concerned, unless they are given the liberty to acquire black slaves, it may be difficult for the Trustees to see their way to send additional white people here at great cost. However, this presentation is obviously wrong and our community has discredited the claim that they cannot accomplish anything with their work, and therefore it is my considered duty to furnish the Honorable Trustees with information as to how we have survived in this country for five years: i.e. that it is entirely possible for white men to work here in the summer and gain their daily bread with God's help and blessing, and perhaps more so than in Germany, once the initial difficulties are overcome. And as the mischief and ill luck caused by the black slaves here is well known, which must be attributed partly to their natural wickedness and partly to the harsh, quite unChristian and barbaric treatment to which they are subjected here, I shall beg the Honorable Trustees in the name of our community not to suffer the importation of slaves into our area and neighborhood.

During the first days in Old Ebenezer we had such people among us for sawing boards, and we surely desire no more of them. In Carolina there is much unrest and fear, because sixty Negroes gathered together, killed some people, and have run off into the woods and possibly even to the Spaniards.[14] What then can we expect in this colony, which is so close to the Spanish? And, furthermore, nobody will be able to keep his belongings with any safety and assurance in his hut or field, since the main attribute of the slaves is to steal whatever they can lay their hands on. The people in Savannah also petition for the liberty to sell their land when and to whomever they want; our Salzburgers dread this freedom, as they can well imagine what kind of neighbors they will acquire in the course of time, if strange people are permitted to buy their land. For this reason I am asking the Lord Trustees in their wisdom and out of their love for poor, honest people, to prevent this unfortunate development. The congregation itself is having a letter written, in German, to Mr. Oglethorpe, asking him both for the acceptance of a new transport and for their initial provision with food, cattle, tools, and good land, as well as for his kind resolution to spare our neighborhood from the importation of slaves and also to prohibit free trade with land and homesteads.

Wednesday, the 14th of March. It has been raining all day today, and our carpenters have therefore been prevented from continuing with the construction of my house. Since it is now planting time, they will have to stop this work for some time, a fact of which I am not altogether unhappy. I had again assembled a few of the men in order to read them the draft of the letter to Mr. Oglethorpe, which according to the will of the congregation will be written in the name of all. They agreed to everything and wished to have some points inserted which might indicate their spiritual contentment with the Lord's guidance heretofore as well as their firm hope of further improvement in their circumstances.

The letter itself has now been set right and corrected, and it may not be unpleasant for our friends and benefactors if it were inserted into this diary:

P.P. "We, the undersigned Salzburgers and inhabitants of Ebenezer, request in our name and in that of our brothers, that Your Excellency show us the favor of petitioning the Lord Trustees to accept yet another transport of Salzburgers into this colony. We have jointly written to Senior Urlsperger and in that letter expressly named those Salzburgers and Austrians whom we should like to have here as our friends and acquaintances. We can state on their behalf that they fear the Lord, work willingly, and will fit into our community. We have let them know that we are much pleased with this country, and that we enjoy in it many spiritual and material benefits over and beyond any enjoyed by other people in Germany, as Your Excellency will be able to see from the enclosed copy. If the Lord Trustees should give them, like us, good land and, at the beginning, some support in provisions, tools, and cattle, and provided that the Lord bless their work, we do not doubt that they will find their sustenance here as we have done and shall be able to lead a quiet and contented life in the spirit of the Lord and in righteousness and honesty.

"True, it is hotter here than in our former country, but not as hot as we had been warned on our arrival; and now that we are accustomed to this land, it is entirely bearable, in that we use the morning and afternoon hours for work, while the hottest noon hours are spent in the shade for all sorts of housework. And, whereas the people in Germany cannot work the fields at all or only very little during the entire winter months, this season is almost the best for fieldwork in this country. We were told in the beginning that rice planting is an impossible or at least a very dangerous undertaking for white people, and a task to be left to Negro slaves but not to Europeans. However, we now laugh at this argument, having seen the contrary to be true. For last year several people among us harvested all the rice they needed for their own and their families' food, and could even sell some.

Should God grant us some funds so that we can be better equipped for rice-polishing, just as in Germany all sorts of mills are used for millet, barley-meal, etc., it will be easy and advantageous to produce rice. We take this opportunity to beg Your Excellency humbly to order several rice strainers of various sizes from Charleston for our joint use, as these cannot be obtained in Savannah. We will be in debt for these to the storehouse and pay them in due time.

"Corn, beans, potatoes, squash, cabbage, etc., have grown in such profusion that they have in part been sold by the bushel and partly fed to the cows, calves, and hogs. If the surveyor, as was his charge and duty, had assigned our plantations to us at an earlier time, instead of doing this only at the end of the last harvest; and if, furthermore, all the members of our congregation had not been sick for so long; and likewise, if we had not experienced such ill luck with the planting of yellow corn from Pennsylvania, we would have been able, with God's blessing, to sell much more corn and use the proceeds to buy the meat and clothing that we now lack. True, two acres of land were surveyed for each family some time back. But there was little rice land among these, and some soil would not bear without manure, which we did not have in the beginning. Therefore, we have not yet had all the benefit of our work which we are sure of obtaining, with the Lord's blessing, now that we have been assigned our plantations.

"We shall plant the best land first, and then will use the poorer soil in due time. Now we shall have the most difficult work, since the land has to be cleared of trees, brush and roots, and we shall have to take much care in fencing it. However, the more progress we make, the easier even this work will be, once we have established ourselves on our plantations. Furthermore, the building of houses and huts both in town and on the plantations has taken much time; also, some of us have earned some money for clothing and other necessaries by helping the construction of the orphanage and its subsidiary buildings, as well as of the house of Mr. Gronau, which was built in the heat of summer, and now of the house of our preacher, Mr. Boltzius. True, this took some of our time from fieldwork, but it was a great blessing, inasmuch as it gave us an opportunity to earn some money right here close to our homes.

"Since, therefore, neither the heat of the summer nor any other obstacle can keep us from our work in the fields, and as we wish to live with each other in good order and peace, we humbly request that the Lord Trustees never allow Negroes to be brought to the vicinity of our town and be used as slaves for the white people here, as we know from experience that neither houses nor gardens will be safe from theft, and that our very lives will not be safe from these savage people. Also, we must humbly beg that nobody be given liberty to buy land near our town, which might lead to our having wicked or disruptive neighbors, and to the expropriation or molestation of the poor among us. Instead, we wish and request that our town and its neighborhood be settled with white people, and particularly with those whose good name and honest bearing are known to us or our benefactors. The Lord Trustees have always been the benefactors of the poor and oppressed, and therefore we beg you to care for us and our community in the future as in the past, so that our descendants may also benefit from the affection you have shown us. We are praying for the happiness of Your Excellency and of the Lord Trustees in return for all your benefactions to us and request your and their continued kindness and favor. We are,

Your Excellency's and Our most Honored General's
Faithful and obedient servants,
All the inhabitants of Ebenezer."

Friday, the 16th of March. Last night we had another hard frost, which has probably spoiled the peaches and similar crops even more than the recent one. The frost was carried by the harsh winds that have been blowing for several days. I have again read to the congregation the letter addressed to Mr. Oglethorpe, which is written in the name of the entire community, and have asked them to sign their names to it, which they have done with great pleasure. This letter has been translated from German into English,[15] and a copy of the letter written to Senior Urlsperger by the congregation in November has been enclosed; a translation of the latter has not been made due to the

shortness of time and the urgency of other matters. We hope
that this will be done in London, so that the Lord Trustees and
the Honorable Society may realize that the members of our congregation are content with God's guidance and use their time
well for the benefit of their souls and for their material well-
being. We have also sent a written report of the present circumstances of the congregation to both the Lord Trustees and the
Honorable Society.

As we have no time at this point to write to London and Germany, we are sending our diary, so that you may be sufficiently
acquainted with the circumstances of our community.

Sunday, the 18th of March. Last night I was informed that a
renegade English servant from Savannah, or perhaps a soldier
from Mr. Oglethorpe's regiment, is in the vicinity of our town
and is lurking among the trees and brush in the woods armed
with a rifle, pistol, and sword.[16] At the moment, the brothers
Zuebli are quite alone on their plantation in this area; and,
while they were in the town to grind their corn, someone went
into their hut and stole several things, as well as upsetting all the
things in their hut and in open boxes. The thief surely is this
fellow who, for want of food, will probably do even more harm.
Therefore, we have done all that is necessary as a matter of
precaution by posting guards both throughout the night and
during today's service.

I consider it a most prudent arrangement by the Lord that
He has miraculously provided for the Salzburgers' plantations
to be so close together that one family can call out to the other in
case of an emergency and ask for help; others in the country are
not so well provided for. We will take care to seek out this run-
away, and for this purpose I have also sent the news to the Englishmen in Old Ebenezer, who like to earn some money. Five
pounds sterling have been promised for every man who is
caught and brought to Savannah.

After the afternoon service I had a most edifying conversation with two men who were edifying themselves by a hut in a
simple conversation from the Lord's word. Then I visited another family, but found only the wife at home, who told me how
the merciful Lord had shown great blessing to her and her husband's soul, but how busy the devil was in making them indolent

and distracting them from the search for the one necessary thing. Her expressions were so strong and convincing that my heart rejoiced, and I received greater edification from her than she from me. May God be praised for continuing to let His word be preached with blessing.

Monday, the 19th of March. The day before yesterday we found enough time to write brief letters to Court Preacher Ziegenhagen, Senior Urlsperger, and Professor Francke. As soon as we have an opportunity, and especially when we have received the promised benefactions, we shall write more with the Lord's help.

Saturday night we assembled those men who had come in from their plantations, and to these we also read the letter to Mr. Oglethorpe, which they, as did all the others, gladly signed and recognized as an expression of their wishes. We have calculated how much corn the dear Lord has bestowed on our community in the last harvest so as to inform the Lord Trustees of this in accordance with Mr. Oglethorpe's wishes. Each housefather stated his share, rather as too little than too much, and nonetheless the grand total runs to 1104 bushels Indian corn, 429 of beans or Indian peas, 518 of potatoes or sweet tubers, and 398 of raw rice. This abundance shall serve witness that Europeans and white people as well are able to work with profit during the summer, and that it is a calumny on the part of those evil men who wish our congregation ill to assert that the Salzburgers do nothing but eat and pray. This had also been reported to Mr. Oglethorpe, who has, however, been fully convinced of the contrary. For, if it were true, according to this widely spread piece of slander which has also been carried to England, that our people do nothing but eat and pray, this beautiful harvest of crops must have been bestowed on our congregation by a special miracle of the Lord, and they should attribute it to nothing but their pious prayer. The letters are being carried to Savannah today, whence they will be forwarded to Mr. Oglethorpe in Charleston.

Tuesday, the 20th of March. The men in the community had agreed to plant all those fields that are close to the town at one time, and yesterday they started on this task. In this manner they have less trouble in watching the sprouting seed, which is often severely damaged by the big birds. During the prayer meeting, the 16th and 17th chapters of Joshua gave me an opportunity to show to the congregation the benefit of God's provisions, in that we are not scattered here and there, as the people in Purysburg are, but live close to each other and thus can assist our neighbors both in the town and on the plantations. This is not the case in Savannah, where almost every one lives in his own part of the woods.

In this regard, the Lord Trustees, our dear benefactors, have acted most prudently in assigning to our people not too much but just enough land to make their living. This will put the discontented and ungrateful among us in the same position as Joseph's children, Ephraim and Manasseh in the said 17th chapter of Joshua, who were dissatisfied with their lot and inheritance, which they called but a lot and a portion, and instead demanded of Joshua cleared and prepared land on which they could live according to the desires of the flesh and enjoy themselves without working in the sweat of their brows. However, they were directed to the woods assigned to them, which they were to clear and thus use for their benefit. The Lord Trustees have also provided that, if a family should not have enough with 50 acres, they should be at liberty to sell these to an honest man and be assigned 500 acres instead.

Wednesday, the 21st of March. When I instructed a woman to earnestly seek a blessing for her daughter from the Savior, according to the example of the woman from Canaan, she told me that last Sunday she had been with her little child outside of the church hut and, when the child was restless, a Salzburger woman had said to it with tears in her eyes: "If you, dear child, but knew what the preacher is just now saying of the woman from Canaan and her daughter, you would not be so restless." She also told me of two other women behind whom she had walked on her way to church, and whom she had overheard praise the dear Lord with humble words for all the spiritual and material goods and in particular for so richly nourishing them with the Lord's word. I was pleased to hear that she uses the example of the pious people among us so well.

This very person also asked me to take N.[17] back into the orphanage, for he regretted with many tears that he had rejected, as if with both hands and feet, the good that the Lord had let him enjoy in the orphanage. I cannot take him back right away, for others may one day follow in his footsteps and cause a similar disorder. Also, he would only be confirmed in his hardheadedness, carelessness, and defiance if he were to be readmitted so quickly, as we have now done out of compassion on several occasions. She should admonish him to do penance. Once his impenitence, arrogance, and spite had been broken by the grace of Christ and he truly repented, before the entire congregation, his repeated wickedness and his contempt for the benefactions he had enjoyed in the orphanage, and once he had promised a serious improvement of his ways, then we might well consider taking him in again.

Thursday, the 22nd of March. In a place in the woods near to the town people found some hog hides and feet, which are a sign that the people who have absconded from Savannah or deserted from Oglethorpe's regiment have killed the two fat hogs that were lost from our town and have taken the meat with them. Since Saturday, when a suspicious-looking stranger was sighted, the people have been on guard, but neither he nor anyone else has been seen again.

My dear colleague had journeyed to Savannah on Monday for the letters and returned home in good health yesterday. By a good coincidence, a child was to be baptized there; and therefore the parents have been saved the inconvenience of giving us the news, and we have been spared another trip down there. Time is precious now because of the work in the fields, and we gladly spare our people trips on the boat.

In Savannah we heard the news that late last week a pirogue[18] went aground in the sea between Port Royal and Savannah, which had carried a captain and sixteen soldiers of Mr. Oglethorpe's regiment who were to be sent to the garrison at Fort Augusta above Savannah-Town. Six men threw off their clothes and saved themselves by swimming; a boat was sent from Savannah last Monday to fetch them. The boat also carried casks of meat for the storehouse and for a merchant in Savannah, all of which has been lost. The soldiers are said to have been Scotsmen who are accustomed to celebrate a bachus feast on Saint Patrick's day;[19] and, as this fell last Saturday, the 17th of March, it is assumed that they made merry on this voyage, ran onto a sandbank, and capsized. There are many Scots in this country, and the preacher in Savannah recently told me the reason for this, namely, that there was little to live on in Scotland, and therefore one is likely to meet Scotsmen seeking a living all over the world, although they pass as Englishmen because of their English tongue.[20] In Darien, a newly built town toward the Spanish border fortification of St. Augustine, close to Frederica, there are said to be nothing but Scotsmen, who also have a Presbyterian minister, by the name of MackCloud.[21]

Today, one of the German servants in our town expressed his great pleasure with this land and used this expression in particular: he would wish not to have a finger left in Germany. This was a country well suited for industrious people, he said, and it is evident that some among our Salzburgers have already reaped more rewards from their labor than many in Germany who have lived there for 40 or 50 years. All his life he had toiled hard, yet had not earned enough to buy as much as a calf. There are many lords in Germany, he said, who all wish to live off their subjects. When he had worked hard all day, he had been forced to cross several high mountains before reaching home, but here all land was flat and well situated.

Now that they have received their own land and thus been able to arrange their housekeeping and farming more suitably, our Salzburgers have only too well recognized the benefits they have received by being accepted into this colony. Since they had not suffered from want of food in their home country but had been well and sufficiently fed and had also been very well cared for in Germany, they found it quite strange at first that they should suffer want and trials in this country. Those among us who stood fast, however, are enjoying the fruits of patience and waiting even now; and they shall enjoy them in even greater measure if they but fear the Lord. Here, too, it is true: "What I do thou knowest not now; but thou shalt know hereafter." In previous times we have often recalled the beautiful expression in that extraordinarily beautiful song: *Solt ich meinem Gott nicht singen*, etc. etc., where it is said: "Thus he shall rejoice after the pain, if (N B) he can wait so long."

It is quite possible that, once it becomes known in Germany

that German people can earn their bread here in this colony and enjoy it in peace and pleasure, just as many people will travel to this country as went in past years to Pennsylvania, where there is now no land to be had. As I was told by a man born and raised in Philadelphia, the farmers there do not enjoy the same conveniences on land and on water and with respect to climate, etc., as in this colony. However, we shall not advise anybody who is poor and has to travel at his own expense to come here at this time, since there is not enough provision and food for strangers in this country, and therefore there will be few who could redeem such poor people from the captains and provide for them. It is quite another matter with the Salzburgers, who were accepted and given free passage here by the Lord Trustees or the Honorable Society and also helped in the beginning with provisions, tools, and cattle.

Somebody told me a few weeks ago that Mr. N. had announced in a letter that last fall several boats with German people had been brought to Philadelphia; but, since nobody wanted to buy them and there was an infectious disease rampant among them, they could not even be brought ashore and many of them had died on board. Almost all of them would have died a miserable death had it not been for the fact that good people in the town had sent them some supplies as a gift from the abundant crops which had been harvested at that time. I could not learn what the ship captains had finally done to dispose of these poor people. Also, they prefer black slaves to white people there, as is true for the English in this country.

Friday, the 23rd of March. A Salzburger woman, who with her husband are almost the poorest couple among us, has told me of several special traces of the fatherly providence of the Lord which she has felt both here and in Germany; and this experience strengthened her in the hope that in His time God would arrange everything for the best in their spiritual and material circumstances. He had listened to her prayers on several occasions, she said, and she did not doubt His mercy; but she was well content if He did not accede to all her wishes, for His will alone should be done. It serves to her own good that the dear Lord made her suffer much want in previous times; and in particular it makes her be grateful for and recognize as a gift of the Lord all things that He might let her come by here and there, which she might well not do if she had everything in plenty. On the occasion of the story of the miraculous provisioning of the Israelites in the desert, she remembered that God had kept her alive without food all day during both hard and light tasks, whereas in her home country she would not have been able to bear going to work without having eaten. Thus "man shall not live by bread alone, but by every word that proceedeth out of the mouth of God."

Now that God is giving her, one by one, the things of the flesh, she has hope that He will do so also in spiritual matters and save for another time those things that He is now hiding from her. A year ago she had remembered from a sermon that an untested faith is no faith at all, and thus God wished to test her faith also. The saying in Sirach 35:21, which we had as an exordium last Sunday, was very dear to her mind. Her entire speech, also with regard to her marriage and household matters, impressed me strongly both as to her great acquiescence to the Lord's will and as to her careful attention to the paths on which God has led her and will lead her in the future.

Saturday, the 24th of March. Mrs. N.[22] was much dejected by the willfulness of her son, and she almost dissolved in tears because all the work that is being done on her three children in school, in church, and in the orphanage still bears so little fruit. She claimed that her prayers for her children must not please the Lord. Several weeks ago she had good hopes for her son; for he had cried and promised much good when she had instructed him, and when he had fallen ill, her admonishments had been even more persuasive, etc. I tried to comfort her and urged her to continue in her prayers for the children, for they please the Lord, even if He does not yet let her see that He has heard her. We now have quite a number of people in the orphanage, whom the dear Lord provides with daily food and care. Many of them pray to the Father in spirit and in the truth, and He will surely let the time come when He will again throw us some material blessings to maintain the poor children and adults and continue this work, which has been started in His name from necessity and from our Christian compassion for the poor and miserable.

A fire broke out in a shed where a Salzburger kept much rice, straw, and fodder; but the neighboring women (the men were working in the field) quickly quenched it. A little child had played with fire and carried a smoldering stick into the shed, and this caused the blaze. In Purysburg whole huts have burned down on several occasions because few people or none could come to help, since they all live so far apart.

Sunday, the 25th of March. Zant is again suffering from a severe affliction on his eyes; he is suffering much pain and cannot see. He is very sensitive to daylight and therefore is forced to sit in the dark with his eyes covered by bandages. He loves to attend the preaching of God's word, and he is very worried because he cannot read anything now or be at the prayer meetings or sermons. Recently I found a pious Salzburger family planting corn on the sick man's field so that he might not miss the planting season.[23]

Today the dear Lord has let us hear much that is necessary from the story of Christ's passion and from the gospel for the 3rd Sunday in Lent,[24] in particular on the preparation of God's kingdom in our souls; may He bless all this in us with His great goodness. The repetition hour was too short to repeat everything the audience wanted, and therefore most was repeated in the orphanage before the children and others who frequently assemble there.

Monday, the 26th of March. In yesterday's repetition hour I saw a woman cry and show signs of great fear, and today I inquired from her the reasons for this. She told me that the cause was her frivolity and negligence. God had done so much for her with His word and forgiven her with such enormous patience; yet He had achieved so little with her that she felt that she was not living in the order to which all must conform if they wish to be saved. He would surely become wearied of her. And another thing hurt her very much too. Namely, that, while she fully felt the power of the divine word which always stirred her heart so much that others could see it in her behavior, she could not in the same measure prove it in her life. This was bound to create great annoyance in others, who might wonder why this woman acts such and such in church and seems to be so deeply moved, yet cannot prove it by her life, etc.

I told her that she need care little for the annoyance that others might feel at her behavior in church, but that her worry should be to find peace for her grieving soul in Christ's wounds. I again explained to her the words heard yesterday: "Do penance and believe," etc.; and I showed that doing penance meant receiving a different spirit from the Lord so that one might hate evil through His grace and love the good which He orders and which pleases Him. Since she was still of a feeble spirit in this respect, it would much pain and grieve her; and that, indeed, was penance. But she should not lose courage thereby or give up everything for lost and flee from Christ even further; but instead she should do as the Israelites did in the desert, who, when feeling pain of the snake bite, looked, upon God's order and promise, at the serpent of brass and thus became well. The Lord Jesus meant her, too, I added, when He said: "Look unto me, and be saved, all ends of the earth."

I also reminded her of what we had said on Saturday in the prayer meeting concerning the sanctuaries. Those poor souls who had incurred blood-guilt accidentally or unwittingly ran as well as they could, in all their fear and terror, up the hills to reach the nearest sanctuary; and there they found peace and safety. She knew of the example in Philippians 3 of Paul, who turned his back on all things in order to seek Christ so that he might be found in Him as in his sanctuary; and he tried with all his might to grasp this treasure ever more strongly. She should do this too, for otherwise she would waste her strength and her spirit in legalistic anxiety,[25] but nothing would come of it until she came to Christ as a miserable soul. "Oh," she said, "I well know how my strength is sapped by such fears; food does not taste right in my mouth, nor can work please; I am becoming ever more incapable in all things," and she urgently requested my prayer on her behalf.

In last Saturday's prayer meeting on the occasion of the ordained sanctuaries, I reminded our listeners what a great blessing it was that the Lord so far has held His hand over us so that none among us has been inadvertently slain or has become even an unwitting or accidental slayer or destroyer of one of His fellow members, although this could easily have occurred in the course of joint construction and other work. We encouraged each other to praise the Lord for having turned such danger from us. I also enjoined my listeners, now that they are again engaging in new, hard, and often dangerous work on their plantations, such as building, joint fence making, etc., to seek the true sanctuary in accordance with the example of St. Paul, Philippians 3, so that, if death should suddenly strike one or the other among them, death would find him in the right place, for else his blood would be on his own head. They well knew that three such sudden deaths had occurred in Savannah. I was much taken by the fact that God ordained these sanctuaries at a time when the Israelites must have needed them most; that is to say, at the time when they were settling in their country, when such an accident could easily have happened while they were jointly building their cities, etc.; and therefore we should all the more carefully benefit from this typical provision made by the Lord in similar circumstances.

Tuesday, the 27th of March. We are now having the most pleasant weather, both sun and warm rains, which make the newly planted corn sprout in a few days' time. This year much land will be planted with corn, beans, rice, and all types of native crops. If the Lord gives His blessing, many a family will emerge from their previous want, which honest souls suffer patiently in faith and hope.

Wednesday, the 28th of March. On our house visits, we now mostly find only the women at home, particularly those with small children who cannot join their husbands in the fields. One Salzburger woman accused herself harshly for her lack of faith and her ungratefulness. She recalled that God had worked on her strongly from the days of her childhood, had led her with her family and countrymen from Popery, and had always granted her a good opportunity to become a true Christian. Also, He had saved her from temptation through her long voyage to America and through her marriage to a godfearing man; and yet things were not well with her Christianity. Her heart was full of sin, etc. Occasionally her heart so oppressed her that, while she might kneel, she could not utter a word, and therefore to relieve her spirit she would have to rise from her knees without prayer and do some work. When again she attempted to pray, she might find it easier; but then she was saddened that she had to succumb at first and that the devil would have won.

I dissuaded her from this wrong worry with the judgment of our blessed Luther, who considered a faithful and patient execution of one's work to be a prayer and God-pleasing service; and I showed her that a Christian would have to use all his advantages in order to fight his way through and defeat the devil. I also told her that it was part of the drive from the Father to the Son if the great misery of her sins was revealed to her, for by this very revelation the Father wished to drive her to the Son as the Physician and Helper, whose sole office it is to save sinners. She was not the first, I told her, whose conversion was a painful thing; all those fared this way in whose souls God wished to lay a deep foundation for true Christianity in the recognition of their sins and lead them into true poverty of the spirit so that Christ might be their One and All. There are people, it is true, who appear to get ahead more quickly and to advance in their salvation, or so it seems; but they lack a true foundation. I said a few more things according to her circumstances, such as to arm herself by prayer and watchfulness against all contrary thoughts and impressions that are in conflict with God's fatherly love and His unspeakable compassion for repentant sinners, also in her feeling of sinfulness, not to be held back by the law and legalistic complaints, from which she would not derive any strength, etc.

Thursday, the 29th of March. In tonight's prayer meeting I was overcome by a seemingly dangerous attack which forced me to interrupt the meeting and send the congregation home. However, the dear Lord heard our prayers and blessed some of the means we had used, so that it all ended better than could have been expected. May He alone be praised and adored therefore! May He teach me to count my days so that I may spend their remainder as days of preparation for a blessed death. By His mercy I have renewed my resolution to penetrate ever more eagerly through prayer and faith into the wounds of Christ as the true sanctuary. May His help be with me!

Friday, the 30th of March. I have been told that wild cats and animals called raccoons have again damaged the newly planted corn in the ground by night as much as the crows and ravens damage it by day, the latter of which can at least be driven away. Here in the woods there seem to be no wild boars, which otherwise would do much damage in the fields.[26] But there are plenty of vermin, which, however, are very shy and run from anyone who makes a hue and cry. Therefore, we have no instances of anyone being hurt by a wolf or bear unless these have been made wild by a misaimed shot. When the Indians hunt for bear, they bring along many hounds, which chase the bear up a tree, so that several of the Indians may shoot at once.

Saturday, the 31st of March. I have heard from the people whose plantations are on Abercorn Creek that they feel their health to be better there than here in the town, despite the fact that they are much inconvenienced by the lack of well-built huts and other circumstances. There are many healthy springs out there and beautiful little wells flowing from the hills, although here, too, we have enough spring water for our needs. We had been worried that the people might be attacked by some new, violent disease once they moved into a new part of the woods; but as necessity and the Lord's providence required it, they did move nonetheless, and they seem to be successful in their endeavor. Thus, our Lord can do more than we ask for or understand. For we shall ascribe such benefits to Him and His fatherly providence, rather than to natural causes.

I talked to the sick Zant according to his spiritual and physical circumstances from John 9:4, whose beautiful words I intend to use in the exordium tomorrow, if it pleases the Lord to relieve me of my hoarseness and strong headcold. He was all the more impressed by these words of our dear Savior, since they were spoken on the occasion of the cure of a man who had been born blind. The good man has much work during this time of planting, but he must suffer the will of the Lord and be patient and obedient, as were the blind man and others whom Jesus helped; and the hour of help shall come for him too.

APRIL

Sunday, the 1st of April. My dear colleague has taken my place in preaching the Lord's word both during last night's prayer meeting and this morning, as my sore throat and heavy cold make it difficult for me to speak. He dealt with the story of the passion both in the morning and in the afternoon; and, although the repetition hour was cancelled, he held the prayer meeting in the orphanage with everyone assembled there and read some passages for their edification. If the Lord had given me the strength and ability, I would have used today's text for the Fourth Sunday in Lent[1] to make everyone aware of the precious time remaining before Easter and to impress on our listeners the work of the Lord Jesus and our duties before Easter. His task was not only to feed the hungry, but above all He was pained by their miserable spiritual circumstances; and He proved to be their Physician and Shepherd (cf. Mark 6:34). Likewise, he was testing the people and His disciples, and finally He granted them their material share, etc.

Monday, the 2nd of April. A Salzburger told me of a young man on his plantation and said that he is responding well to instruction and has become quite regular both in prayer and in his tasks; yet he has noticed that, once together with frivolous young men, he returns to his previous frivolity. There is much blessing if one works on the other in the spirit; and this can well take place during their fieldwork, since their plantations are close by.

By now, all in the community are provided with quite good land, and there are still some plantations left over which, although not as large as the others, are not to be despised and, with the help of the other inhabitants of our town, can well be turned into useful land by industrious people who may eventually join us. We two are the last; and, in order to avoid all semblance of suspicion or offense, we hesitated to make our choice until all our listeners, who must sustain themselves by the work of their hands and the product of their fields, had been provided for according to their wishes and desires. But, as we have the right to acquire a piece of land for ourselves, we shall not ignore this benefaction but intend to take the two plantations closest to the town, which, to be sure, are useless now, but may well become useful later, when enough manure has become available. Nevertheless, some tracts are convenient for planting rice and corn, but we shall not undertake anything with these until our families consider it advisable, without our involvement.

There is much grass here, and it would become even more abundant if the ground were worked properly; and therefore we have been advised to use these two plantations, which lie right next to each other, for raising cattle. But we shall not become involved in matters of raising food; on the other hand, since we cannot do entirely without servants, we shall let these do what they can and may. Because they are honest and faithful, we have no worry. For several months now, I have benefited from the services of an honest and faithful fieldhand[2] who, although he is already fifty years old, has much experience and makes as much effort with the land as he is able.

Tuesday, the 3rd of April. It is said that Mr. Oglethorpe intends to travel by land from Charleston to Savannah and will inspect the sawmill and the Trustees' cattle in Old Ebenezer; and, presumably, he will pass through our town afterwards. He has not been here since we settled at this place. Our people would much like me to ask him for his help in erecting a flour mill, and I shall see if an opportunity for this arises during his visit. True, a mill has been constructed and is driven by two strong men, but it does not permit making more than 1 bushel a day of clean flour, and therefore they lose much time with grinding. Others who cannot spend their time on grinding must eat coarse-ground corn, which does not agree with them too well. If we had a good flour mill, our people could use the Indian corn to much better advantage than is now possible and would have to use much less wheat flour, which costs much money.

A barrel of wheat flour, which is not much whiter than good rye flour in Germany, usually costs about 24 shillings sterling, or more than 10 florins in German money; and such a barrel contains no more than 3 bushels or English measures, each bushel being counted as 32 quarts. The rice, too, yields good flour, and the people here often mix this with Indian corn-meal for baking. Near our town there is not only Abercorn Creek, but also other constantly running small streams on which it should be quite feasible to build a good flour mill, at least with a millrun.

Two of the carpenters who are building my house are well-versed in mill-building, and we have a Salzburger in the orphanage who is devoted to its service, and he is a trained miller who well understands milling.[3] If the dear Lord wished to provide some funds for the orphanage, we could have a flour mill constructed at the expense of that institution, which would then also be responsible for its maintenance. Everyone would be prepared, as is only fair, to contribute mill fees either in kind or in money; and thus we could slowly repay the initial costs.

It would seem that neither in Savannah nor at any other location in the vicinity are the circumstances so favorable for the construction of such a flour mill as in our area, inasmuch as the tides do not run up here. Also, since the carpenters would have industrious and faithful helpers in their task from our Salzburger group, the costs would not be very high. If we had but the tenth part of the money spent on the sawmill in Old Ebenezer, we would be able to construct both a flour and a sawmill; and, hopefully, it would last longer and be of greater usefulness than is to be hoped for the mill there. At the present time, however, there is probably little hope of getting any funds for this from Mr. Oglethorpe, as money is scarce. Who knows how the dear Lord will provide help in this matter.

Wednesday, the 4th of April. We now have only a few children in the school, as they are needed all day in the fields to guard against the ravens and crows that scratch up the newly planted corn. However, they are being sent to the prayer meetings most of the time, so that they do hear something every day for their edification.

Thursday, the 5th of April. A woman complained of her lack of real and deep sadness regarding her sins. She wished to experience such sadness in the measure of the plentiful sins she committed in childhood and youth, when her church-going, singing, and all other spiritual exercises had been nothing but sin, as God now has made her realize. He is revealing ever more sins to her conscience, particularly during prayer, which she then confesses to the Lord with tears; and she would much desire at these times, when all is being revealed and made alive to her, to have one of her teachers by her side so she could confess to him too. She often remembered her wickedness and the persons with whom she had sinned, and she now fears that they may well testify against her on that great judgment day that she gave them opportunity to sin but not to repent.

I admonished her to pray for those fellow sinners whom she remembered and assured her she need not fear their accusations. Instead, if she truly converted, she would shame them all the more with her example, and they would have no excuse for frivolously rejecting the mercy which God had so often offered to them as well as to her, whereas she would be raised before angels and men by the unspeakable compassion of the Lord, which had so strongly worked on her. I also showed her the right manner of penitence or conversion to the Lord and showed that legalistic fear and sadness for her sins is not the salutary remorse and sorrow that leads to salvation. If God gains so much in us that we recognize our sins as sins, feel them, and tear away from them by the strength of God's mercy and turn to Christ and His dear reconciliation with a yearning, longing, and confident heart, and ask for Him as the highest treasure of all, then our conversion and rebirth will have occurred in truth. Then the true struggle will really begin: for the more a Christian grows in the recognition of the glorious and blessed Savior (for which we should pray fervently in accordance with Ephesians 1:16), the more hostile he becomes toward his previous life of sin and against the nature that still lives and rages within him. This is confirmed by the example of the Samaritan woman in John 4.

Friday, the 6th of April. In yesterday's prayer meeting we considered the resolution of the 21st chapter of Joshua and learned that the servant of the Lord, Joshua, renders glorious testimony of the Lord's faithfulness in fulfilling His promises, which He had made to the fathers and their descendants, the Children of Israel, concerning the land of Canaan. As we have noted in the course of the story, there were many initial trials because of which faithless and materially inclined Israelites grumbled and complained and said, much in the manner of other wicked people in our time, that God had promised us much, and in particular a land where there floweth milk and honey, but none of these promises has been kept, not even their tenth part is true, oh, if only we were in another place, etc.

Those, however, who withstood the trials and waited for the fulfillment of God's promise in faith and patience, such as Joshua, Caleb, and others, could now pronounce and repeat this testimony in honor of the faithful Lord and for strengthening the faith in others. That which could not be said of the settlement or establishment of the Israelites in the first, second, or third year (for God does everything in His own time), that could well be said in praise of the Lord and His providence in the seventh and subsequent years, as long as they feared the Lord. We sang in conclusion, with hearts and mouths, *Gott hat alles wohl bedacht, und alles, alles recht gemacht, gebt unserm Gott die Ehre*.

It deeply impresses us to find our circumstances and previous experience as good as replicated and confirmed in the Lord's word. On the occasion of our house calls we often hear that such details go to the hearts of these eager souls as especial evidence of the divine providence over us, which others have also experienced; and they also remind us of our duty and encourage them in their trials and strengthen them in their patience.

In tonight's prayer meeting we again learned from chapter 22 several points which may serve much good among us. The children of Israel in the land of Canaan were much concerned that the altar to be erected by the three and a half tribes might cause apostasy, a schism in the true religion, or idolatry. This should show us that we too should take great care in our new arrangements in this country that all objectionable conduct be controlled right off before it can grow into a strong stream. And as they were prepared, for the love of the Lord and the salvation of their brothers, to relinquish to them part of the inheritance already allotted to them and be content with smaller shares rather than acquiesce to such disorder in their religious affairs, our listeners will receive a good example of how they, too, should practice self-denial with regard to their plantations and such temporal goods as the Lord may have granted them, for the glory of God and the benefit of their brothers who may follow after them and who may wish to live with us close to our church and school.

Who knows how well this beautiful example may serve us when another transport arrives? Because the three and a half tribes, who had to leave the holy services with a heavy heart to move into their new land, so carefully provided for a share in the true service for their children and children's children so that these might remain within the true church, this example not only shames many hundreds of so-called Christians in this country and in this region, who care little for church and school and seem to value their plantations and cattle more highly than their children, but also reminds our listeners of what is necessary, namely, that their foremost concern should be that the purity of the Lord's word and the Holy Sacraments be preserved until the end of their days and for their most distant descendants.

If parents and adults are careless in providing for the salvation of souls and the maintenance of holy services, their children will follow soon; and then there will be the judgments whereby the Lord will remove the candlestick from its place.[4] This, too, may well serve to remind our listeners, who are gradually moving to their plantations to set up their households there, of their duty, since we have heard how Joshua admonished the three and a half tribes who departed for their inheritance to be industrious not only in material things, such as in their field work, in fortifying their towns, etc., but above all in their fear of the Lord and in their honest love for Him, which necessary admonition he repeated solemnly several times before his end (see chapters 23 and 24) and above all warned them faithfully and in a fatherly way of all things that were in conflict with the practice of God-fearing men.

Saturday, the 7th of April. In the last few weeks it has been quite cold, and last night we even feared a frost. This has been averted by the dear Lord, however; for otherwise much would have perished in both the fields and the gardens. May He be praised for this and all His other help. It is most astonishing that the recent frost killed off all the shoots of the cultivated vines, whereas it left the native or wild vines unharmed, and even the smallest and lowest among them bear a large number of grapes. In the garden near the storehouse, which was given to Mr. Thilo last year, we found a young vine whose branches, even the thinnest, were so full of small grapes that even the people who had grown grapes in Germany could not remember ever having seen anything like it. Since the native vines grow so well here and bear so richly, we shall plant many of them in our gardens next fall with God's help in order to see if they can be trained and domesticated.

This morning before dawn my dear colleague travelled to Savannah in order to preach God's word to the German people there, if it pleases the Lord. May God give him strength in body and soul to do much good in His name and for the salvation of the souls there. The hearts of most of them are as hard as a rock, and they have so many prejudices that the strength of the word cannot enter. We also hear how God is after them with many physical judgments and harsh chastisements, but they will not feel this and consider themselves innocent and their afflictions as a cross.

Sunday, the 8th of April. By the grace of the Lord, the beautiful words of Jesus from today's gospel: "Verily, verily, I say unto you, if a man keep my saying, he shall never see death," etc. have been so blessed in my heart as well as in the hearts of my avid listeners that we could make up for what we had neglected in previous times in our earnest search for salvation, in which endeavor the dear Savior Himself is offering us His divine strength and assistance. It is a great comfort to us that it is not too late yet; for it is written that, if someone, be he the greatest sinner, shall keep My word, even if it has not been done before, etc. As an exordium I took the words from Hosea 13, "O Israel, thou hast destroyed thyself; but in me is thine help," etc., which have always much impressed me.

In the afternoon I dealt with the portion of the passion story from Matthew 27:11–26, which was next in order; and I have much reason to praise our faithful Savior for His kindness and gentleness, for He not only gave me strength for my sermon but also awakened all our hearts through these words of His suffering and through the means to our salvation so dearly merited for us, to give praise with words, heart, and truthfulness.

A woman told me that after the sermon on the 20th chapter of the Revelations of St. John, from which the 6th verse had been quoted, she had re-read the text by herself and had been much dejected by the last verse, "And whosoever was not found written in the book of life," etc. She had been thrown into a great sorrow because this had stirred something in her conscience that had always caused her the greatest grief. But God had placed such a blessing in her heart from the story of the passion that her heart had grown lighter and she had been encouraged in her struggle. Lighthearted men and women think little of the consequences of yielding to lust in one's youth and of sinning against God and their consciences, and of how painful it will be afterwards when they wish to atone in order to gain mercy and an assurance of the forgiveness of the horrors they have committed. Oh, but that all would let themselves be warned! Psalms 50:21–22. In the conduct of their Christian lives, such people fare as do those who once broke an arm or a leg and who always feel the pain anew when the weather changes, although the broken bone may have been mended. There you must learn the grief and pain that come from leaving the Lord your God.

Monday, the 9th of April. Last night my dear colleague returned well and sound from Savannah. To be sure, he again had many listeners to whom he preached the word of the Lord twice; but he brought few good tales of these miserable and wayward creatures. The word seems to them as a burden that is too heavy, and they use many excuses to rest undisturbed on the bed of their sins. Disregarding their poverty, they continue in their old German customs on the occasion of weddings and baptisms, where they get together to drink, eat, and engage in all sorts of godless ways to their heart's content and to excess, living all the while in all kinds of vices. Since they have not shown any improvement after partaking of Holy Communion, we much fear giving it to them again, and therefore this service has not been held for some time.

In Savannah most foodstuffs, in particular meat, have become quite scarce and dear; and hence it will be good if the people in our town take up cattle-raising, in which enterprise they should eventually become more successful than heretofore, now that we have more fodder for the cattle and more corn and beans for the hogs and the poultry.

The people in Savannah do not know of any reason why no ships have landed in Charleston for the last three months, for at this time they usually come there for rice. The long delay in getting letters and news from Europe may well be due to the lack of an opportunity to forward things. As great as is our present longing for news, as great will be our pleasure and edification once we again see a few lines from our Fathers and friends.

Wednesday, the 11th of April. A woman who can read but little and desires a true benefit for her soul from the Bible verses is having those verses that are taken up in the congregation on Sundays underlined in red ink. I was much pleased that she had committed many to memory from repeated hearing and reading, and I had to underline these for her, together with others which she found edifying. I heard that her neighbor occasionally comes to her hut and inquires as to how much she has retained from the sermon.

A woman here has had a lame foot for a year; and, since nothing seems to work, she has shown the foot to an Indian who showed by his gestures that he wished to help her. He asked for a glass bottle, which he broke, and then sharpened a shard to a point as for a lance. He then punctured the skin around both swollen ankles, as is done for bleeding; but, when no blood flowed, he sucked it out by mouth, and this caused her some relief.

Thursday, the 12th of April. Yesterday toward evening Mrs. Schweiger gave birth to a young daughter, who was baptized before the prayer meeting. The woman has had many epileptic seizures; and, since God has helped her with all this, He deserves praise for it. The French woman is said to have again rendered very good services on this occasion.

Our servant showed me a vine which he had pruned this year and cared for with much attention, so that he hopes for a good harvest of grapes this fall. The vine was old and thick and had borne many shoots even last year, which the man had put in the ground during the winter and thus preserved. In the spring, each of the plantings had greened and started to bear grapes, which even now are beginning to blossom; the man is much surprised by this, as he had seen nothing like this in Germany. These vines are planted in a very inconvenient spot, and we fear that thoughtless children may damage them and tear off the green grapes. If not, these grapes may become quite large and give proof of what knowledgeable people can do in this country in matters of wine-growing. We shall replant the vines in the fall in a better place.

Friday, the 13th of April. This week most of the men in the community are busy on Abercorn Creek in erecting a common fence around their new fields, which some of them intend to plant this year. In this country every plot must be well fenced, since the English let their cattle and horses run free in the woods. The hogs in particular would do great damage, because they cannot be kept here as in Germany for lack of proper arrangements and the money to pay swineherds. If there were only a beaten path, we would much like to visit the men in the fields. But everything is gradually coming to better order.

My dear colleague is often visited in his house by many of our listeners, in particular the truly honest N.,[5] whom he himself visited today in her hut, finding much edification there. (1) He was particularly impressed with her serious concern for her own soul; she takes her prayers, vigils, and struggles very seriously and tries to become ever more similar to her Savior, yea, to crawl quite unto him. (2) He was also impressed with her honest concern for the souls of her children, for whom she prays incessantly, admonishing them and turning everything to their use. She employs well the saying: "What I do now, you do not know," etc., which she has heard on several occasions in the prayer hour, for the purpose of learning how all the dark pathways on which the Lord has walked with her have truly been for the best of her soul, and thus He will continue to act for her and hers. She considers it a precious benefaction that our glorious Lord has brought her here to this country, to a quiet lonely place, and to the abundant preaching of His word.

Saturday, the 14th of April. I learned from two Englishmen that Mr. Oglethorpe has returned from Charleston to Savannah this week; therefore, the rumor that he would travel by land to Old Ebenezer and thence to our town was not founded. Tonight we read, God be praised, the conclusion of the 24th chapter of Joshua and thus have finished the whole book. May the dear Lord be humbly praised for all His assistance and blessing which He bestowed on us during the contemplation of the beautiful Bible stories and other glorious truths. May He leave us His grace from this until our blessed eternity. When Joshua recollected the many benefactions received by the Israelites and their ancestors, we remembered the abundant good which our faithful God has shown us in previous and present times according to the three main articles and which resemble in the main those received by the Israelites. Just as they were led to join each other in an upright fear and in the service of the Lord, we too, in considering the rich enjoyment of God's beneficence, have ample cause to gratefully remember our duty to return the love of our good God, who loved us first when we too wished to hear the comforting words from the mouth of the Lord which Joshua, Moses, Eleasar, and all the saints who profited from the talent entrusted to them have heard: "Well done, thou good and faithful servant," etc.

Sunday, the 15th of April. I have been quite feeble physically for the last few days; but, when I attempted the sermon in the name of the Lord, He strengthened me so much that I could also hold the repetition hour later in the evening. We have truly learned that, if we attend to the ways of the Lord, He can generously do more than what we beg for or understand. I have also noticed that the kind Savior has placed His blessing on the preaching of His word.

Two men from Old Ebenezer who work on the sawmill in the service of the Trustees complained to me that their master, one of the two millers there, had pressed them to go to Savannah this week, thus making them miss celebrating Holy Communion and Easter. I told them how I would act through God's grace, namely, I would hold my duty to God higher than that to men, which befits all Christians, and thus rather suffer in the flesh than sin against God and conscience. Mr. Oglethorpe much likes our holding a service for the German servants in Savannah every four weeks, and therefore he will hardly like to see those prevented from attending services who live close by in Old Ebenezer. A pious man from the congregation had been called to Old Ebenezer yesterday for important reasons and had to spend half of the day there today; he could hardly find words to complain about the great disorder in which both men and women live there. He took this opportunity to thank the Lord for his salvation from all temptations to sin, which had been his recognition of the good that God bestows on us in our solitude.

Monday, the 16th of April. N.N. notified me that he wished to go to the Lord's Supper this coming Friday, and on this occasion asked me from his simple heart to devise such a prayer for him as would fully express the state of his heart, which he has revealed to me so far and will reveal further. True, he said, there were beautiful prayers in Johann Arndt's *Garden of Paradise*[6] and in Haberman's prayer book as well,[7] but none was fully applicable to the state of his soul. He wished to follow the advice he had recently heard publicly and again a few days ago from my dear colleague, and to present the state of his heart in a simple manner and in his own words to the dear Lord; but in praying he would tend to forget some things which he had wanted to request or for which he had wanted to thank the Lord, etc. At another time, he asked me for a prayer for his ministers; and, as he found one he considered suitable in his prayer book, he had marked it carefully. He also told me that he was using the *Treasure Chest*,[8] which he had borrowed from me, to good purpose. Whenever he had no time to read, or was about to leave for or return from work, or whenever there was an inner or outer disturbance, he would take along one of its sayings.

Tuesday, the 17th of April. In recent weeks, N. has repeatedly indicated that he wished to go to Holy Communion next Friday; and therefore he came to see me again today. However, I begged him to consider his condition and said he would find that he was not truly prepared for such a holy and important matter. We were now almost upon the holiday on which God would give him opportunity to hear much good; and the dear Lord had surely kept a blessing in store for him, which he should above all not reject, as on previous occasions. I explained to him why we could not let such people as him simply run to the Lord's Table, and that this was not with any intend to hurt them but rather to do them good and restrain them from the heavy sin of an unworthy enjoyment of the Holy Supper. Instead, we wished to bring them to reflection and true improvement in regard to the dangerous state of their soul. He well understood our admonishment and accepted the advice to pray with greater industry than before, and to pray as well for the right thing for him: that is, to pray for a repentant heart, to free himself from frivolous companions and profligate living and, instead, to seek the friendship of one or the other pious member of our community, and to take some pains with such prayer.

Wednesday, the 18th of April. More than a year ago Riedelsperger lost a large ox, which returned to our herd yesterday. The beast was not branded, and therefore he could easily have lost him. It is to be butchered today, and the meat will be sold partly to the orphanage and partly to others in our community; and this is a true blessing in view of the high price and scarcity of meat these days.

This year almost everyone is complaining that, during their work in the fields and even in their huts, the people are plagued by large and small gnats. This pest is much more abundant this year than formerly, and those living on their plantations on Abercorn Creek find little rest from them even during the night in their huts.

Together with some of the carpenters, a few men from our community are busily engaged, despite their plentiful fieldwork, with finishing the living room in my new house, as they are well aware of the inconvenience that I suffer from pests and other causes in my present hut. Once the fieldwork is over, the carpenters will surely get together to lay the floors, make shutters, doors, stairs, and the kitchen, all of which are still lacking. In the beginning no one could have imagined that this house of one story could have required so much work and time, even though it is quite spacious, comfortable as a dwelling, and durable. Had I realized all this in advance, I would probably not have resolved to undertake this construction, although it is dictated by dire necessity.

Toward evening we had a thunderstorm and a fine, fruitful rain which is much needed for the crops, which have wilted in many places because of the recent, long drought. When there is no rain for long periods, the wells dug by our people tend to run dry; in the orphanage, however, the well has, with God's help, been so well constructed that they have enough water all year around. That well is quite deep, and therefore its water is quite fresh, clear, and of good taste; it also agrees with the people who drink it (since we lack the capacity to brew thin beer).

The water level is only about three feet, and it neither rises nor falls, regardless of whether there is rain or drought. Even when the Savannah River is at its height, the water in the well does not rise; and likewise, when the river is low, the water in the well does not fall. We do not know the reason for this.

Good Friday, the 20th of April. As is our custom every year, we have spent this day as a high holy day in singing, praying, and a threefold preaching of the Lord's word. Also, we have held Holy Communion, at which we had fifty-six communicants. The story of the cross, which is a folly to those who will be lost, but God's strength for those who will be blessed, has been the most prominent, indeed the only, topic presented today; and may the Lord bless it in all our listeners for their true salvation. In previous days during the evening prayer hour we have suspended the reading of the Old Testament in its proper order and accommodated our sermon to the present time. In two prayer meetings I have tried to present the humiliated and exalted states of David, the man according to God's heart, as a fitting prefiguration[9] of the two states of our King of Mercy and Redeemer, Jesus Christ, and to present the image of the heart of David, which was so inclined to forgiveness, as a parallel to the Heart of Christ, which gives forth nothing but reconciliation and mercy. I also presented 2 Samuel 19, as was our duty. May the Lord transfigure Himself in His Jesus love in all our souls!

One of the German servants among us who had also gone to Holy Communion had cursed while herding the cattle, as I was informed before last night. When I had him summoned early yesterday morning, before we went to church, and presented him with this abomination, he did not deny it but with tears accused himself of this and other gross sins; and he promised to see me at some other time so as to relieve his heart. Yesterday after the sermon he met me and said that the Lord had touched his heart; he would much like to confess to me if only we could find an opportunity as is available in Germany in churches and vestries. The expression he used in this regard well showed me that he has an almost idolatrous belief in such external means as simply going to confession and absolution. As we are lacking a good house for congregating, my house will prove a good spot for our listeners to come forth more freely with an open and repentant recognition of their sins. This is also quite necessary for those souls who take their salvation seriously and are driven to it by their conscience. There will be no way of finishing my room this week after all, as the workers have been prevented by some other matters. I shall not press them, but gladly stay in my hut, as I do not in any event approve of the people taking on too much work during this week, particularly as we get closer to Holy Easter.

Saturday, the 21st of April. We again held our preparation for Holy Easter in the orphanage, where we have a beautiful opportunity to pray on our knees to our God and Father, reconciled to us in Christ, once we have dealt with the divine word and have refreshed our hearts from it. We used for our purpose the beautiful examples from John 12 such as the divinely simple Mary, her brother Lazarus, so dearly beloved by Christ, and the entire multitude who led Jesus, the King of Mercy, into Jerusalem with shouts of faith, love, and joy. However, our talks dealt particularly with the heartfelt desire of some Greek men who dearly wished to see Jesus on the day of Easter. We thereby learned for our instruction, edification, and imitation, that even then our merciful God had extended His hands beyond the Jewish people, as His heart longed for the salvation of all men; and just as the devil and his tools were vexed that everyone followed the Savior, just as great was God's joy at this example of His work.

The Greeks had come to Jerusalem to adore the Lord and receive more instruction and guidance for the true recognition of Israel's God; and, since they had learned much that was strange and noteworthy of the Lord Jesus on this occasion, they longed as poor heathens for His closer aquaintance, company, and instruction. Thus they give us a beautiful example to which we should direct our spirits at Easter in particular. They were not content with good thoughts, wishes, and resolutions, but used the means to see Christ: for they addressed Philip, etc. And, as this apostle united with Andrew to present the desire of these Greeks jointly to our Lord Jesus, we revived ourselves with the words in Matthew 18:19, "If two of you shall agree on earth, etc.," to appeal to the Lord Jesus together during our prayer meeting, so that we might see Him and come to His living understanding; and to this end we admonished both parents and children and all neighbors. We wished to rejoice in the light of this example of the two apostles and thank the Lord for any opportunity to lead souls to Jesus in these days and to bring them to recognize Him. May He be transfigured in all of us; for He Himself says that the hour has arrived that the Son of man should be transfigured among Jews and heathen alike, having laid the ground for this by His death and resurrection and merited all the goods of the Kingdom of the Lord.

Monday, the 23rd of April. One of the German servants who works as a herdsman among us drank some stagnant water in the woods yesterday and had some terrible pains in his abdomen last night, so that it was feared that he would not survive the night with these pains and the distension of his belly. However, the Lord blessed a few enemas in him, so that the pain subsided around midnight and he is well on the way to recovery. I asked him today what he thought of his chances of salvation had he died yesterday. He said that he believed he would have gone to Heaven, for he had truly reconciled himself with God and man in Friday's Lord's Supper. If he only did not have to herd cattle, but could live in the town like other people, close to God's word and by the work of his hands, he would live as piously as he has seen others live here, whose example edified him, etc.

I asked him nonetheless if he had in fact read the two chapters from Arndt's book on *True Christianity*, namely book I, chapters 2 and 41, which I had recently instructed him to do. And, when I learned that he had read only a part of them, I read the aforesaid second chapter to him and his wife myself, showing him how salvation presupposes true faith and true faith presupposes a true conversion. And it was the first part of conversion to fully recognize our original sin, faithlessness, and other abominations that are found in our hearts; those who do not become Christians by this route, I said, are not true Christians, all outward appearances and exercises notwithstanding. I admonished him and his wife to think along these important lines after I had left and to beg the Lord to place them before the mirror of His word and thus make them see the rotten state of sinfulness in which they lived. When I return, I shall see whether he and she have accepted my advice. We always insist with our listeners that they should each, in accordance with the guidance of the divine word, recognize the true state in which he finds himself, and whether he has in fact converted or not. For otherwise they cannot hear the word with true seriousness; rather some are so blind that they will find comfort in Christ and hope for eternal life without, and against, God's order.

May God be praised for giving us the strength to pronounce the comforting gospel of the resurrection of our Savior and its harvest for us during these two days. Our listeners have attended our sermons diligently and attentively and have let nothing distract them. In the orphanage, my dear colleague read the late Prof. Francke's open letter regarding Christ[10] to our listeners in the evening so that the salvation-hungry souls among us would use this means as well to further their recognition of their Savior and be constantly strengthened and reinforced in the true faith. May the Lord bless this undertaking! In today's repetition hour I found it necessary to recall publicly the old leaven in which some of our listeners are mired and to warn the congregation against participating in their offensive conduct. In conclusion, we had just read the 17th chapter of Jeremiah, as it came in the order, wherein the defilement of the Sabbath is harshly punished; I made reference to this and warned the congregation not to be frivolous in such matters, as the defilement of the Sabbath belongs among those vices which bring God's curse on town and country.

Tuesday, the 24th of April. A captain whom I do not know informed me in a letter that he had jailed an indentured servant who had escaped from Savannah to Charleston;[11] and, as he learned that the man had spent some time in our district and woods, he assumed that he had probably caused damage by theft here as in other places. This is all too true, in that he broke into the Zueblis' hut on their plantation, and stole food as well as tools and clothing. In addition, a hog was shot dead and another wounded, for which the said servant is probably also responsible. I shall report all this to Savannah on the first possible occasion. The heads of the community came to me to discuss some of the offenses committed before and during the holidays and to inform me of their own and the congregation's opinion in this respect. It is considered preferable to remove N.N.N. from our place rather than have them punished here or in Savannah. We have tried everything for them; but no improvement has resulted, and it is getting worse and worse with them.

Thursday, the 26th of April. The pleasant weather continues and is so fruitful that we have much reason to thank the Lord. The crops are growing beautifully in both the gardens and the fields, and thus the dear Lord gives us green and pleasant hopes of a good harvest. The squirrels are a great danger to the sprouting corn, in addition to both crows and raccoons; and they do much damage. Last year there were no acorns, and therefore they are forced to seek their food in the fields. My dear colleague told me that he had occasion to talk to some of our listeners and ask them for the Easter blessing that God had offered them through His word; these told him to the praise of the Lord that He had done much good in them through the gospel and had taken pity on them. In view of the grief which the disorder and constant impenitence of some people causes us, this has much strengthened us. We notice here, too, how Satan causes much rascality before and during the Holy Days in order to cause harm among us, as he well knows that the Lord, the Lover of all these dearly bought souls, is abroad on these days to extend His kingdom and to attract the souls to Himself.

Due to my present feeble condition, which requires me to take walks,[12] I cannot visit much among the people, which normally affords me much pleasure.

Friday, the 27th of April. Mr. Oglethorpe and many other impartial people in Savannah well recognize the damage that wicked and disorderly people cause by both word and example and what a benefit it is for a young colony if it is cleansed in time of such offensive, seductive, and malicious people; therefore people in Savannah are happy if such people leave.

Sunday, the 29th of April. Praise be to God, who is still providing the means for maintaining the children and other needy people in the orphanage, even if there has been no lack of trials in this respect. By God's grace, the manager of the orphanage and his wife are of such a disposition that they gladly accept everything that comes across their way in their task, and both pray and work indefatigably.

Monday, the 30th of April. The blossoms are falling off the vines from which we expected some fruit this year as a proof of their hardiness: these vines were planted only last fall and they are now faring as do the young peach trees, whose blossoms also tend to be shed during the first year. On the other hand, there is a peculiar thing to be observed in this country, in that the wooden part of the vines grows fast and strong during the first year; what takes twelve months here requires three years or more in Germany. It is most pleasant to observe the sight on both sides of the river from the boat, because vines have grown right high on the trees and are covered with little grapes. It should be quite possible here to grow, in a short time, the most beautiful arcades made of vines, and in this manner, as Mr. Oglethorpe recounted recently, they would bear best, for in this hot country they must be trained to grow high off the ground and they must not be pruned too much so as to protect the grapes from the heat of the sun.

In our vicinity, there grows a fruit resembling the red cherry in Germany which has a sourish taste and has already ripened.[13] These contain three or four little seeds similar to those in grapes. They are quite abundant, although they are quickly picked off by the birds. They grow only in wet ground and swamps, which are called marshes here. We would also get a lot of a kind of black cherries, that is, black mulberries, if these were not picked off by the birds before they ripen. We have not seen any fruit on the white mulberry trees, although we planted a number of them in our gardens. This year a late frost withered the first leaves and therefore probably prevented their blooming.

Last week we started the book of Judges in our evening prayer meetings; and we have used the events recounted in the first chapter according to our circumstances, in all simplicity. In particular, we have seen the beautiful fruits that faith and obedience to God's orders will bear, and in contrast the evil caused in the land by disbelief and disobedience. Today we treated, from the first part of chapter 2, the noteworthy penetential sermon which the angel of the Lord, the prince over the Lord's army, the true savior and good shepherd, addressed to the Israelites assembled at Silo and which, although causing a strong emotion among the people, went unheard afterwards and did not bear any true and lasting fruit of remorse and penitence.

The contents of this sermon reminded us of the many blessings the Lord has shown us in Germany, on our voyage at sea, and in this country, yea, even sooner, by His acceptance of our souls into His merciful covenant in Holy Baptism, and how He promised us many valuable goods in His word. Therefore it is a mean and irresponsible ingratitude to insult the Lord, who is essential and original Goodness, and who has never treated us ill but only well.[14] Among such insults are not only the sins of commission but also those of omission, as can be seen in the case of the Israelites; and, as it is not said in the Bible that any among the Israelites had become embittered at this sharp sermon of penitence and at the revelation of their sins, it is to be hoped and desired that none among us should become embittered thereby, although this is only too obviously the case with N. and his wife, to their own harm.

MAY

Tuesday, the 1st of May. Now that one of the rooms in my house is ready so that we can live there, I have moved in today. May the dear Lord make this dwelling serve for His praise and my spiritual and physical well-being, for which He shall be earnestly implored by me and other honest souls who shall join me here in prayer. May He support mine and our good intentions with His mercy. The carpenters and other laborers are now in the midst of their field work and will hardly be able to finish the house for several weeks.

In tonight's prayer meeting we discussed the second part of the second chapter of Judges, which describes the circumstances of the Israelites in matters of religion and their external affairs under the government of the Judges. We have again learned much for our instruction and warning, in particular as we were shown how it happened that the children of Israel gradually degenerated and turned into a generation entirely different from that of their pious forebears. Much damage is caused by traffic and communion with those whose minds are directed at the world and the flesh. They occupied their plantations in peace and with much pleasure as long as they served the Lord and kept unsullied by the world.

Wednesday, the 2nd of May. Yesterday, a German man from Old Ebenezer asked me to baptize his child; and he chose a few honest people from the community to serve as witnesses of the baptism. As it is too difficult and also dangerous to bring such a small babe here to our place, we travelled there with the witnesses.

Thursday, the 3rd of May. A man who was walking to his plantation this morning, carrying a heavy burden on his back, told me that before departing he had recalled to his mind the 139th Psalm, which edified him much. We often remind our dear listeners to arm themselves against all exterior and interior temptation with the word of the Lord, so that they may not become slothful and lazy when they are unable to attend our prayer meetings for some days or even weeks at a time, but must be content with that which they hear on Sundays; other-wise, they may well be harmed in their souls and their Christianity, all outward signs of industriousness notwithstanding. I had to talk to another man this morning in his hut; and he was most eagerly waiting for me to pray with him and his wife, which he clearly preferred to all his work, although this brooks no delay at this time.

I intend to travel to Savannah early tomorrow morning, although I am still feeble physically. It is an easy matter for the Lord to strengthen me in body and soul during my journey and my ministrations in Savannah, as He has done on several occasions. Several of the German people there wish to go to Holy Communion this coming Sunday, and therefore I must take time to talk to each of them separately. I know most of them better now than previously; and, since for most of them the use of the Lord's Supper has led to no external, let alone internal improvement, we shall, with the aid of the Lord, work on them in love and seriousness through God's mercy and keep back those among them who are obviously grievous sinners and show no desire and seriousness in their true improvement. Those poor people do not wish to be convinced that they are rotten through and through and far from being Christians. They are full of prejudice.

Friday, the 4th of May. During my visits, I spoke in particular with one person who loves the Lord Jesus from the bottom of her heart. She is among those of whom the Lord Jesus says, "Blessed are the poor in spirit, for theirs is the kingdom of heaven." She said that someone had visited her yesterday and had said that she could not pray at home for she was too miserable and so she wanted to pray with her. But she herself had thought she too was worthless, and thus two miserable souls would be together. But the dear Lord had not let their simple conversation and their poor prayer go without blessing.

Even now when I visited her I met another person there in whose heart the Lord Jesus has started His work. It is most pleasant to speak to such simple people, for one can conduct oneself with them in a simple and open manner since we know of their honesty and are assured that in truth they are concerned only with the edification of their souls. I read to this woman what is written on page 33 of the *Treasure Chest*,[1] which the dear Lord had just blessed in my soul. I also spoke to another woman who would like to be saved but does not know how to go about it; she thinks the reason is that she cannot read. I therefore showed her what the dear Lord Jesus wants of her, namely her heart; and, if she were to give that to Him at His request, He would do with her as He wishes and that would settle it. If she would proceed thus in all simplicity, she would surely be able to tell me something of the Lord Jesus, to his praise, on my return.

Saturday, the 5th of May. Recently, at the end of the prayer meeting, I saw a couple of honest women walk together engaged in conversation. And, as the path they were taking was not on the regular way home for one of them, I asked her why was she walking on this path at this time? She replied that she was discussing with the other woman how she could well apply that time which is left for her to spend in this world by God's will, for they had been so especially awakened in the prayer meeting. Since they had little opportunity to talk with each other because of their many tasks, she was making a little detour on her way home so as to talk more with the other one in this regard.

Today the dear Lord ordained my coming to one of the Salzburgers, whose soul is in a sad state. I asked him how things went with him, and he replied, "Quite badly," for he kept thinking that he had missed God's grace. I showed him, however, that this was a deceit of the devil, who thus wished to deter him from seeking the Lord in all seriousness. The dear Lord gave me further grace to show him, by the example of the prodigal son, that, if he were to start out with the latter in all truth and go to the Father, confess everything to Him, and seek His mercy with a repentant heart, He would not reject him and treat him harshly, but instead accept him with a thousand joys, forgive everything, and make him into a blessed man. This seemed to please him, and he promised to accept this good advice. May the Lord help him in this and bless him so that he may render unto Him his whole heart in order that He may make it the way He thinks right.

Sunday, the 6th of May. May the Lord be praised for having granted us on this day the grace and the strength to preach His dear word. May He become ever more known among us as the good shepherd who gave His life for us, and may He bless His word for this purpose so that finally all those in Ebenezer may say, in the praise of their Savior and for the edification and encouragement of others, the words of Psalm 100, verse 3: "Know ye that the Lord he is good: it is he that hath made us, and not we ourselves; we are his people and the sheep of his pasture." Amen, may it be thus, Amen. In the prayer meeting at the orphanage we considered, as we often do, the mission work in the East Indies[2] and addressed the Lord jointly, begging Him for further blessing of this work, as well as reminding the Lord Jesus, as our good shepherd, of His dear promises which He made in today's text, John 10:16, begging Him that He might soon grant their complete fulfillment.

Monday, the 7th of May. An honest Salzburger woman recalled what the Lord had done for the Salzburgers by leading them from Popery. "Oh," she said, "there we found such hirelings as we were told about in yesterday's text; but nothing was told us then about the Lord Jesus as the good shepherd. But now we are on His green pasture." She did not know how to belittle her own merits enough and did not trust herself at all. She could not deny, however, that the Lord had accepted her and had to admit that the Lord Jesus had taken hold of her entire heart and that, through His mercy, she had nothing to care for but to know Him ever more closely and be entirely His own. She said that things progress gradually and that He is leading her ever further. My dear colleague recently said that, if one cannot examine one's own condition, one should ask one's minister or another Christian to do this. She recalled these words and said that to this end she would come and have herself examined, so that she might remain undeceived and arrange her prayer accordingly. I replied briefly to this according to her circumstances, as she was just then called to meet the returning cattle.

Tuesday, the 8th of May. The dear Savior helped me not only to be in good health in Savannah but also, with His assistance, to be able to work for the good of the German people there in several matters. The storehouse keeper, Mr. Jones, has had a separate little room built wherein I could talk alone with these people and work on their souls, which on this occasion I did especially for those who wished to take Holy Communion. With divine assistance, I hope much from such private exhortations and discussion with these people, who are grievously lacking in the recognition of their souls and of the path of salvation.

I learned here with certainty that a man left his wife in Germany, lived with his maid servant in open sin during the voyage, and has now been married to her in Savannah. Neither of them denied this but sought to offer excuses for their acts, in particular the man, who argued that his wife in Germany was a wicked woman, had dissipated his entire temporal property with her family, and then had refused to join him in going to America. Both the authorities and his minister had advised him to leave, etc. I presented their abomination to them with the words: "Whoremongers and adulterers God will judge." I also declared the marriage which they had obtained here under false pretenses for null and void and admonished them not to cohabit or remain with each other any longer, for this would constitute further adultery and sinful fornication and thus bring manifold judgments of the Lord on their heads, such as they now had to endure in their bodies with their present very strict masters.

As I had not discussed this very grievous matter with the authorities, I refrained from dealing with it publicly. This will be done shortly, however; and it is all the more necessary since I have been informed that the civil authorities do not deal with such matters as belong to the bishop and his court. I have also been advised to persuade the man in all kindness to relinquish the present woman, all this apart from the fact that the question whether their masters would consent to such a separation is still open and depends on the latters' good will.

There was another unpleasant occurrence: A maid servant, of Popish beliefs, who also belongs to these German people, has committed fornication with a Jew;[3] after she had borne a child whom she had baptized by the English preacher, she had then run away, probably to join her Catholic co-religionists in St. Augustine, and had left the child in the Jew's house. The Jew does not wish to acknowledge the child, although he is without doubt its father, and for that reason has let it almost die of starvation. He was called before the authorities on this account and instructed to care for the child. He is to get some help in this regard from the storehouse.

From Charleston, I received a package of letters, which have come from our Fathers, benefactors, and friends in Europe. There is again much that is edifying in these letters; may the dear Lord bless it in us and our congregation. We are also advised that presents from Augsburg and Halle, of which we had already been informed in previous letters, will be sent from London to our congregation with the first available ships. We wish to thank the Lord for these gifts in advance. The dear Lord has also blessed the intercession by Court Chaplain Ziegenhagen on behalf of the German people in Savannah, in that some benefactors have given help toward the purchase of some necessary books for them, which we will receive among our other presents.[4] Some time ago we gave them some Bibles, New Testaments, psalm books, catechisms, and reading primers, so that they are all more or less supplied. Also, some of them have received old hymnals and copies of Arndt's *True Christianity*, as much as our supplies permitted.

We are often asked for sermon books so that they might read to each other from them in their small meetings on Sundays. The small Sunday sermons by the late Prof. Francke[5] were lent to Purysburg some years ago; and we cannot ask for their return, as some of the people there use them for their edification. True, we have a few edifying postils, but we need them for our own edification and reflection. However, I intend to bring or send them, every four weeks or so, a few separately printed sermons by the late Prof. Francke or Pastor Freylinghausen, which should give them ample opportunity for edification, if they are serious about this. Perhaps we shall also have a sermon book one of these days so that we can serve them in this respect also.

The German children in Savannah are made to work, and they are not given enough time to go to school.[6] Maybe one day the dear Lord will bless our intercessions in this respect with Mr. Oglethorpe. Many of the German families implore me to help them to come to our place or at least to Old Ebenezer, where the Trustees also require servants, so that they and their children may be closer to church and school. Some among them are of good intent, and the word of the Lord is taking its effect among them slowly but surely; but we are not in a position to help them. The herdsmen whom we took in, as well as some little girls and elderly people who have been taken into the orphanage out of Christian compassion, require considerable expense for food and clothing, for which the Lord Himself will eventually provide.

Some of the people are quite severely treated in Savannah at their place of service and do not receive the wages promised them. We spoke to the authorities on their behalf this time and have been able to obtain some advantages for them. The English and Jewish people in whose service these Germans are do not have many means to provide for their servants, yet they are nonetheless made to do hard and heavy work. Some have fared better, but their work and conduct is quite bad.

Wednesday, the 9th of May. This evening in the prayer meeting we began reading the edifying letters that have come to us from Europe this time and using them for our joint instruction. Our faithful Lord, who in previous times has let our and our listeners' hearts be blessed by such heartfelt letters, will again cause some good to come of this for His praise and our furtherance in Christian belief, so that our dear benefactors, who so kindly care for our true well-being, may also find therefrom a good fruit in blessed eternity. May the good Lord bless and reward them for their love, which they have proved to us and the congregation by writing such dear and sincere letters, of which I can in truth, as before the face of the Lord, assure that our faithful God has amply blessed them in our souls and caused our mouths, eyes, and hearts to bring forth many sighs and tears, and many prayers and praises of the Lord and requests for His succor.

Our listeners heard that some of the contents of the letters received would be read; and therefore nobody seems to have valued his housework and other business more highly than attending our meeting. It must in any event be said that our regular evening prayer meetings are diligently and regularly attended by those keen on their salvation, however heavy their daily tasks. The Israelites were forced to rise early for the sake of their material manna, and our dear listeners willingly go to bed a little later for the sake of their spiritual manna, the sweet word of the Lord. As an exordium, the words of David in Psalm 23, "the Lord is my Shepherd, I shall not want," much impressed me, and I wish sincerely that every one could speak the first words from our dear David in truth, so that he might repeat the next following words, i.e. "I shall not want," without inner contradiction, and in the praise of the Lord. Even the cross, physical want, and trials, are benefits bestowed by the Lord, by which we should be made to resemble Christ, and which the lambs of Christ should not lack any more than other benefits.

At this time I awakened our listeners to reflect on what the Lord has done for them all unto this day, and bade them consider whether the Lord had not shown Himself as a good shepherd in His threefold office of High Priest, Prophet, and King. It was a very special blessing that He had inclined to them the affection and love of so many honest Christians in Europe, and particularly the care of some of His faithful servant-shepherds. It is now quite obvious how honestly and affectionately they pray, care, and speak for us, and it will be made abundantly clear only in blessed eternity how much good has flowed to us from their dear and eager intercession.

We are so often inclined to single out men and external causes for the many happenings of our lives; but this brings about much sin, for we should attribute all to the Lord and His all-governing power and wisdom. For our watchword shall be: "The Lord is my shepherd, etc." "This is Immanuel," of which we were reminded by the words of our dear Prof. Francke,[7] who wrote that the news from our place, although still giving rise to some misgivings because of the war, did not leave him in any doubt that the Lord, who had brought us here with our dear listeners, would protect us here also and show us His faithfulness and bounty, of which He is capable beyond man's imagination. God has done it, all glory to Him!

We were most pleased to hear that the labor of the Lord is being continued in the institutions of the Halle Orphanage;[8] and I took this occasion to recount again all the good that the dear pious Lord effected through the said Orphanage, both in internal and external matters throughout the world, and that we too partake in these blessings, in that not only many physical blessings, which are again detailed in these letters, have been collected for us there, but also many prayers are said on our behalf. In particular, I told the children before the entire congregation that I believed that many pious children of their own ages who had heard of Ebenezer were including them and us in their prayers and that this should make them reflect seriously. I awakened the entire congregation to pray ever more assiduously for the University and Orphanage at Halle as being most useful and dear works of the Lord. This we will continue to do with the honest souls among us in my new house, which shall soon be ready; and we again invited them to this endeavor with God's grace.

We were much pleased by the news of the physical and spiritual circumstances of the Salzburgers in Prussia,[9] and it is a pity that the excerpt of a letter from pastor Breuer mentioned by our dear Professor was not included. In this connection I reminded the Salzburgers that they were obligated to be grateful to God, faithful, and eager in their use of the light of the gospel which they had received; for God had performed a true miracle in leading them and their compatriots from their country, as would be fully recognized only by future generations. And, as the Salzburgers in Prussia are so serious in seeking their salvation, this should encourage them all to a faithful imitation so that none of us might be missed at the place of the perfectly just. All the saints in heaven and earth call out to us as if with one voice: "Those who wish to be saved must be most serious about it and not refuse to resist even unto their blood," etc., for they shall be rewarded one day.

We are also rejoicing that Sanftleben has retained, and proven by his deeds, the grace that the Lord has given him through His word; we shall use this news for the good of the congregation. We are all much pleased that he wishes to return here, even though he does not yet know that the dear Lord has so clearly improved our physical circumstances. Our dear Mr. Berein, in his edifying and most pleasing letter, gave us more detailed news about Sanftleben, his voyage, and his circumstances. He also let us know that the Honorable Trustees will contribute £100 sterling for the transport of several Salzburger artisans and unmarried women, who are to be recommended by Mr. N.[10] This, too, causes us to praise the Lord; and we trust that He, who possesses the key to the hearts of all men, and even more to their chests and money-boxes, shall easily find ways to help if a whole new transport of honest people is to come here.

Thursday, the 10th of May. We have much pleasant and fruitful weather this spring, and the crops in the fields look well. It is not hot, and therefore the people can work well in their fields throughout the entire day. However, there is great damage caused by the fact that formerly, due to the delay in surveying, our people were forced to clear and plant various plots here and there and therefore cannot guard every place where there has been planting. As a result, the seeds are dug up by a kind of wild cat[11] at night and by crows and other birds during the day. This could be prevented if their plots were all together, as they will be in the future. Some people have already planted some part of their plantations; but, since they have much work here and cannot stand guard out there, not much will come of these crops. Some even live out there, and have either given away their land close to town or are now suffering losses on those plots that are planted here. Where they cannot continue with the corn, they will be able to plant all the more in beans and pumpkins, as these are not damaged by the aforesaid vermin, at least in the early stages. However, when the beans are high, they are the target of the deer and turkeys. Once most of the wood has been cleared on the plantations, the crops will be harmed less.

The wild cats, or, as they are called here, the raccoons, do not live only in the forest but also in holes and in hollowed-out trees on the ground. They only attack the new corn when it is still in the ground. True, the squirrels too dig it up and cause much damage, but mainly by tearing out the stalks. The rice is picked from the ground by small birds resembling sparrows; and, once it is ripe, a larger kind of black birds, called starlings, come in large flocks and rip off whole heads of rice with their beaks.[12] Once they can use a plow, the people will likely plant German seeds such as wheat, rye, and barley; these grow so well in the gardens, where they have been planted in abundance this year, that the people are amazed. For this kind of cereal to grow, however, the land must be well worked, which cannot be done with a hoe, this manner of working taking too much time. In contrast, planting Indian corn and beans requires only the digging of large holes in the ground, although care must be taken later to chop down the grass, which grows up afterward, or the plants will be choked. A plow could also be used for planting rice, as there are no logs or heavy roots in the swamps used for this crop. However, a plow is quite expensive in this country,[13] and horses and oxen are in scarce supply. We plan on supplying the orphanage with these things by and by, provided that the Lord will give us help in this respect; and this may then serve as an example to others.

One of the German servants among us, who had not often been ill in Germany, is suffering much from quotidian fever. However, he considers it a blessing of the Lord. As a result of His word, he has become aware of the terrible sins in which he had been mired since his youth; and, now that he is suffering in his body, he has had time to reflect and to become deeply repentant of his sins, not only of the more gross ones but also of those which he used to consider small and insignificant. I told him today that it was the mercy of the Lord if He opened his eyes and let him recognize himself in his full misery; by this, He prepared the rotten souls so that they might come to His Son as miserable and bent sinners and be refreshed by Him. However, he should be on guard against all consolation coming from himself, but rely instead on begging and crying and praying, so that his natural perdition and the terrible abomination of his heart might be ever more clearly revealed to him. Thus he would come to true repentance, and comfort would be forthcoming. For Christ has ordered us to preach penitence and the forgiveness of sins; therefore penitence would have to come first. It was comforting not only that the dear Savior had ordered that both be preached, but also that it is written in Acts 5 that "Him hath God exalted with His right hand to be a Prince and a Savior, to give repentance to Israel, and forgiveness of sins." This means, surely: "Look ye, I (the Prince and Savior) am among you every day," etc., that is, to give the people that grace which the teachers of the New Covenant announce.

Friday, the 11th of May. Last night in the prayer meeting we edified ourselves from the very kind letter of our dear Court Chaplain Ziegenhagen. In it we again found many signs of his fatherly love and his untiring care and intercessions on our behalf. He also mentioned how affectionately the dear Mr. N. and Prof. Francke are inclined toward us and our dear congregation, and how Mr. N. likewise sought to work on our behalf. This again awoke us to praise the Lord, and we strengthened each other in our confidence of His divine goodness. As He so kindly inclines the hearts of His servants and children to us so that they care for us as for their children, His fatherly heart itself must surely be full of love and pity for us; and this should move even the most impenitent sinners among us to do battle with the prodigal son in their souls and to return to seek the mercy and favor of such a pious Father as this one. Oh what a blessing not only to be called a child of the living God but to be in truth His child! The letter which our dear Court Chaplain Butjenter addressed to me also provided us with many a thing that we can apply to the common good in future circumstances. May the Lord in His mercy give His "yea" and His "Amen" to all the good wishes uttered on our behalf, and may He amply repay our dear Fathers and benefactors in this life and in eternity for all their love and kindness shown to us.

A German man from Old Ebenezer has placed his daughter in our school, as she cannot be used for field work because of her physical weakness; for else both children and adults are bound to serve the Lord Trustees. These people are quite poor, and it would have been well if we could have accepted the child in the orphanage and cared for its needs there; but this is not within our ability and therefore others as well as we must wait for the help of the Lord. The establishment is conducted as economically as possible, but to care for the needs of a crowd of children and adults such as we now have in our care, much is needed. May the Lord grant us this according to His kindness and wisdom!

Saturday, the 12th of May. Some in the congregation have tried to bring in the bees which are found in the woods in high trees and to place them in barrels resembling beehives or baskets; and several times this has proven successful. They cut down the trees; and, if they fall in the right direction so that the bees are not killed or drowned (for they usually have their hives in trees close to the river or in the swamps), the people try by all sorts of tricks to make the bees go into a barrel smeared with honey and flour, which they carry home during the night. I have been assured that the bees here swarm three times a year, since they bring in honey almost throughout the entire winter, and therefore it would be most profitable if they were to remain in the aforesaid barrels.

One of our herdsmen seems loath of his work and offers himself and his wife for all other kinds of work, if only he can be relieved of herding the cows. He had sent his wife to me for this purpose; but I sent for him in person, as I wanted to hear the reasons for which he wished to give up his profession. As an excuse he spoke above all of his great fear of the many snakes, for he encounters them constantly and can hardly take enough precautions. I reminded him of the 91st Psalm and urged him to constant prayer, in which he should give himself up to the Lord and His wisdom. If he felt that this would help, we were prepared to have leather leggings made for him instead of his woolen ones, for these would surely protect him against snake bite.

This man had offered his services to us in Savannah with his wife and begged me with many words to take him in as a herds-man and said he would serve the community faithfully. He had also herded cattle in Europe, he said. As he is employed in his profession, and offered himself to herd the cattle, we can hardly relieve him from his work and start him on something else. The community would suffer much loss as a result of this, I said. Once he had served his time faithfully, I reassured him, he would find the benefit waiting for him at the end of his term of servitude. He sees even now how the people in the community are kind and generous to both him and his wife, provided that he carries out his duties faithfully. We have heard no complaints of the other herdsman,[14] his wife, and his son, who guard the other herd in the woods; the cattle are said to be in good shape.

Sunday, the 13th of May. Two mothers brought their chil-dren to church today for churching, Mrs. Schweiger in the morning and a woman from Old Ebenezer in the afternoon. The German people also like us to remind the churching moth-ers of their duty, as is our custom, and to pray with them pub-licly and to thank the Lord for His kindness to mother and child.

It was announced in the congregation that we intend to hold Holy Communion again in a fortnight's time for those who show an honest desire for it and will worthily prepare them-selves. We are now in the pleasant period between Easter and Whitsun, where we not only see the Lord's blessing in the green promises sprouting in our gardens and fields, but also receive beautiful opportunity to prepare ourselves in an evangelical manner for the holy feast of Whitsun and for the Lord's Supper from the beautiful Sunday sermons, which are mainly based on the notable and highly edifying last words of our dear Lord Jesus.

Today I took as a text the very beautiful and deeply moving and fortifying words of our motherlyminded Savior: "And ye shall be sorrowful, but I will, etc." In the afternoon, my dear colleague started on the first article; may the Lord bless this discussion as well as all other presentations. I heard yesterday from someone in the congregation that the Lord had indeed blessed our recent contemplation of the Ten Commandments, and in particular of the 9th and 10th,[15] for a better recognition

of our innate misery and of the sinful lusts which frivolous people consider as trifling matters. We also know from manifold
experience that the industrious application of the truths of the
catechism has created much edification and strengthening in
our Christianity. Therefore I cannot accept how some people,
who have started a school in N., can be so presumptuous as to
ban the entire catechism from their school.[16] They will not suffer the catechism to be either read or learned by heart, as I was
recently told by children and parents in N. And a little girl
added, "They never pray 'Our Father who art in heaven.'" Instead of the catechism, they give the children a little hymnal
printed in N., in which there are some songs which the children
must learn by heart at home, etc.

The conduct of these self-assured people reminds me of a
letter which an honest preacher, experienced and skilled in the
struggle of Christ, i.e. the dear Rev. Sommer, wrote about
Luther's *Small Catechism* in the two years of his confinement. An
extract of this letter is reprinted in the *Fifth Contribution* to the
Building of the Kingdom of God, page 564.[17] The whole letter is
beautiful and well worth reading; but I shall quote only these
words: "In particular, the *lectiones*[18] from his *Small Catechism*
have never tasted as I taste them now, and I have never before
found as much in them as I now find daily, whenever in my
loneliness I find occasion to meditate on them. Likewise, only
now have I truly recognized how good it is to sit in the last row,
and also what our dear Savior wishes to say with the words, 'if
the old people would only turn back and become as children,'
etc. If we should become children again in our old age and return into the catechism, we will not be rid of it," etc.

Today for the first time I had the school children with me in
my new house to sing with them and pray concerning the words
heard in the sermon. I told them how much I yearned to lead
them to pasture as the lambs of Christ and to lead them to the
good shepherd who loves children so much. I warned them
against frivolity and the mere outward practice of singing and
praying; and I assured them that, if only they would undertake
seriously, in this house, to serve their Savior with an honest
heart together with me, He would serve them in turn by dis-
tributing His spiritual and even material blessing. He knows, I

said, their want and poverty; and it is easy for Him to lay a gift in my hands that I might distribute among them in this house for His praise and for their joy and for the alleviation of their want.

Monday, the 14th of May.[19] Last night, at the time when we customarily hold our repetition hour, I consecrated my house, which is almost entirely finished, with God's word and prayer. On this occasion, all our dear listeners were present. Since the beginning of the year, when the carpenters started on this work, these words, of which I reminded them on several occasions during their work, have been uppermost in my mind: Colossians 3:17, "And whatsoever ye do in word or deed," etc. These beautiful words, and the preceding verse 16, I chose for my text so as to edify myself and our assembled listeners with some appropriate thoughts. They also were most fitting on this Jubilate Sunday, and we had much edification from them by God's grace. My main theme was what ministers and listeners would have to do if they wished to be furthered in the good works they have begun and properly prepared for blessed eternity: They must (1) properly use the means of salvation and in particular the dear word of the Lord, and (2) fit their entire conduct in accordance with it.

In the application I told my audience of the resolution made before the Lord, namely, to serve the Lord in this house with all my heart and, through His grace, to be most useful to our dear congregation. It would please me and accord with the main purpose for which this house was built, if they would treat the Lord's word with me in accordance with Paul's prescription here in this house too, so that we might further each other in the good and be properly prepared for blessed eternity. I reminded them that it has at all times been most useful and blessed if listeners are in communion with their ministers and use their houses, as far as circumstances permit and suffer it, for their edification. At the same time I cited some words of our dear Apostle Paul, from Acts 28:30–31, 2 Corinthians 11:28, and Acts 20:30–31.

I also told them of the blessed effects of the private conversations with Prof. Francke in Halle on all those who were being prepared for the ministry and who came to see him in his study weekly on prearranged days to talk with him about the state of their souls. I also told of what I had observed in Tommendorf in the case of the late Pastor Mäderjan, in that the people there did not only come from near and far to attend church regularly, but were edified in his house, several talking to him privately in his study concerning the state of their faith, and that this had brought about much blessing and a furtherance of the good. Finally, we fell on our knees and praised God for all His previous blessings; and I prayed for a special blessing on those among our listeners who had done some work on this house for no other recompense but their love for me. My listeners in turn helped me to pray for a blessing on my office and house, and also for the payment of the costs for it; and the entire occasion was concluded with praise for the Lord, to my great refreshment and fortification.

These words of our prayer impressed me particularly: "He has arranged everything well, and done everything right. Give glory to our Lord." And we must all repeat this if we only think of His guidance in this country. He has arranged everything well so far, and will continue to arrange everything well. May His holy name be blessed from eternity to eternity. Halleluiah. Ebenezer, the Lord has helped this far.[20] I only wish that the carpenters were finished with the kitchen, the doors, and the windows and that I could use my study for my own purpose. However, I do not doubt that, once this is possible, the dear Lord will grant me some blessed hours with my dear listeners in private conversation. In previous times, many have been too shy to come into my hut and reveal their hearts and what oppressed and pained them; *ratio* is in *promptu*.[21] Here, everything is well guarded; and my study will serve in place of a confessional, lectern, punishment, and comfort chair.

A firewall of brick will have to be built between kitchen and study so that the fire in the kitchen cannot damage the house and so that I can have a small stove built in my study, which is yet some time away.

Kieffer's son in Purysburg is asking for a primer so that he might by and by be able to teach his father's two Negroes how to read.[22] He said that he was eager, both during work and on other occasions, to give them some instruction in the recognition of the Lord, and that one of them in particular was most eager. However, they did not know much German and so not much could be taught to them at this stage.

Tuesday, the 15th of May. Today, the disorderly shoemaker N.,[23] who had been admitted to our community together with other servants from Captain Thomson's ship for Christian reasons, was ordered to return to Savannah to the service of the Lord Trustees together with his wife. We had advanced him, for leather and provisions, as much money as he demanded; and he has slowly worked off this loan. However, his work did not well serve our people, who must earn their money in the sweat of their brows. And, since he is a most offensive man and we have tried all means to improve him, whereas he gets worse every day, we recently asked Mr. Jones,[24] who is in charge of Mr. Oglethorpe's affairs in Savannah, to remove this wicked and offensive and harmful man. He tried his best to forestall this and would gladly have forced himself on our community if they had but suffered him. I bought the leather from him for the orphanage so that he might have no excuse; and I also paid for the shoes of those few in the community who were not now able to pay for them. To be sure, this procedure may seem rough, but it is in accordance with his contract and in the interest of good order, which must be preserved in the community, and the honest members have themselves asked to be rid of him. We do not doubt that this seriousness will impress other disorderly people, at least for a while.

Zettler had wished to learn shoemaking from him; and to this end he had bound himself as an apprentice to him for two years; although he has not finished his apprenticeship, he has learned enough so that he can do the cobbling for us and also make coarse shoes, of which we have greater need than of anything else. He lacks tools and hemp, but help will come in this respect also. His conduct is satisfactory, and the community will be better served by him than by his master. We have hopes that Sanftleben will bring us a good and conscientious shoemaker and that Zettler may finish learning the trade from him.

Wednesday, the 16th of May. We have now finished writing some letters to Europe, which are to be forwarded to Savannah next week together with our diary. We have been given permission to borrow our salary for this semester on a note, as well as another sum for our orphanage and congregation, which is to arrive through the intercession of our esteemed Prof. Francke. On this occasion, our letters will surely be sent off. We have written to Court Chaplain Ziegenhagen, Prof. Francke, Senior Urlsperger, Court Chaplain Butjenter, Counsellor Walbaum, the praiseworthy Society, and Mr. Berein. May God bless it all.

This morning I had wished to visit some of the people during the field work; but I was delayed with a sick little girl and a young man, and meanwhile the people had gone home for dinner. I met three men who were coming from the widow Arnsdorf's land, where they had helped her plant rice; this is truly a work of love. She is living well and honestly and is much esteemed and loved by the Salzburgers. Sanftleben, too, has done much good by her; and he will be surprised at his return how much the dear Lord has blessed her in the management of her house and land. She is much better off in all respects than when her husband was still alive, and she suffers want in nothing. Pious people who practice their profession in Christian orderliness will surely find their sustenance among us, but there is nothing to be gained for disorderly ones.

N.N. accompanied me to his field; and, since his work causes him so much trouble and still brings little result (as shown by the state of his corn, which is far behind that of the others), I told him and his wife that the blessing of the Lord was not on their house. Should they convert to Him, and should this all-powerful Creator of heaven and earth become their Father, all would be better; without Him, however, and as long as they remained His enemies, all would retrogress for them. They said nothing to this. In their poverty and contrary circumstances these poor people blame others. They would have us provide them with money, food, and clothing; but this is not within our power, nor would it be well applied in their case.

Thursday, the 17th of May. A little girl had been suspected of theft, and everyone was after her; for many circumstances indicated that she was the culprit. When another girl, who had in truth become guilty of theft, saw how the first girl was to suffer despite her innocence, she admitted that she herself was guilty, but the other innocent. She could no longer see another child suffer on account of her misdeeds, she said. She had once seen a little piece lying on the ground and had picked it up; and, since nobody had asked for it for several weeks, she had kept it. True, in the beginning she had wished to say she had found money in the bedroom; but, because she had delayed too long, she had been afraid to make a clean breast of it.

At noontime we had the men assemble to discuss some material matters. The English boy[25] is of little use as a herdsman, since he has no liking for this work and would rather do other, even the most difficult tasks. Therefore, Schartner should again be appointed herdsman. However, since only very few in the community are able to support him, and since the cattle, which are the greatest asset of our people, must be cared for, we might be willing, in reliance on God's plenty, to take him into the orphanage and there provide him with food and clothing, on the understanding that he will voluntarily agree to accept everything without complaint and faithfully attend to his profession. He has already kept the cattle in Old and New Ebenezer, and he is unfit for fieldwork. He has also planted little this time, and everybody is agreed that his spiritual and physical well-being would be furthered in this way. May the dear Lord Himself indicate what is to be done. We gladly do what we can for the love of the congregation, and we have hope that the Lord will also provide the means for us to do something. The English boy has promised to work faithfully in the orphanage, and he has much strength and skill.

We have had a penetrating rain, which has much refreshed our fields again. Since the wild cats[26] will not let the corn come up in some locations, our people take out the grown stalks from those places where the corn is too thick and transplant them to empty spots, just as cabbage and greens are transplanted. We have already noticed for several years that this is a practicable method and that the corn shows no difference at harvest time. For, once it is several inches high, the animals no longer attack it. The squirrels, which do damage only during the day, are easier to scare away. Necessity is the mother of many good inventions.

Friday, the 18th of May. I found a woman doing a small but important task; and I encouraged her to do all her work, even the smallest things, in the name of our Lord Jesus and for His glory. She wished she could do that, she said, and she strove mightily; but she still found herself quite corrupted. Whenever she would attend a sermon or prayer meeting, her unusually great perdition was revealed to her: she had been full of sin since her youth and had so insulted the Lord that she now had to marvel at His great patience and forbearance. He could have long since cast her into hell, had He but wished it; but instead He had always waited for her penitence. Now she was much chagrined that she was still living so little for the glory of the Lord, and still sinned so much, although against her knowledge and will. She was often much depressed by this and wished soon to be where God could be praised without sin. She cried over these words. I gave her a little verse: "The Lord hath pleasure in life," likewise, "Blessed are the poor in spirit," (i.e. those who keep nothing before their eyes but perdition and consider themselves unworthy of all mercy and gifts). It is also said, "Blessed are they that mourn," for it is one thing to be poor in spirit and to mourn, and whoever is found in this state is not lacking blessing but is blessed. If it were said, "Blessed are the happy, the comforted, and courageous souls," this would deprive her of courage, but not otherwise. But she should not only look upon her perdition, but also upon the Savior who has come for the good of the sinners, for Paul also had held onto Him when he sighed, "O wretched man that I am, who shall deliver me?" and had praised God for His helper's blessing.

I reminded her of what we are now discussing in the Bible story, where we have seen that, in response to their loud complaints, the Lord gave these wicked people saviors, although they were not worthy of it, and had proven Himself gloriously to them. We, however, had a greater Savior, whom God had given to us and who is surely not without strength. She also told me that she often loses the feeling of God's grace when faced with her perdition and that this drives her into prayer. She will not stop praying, she said, until she again feels some of the grace of the Lord, etc. This woman proves her seriousness in Christianity and approaches her goal and treasure ever more closely.

This afternoon we had a heavy thunderstorm and a long, lasting rain. Once the lightning and thunder were so strong that it seems a tree close to our town was struck. Praise be to God, who until now has turned all harm from us. So far we have not heard of any occasion in this country where a house or a hut was struck by lightning or somebody was harmed.

Sunday, the 20th of May. In considering the prophetess Deborah's song of triumph and praise in the 5th chapter of Judges, which was sung at their thanksgiving feast for the glory of the great Lord and the edification of the Israelites and which describes the pitiful condition of the Israelites, a condition improved by the grace and miraculous power of the Lord, we reminded ourselves in yesterday's prayer meeting of the physical and spiritual blessings we have received during our sea voyage and here in this country above all other people and without our deserving them. This should give us cause to hold a thanksgiving and memorial feast, not only publicly once a year, but often in our hearts.

In verse 2, the prophetess praised the Lord that Israel was free again and that the people had agreed to it. All of us can see what a noble gift of the Lord freedom is by the example of others in this land, who are sold after their sea voyage; whereas the dear benefactors in England and Germany were willing to bring our listeners in three transports from Germany to England and thence here, with much love and free of cost, and to support them until they could support themselves. I reminded them that others who also wish to join us may not fare this well, inasmuch as both willingness and funds may be lacking; and we could be sure that many would thank the Lord if they were to receive but half of the good that was bestowed on us. And since we did not experience any of the want and misery which the children of Israel suffered under the tyrannical king of the Canaanites, but could enjoy our divine services and our work in peace and enjoy the Lord's blessing with a contented heart, the experience of the Lord's providence should lead us to eager praise of the Lord, following the example of Deborah and others, so that it might be said: "May my heart be God's vale of praise," etc.

N.N. from N.[27] visited me and asked to receive Holy Communion next Sunday. I told him that I did not like to refuse strangers who wished to take the Lord's Supper here and therefore would not object to his desire. However, I begged him to examine himself carefully so that he might not go to judgment but to a blessing. I knew that God had worked hard on his soul; but I also know that his common sins were an equal acceptance of the world and frivolous company, so that he is quickly deprived of all the good that the Lord has built in his soul. I told him from the previously treated texts from the Book of Judges that the most common sins of the Israelites had been forgetfulness of the Lord, their Benefactor, acceptance of the world, and idolatry, and that these had led them into their physical and spiritual perdition. Thus is was with most Christians, who accept as sins many gross things, but not the acceptance of the world, sinful customs, workmen's habits, and similar acts of participation.

Monday, the 21st of May. There are many among our dear listeners to whom the Lord has shown His mercy, and who gladly attest this in His praise. However, they are never satisfied with themselves and cannot complain enough about their misery once they start talking about it; and therefore they wish to realize it all the better, so that they may all the more surely claim the good which is promised to the miserable. I advised one of them to look eagerly upon the crucified Christ, for then he would learn how to become even smaller. The more we savor the love of the Lord and participate in His mercy, the lower we become. If there is anything good in our hearts, we must blow on it constantly so as to make it glow. Yes, he answered, if he were not to do that and bare his heart before the Lord in prayer, he would decrease more and more; but the more closely he learned to know the Lord Jesus, the more he savored His love, and his desire to stay with Him forever and consort with Him grew greater and greater. The Lord has blessed what we preached on the preceding day in many souls, as I have been told. May His name be blessed!

Tuesday, the 22nd of May. A man and his wife came into town from their plantation and visited me this afternoon. I read him a chapter from Johann Arndt's *Book of True Christianity*, spoke in explanation of the text, and then prayed with them. The man had been here yesterday and had asked whether he could see me this afternoon, because then his wife would be here too. Among other things, he told me how he enjoys spending a whole day in town on Sunday to hear God's word. On another occasion he told me that he often thought of last year, when he had given me to understand that he would have a bad harvest for lack of rain; for soon thereafter the wind had shifted and rain had fallen and the dear Lord had given him a plentiful harvest. This, he said, caused him to be quite ashamed.

Wednesday, the 23rd of May. Both the receipt of our salary and the forwarding of our package of letters required me to travel to Savannah very early Monday morning, whence I returned, thank the Lord, this noon, healthy in body and soul. Mr. Purry, who is prepared to accept our note on the salary, was not home; but I could not await his return from Mr. Montagut's plantation because of our present communicants, so I shall transact my business with him when I travel again on behalf of the German people. In the meantime, however, I was able to obtain from his store all supplies needed for the orphanage, the community, and our own needs.

In Mr. Oglethorpe's envelope Mr. Newman had written us a letter in which he announced that he had talked with the famous London merchant, Mr. Simonds, in regard to our salary, which we are to borrow on a note here in Savannah. That gentleman had been quite agreeable to the payment of this sum through Mr. Montagut and Mr. Purry, who are his agents here and trade in his name; and he had promised to give the necessary instructions. I gave our letters to Colonel Stephens, who will forward them shortly with his letters to the Honorable Trustees. He told me that a ship had arrived in Charleston to deliver some trading goods and was to proceed to Georgia from there. The ship had sailed from London in February; and it therefore can be assumed that our gifts, of which Court Chaplain Ziegenhagen again made mention in his last letter, dated from December, will have arrived. In the congregation, many prayers are said that the dear Lord may preserve these blessings and let them reach us safely. These long awaited gifts will be all the more appreciated, especially since many of our listeners badly lack summer clothing.

In Savannah I had to baptize the child of a Reformed family. The man is a servant of the preacher there, Mr. Norris, who had offered to baptize the child once it saw the light of this world. For this reason the German man had postponed the ceremony of Holy Baptism for several weeks, in the hope that the English preacher would return shortly from Frederica, whither he had travelled. An Englishman had tried a fortnight ago to persuade me to join a young couple for whom Mr. Norris had pronounced the bans but whom he had not yet married. However, this does not pertain to my office. I had once asked the preacher whether, in *casu necessitatis*,[28] he would agree to my performing some services for the English in Savannah, but he would not consent to this.

Mr. N.[29] had written a very kind letter to both of us, which was given to me in Savannah. The letter dated from October; and since he promised to be back in Georgia within seven months, with God's help, we are now expecting him by the first boat. He wrote, among other things, that he had written to Prof. Francke,[30] as promised, and had also composed something in which he was asking for a contribution toward the construction of a church in Ebenezer. Mr. N. has also returned from Germany and I was told that God had given him the grace to take a better look at the gospel and search for justice only in the blood and wounds of Christ.[31]

Thursday, the 24th of May. Both recently and on this occasion, I heard that Mr. Oglethorpe had promised those people in Savannah who would work industriously and harvest corn, beans, and potatoes a present of 2 shillings sterling for each bushel as an encouragement for further industry, and that they should keep the produce for their use. I inquired with those in charge of Mr. Oglethorpe's business in Savannah whether this favor was also to be extended to us, but I could not receive any assurance in this respect. However, Mr. Jones, the storehouse keeper, will inquire into it.[32]

Friday, the 25th of May. I heard a woman pray and sigh, even before I had reached her room; and she told me in tears that she had read that the Lord demanded that no idle talk should come forth from our mouths, whereas she said many a word that could well be omitted, etc., and thus she found many sins whereby she transgressed the Lord's commands. "If I could only," she continued with upraised hands, "be rid of all my sins at once! I have so often insulted the Lord since my youth," etc. I told her that a believer would be free of all his sins in his justification; and then there would be nothing damnable left in him, since he would be freed from the bondage of sin through the conversion in Jesus Christ, the strangled lamb of the Lord. From then on, in the course of his Christianity, he would shed all sin that might stick to him and make him slothful, the more the longer. If we were to ask all true Christians in present and former times what had been their daily exercise of Christianity, we would hear that, through God's grace, they had let this be their worry: to extinguish the Old Adam with his lusts by daily penitence and remorse, so that the New Man and the spirit directed to Christ would emerge ever more strongly.

She should not ask what God Himself does not ask, that is, to be rid of all sins in this life so that she would no longer require any struggle; for that could only be expected when the just rise in the life beyond. In the meantime, I said, she should not lose her courage if she recognized more and more her sinful and rotten heart and had to struggle with it; because this was a great blessing, for which she indeed prayed. Therefore, if God revealed her sins to her in her prayers, He meant well and she should hasten to Christ, the Physician and Savior. This reminded me of the beautiful song, *Eins Christen Hertz sehnt sich nach hohen Dingen*, etc., wherein she would find it indicated in the very first lines that she no longer belongs to this world but to the Lord Jesus. And, since she is always worried that God might yet reject her for her deep perdition and become loath of her, I recalled to her the end of the first verse: "Once He begins, He continues and achieves;" also, in verse 2, "The Lord so dearly loves the poor worm even if it, like Jonas, should flee from Him, He will still love it and will not let go of the child of sin, but seek to embrace it."

I reminded her that she had told me several times of her frivolity in Salzburg and of her damnable condition, and I asked her whether God had not indeed run after and followed her even though she had gone away from Him. How much less would He leave or reject her now that she is no longer fleeing from Him but wishes to come closer and now that her greatest sorrow is being prevented from this by her sinful weaknesses, etc. Finally, she told me of some instances when the Lord had blessed her heart by unspeakable joy and assurances of His mercy, but this changes constantly.

Another woman, who had been bedridden for several weeks, recognized well that both came from the Lord: health and sickness, good days and bad (or at least those that seem bad to our flesh); He always had a salutary intention of freeing man from this world and drawing him to Him. He achieves more through sickness and contrary circumstances than through true blessings, etc. I reminded her of the saying: "The ox knoweth his owner, and the ass his master's crib, but," etc. She said this verse was the first that so impressed her in Salzburg that she remembered it as often as she went into the stable; for she had always fed the cattle and been good to them, and they had looked around after her, but had not done so for strangers. Another Salzburger woman living close by joined us and brought her little child along, and thus our joint prayer was increased. The simple but warm words exchanged between these people impressed me much, for there was nothing but Christian simplicity, frankness of the heart, willingness to serve each other, etc.

Saturday, the 26th of May. We now have rain every day, accompanied by thunderstorms; and yesterday's rains were very strong and prevented us from holding the prayer meeting, which I would have liked to hold in preparation for Holy Communion. In the order of the gospel we are now having the 6th chapter of Judges with its noteworthy sermon of penance, which one of the prophets of God held for the Israelites and wherein both the acts of God regarding His people and the acts of His people with regard to Him are stated briefly but impressively. Our actual preparation and penance and confession concerned the first verse of tomorrow's text, John 16:23, the words of which may well be called the golden scepter which the Lord Jesus extends to His orphaned, aggrieved, and deprived children.

Sunday, the 27th of May. Today, fifty-two persons celebrated Holy Communion, and we wish from the bottom of our hearts that the Lord may bless this dear feast in all of them for their eternal salvation! Although our dear listeners are in the midst of their fieldwork, they do not let themselves be prevented from the industrious use of the means of salvation and an industrious attendance of all occasions for edification; and this pleases us very much.

Today, I was visited by a child whose brother-in-law had taken her from the orphanage for business reasons. She had joined the other children in prayer and prayed herself in a heartfelt manner and with many tears; she remained after the prayer and asked me plaintively to take her back, as she preferred the orphanage to all other opportunities. She promised to be pious and industrious and obedient, and therefore I simply did not have the heart to refuse this poor orphan. We have a rich Father, and He will surely be able to provide for this one as well as for the others. Today's epistle contains the beautiful verse: "Pure religion and undefiled before God and the Father is this, to visit the fatherless and widows in their affliction," etc. God, who is pleased by charity, will surely give us the strength and the means to exercise such charity.

Monday, the 28th of May. For those among us who like to cause discord, it may be a great affliction that we two, by the grace of God, stand as one man and act from one principle and for one purpose, so that they cannot find a *patrocinium*[33] for their disorderly intentions and actions in either of us. It is most salutary and contributes much to mutual agreement and to the furthering of the best interest of the congregation if preachers who work with one congregation take pains to consult with each other on what is required in this or that doubtful case, where caution must be exercised. For, if the listeners find no contradiction among them but see one act like the other, honest spirits are strengthened in their confidence in their teachers; and the evil minds are all the more surely put to shame and prevented in their disorderliness. *Concordia res parvae crescunt*, etc.[34]

Flax, barley, and peas are already ripe and being harvested; and therefore our people can use these fields twice a year. They are now planting either Indian beans or sweet potatoes, or, in a few months, turnips. They use the fenced land for all sorts of purposes, whereas in Savannah and Purysburg many beautiful plots near these towns are uncultivated and Purysburg looks more like a forest than a town. In Savannah, too, little is planted; and we hear that the people there still tend to move away and to find their living elsewhere.

Tuesday, the 29th of May. A sick woman praised the goodness of the Lord, which ruled over her even during her illness, in that she had been led much deeper to the bottom of her heart and brought closer to her Savior. In our conversation, we mentioned the song: *Schwing dich auf zu deinem Gott, du betrübte Seele*, etc., which fitted the circumstances of her soul right closely; and she was thereby much strengthened in her trust in the fatherly love of God in Christ. She finds much refreshment in the song: *Jehovah ist mein Hirt und Hüter*, etc.; and she wishes that, if she should die in a state of grace thanks to the grace of God, this song should be sung at her funeral.

For some time now meat has been quite dear in this colony and very scarce. As the orphanage, too, is suffering want in this respect, the dear Lord has ordained for two large, six-year-old oxen to join our herd. They belonged to a merchant in Savannah who is about to leave this colony, and he sold them to us for £6 10s and I have been assured by our people that the orphanage has fared very well in this purchase. I must borrow the money for this, because the £25 which I borrowed on a note upon the instructions of Court Chaplain Ziegenhagen, and which were meant as a present from Prof. Francke, were used partly to pay old debts and partly to buy linen for summer clothing and other necessaries and foodstuffs. I received a good admonition these days when somebody repeated the verse: "Casting all your care upon Him, (on Him Whose hand is powerful) for He careth for you," 1 Peter, 5:7.

Wednesday, the 30th of May. This afternoon we had a strong wind, accompanied by heavy rains and thunderstorms, which bent the tall corn to the ground and blew over some of the fences. The ground here is very loose and soft and is quickly made even softer by the rain; and therefore the corn is bent quickly, and even trees in the forest are easily uprooted. This storm arose quite suddenly and unexpectedly, and we will have to hear whether there was any damage at sea. The wind came from the south, and thus was all the more dangerous for the ships which recently left Charleston or its vicinity. The sailors fear the coast more than the winds or the open sea.

Thursday, the 31st of May. We have received much edification today, both from preaching the Lord's word and from the visits of our dear listeners, for we have learned that the Lord has let His words find a good place in their hearts. On the other hand, there has been much disquiet because of certain circumstances; but the dear Lord has not let this affect our edification or that of the others. The English here do not observe Ascension Day, and they attempted to force the German people in Old Ebenezer to work on this day too; but some refused to do this and instead joined us in church. We hear many complaints regarding the disorderly and offensive ways of some of the Germans there, who act as badly as the others in every way and are therefore a great burden through their wicked words and example for those who are better than they are. Since we have learned of their offenses, such people have not had the heart to come to us to register for Holy Communion or to be seen by us.

My dear colleague had reached the elevation of Christ in the second article; and, as he had occasion to discuss the teaching of the ascension of Christ and His sitting on the right hand of the Father, I chose the two most impressive verses from Mark 16:15–16 as a text and preached on the loving arms of our Lord Jesus, which are open to receive all sinners; here, I based myself on the beautiful words of our dear Savior in John 12: "And I, if I be lifted up from the earth, will draw all men unto me." May God be praised for all His help and blessing.

JUNE

Friday, the 1st of June. The time has come again to preach the word of the Lord to the German people in Savannah, and therefore I plan to depart toward noon. I would like to let my dear colleague undertake this journey this time, as I have felt quite weak and listless physically for several days. However, on my last visit I was unable to settle matters regarding our salary and some other bills, and I must also address in public the matter of the man who has recently married his whore[1] in Savannah, although he has a wife in Germany. In this regard I shall have to publicly declare the marriage null and void, impress on them from God's word the serious sin committed through their fornication and adultery to this day, and again see whether it cannot be arranged to have these two disorderly people separated, whether through the intercession of the authorities or by the consent of their masters. May the Lord strengthen me and bless my undertaking.

Saturday, the 2nd of June. When I asked N. what the dear Lord had bestowed on her as a blessing on the Day of Ascension, she said that the dear Lord had much refreshed her, and she had felt as if she were already in heaven with our Lord Jesus. It can be seen from all her gestures that the Lord Jesus has especially refreshed her from what we have preached from the New Testament. She said she was especially happy that the dear Lord had brought her to this country. She had not wanted to go at all, and for that reason she had not wished to have herself inscribed for the voyage to America; but her husband had said that they should present their plans to the dear Lord, for He would arrange things according to His wisdom and for their benefit, and therefore it had gone well.

Sunday, the 3rd of June. Praised be the Lord, who on this day has given me strength to pronounce His word. He will surely not let this pass without His blessing. The Holy Spirit itself will bear witness of the Lord Jesus in our listeners' hearts and thus they will learn to recognize Him. In the afternoon we were to consider the third article of the catechism, half of which I examined with my listeners; this fitted today's text very well, as well as our preparation for the feast of Holy Whitsun. May the Lord bless all this in His great mercy!

Monday, the 4th of June. Having arranged my affairs in Savannah and in particular discharged the duties of my office with God's help and blessing, I left there last night and returned to our Ebenezer shortly after lunch, in better health than when I left. May the dear Lord be praised in all humility for all His assistance, for the strength given me, and for His blessing; and may He give rich blessing to all which has been placed in the hearts of the people there in His name! As the German servants in Savannah had neither opportunity nor permission to celebrate the feast of Christ's Ascension nor to hear something of the dear benefits of mercy which flow therefrom, I spent considerable time in the morning on the beautiful words of the

68th Psalm: "Thou hast ascended on high," etc., so as to show my listeners the blessed fruits we stand to expect from the loving heart and hands of our glorious and splendid Savior. Every one could and should demand gifts according to his circumstances, and thus change from a renegade knave to a temple of our highly praised and ever-to-be-loved Lord.

From the text for Exaudi Sunday[2] I used the first verse as the basis for our edification and treated of the both important and comforting teaching of the divine nature and office of the Holy Ghost. As the time for treating and applying this weighty text was too short, we continued this necessary and instructive discourse in the afternoon. The dear Lord also let me realize that His word had found acceptance. Four weeks ago several people had asked for testaments and catechisms, which were distributed after the sermon, along with some primers for the children. The children are not permitted by their masters to attend school, and the schoolmaster who lives among them also is not permitted to use even a few hours of his time for the children. Instead, he must work like the other servants. So that they may not grow up entirely ignorant, some of the parents intend to instruct them as much as they can from the books they have received.

Some of the people who live out on the plantations are encountering difficulties in coming into town to attend church when we come to Savannah on their behalf. If Mr. Oglethorpe were told this, he would surely not be pleased. The people also complain much to us how ill they fare in regard to their food, clothing, and conditions of work; and, since there are a number of honest souls among them who are eager for the good, I have much sympathy for them and would like to help through my intercession, if only something could be done. In the meantime I shall do what I can once I return to Savannah and see Mr. Oglethorpe.

I dealt publicly with the wicked man who had married his maidservant, with whom he has committed fornication for some time. I declared the marriage, which had been obtained surreptitiously and, as it were, by theft, to be null and void and explained to the man the verse, "Whoremongers and adulterers God will judge," and also Corinthians 6:9–10. I also admonished both him and her to do penance and to abstain from each other completely and entirely, and I finally admonished the other people there to remind these wretched people constantly to refrain from their wicked conduct and do sincere penance, and to pray for them. I also showed the seriousness of the sin which those people placed upon their consciences who had not said anything even though they had known something of the disorderly conduct of these people, for whom the banns had been pronounced and who had been publicly married.

After the afternoon service, the woman came to me with another man and showed her repentance and stated that she was willing to free herself of the man, if she were only given permission to go somewhere else instead of having to stay near him. I admonished her and let her go. I also spoke to some friends in this matter to have them intercede with the masters of these two people, since I as a stranger would not have their ear; however, I was told that I would have to wait for Mr. Oglethorpe, since nothing could be done without his authority.

Tuesday, the 5th of June. A woman to whom I spoke while she was at work in the fields responded to my greeting and wishes with a right lovely answer and testified with much joy and praise of the Lord that God had done much good to her soul. She also said that in passing a man had called to her, "And I, if I be lifted up from the earth, will draw all men unto me," etc., and had admonished her not to forget the good the Savior had recently caused to be preached on these His very words.

This morning I married the locksmith Georg Bruckner, a young Salzburger, with the oldest daughter of the watchmaker Mueller, Johanna Margaretha. The text was taken from the words of the 68th Psalm, which had impressed and edified me when I recited them to the German people in Savannah. Whoever is or is called man shall have gifts from the Father through the hands of the mediator, and therefore also young newly married people, provided they seek them in the order in which they are instructed from the gospel.

Wednesday, the 6th of June. As our evening prayer meetings now end only toward nine o'clock and our listeners can therefore not come to our house afterwards for private prayer, they have begun to use the noon hours for this purpose, since they cannot work then because of the great heat. We sing a song, then read some Bible passages and use them for our edification, and then some speak a prayer. Everything on these occasions is conducted in a simple and heartfelt manner. I shall shortly go over the most edifying last sayings of our Lord Jesus from John 14 to 17, from verse to verse, with these dear friends in a simple manner. They will surely like this; for they have heard many a precious heart-penetrating truth from the recent Sunday sermons, which were based on this text.

When I read these chapters out loud today, I was reminded again of what I had read last week in Savannah in a printed sermon held and printed by N.N. in N.;[3] this had seemed to me something new that was not founded upon the Scriptures. He speaks therein of the faith that justifies and saves and claims that this was not held by the apostles as long as they had been in the school of the Lord Christ prior to His passion. Here, he seems to confuse the verses that speak of the faith that justifies with those that deal with faith in miracles, nor does he touch upon the witness that the apostles themselves gave of their living faith in the Son of God, the Savior of the world, such as John 6:69 and Matthew 16:16–17, as did the Lord Jesus Himself in these His last speeches and in His high-priest's prayer.

An honest man in N. had just recently told me that Mr. N. had changed much and had better learned to look the gospel in the eye; for he now sought nothing else but to obtain his justification in Christ and from sheer grace. I also see from Mr. N.'s letter that he no longer is an opinion-monger, no longer loses time with ancillary arguments, but keeps his eye on the heart of the matter in his Christianity.

One of the German servants[4] in the orphanage became ill and had me called to his side, just as I was about to conduct the customary meeting in the orphanage. He bore witness that much had recently passed through his soul that had caused him much struggle and fear. His youthful sins were awakening, he said; and he had begun to realize that the Old Adam would have to pass and everything be renewed if he were to gain entrance into heaven. I hope that this will prove true for him. The Old Adam is completely degraded by the word of the Lord as it is preached among us, and he is referred to the cross of Christ;

to this belongs also all self-made justification[5] and piety, so that Christ might be all and everything. This man also has a sick son who is servant to a Salzburger; some time ago this boy had given signs that he would convert to the Lord, but his dishonesty has been revealed in some matters. However, we would gladly be patient with this if he were only to come to a serious change of heart in the end.

Thursday, the 7th of June. Today I received a gift of two beehives, which were brought from the woods by the herdsman and by a servant of the orphanage. Now that a start has been made to take the bees from trees in the woods and make them settle in barrels or chests, there will be many bees in our community. The more our people become acquainted with this country, the better they know how to use the things they find here, and they find that it is true that this country has many advantages over Germany in many respects. Recently I was told something about a kind of oats that grow in the woods, particularly in marshy spots.[6] Some time ago, when travelling to Savannah, I saw this plant myself on the river banks and was much amazed by the grains, which are full of meal, and by their sweet taste. However, as these grains grow on long thin reeds, we did not think much about them because we thought they were seeds which were not good for anything else. We now have heard, however, that the Indians gather whole sacks full of this grain, that some people in Old Ebenezer fatten their hogs with it, and that a man in our congregation uses them for chicken feed, and therefore we will surely learn to make better use of these American oats in the future.

We are still having the most pleasant and convenient weather we could desire, and the crops in the fields are ripening better than ever before. Consequently we hear many of our people thank and praise the Lord for this benefaction. Oh, but that in these days the spiritual field in our congregation may also become green and fertile, so that young and old may grow like the grass, and like the willows on the water courses, for which end our faithful Lord has promised us His spirit as a refreshing and richly yielding water. During the evening prayer meetings the Bible stories also give us an occasion for preparing for the Holy Feast. May the Lord bless this in us! The dear souls who now come to me daily for their joint edification have been made eager for grace by the Lord; and the Savior who has called, "If any man thirst," shall surely not let them go away empty.

Friday, the 8th of June. A woman cried and complained bitterly that things in her house were not going in such proper order as she wished. On Sundays her family would be guilty of much neglect and would miss the repetition from the sermons; everyone went his own way after the public service, etc. I resolved to speak in this regard to her husband and children, who were not home. In the meantime I admonished the woman to pray for her family, also to speak kindly to her husband to try to move him. I asked her to remind him of the verse: "Because thou art lukewarm, and neither cold nor hot, I will spew thee out of my mouth," etc. Oh that God, who is so fiery and ardent in His love for us sinners, may ignite in us a true fire of love for Him and among ourselves, so that it might burn hotly in Ebenezer and others might be ignited by this flame! A sick young man whom I visited again today said that he felt much better and stronger because I had visited him Wednesday and today, spoken to him from God's word, and prayed with him. May God strengthen us in body and soul so that we may be useful to our listeners.

Saturday, the 9th of June. An English woman from Old Ebenezer brought a barrel of rendered beef fat for sale, both today and once before; however, since there is little money here, she probably earned little money. Our dear people use as little as possible for food and clothing so as not to make any debts. They are often offered credit both in Savannah and Purysburg, and the people there like trading with them; but they do well not to engage in borrowing. When God gives them much, they have much and praise Him for it; if He gives them little, they use that to good advantage; and, with God's blessing and advice, they get as far with that as others with all their money and stores, but they remain without debts. The construction of my house has been of some help to many among them, and God is praised therefor. If only the dear Lord would provide me with something from the well of His grace so that I might pay all those workers who are still waiting patiently!

In preparation for Holy Whitsuntide we had the beautiful

words of the Lord Jesus from John 14:16–17, "And I will pray the father," etc., in connection with which we treated the inestimably precious gift of the Holy Ghost, in regard to (1) the giver, (2) the gift, and (3) the takers or recipients. May God bless all this for the sake of Christ, free us from the spirit of this world, and instead fill us and our hearts with His spirit! We held the preparation hour early, so that we might come together for our joint prayer at the time of the prayer meeting at the orphanage.

Sunday and Monday were the Feast of Holy Whitsuntide. Two German men from Old Ebenezer complained that orders had been given from Savannah that, except for Sundays, they were to have no other holidays but attend to their work every day. Their master had complained that they wished to come to our town for the service on Ascension Day; he had not permitted this, and in addition he had complained of them. These servants of the Trustees are given every Saturday for their own use and have offered to work on that day if they are given the opportunity to attend services on those feast days which occur throughout the year. If Mr. Oglethorpe were close by, we would talk to him on their behalf and inquire into this matter. Little or nothing is made in this country of the regular Sundays, so how can we expect that other holy days be honored? Only one day each is allotted for celebrating Christmas, Easter, and Whitsunday; and nothing is made of the other occasions, such as Christ's Epiphany, His Ascension, etc. But through the grace of God we have again learned on the last two days what great use can be had from the celebration of such holy days for those who are serious about the salvation of their souls. The dear Lord has awakened us strongly by His precious gospel of the unspeakable love He holds for us sinners; and He has let us recognize how well He means with us and what we are still lacking, and that the path is wide open for us to become partakers of the grace and communion of the triune of God in truth. May He preserve this blessing in us and teach us never to forget the acts of mercy that He has done for our souls.

Even before the holy days, the Lord had made several souls hungry and eager for His grace; and these have waited upon the actual bestowal of this same and precious grace with a serious use of the means to salvation. Praise be to God, who has not let them wait and hope in vain. In the repetition hour our faithful Lord has bestowed such a blessing upon me that I cannot praise Him enough. May He only make me right faithful, so that I will receive more and more and so that, by His blessing, I shall become more and more capable for the praise of His glory and the salvation of our dear listeners. In the place of the catechism, my dear colleague had as a text two verses that are well suited for the occasion, i.e. Corinthians 13:13 and Numbers 6:22–27.

Tuesday, the 12th of June. After Sundays and holy days, it gives us great pleasure when our dear and kind Lord lets us realize while visiting our dear listeners that His word has been preached with His blessing, of which I experienced a beautiful example today. A man told me that he had believed he had previously celebrated Whitsunday with blessing, but this time the Lord has bestowed on him a special act of mercy so that he can well say that he had never before celebrated Whitsunday in such a manner. He would have gone to his plantation today, but he feared that he would be distracted; and therefore he wishes to let the gift he has received take root quietly. Also, a woman had been in much unnecessary distress and fear during the holy days, which had been caused by some careless neighbors who had made a groundless accusation. Therefore she had not benefited from the sermons as she should have done. I showed her the way she could come to peace of mind and to rest. Since several unpleasantnesses had occurred in her house with regard to her children, she remembered the conclusion of the Tenth Commandment, where God threatens to visit the sins of the parents on the children to the third and fourth generation; and on this occasion the sins of her youth had stirred strongly within her.

Another woman was much depressed and complained with tears that, despite the rich love of the Lord and His great and dear promises, her heart was still empty, so that she sometimes felt that she would never break through because she was so corrupted; her, too, I was able to lead on the right way with God's grace. Because of her physical weakness she has not always been able to attend the public preaching of the divine word, and therefore her husband has faithfully and simply repeated to her what God has given him for his edification. We notice here and there that good people stress their Christianity more by exercising their Christian duties than by simply placing themselves at the breast of Christ in simple faith and sucking in His mercy and thereby being prepared for all good works. Then, upon realizing their weaknesses and their lack of strength, they are full of legalistic fears and distress and close to despair.[7]

A sick man recounted how he had sighed for grace on his sickbed and had gone to sleep with the grieving thought whether there was any grace left for him; and in his sleep it had appeared to him as if a door had opened in a large house and a virgin dressed in white had pointed out to him the 22nd Psalm; he himself had noticed on his right hand a bloody thick welt. He asked me what I thought of this dream. He had read the psalm by himself, and I showed him how he could use its glorious content according to his circumstances. He should continue to implore the Lord for a repentant recognition of his sins, so that he might see the truth; then the Healer and Savior of poor sinners, of whom such comforting words are said in this psalm, would become most dear and close to him. The psalm also says: "The meek shall eat and be satisfied; they shall praise the lord that seek him," etc. Also, he should cling not to a dream but to the Lord's words.

Wednesday, the 13th of June. In yesterday's evening prayer meeting we concluded the impressive story from the 7th chapter of Judges, where we heard that: (1) Gideon and his three hundred men were a beautiful prefiguration[8] of Christ and His servants in the New Testament, who fought and vanquished the enemies of the church not with weapons of the flesh but with the sword of the Lord's word, which had flown from their mouths and pens, and with the resounding sound of the gospel. They had contained their treasure, their light and their strength, but did great things. (2) It had always been God's way to accomplish great deeds through little things despised in this world, and many a time a small beginning has finally come to a glorious and miraculous conclusion.

In explanation, and to show that even today God takes such paths with those who believe and whenever it is required for His glory and the well-being of His church, I told my listeners, to my own great joy, not only what the Lord had accomplished in the Halle Orphanage through the service of His dear and chosen fighting arm, the late Prof. Francke, in that he had caused the foundation to be laid for such large institutions at the expense of only a few guilders. I also recounted what I learned of the most honest Mr. Elers, who now rests in God, and his newly started bookstore, which set out with one printed sermon and had so expanded with the Lord's blessing that now many poor, both within and without the Orphanage, are refreshed through it in many ways. I have been told that this blessed man, when he came to the Leipzig Fair for the first time, had his windows broken by his enemies during the night. His servant, whom he had with him as Gideon had the boy Pura, became quite fearful and aggrieved at this; but the blessed Elers calmed him with these words among others: "He should but be quiet and wait in the faith; the very people who now throw stones into my room will one day bring me money." And this, in fact, occurred, as the bookstore prospered under the Lord's blessing.

We have occasion to converse with our listeners both privately and publicly in the most simple manner, and we make use of many things serving their and our edification. On Whitsun Monday, we read publicly the 52nd chapter[9] of Jeremiah, which followed in the order; and I was much impressed by its 50th verse: "Remember the Lord in a far land and let Jerusalem be in thy heart." May the Lord himself remind us often of the good that we have enjoyed richly in Halle, both physically and spiritually, in which our congregation shares even now, in that much has flown from the blessings there to their benefit and that of the orphanage. May God be praised!

Thursday, the 14th of June. This morning I was visited by a smith from Savannah who had previously asked me to assign to him a 15-year-old boy from our community, to whom he wished loyally to teach his trade and whom he wished to keep as his own child. However, I could not propose such a child to him either the last time or today, because the parents here urgently need their grown children. Also, I cannot really advise them to remove their children from God's word and proper supervision and let them go to a strange place among strangers. We are still hoping for the arrival of some much-needed artisans, so that the young among us may be instructed by and by in some of the useful trades. An Englishman told me that a week ago Saturday two ships had arrived in Charleston, one carrying German freemen who had been sent to this colony by the Lord Trustees and who were expected shortly in Savannah. If these are not the people destined for our community (as we always hope), we shall at least expect on this boat the gifts which have long been on the way and which would cause great joy to us and our dear listeners in this time of want.

While I was in school, the oldest Zuebli[10] came to me and told me that the English servant who some months ago had stolen several things from their hut had returned and again stolen some items.[11] He had met him face to face; but, as his brother was out in the fields, he had not been able to do anything. This fellow has escaped from prison in Savannah and will again cause much damage. I immediately wrote to Old Ebenezer and asked the Englishman living there to send some of his people on horseback to search for the fellow. It has rained heavily this afternoon, and we also had a thunderstorm, so that our people were prevented from going out to look for him. Also, he has probably left our area, as he was surprised in the act of stealing. We are very sorry for the two Zuebli brothers, who already are among the poorest here, and I shall ask Mr. Oglethorpe to extend some help to them to make good for the loss they have suffered. It is not within our power to help them with anything more than what they have already received. It was their choice to seek out their plantation in an isolated spot on Ebenezer Creek; and, as they have no neighbors, nobody can help them in case of need.

I talked to some of our listeners and heard again that the good and pious Lord has bestowed a great blessing on them during the Feast of Whitsuntide, for which they praise the merciful Giver and vow to undertake their Christianity with greater seriousness thanks to His grace. A young man who has heretofore been confined by his fearful and legalistic ways gave witness that, by God's grace, things were going much better with him these days; and he recognizes well that his legalistic efforts and works cannot really lead to a good end. He could not enjoy his Christian faith, he said, everything he did was done with resentment, he had no strength to resist sin, and, when he contemplated his weakness and previous sins, he experienced nothing but pain and fear, etc. I told him that he should turn around and become like a child and, like the small newborn infants, suck the unspeakable grace of the heavenly Father, which is open to all sinners, from the loving breast of Christ; also, he should make this grace his own in faith and humility as a poor repentant sinner, and not give way to the objections of his wicked faithless heart. If he should then become stronger in his grace and the love of Christ and continue to grow, he would also garner the strength to embrace his Savior with childlike affection and live in His glory. Thus he would also learn the great patience and forbearance which the Savior shows to His weak children and infants. In this connection, I referred him to the very evangelical sermon of the blessed Prof. Francke, which is so comforting to fearful sinners, wherein he speaks of the kindness of the Lord Jesus in accepting the sinners and which was held on the beautiful text in Matthew 9:9-13.

Friday, the 15th of June. Yesterday lightning struck two trees in two spots quite close to our town; one was completely demolished and large chunks of wood were strewn around. Praised be the Lord, who does not avert his kindness from us but renews it over us on each and every day. We are in His hands with our houses, huts, and all possessions, may He deal with us in the future not according to our sins but to His saving grace. The weather is quite fruitful now and most convenient for planting sweet potatoes. The beans have suffered in some spots from the heavy rains, but they will recover by and by. The deer invade our fields at night and eat off the young beans. All of this is happening for some good reason, and we look upon such things as a necessary exercise and trial of the faith.

The old carpenter who has been spending some time in our town has fallen ill; and, as he is already a man of some age, his end will not be far off. He can speak of true conversion to God, and today he told me of the mercy which the Lord has shown to his soul. He had been much attached to this world until his twenty-seventh year; and, because he was a man of natural understanding and skills, he had been dear and pleasant in the eyes of other worldly people with whom he had enjoyed the pleasures of the flesh. In particular, he had much sinned with his comrades by drinking, gambling, and such on the days of the Lord. But, in the very course of his sins, the Lord had dealt a harsh blow to his conscience, so that he had to leave the company in which he found himself. Later, he had wanted to rejoin his companions; but, whenever he had gone, he had been stricken with anxiety and had cried much. His sins and God's anger at them had rested so heavily on his conscience that he had considered himself as lost and had spent three years as a despairing man in much fear and terror. A young preacher had become aware of his state, and this man had not only visited him constantly but had called him to his quarters twice a week. These ministrations had by and by been so blessed by the Lord that he had learned to believe that God wished to let this sinner, too, be redeemed in Christ. From this time on the work of the faith had started in his soul, but also tribulations and rejection, etc. This man is an eager and diligent hearer of the divine word among us and sets a good example for others, so that we have no reason to doubt the good foundation in him. He sends his only son to school, and this boy shows much promise and has good ability to learn.

Saturday, the 16th of June. The younger N.[12] has composed a supplication to General Oglethorpe in which he presents his and his brother's great poverty as well as the theft that has afflicted them twice; he begs to be granted some help in the form of provisions from the storehouse. I accompanied this petition with a testimony on the good conduct of these two men among us and added my request for help on their behalf. Although we wish we could do something for them, this would exceed our means entirely, and we ourselves must wait upon the help of the Lord. A woman who had heard of the misfortune of the two brothers told me of her regret at being unable to help these and other poor people. However, since she is praying for them, this too is an act of love and a good work. The N.N. have planted some crops, to be sure, but it is little; and, as they have settled in the middle of the forest, the shade from the surrounding large trees hinders the growth of their crops. Nor have they had the time and the strength to fence their field, so that not only the deer but the pigs which run from our town into the woods have free access to their plantings; although they have not yet done any damage, they may yet do so. May the dear Lord have mercy on them and direct the heart of N.[13] to open to their great need.

This afternoon I and the foremen of the community had the wicked and spiteful N. before us so as to refer him to his duties with good but serious words. Until now he has considered me too harsh because I was not able to overlook his offenses. Because he had been heard to say that others also felt that I had been too harsh and thus unjust toward him, he was asked to state, before these men of the congregation, what people he meant by this, so that I might talk to them myself and forestall a misunderstanding. However, he could not offer any names but the single one of N., who indeed often meddles in matters that are none of his concern and pretends to be very clever and is therefore not very highly regarded in our community. Inasmuch as he has harmed the boy N. with his idle talk and made him even more obstinate, there will surely be an opportunity to place this vexing matter on his conscience; although I prefer to be careful not to embitter him, since he already takes offense at the smallest thing. He moved to his plantation some time ago and is said to live in much discord with his wife, a fact which both of them keep quiet. May God convert him, although he puts many obstacles into his own path.

Sunday, the 17th of June. Last night I was afflicted by heavy vomiting, which made my throat quite too sore for talking and has enfeebled my entire body. Therefore I had to ask my dear colleague this morning to present in my stead what he had prepared with regard to the last part of the third Article. With God's assistance I sufficiently regained my strength this afternoon to preach on the third verse of today's gospel from John 3:1 ff., on rebirth, its necessity, nature, and blessing. May the Lord let me see the fruit of this and find it before His throne.

Monday, the 18th of June. The dear Lord has placed such a beautiful blessing on yesterday's preaching of His word that some faithful and grace-hungry souls came to us this noon to continue their edification and seal everything with a prayer and the praise of the Lord. I read something to them from the beautiful little book[14] of the late Dr. Richter concerning the rebirth of the soul, and our dear Lord graciously let mention be made therein of the evangelical growth in the received gift of the new birth. This is most important for some who tend to engage in mere legalistic activity with regard to the good received from the Lord. The verse: "In returning and rest shall ye be saved; in quietness and in confidence shall be your strength," etc., was most impressive for us.

Saturday a sick woman had asked for me; but, since I had been prevented from visiting her, I went to her today, which still served her well. She was suffering from fever and praised the Lord for revealing to her the sins of her youth and for working faithfully on her so as to make her into a new creature. When she has a little strength, she uses it to pray to her Savior, who also does not fail to hear her. When her husband and I fell on our knees before her bed to pray, she also moved to her weak and feeble knees in her bed; and when I admonished her to remain still, she said she would not wish to please the Old Adam by lying down; she, too, wished to humble herself, etc.

Tuesday, the 19th of June. The wicked fellow who has stolen several things from the Zuebli cottage is still said to be in our neighborhood. Many watermelons that have not even ripened have disappeared from the gardens, and surely this miserable man must be forced to eat these from hunger. We have had rain every day, so that our people have been prevented from searching the woods. But, as the sky cleared this afternoon, all of the men in the town who have guns have gone out, both to hunt for this man and to chase off the deer that are doing so much damage to the beans. After four o'clock we had a strong thunderstorm and much rain, which probably incommodated them greatly during their search.

The Lord knows what we need before we tell Him about it; and, since our fields need dry summer weather after all this rain, He will surely give us this grace if only we pray for it in faith and wait for it with patience. Beans, gourds, and melons all suffer much from this wet weather. Last year, the rains stayed away too long and the crops did not mature well; but God showed us that He can do abundantly more than we ask or understand, and many of the people still have food from the blessing we received in the last harvest.

I found a recently arrived married couple sick in bed and talked to them according to their circumstances. Things are still going badly with them; and, since they have brought many prejudices with themselves and have comfort to spare,[15] it is difficult to convince them that they are rotten and damnable sinners and must crawl to the cross. May God bless all that which we have said to them in advice and prayer for the sake of their souls.

Wednesday, the 20th of June. Our men who went yesterday to look for the thief combed the entire woods for him, particularly in the vicinity of the Ebenezer Creek, but could not find him. I received news from Old Ebenezer today that we no longer have to fear anything from this thief, as he has left the area and gone his previous way. We also have everything well secured and do not need nightly watches, so that the toilers sleep under the shadow of the wings of the Lord after their daily labor, for He as the guardian of Israel neither sleeps nor slumbers; thus, they sleep quietly and securely after we have recommended ourselves to His saving grace in the prayer meeting before bedtime. Today and yesterday we have been unable to hold a prayer meeting because of the rainy weather.

Perhaps the dear Lord will bless the loving efforts of Mr. N.[16] to collect some money for the construction of a church in our town, so that the church can be built in a location that is convenient for all our listeners. At present the meetings are still held in the old hut which Mr. von Reck had built by the joint labor of the Salzburgers on the Savannah river. This spot, however, is out of the way for most of the people and difficult to reach in the dark of the evening and during rainy weather.

Thursday, the 21st of June. In the afternoon hour between two and three, I have instructed the children who are to be prepared for Holy Communion in the larger Order of Salvation, ending with the appended *Golden ABC*.[17] Now that I have finished this, I thank the dear Lord for all the help He has rendered in this regard and call upon him in the name of our Lord Jesus to place His grace on all the truths presented in this catechization, so that these children may not only grasp and retain this holy Order of Salvation, word by word and letter by letter, but accept it within their hearts so that they may become new creatures and children according to the heart and mind of the Lord. Three girls and one boy have been rendered quiet and attentive by the grace of the Lord, and I have much hope for the change of their hearts and their proper preparation. Provided they become and remain faithful to the Lord Jesus, I intend to let them go to the Lord's Table on the next occasion, after previous examination and confirmation.

I kept the boy with me after the lesson and admonished him to use the means of salvation earnestly as well as to faithfully apply the grace he received; I also inquired into his company, and whether he visited his neighbors often to be edified by them, as I know that they are true Christians. Here I learned that there had been a misunderstanding between his mother and one of the neighbors, which had not yet been cleared up although the mother had sought peace and reconciliation. I shall look for an opportunity to inquire into the matter and make peace. The abovementioned children as well as the others could not come to the preparation hour during the planting season, as they must help their parents in the fields; but, since most of them did go to school several hours a day and all were made to attend the daily prayer meeting and the public services, they have never been without the opportunity for a true preparation. I therefore plan to repeat the dogma of the Holy Communion with them according to the instructions of the catechism, so that they may gain a full understanding of this most important sacrament and be all the more motivated by its importance and great helpfulness to prepare for it properly with eager and zealous prayer.

A little girl asked for some linen for some clothing and at the same time begged to be admitted to the orphanage, etc. On several previous occasions I had wished to accept her among the orphaned children, but her mother preferred me to make provision for helping her outside so that she could stay and help with her housekeeping tasks. This was not possible, however. Now that the mother is willing to let her go, the orphanage is so filled with children and other of the poor that we will have to refuse several applicants unless the Lord shows us new traces of His grace. Until now, the dear Lord has always provided, although the housekeeping in the orphanage had to be arranged along the most frugal lines, wherein the manager and his wife do the best they can.

Friday, the 22nd of June. The dear Lord granted me much edification today in the meeting, which is held twice weekly in my room. When he first arrived, Simon Reiter could not read a single word and appeared simple and maladroit to us and others; but after he turned to God from the bottom of his heart, he has not only learned how to read but utters the words of his prayers with such strength and impressiveness that they cannot be but edifying and joyful to all those who would listen with a devout heart. When I heard him pray today, I thought of our dear students of theology in Halle, and I wished to God that they would not be content with outward and literal scholarship, but would go to the school of the true instructor, the Holy Ghost, so that they may become *theodidaktoi*[18] and thus make their talent right useful to their neighbor. At the time I was there, it was easy to see that, in many cases, both words and prayers came from the mind instead of flowing from the dear treasure of the heart, and this yields but little good. True Christianity, and the new birth that lies at the bottom of it, are an ornament that suits everyone, even the most simple, and renders him useful to both God and man. How much more will it not then befit a student of theology, and how much good would not flow therefrom for others if these were all to become thus.

Saturday, the 23rd of June. We have had rain every day for some time, and the ground has become quite soggy. I have not heard that much damage has been done to the crops so far, and we trust that the dear Lord will maintain and protect the blessing He has shown us. Doubtless, the honest members of the congregation call upon Him with much zeal in this regard, and they have the most certain assurance that they shall not pray in vain.

I found the manager of the orphanage in confident spirits today, and he told me for the praise of the Lord that He lends more and more of the grace that is required to cope with all circumstances that tend to arise in such an institution, however small it may be. He and his wife have learned, he said, to suffer want in the school of Christ and to acquiesce in everything the

Lord ordains as His servant and bondsman. He knows how to show love and forbearance as well as strictness, each at its proper time, and God blesses his labors. It will be necessary for me to speak to the adults in the orphanage in the course of the next days, and I will do this more often in the future, so that all may agree with each other and each be obedient to the other in the love of God.

A small misunderstanding and some ill will had arisen among three pious souls because of a boy, which had prevented them from attending yesterday's meeting in my house in the right spirit; and this had caused them grief and disquiet. But they soon talked about the matter in question in a friendly way and reconciled themselves on their knees before the Heavenly Father, so that my intercession was not necessary and I only learned of the matter after it had been settled. It is truly a great advantage if people do not forge ahead and insist on their imagined rights, but instead attempt to settle discord before the Lord; else, things get difficult and division arises.

Sunday, the 24th of June. Last evening after the prayer meeting we had the pleasure of receiving a goodly package of letters and other news from Europe. They had been waiting for us for several weeks in Charleston and Frederica; and, since they had reached the hands of Mr. Oglethorpe, he forwarded them to us with the following words: "God be praised, we have obtained £40 from Europe to be payd to you towards the Maintenance of Saltzburgher Widows & Orphans, & £30 to Mr. Gronau for to be laid out in Building him a Dwelling-House for his Ministry. have sent up the Money to Mr. Jones in the trustees Sola Bills by Mr. Kellaway, etc." [19] God be praised for this blessing, which we least anticipated at a time when money is quite rare in this colony.

The letters which we now received were from Court Chaplain Ziegenhagen, Secretary Newman, Prof. Francke, and Counsellor Walbaum; and all contained much that causes us to praise the Lord. Among other items, Mr. Newman advised that three honest merchants from N. had forwarded £10 sterling to the Honorable Society for the good of the Salzburgers, with the request that the Society see to it that the money be used for the good of our orphanage.[20] Oh how great is the mercy of the Lord! His fountains carry water in plenty, and He knows when to refresh us after all our want and trials. The manager of the orphanage and I had agreed some days ago to slaughter one of the oxen we bought recently, as there was a lack of meat in the orphanage and there was no money to buy anything in this time of want, when everything in Savannah is both rare and expensive. However, the horse needed for bringing in the oxen could not be found, and now the Lord lets us know that the money has arrived for the orphanage and therefore we can keep the ox until the heat has passed and it has been fattened in the pasture. We use even the smallest circumstance to strengthen our faith, for indeed all is within the providence of the Lord.

Court Chaplain Ziegenhagen confirmed Mr. Newman's announcement that the dear Mr. N.[21] is sparing no pain to act on behalf of us and is being quite successful in this; and therefore there is reason for hope that on his anticipated return to Savannah he will bring some money for the orphanage and for the construction of a church. Court Chaplain Ziegenhagen also mentioned Sanftleben and several women and a shoemaker, who were en route from Augsburg to Holland at the time of his writing. And today at noon I had a note from Sanftleben that he and several others had arrived in Port Royal last Tuesday from Charleston, whence he intends to travel to Savannah on the first occasion offered by water and asks us to fetch him shortly from the latter place. For this, too, praise be the Lord!

The letter of the court chaplain also mentions that the four chests with all sorts of gifts from Augsburg and Halle had not yet arrived in London, and that it must therefore be presumed that they were lost in or with the boat on which they had been sent. If this be true, we shall say in faith and humility, "The Lord gives and the Lord hath taken away," and we hope that the dear Lord who restored his lost goods and children to Job after his many tribulations shall also find means and ways to let us partake of His blessing in some other way. In His government He doeth nothing without reason. A pious Salzburger to whom I recounted this story, upon learning how much had flown in physical blessings to the orphanage and with it to the entire congregation, remarked that God was wont to add salt to the sugar. Apart from this, Sanftleben's arrival is bringing further blessing to us, the orphanage, and the whole congregation. Dear Prof. Francke as well is equally untiring in his concern for us and comes to our aid with all sorts of good inspiration, edifying news, and advice, and also material assistance, for which may the Lord Himself repay him. And our esteemed Counsellor Walbaum too has again thought of our congregation with re-newed and tangible affection by forwarding us through Sanftle-ben the sum of 25 Reichstaler. May the dear Lord help us to receive His gifts not only as is written of the rich man in the gospel, but to cherish them in His praise and with heartfelt thanks and a new resolution to dedicate ourselves to His service with all our heart and soul, so that they may produce much useful good for the praise of the Giver and the best of our neighbors.

The poor among us had looked forward eagerly to the linen and other gifts of which Prof. Francke and Senior Urlsperger had made repeated mention in previous letters; now that their hope seems to have been in vain, they will feel some grief, as the shortage of linen in particular affects them much. I have tried to encourage them in today's repetition hour wherein we read the edifying letters of Court Chaplain Ziegenhagen and Prof. Francke for the good of the congregation. For we have a Lord for whom nothing is impossible. If it should serve His glory and our good, He can bring up the lost presents from the bottom of the sea as easily as He can compensate for our loss in some other way. I reminded them that nobody would have dared hope that my lost gown and the box of letters would have been returned to me, as in fact occurred.[22] In the repetition hour, I informed the congregation of the edifying content of the letters and of the beautiful blessing that is forthcoming for the orphanage, in which the community will also share; the Lord let this pass with great edification and strengthening of my faith. In the evening, we assembled in the orphanage to sum up all that we had heard from our letters in prayer and to present it to the dear redeem-ing God and Father in heaven, as did Jephta in Judges 11:11, whereof we have been dealing in our prayer meetings these very days. The children were more attentive than usual; and, as quite a crowd had assembled, we praised the Lord for His bless-ings, prayed for our dear benefactors and wished before the

Lord that Sanftleben and his dear companions might arrive at our place in good health and spirit and for their and our furtherance in the faith.

Because of the continuing rainy weather, these dear people will be waiting for our arrival in Savannah with great impatience, so my dear colleague travelled down there in our small boat tonight, to welcome them kindly in the name of the Lord and to make arrangements for their needs and transportation. Tomorrow morning our Salzburgers will travel down with two boats to fetch them and their belongings, for which undertaking everyone has shown the greatest willingness. It seems that Sanftleben's note reached me quite late, else we would have taken steps last week to wait for them and his people in Savannah, so that they could have been received immediately by our boats and brought up here without having to witness bad examples in Savannah and have their minds befuddled by all sorts of unfounded gossip from the wicked Germans there. I hope that Sanftleben has used all necessary precautions. The chances of being misled in this country are quite great.

At noon, I was visited by three Englishmen, who are on their way from Fort Augusta to Charleston on matters of commerce. They asked me to have two people in their boat married in my house; but I refused them, as I have done before with all such people. It is not my office to become involved in such marriages, which are usually surrounded by suspicious circumstances. I inquired from them of Mr. Falk, who once pretended both in Savannah and here to have been ordained by a bishop in Sweden and sent here to America as a minister. As he could not get anything accomplished in Savannah, he travelled to Savannah-Town; but, as one of these Englishmen told me, he never made it there and instead stayed for a while in Palachocolas, where he baptized children and tried to set up some kind of divine services for the English and the Negroes there. However, he proved somewhat dishonest, and therefore he was made to leave and travelled back to Charleston. Although the road leads past our town, he has never come back here.

Monday, the 25th of June. There is again a rumor that Mr. Oglethorpe intends to travel to the Indian Nations or to Savannah-Town, and for this purpose several strange Indians have come down the Savannah River. He will surely use this occasion to inspect the mill, as his itinerary will take him past Old Ebenezer by land.

H. Floerel's wife was delivered of a young daughter this morning, who was baptized at noon. Two pious women assisted her in her hard labor, who jointly with her husband fell to their knees in the hour of greatest danger and prayed for the help of the Lord. Since the three had jointly promised the Lord to praise Him today in our meeting for the help rendered, they all came to my room for this purpose, where the husband prayed quite from the bottom of his heart and praised the Lord, as well as remembering, in moving words and before the face of the Lord, our dear fathers and benefactors in Europe; he was joined in this by others who were there for prayer. May God be praised for these blessed noon hours during which we meet Mondays and Fridays.

From a little letter of our dear Prof. Francke, we made good use of the news of the blessed departure of the dear servant of the Lord, Pastor Freylinghausen; and I told them what a treasure he had been to the Church of Christ and particularly the dear city of Halle, who are both now deprived of this noble jewel. I have learned from him and all his works with which I am familiar, the Lord be praised, what the Savior intended with these words: "Except ye be converted and become as little children," etc. At the conclusion of our prayer we sang a few verses from the beautiful hymn by this very Freylinghausen: *Wer ist wohl wie Du*, etc., which touched me particularly on this occasion. In this connection, I am reminded of the devout expression of the late Pastor Mischke, as recounted in the story of his life, i.e.: "The closer he came to his end, the more impetuously he penetrated into Christ and His mercy,[23] so that he in truth accomplished what he used to answer in his days of health to the question: How would he act once the bridal coach which he so eagerly awaited would come? And he was wont to answer: I shall then once more cleanse myself thoroughly in the blood of Christ, and shall dress in a white shirt, which is the robe of Christ's justification, and then I shall mount that coach joyously." That truly means: to prepare oneself for glory!

Tuesday, the 26th of June. Among the unmarried women ac-

companying Sanftleben is the blood sister of our Mrs. Landfelder, by the name of Elisabeth Wassermann. Since she is being
taken in by the Landfelder woman pending future arrangements, I admonished the latter well this morning, particularly
with regard to working on her sister by word and example so
that she might be led into that order of things from the very
beginning in which she can please the Lord through Jesus
Christ and become blessed. Outward quietness and proper de-
meanor, as well as an industrious use of the means of salvation,
are not decisive in our work of grace. Instead, according to the
meaning of the exordium of last Sunday, Deuteronomy 30:19–
20, a man must reach the point of believing in God and his
Savior through the word of the gospel, and his faith must be
proven through love, love through obedience, and obedience
through an attachment to Christ, as we have seen in the example of the dear Apostles of the Lord. Thus one obtains the possession and enjoyment of the promised land and will partake of
grace and life both here and in eternity. She was well pleased by
these words and promised that she and her husband would pray
diligently so that she too might partake of this grace.

Since I had communicated the contents of the edifying letters
we received last Sunday in the repetition hour for the good of
the departing members, I repeated the sermon on the regular
text in yesterday's prayer meeting. May God bless all this for the
sake of Christ! After the prayer meeting, six girls visited me for
prayer, whose hearts the dear Lord has touched these last days.
I told them that the devil had much harmed them through frivolity and that they should watch their thoughts, eagerly sigh to
the Lord, carry a good verse in their minds at all times, and pray
to the Lord several times during the day, as well as visit me
frequently. Then I would not doubt that God will continue and
ground ever more firmly His work in them which He has com-
menced on several occasions. Upon their return, I shall tell
them from the pleasing letter of the dear Mr. N. some things of
the highborn children of the noble Count N., since I had mentioned something of their edifying example just yesterday. Mr.
N. uses the following expression concerning these children so
highly born in the Lord: "There is none left among the Count's
children who is not confidently enjoying the Lord, his Savior;

and their number is now being augmented by the recent marriage of the young Count at N., with the most proper and demure Countess N. May our Lord be praised."

Rauner well notices that the blessing of the Lord is not on his house and matters are retrogressing with him in many respects. I admonished him to see to his true conversion, for then he would partake of His blessing in both spiritual and material things, as he has now heard repeated several times. However, since he and his family have until now elected the sins and temptations of this world, he also has to bear the curse that is attached thereto and therefore must blame himself for all misfortune. I also admonished him regarding his disobedient and reckless son, whom I have ordered to come to me tomorrow to give him some necessary clothing from the orphanage and to admonish him on this occasion. I told him that I had noticed two external errors in his education of this wicked boy: (1) that he was never of one mind with his wife; (2) that he often failed to have the boy accompany him at work and indulged him too much in his will and in the use of his time. The major reason why their children have not turned out well, however, is the unrepentant and mistaken state of mind of the parents. In previous times, he spent much time in the company of some wicked people in Old Ebenezer; and I was glad to hear that he himself had realized that this had done him more harm than good and that he vowed he would dispense with such company altogether from now on.

N.'s wife had an edifying and warm conversation with me today which bears witness of her growth in Christianity. She also told me that her husband had recently returned home much moved and shed many tears over the words of the Lord that had penetrated his heart. He has left for Savannah with others of the men to fetch Sanftleben and his travel companions. Prior to the voyage, he prayed to the dear Lord to protect him from unnecessary gossip, since this was an easy temptation in the company of so many people and he might therefore sin easily. She told me that young people had come to the hut on several occasions and started gossiping, but she had chastised them for that and they had stayed away subsequently.

Wednesday, the 27th of June. Last night my dear colleague

came back home and brought with him the new shoemaker,[24] who seems to be a most honest fellow. As he cannot have anything built now, he will use my old hut in the meantime, and a Salzburger woman in his neighborhood will wash and cook for him. The Lord Trustees have made him a present of leather and wax worth 19 shillings 10 pence, and he has obligated himself to make shoes for the orphanage from this for half price. Mr. Verelst is also bearing in mind the 40 pounds for the orphanage and the 30 pounds for my dear colleague's house, which were mentioned in Mr. Oglethorpe's letter a few days ago. May God be praised for all His munificence!

In the morning towards nine o'clock the two boats with Sanftleben and the unmarried women arrived. They first came to my house, where our first concern was to sing a joint song of praise and call upon the dear Lord in humble prayer for His blessing on our faith and our external professions, to praise Him for all divine assistance experienced on land and on water during the voyage, and to ask Him as well for forgiveness, in the name of His son, for all offenses and sinful weaknesses. Then a meal was prepared for them which everyone attended in good spirits and with much joy. The women soon found their friends here with whom they will stay until God shall provide for them in other ways. Mr. von Reck gave Sanftleben his hut, where we have until now held school; we will now have to move somewhere else for this. That which the dear Father in heaven has intended for us through the hands of some pious benefactors in Augsburg, i.e. linen and several items for clothing, as well as useful books, had to remain behind in London for the time, as the customs officials at first did not wish to let these goods pass; however, we have grounds to expect them later. Also, the letter of dear Court Chaplain Ziegenhagen gives us new hope regarding the four crates which we recently had given up for lost.

These good people came from Charleston to Savannah in an open petiagua[25] and therefore both they and their belongings have suffered much in the rainy weather. When they arrived in Savannah, the storekeeper, Mr. Jones, had just traveled to Frederica; and, since there was nothing in the storehouse anyway by way of provisions, all that was given them was a barrel of flour.

In our letters, no mention is made of their sustenance during the first period after their arrival, except that Sanftleben told me that the Lord Trustees had promised to arrange things for them as had been done for the first Salzburgers. According to news received from the Court Chaplain, Mr. Vernon is said to have recommended them to Mr. Oglethorpe; and we will probably learn shortly what kind of provisions will be made for them from the storehouse. From the letter written to the Court Chaplain by Senior Urlsperger, which contains a complete listing of all things given to Sanftleben for us, we see that despite the pitiful conditions in Germany, where there is much want and expense, the Lord is remembering our congregation with His blessing and is bestowing one material blessing after the other on us through well-meaning hands and in accordance with our needs. The house of the esteemed N. is indefatigable in proving their true love and care for us, and we will eagerly call upon the heavenly Father in the name of His son so that He may place His blessing on them now and in eternity.

We have been honored by a most edifying letter of Lady N.;[26] may the Lord bless it, in us and ours. Also, the esteemed Mr. N. wrote us and gave us news of his charitable gift, which Sanftleben has brought with himself in the form of a sum of money. May the dear Lord strengthen the dear Mr. N.N. in his heavy burden of business at home and abroad and may He let him, as all His faithful servants, enjoy even here on earth the beautiful fruit of the precious divine prophecy in Isaiah 3:10: "Say ye to the righteous that it shall be well with them: for they shall eat the fruit of their doings." In the crates left behind in England there are said to be several other letters addressed to us which we would love to read soon. Sanftleben is quite busy today unpacking his belongings and being visited by the Salzburgers, who are eager to learn all the news from him; and we will therefore have little of his company today. We have had pleasant weather in the last few days, so that our dear guests have arrived safe and dry, but the rain is starting again. God will make all turn out well for us, including the weather.

Thursday, the 28th of June. I hear that useless people in Charleston have talked a lot with the women who arrived with Sanftleben and have tried to prevail on them not to continue on to Georgia, arguing that there was nothing but want and misery here; and this had caused some disquiet in several of them. I believe that they will like everything they find here, however, as they are being accepted with much love by Christian folk and are enjoying all sorts of good favors. Sanftleben has also brought a gift of money for the orphanage and the two of us. Praise be to God, who always knows the means to make good our want and to relieve us from misery. He told me that dear Mr. N.N. had told him I should have a room of my own, even if he had to have it built from his own money. May God repay him for his love!

The carpenters are again seriously at work finishing my house; and therefore I will not only have a good room for study, prayer, and conversation with my dear listeners but also a warm sickroom, since the walls are 5 inches thick and they will set up an iron stove, which has cost me 2 pounds 14 shillings and which can be conveniently arranged because the kitchen is right in the middle of the house. The cause of the long illnesses and frequent weakness among us is above all the fact that in the winter time it is difficult to raise a right strong sweat and maintain a constant light state of perspiration, as the huts are not built to keep out the cold. How much good I have already felt from the use, by day and night, of a proper living room, in which my family will be able to conduct their household affairs in the future, and how much my health and my office have benefited from it! May God be praised; may He also provide us with the costs for the house! At present I have only one window with two casements, each three feet high and two feet wide. If the dear Lord does not send glass from England at reasonable cost, for which I asked the dear Court Chaplain Ziegenhagen several months ago, we will have to see to buying something here, for without glass windows my purpose will not be served. The glass made here is of low quality and quite expensive.

The dear N.N. has sent us his portrait, which I showed to a woman who is seeking the Lord, without telling her whose likeness this was. However, at the very first glance she said, this one I know best, for he had done much good to me, etc. We hear that many other likewise well-intentioned Salzburgers have become quite worldly in Germany and that there is now little difference between them and other vain artisans or similar people. For this reason they are held in low regard and even mocked by their compatriots who have left the pleasant material conditions there and come here. Such people will cause much grief to faithful ministers in whose lap the Lord had delivered the souls from Salzburg.

We learn from a letter addressed to us that it would be well if we would not only make a general acknowledgment of the gifts received, but also render a more detailed account, for the pleasure of our benefactors, of how the individual gifts of money and other things are being used. I would dearly love to include such a detailed account of all moneys so far received in this diary or in our letters, if my time and my physical strength were only to permit it. Those sums that were intended for us as a gift we have not specifically reported in these diaries; and because, in accordance with the intention of the benefactors, we have used the money intended for the congregation whenever the circumstances required it, we have only acknowledged the proper receipt of such sums and recorded them in our ledger of income and expenses, without giving specific notice when and by whom these were sent. From now on, we intend to be more specific in recording all circumstances concerning receipt and disbursement; and we will attach our statements of account to these diaries in the same manner in which we have so far kept them for our own purposes.

In tonight's prayer meeting, after a brief repetition of the story of Jephta, I read out the impressive passage from the letter of Mr. N. to Court Chaplain Ziegenhagen, wherein he lists the especial instances of divine providence for our congregation, in that God had awakened several generous hearts in N., who had eagerly collected beautiful gifts of books and clothing, although they had their hands full with their own affairs, all sorts of special levies, and the poor of the city. His manner of expression was most moving and touched my heart, as well, I hope, as that of our listeners. The blessing mentioned has not arrived yet but is still in London, and we will expect it as well as the other crates sent from Halle and Augsburg in faith and hope. Some people seem a bit dejected that Sanftleben has brought nothing for them to relieve their want, although they had been promised that recently. They will now expect with new hope the blessing that is always needed.

After the prayer meeting I distributed the fifty bottles of Schauer balm[27] of which Mr. Johann Schauer made a gift to our community. As he said in his fine letter, he was prompted to make this gift by my letter of thanks, from which he learned how highly the Salzburgers esteem this balm and with what good effect it has been used in many instances. In previous times, the esteemed Mr. N. had sent this balm to us on several occasions; and, since we had not been informed that these were his presents, I erroneously thanked Mr. Schauer for them, which error has turned to our best through God's providence. There is more of this balm in a crate which remained in London, which Senior Urlsperger is sending for our own purposes. May the Lord be praised for everything! We have not received a letter from the most esteemed Mr. N. in either the previous or the present package; but we presume that something will be in the aforementioned crate, and we will be most pleased to receive it. Sanftleben told us that several letters were contained in it.

On several occasions in our meetings we have remembered the dear family N., which is indefatigable in their good deeds on our behalf and that of others. We again remembered them today, as their gentle gifts are again to refresh the poor. The children and adults have hardly used up what they received in previous times from their hands; and now they will again benefit from something, my own house included, praise be the Lord. Their letter is most impressive for me, and I shall read it tomorrow in the meeting at my house to those honest souls who appear with me before the Lord with prayers and thanks on behalf of our dear benefactors. May the gracious Lord crown them with His blessings, as with a shield, and let them savor the fruits of their works here and in eternity!

Friday, the 29th of June. In today's meeting at my house several beautiful letters were read, which truly awakened us and encouraged us to the praise of the Lord and to prayers on behalf of others. As we again learned something of the munificence of some pious rich men toward us, I recalled the beautiful passage from Job 31 : 16–20 and showed those present that the example of Job should serve not only for the rich, but also for poor people, including therefore our Salzburgers, who could learn their duty from the example of the poor cared for by Job, namely, to bless our benefactors when enjoying the gifts received from them. We therefore again undertook today to remember their names before the Lord.

N.N. told me yesterday that in her physical and mental weakness, his wife sometimes upset herself unnecessarily about this or that matter so that, once she recovered and reflected on her conduct, she was all the more aggrieved by her faults. He, too, was at our house today and, because the beautiful letter of the esteemed Lady N. contained the saying of Psalms 91 : 14–16, which had been briefly applied to our joint edification, I made this sick woman, who is honest from the bottom of her heart, partake of this edification through her husband; and she is finding counsel and comfort therein for the condition of her soul and her body. A weaver from N., a journeyman called N., also wrote to us and gave us most edifying news of the blessing which the merciful Lord places on His servants there in the administration of their office. He seems to have a right good foundation, and he writes most edifyingly from the fullness of his heart. He is a weaver by trade and shows much eagerness to come here, if the Lord should ordain it. There is little he could do here in his profession, although he seems to believe differently. We have several weavers among us who have had to turn to field work. Once there is more hemp and flax planted in future years, then some weavers might well find work. We would have much liked to have Sanftleben with us to have him talk about his journey for our edification, but he missed the hour and will visit us shortly.

Saturday, the 30th of June. Last night the honest N. told me something about his sick wife, which prompted me to visit her today. She had recovered somewhat in body and spirit and told me that during her severe pains she had been in great fear of her conscience, for her conscience had told her that she had not so far been honest in her intentions toward God and, if she were to die now, as it had appeared to her, she would not have been able to find secure comfort in her Savior; and she cried bitterly when telling me this. Because I know her as a repentant soul eager for salvation who in her previous struggles has surely had only one goal of saving her soul and making sure of her salvation, I sought to encourage her wounded heart and fearful spirit by all possible means through the gospel. While talking to her, I was reminded of the words from 1 John 3:20, "For if our heart condemns us, God is greater than our heart, and knoweth all things." I reminded her that she could consider what the dear Apostle says of himself and other believers, that is, that their hearts had reproached them as well, refused them the grace of the Lord, etc., but he had added: "God is greater than our heart, and His word should count more for us than the voice of our deceitful hearts." Therefore, we should always examine all that our heart and mind tell us in the light of the Lord's word, for what agrees with it is right. But, when our conscience tells us, "You are damned because of your great unfaithfulness and your weaknesses, Jesus and His merit do not touch you, you have waited too long," etc., we must overcome and suppress such notions by means of the merciful promises of the Lord, which cover all sins and sinners through the merit of Christ. Let His word be your sure ground, even if your heart speaks more loudly, etc. I reminded her of the words which I had sent home with her husband yesterday: "Him that cometh to me I will in no wise cast out." Here the Savior does not describe how a sinner should look when he comes to Him (for if he were to come to Him better than a worthless sinner, he could never come), but rather He wishes to have all sinners; and it is His office, which He carries out with thousandfold joy, to bring to a state of grace all sinners, the arch sinners, and the villains, and to deliver them from sinning and all sins. And, if this word is prefaced by the words that only those come to Christ whom the Father pulls, then it is clear that this is the Father's very means of doing so, namely to present the sinner as such to his conscience, and to convince him of his misery so that he will believe that he needs a Savior and is longing for him, etc.

I remembered the words from the *Treasure Chest*,[28] "When the dove did not see where to rest its foot," and I read them to her with the verses printed underneath and said: "Such was the love of Noah for the dove that he took it in, for else it would have perished; how great then is the love of the Savior for saved mankind, and in particular for those in whom He has started His work, since He has used His divine blood for them and has laid down an eternally valid ransom for them. He will not let go of the soul, for He loves it too much." She said that she felt like the Children of Israel in the desert, in whom spiritual and physical need came together because of their sins. I replied that she should not only use this but also another lesson as an example; that is that God, in His unspeakable mercy and despite the many sins of the Israelites, had given them a sign of grace in the form of the brazen snake, and thus a prefiguration[29] of the Savior (who became a worm for us and was to be hanged as a banner and sign of grace), etc. And now it is said from the mouth of the soul-hungry Savior, "Turn to me (with your snake bites and wounds), and you shall be saved until the end of the world," etc. Finally, I prayed with her and recommended her to the mercy and care of the good Shepherd and Redeemer.

At present there is no meat to be had in Savannah; and, because the newly arrived people as well as the orphanage are suffering want, we had to butcher one of the recently acquired oxen, which we would otherwise have deferred until the fall. Not only did we distribute as much as will be necessary for the first time to those who arrived with Sanftleben, but in addition a meal was prepared for them today in the orphanage, so that we may show them also in this way the deep love that we feel for them. We have also let the sick have a little fresh meat.

JULY

Sunday, the 1st of July. I was alone today, since my dear colleague, Mr. Gronau, left yesterday for Savannah, where he will teach the word of the Lord to the Germans there. Despite my feeble physical condition, our merciful Lord so comforted me and made me so joyful during the preaching of His word that I could present to my dear listeners the sweet fatherly heart of God in Christ toward both Jews and heathen and all mankind. I also carried out the will of my Savior in beckoning and urging my dear flock, also the newly arrived among them, to come to Christ's kingdom of mercy and God's richly prepared table of grace, where everything is prepared for one and all according to the needs of each. I added that there was no reason for any among them to delay; for nothing is to be preferred to the call to the Lord's Supper, not even the most important affairs pertaining to one's daily profession.

My main intention was directed at an explanation of the exordium for today's gospel for the 2nd Sunday after Trinity—namely, "Blessed is he that shall eat bread in the kingdom of God"—wherein I first treated of the important connections between this text and the preceding ones and then showed both what is meant by the words, eating one's bread in the kingdom of God, and also who can actually enjoy it. In the exordium I explained the verses Matthew 8:11–12, "And I say to you that many shall come from the east, etc." In the application I stressed the two verses from 2 Corinthians 6:2, "Behold, now is the accepted time"; also, Hebrews 12:15–17. The afternoon service had to start somewhat later than usual because of a strong rain; and this was very useful for me not only because it permitted me to regain my strength, but also because it was cool and agreeable in the church after the rain.

Our assemblies were well attended on both occasions; and, because I could not hold the repetition hour in addition to the afternoon catechization, I took the occasion to repeat the most important points at this time. Praise God who blessed this first in me and then, it is hoped, in the others. In the evening prayer meeting in the orphanage, where a large number had assembled, I used some time before the prayer to read some passages from the detailed reports from some Salzburgers in Prussia, whose names were given, those reports having been sent to us by Prof. Francke. In particular, much mention was made of old Mr. Rottenberger and his two sons. Rottenberger has an honest son here, who is skillful in many things and of great usefulness to us. He is much pleased by the Christian conduct of his loved ones, which serves as an example to be followed by others. Similarly, the names of several who were mentioned in this report are known to some of our listeners here.

Monday, the 2nd of July. Sanftleben and Ulich, the shoemaker, told us for the praise of the Lord that they had fared well during their passage at sea and had not lacked anything. The captain, a man called Hermann,[1] had shown them so much kindness that they could not have wished for more. Such reports are quite rare and would indicate that this captain had received favorable recommendations concerning these passengers. Two of the women, Lackner and Wassermann, who usually are of good health and a strong constitution, suffered much more from sea sickness, both in duration and severity, than others. An unhappy incident afflicted the Berenberg woman while they were at sea; one of the women spilled grease from a pan while they were cooking, almost setting the kitchen on fire. Because this caused much alarm, hurrying to and fro, and running about, the Berenberg woman attempted to climb down through the hatch from deck into the ship. In her confusion, she missed the steps and fell down head first, causing her to lose her speech and upsetting her mind. It is reported that nobody saw her fall and therefore nobody came to help her. In her confusion and loss of consciousness, she crawled into a dark hole somewhere in the boat; and, when she was missed, they looked for her everywhere. Finally she was found in a dark corner. As she looked quite ill and was unable to talk, Sanftleben had her bruises rubbed with Schauer balm, and the good Lord so blessed this application that she started talking again after twenty-four hours, and now she shows no signs of her injury. I have tried to persuade Sanftleben to write out his notes on the events of their voyage up to their arrival, first in Charleston and finally in our community, so that we may forward them to Europe next week with our letters. He has promised to do so.[2] He was with us today in our private meeting, and he told us several of his observations about the kingdom of the Lord, as noted in Halle, Saalfeld, Augsburg, Sorau and other places. Among other matters, I was much pleased to learn that, in the Orphanage in Halle, he had joined in prayer and the praise of the Lord with several pious students who still remembered me. He gave a pleasing testimony of their simple and honest ways. As the honorable Mr. B. E. showed himself particularly gracious and generous toward Sanftleben, and because he is among our most esteemed benefactors, our assembly wished that he and his entire family might realize the true goal of their faith, the salvation of their souls, and may be crowned forever at the end of all their struggles.

Shoemaker Ulich has taken on Zettler as an apprentice upon the latter's request and wish and has promised to teach him the shoemaker's trade within a year and a half, provided that he shows himself to be orderly, obedient, and industrious. He will not be charged for his apprenticeship, nor will he have to provide for his food. The boy is big and strong; and, because he had already learned some things from the previous shoemaker who was returned to Savannah, he can be expected to be of service to our new shoemaker and will have to serve only briefly; he will surely learn a right decent trade from this skillful man. The matter was agreed and decided in my house this morning and properly recorded.

Tuesday, the 3rd of July. We again have dry and warm weather which is very useful for our land after the long rains. It seems that the Lord will provide a good harvest this year except for the beans, which have been much damaged by the rain and have also been ravaged by the deer. There are several Indian families at our town, who will probably chase off the deer. These Indians had among them their king, an impressive man of obvious wisdom; and they all visited me upon their arrival. Since I had given them some food and drink for refreshments, they returned today with some meat and asked for our boat.

As much as our strength and time will permit, we shall write letters to our Fathers and benefactors this week so that they may be informed of the safe arrival of Sanftleben and the others. As there are apparently many letters in the box left behind by Sanftleben, we will have to be forgiven for not answering them at this time. With God's help we will do so shortly, when we can announce the receipt and application of the gifts sent to us.

Wednesday, the 4th of July. I found three pious women with Mrs. N., who were helping her and her small child. I learned that the poor condition of the patient had improved; and, since many other children of the Lord had prayed for her (which she esteems highly), I told her that her improvement had been the fruit of her own prayers and those of other faithful souls. I also repeated to her the verse which God has blessed in me in connection with the story of Samson in Judges 13:8–9, "He will fulfill the desire of them that fear him,"[3] which is surely a special privilege of those who fear the Lord and shows the magnificence of the love of the Father in Christ for His children. (John 17:23, Sirach 10:27.) She replied in a low voice, "Oh, if only I were one who feared the Lord"; and I answered that it is written in Isaiah 65 concerning those who are the true servants of the Lord and upon whom the Lord looks with favor, "I will look even to him that is poor and of contrite spirit, and trembleth at my word." Then she could not object anymore, for this verse well expresses her honest but fearful and apprehensive mind.

A woman joined in and added that she had recently heard a verse from me and had seen that I liked it well and held it dear, i.e. "The same Lord over all is rich unto all that call upon him." She exclaimed that she would never forget this verse but would pass it on to all those dear to her. For even if we be poor and have nothing much in spirit or in flesh, we do have a rich God in Christ upon whom we can call, for He has enough to cure all our want. And I added that it was an error of all those who fear the Lord that, when God reveals to them their misery, want, and deficiencies, they are discouraged thereby and ready to despair, claiming that God will reject them for their utter lack of virtue, etc. However, they should instead recognize it for a special grace of the Lord that He stirs up the wickedness in their hearts and reveals it to them, for by this He wishes to drive them into the arms of His mercy and to the blood of conciliation shed by His son, as well as to render them right poor and small, so that they might humble themselves deeply before Him and search for His grace in hunger and thirst, for this is the surest way to heaven, etc.

I again repeated to the children in the orphanage what I recently proclaimed for the praise of the Lord in public assembly, namely, that this time the dear Lord had opened His generous hands so richly for the orphanage that even those children for whose sake this institution was established and is being continued would have ample cause to recognize the fatherly providence of the Lord in heaven and praise Him highly for it. Thus I sought to admonish them movingly to show gratitude to God and man, and in particular a true and honest fear of the Lord. In external matters as well, I made and recorded some arrangements for furthering the interests of the children and good order in the entire institution.

Once the patients have improved so that I can again instruct children and adults jointly, I shall take up all the matters in more detail that are necessary for the greater glory of the Lord and their own welfare. May God give us the wisdom to conduct ourselves in this respect in such a manner that the purpose for which this institution was erected, contrary to everyone's thoughts and expectation, and maintained until now with His assistance, can be realized in both the young and the old. The statements of dear Professor Francke in his letter of 15 January of this year have been most impressive for us and our helpers in the orphanage; and through God's grace they encourage us to continue working with our lambs, even if we do not immediately recognize the blessing that this involves. He writes thus: "May the Lord in His mercy direct that all the children who have been accepted in His name shall be reared in His praise and become plants of justice. With youth, one must needs work in the hope of the future, for in youth good resolutions quickly vanish again. However, the effort and work spent on them for the sake of the Lord is never in vain; and therefore we must continue and persevere in prayer and searching, with admonition and loyalty, while awaiting the blessing of the Lord in this as in all other things."

Thursday, the 5th of July. This morning N. and his wife came to us for private communion. They are both weak because of the fever; and, as they cannot join the others in the congregation at the Lord's Table next Sunday, they requested to be admitted today. They both humbled themselves abjectly before the dear Lord for the many sins committed since their youth and seemed most eager for salvation in Christ. They also showed great joy that God has bestowed on them such great mercy in the form of His Son's Last Supper, and declared that they would be grateful for it for the rest of their lives.

A woman from the orphanage came to me afterwards and wished to speak to me in private. Her heart, she complained, stayed hard throughout her prayers and showed not the least sign of God's grace. She crawls on the ground like a dog during her prayers, and coos like a dove;[4] but nothing improves matters. She would have to confess to so many sins that it could not pass without many tears, and therefore she wished to be alone with me. God had shown her so much physical grace through the gifts that He had bestowed on the orphanage that this made her remember all her sins, and therefore she had to consider herself entirely unworthy. She did not deserve all the good she enjoyed, etc. I encouraged her spirit with the help of the gospel as much as possible. She listened to each comforting word with much eagerness, as if she wanted to devour it.

Friday, the 6th of July. This week a number of letters have been written to our Fathers and benefactors, i.e. Court Chaplain Ziegenhagen, Senior Urlsperger, Professor Francke, the Honorable Society, the Lord Trustees, Court Chaplain Butjenter, Counsellor Walbaum, and Mr. Manitius. Senior Urlsperger has been asked to render our thanks to the esteemed family N. and other benefactors for all the clear signs of their kindness and to apologize on our behalf for our present failure to write. We shall soon express our gratefulness personally, once we have received the things that were sent as presents, because then we will be able to report their condition at their arrival, whether they reached us in good shape or were damaged. Mrs. Landfelder, née Wassermann, and her sister, who recently arrived with Sanftleben, have asked me to thank both Mr. N. and Chaplain N. for all the favors shown to them, in particular for their offices in sending the sister here, accompanied by a pleasant gift of *Pomesin*[5] for herself and Mrs. Kalcher. In their simplicity, they asked to have two verses sent, that is, Psalms 46:2 and Psalms 47:3; and they wish the Lord's blessing on them[6] and the honorable Mrs. S. in return.

During dinner time, my room was filled with the dear souls who, along with us, are preparing themselves with prayer and imploration for the intended partaking of Holy Communion. For our joint edification, I read to them before our prayer the refreshing letter of Mr. Manitius, who is working in grace with the Jews. Praised be the Lord, who awakens us from nearby and afar, to perceive our salvation. After the prayers, I gave each one a copy of the beautiful song, *Mein Heyland nimmt die Sünder an*, which has reached us this time in many printed copies. God willing, I shall use it for my benefit and that of the others in the preparation tomorrow, since it so well suits the glorious gospel for the coming 3rd Sunday after Trinity.

Saturday, the 7th of July. The living space in the orphanage is getting more and more crowded, and the manager told me that toward harvest time, in view of the rich rice harvest that is expected, he would require a threshing floor and a good storage space for the corn, beans, and other physical blessings, as well as for fodder. From the enclosed accounts our Fathers and benefactors can see that there is no money for this. If, however, we are forced to build something to accommodate our supplies, we will go ahead in the name of the Lord and wait for His blessing to defray the expenses.

Sunday, the 8th of July. We had a strong rain at night, as well as much wind and thunder, which prevented us from holding our repetition hour. Yesterday a strong rain fell during the preparation hour and forced me to stop my sermon, the noise of the water on the roof being so strong that one could not hear one's own words. God will surely help us soon to find a better place for public assembly.

Monday, the 9th of July. Today we made a bundle of our letters and diaries, and we shall now give them into safe hands for delivery in Savannah. May God bless everything that has been written.

At noon, I had the men of the community come to my house to discuss various matters. As they still have much work close to the town, only very few will be in a position to begin their households on their plantations. In the meantime, those trees that throw too much shadow on their neighbors' property will be cut down so that all those who have already moved out or are about to move will not incur any damage. A common fence was built already in the spring; and therefore all that is needed now is to prepare the land for planting. Those few who are already living on their plantations would like to have more people move out so that arrangements can be made to have public services held there on Sundays and once a week. In rainy weather the roads there are very poor; and therefore quite a number of arrangements would have to be made before one of us could go out every week and preach there. All beginning is hard, but with God's grace things will arrange themselves in due course.

Tuesday, the 10th of July. Ulich, the shoemaker, announced that he wishes to join Margarethe Egger in wedlock; and for this he wishes to come to me with her this week once more and be married next week. N. [Pletter], a true Israelite in whose heart there is not a wicked thought, intends to marry N. [the Wassermann woman], for which reason he came to me today to get some advice. As weak as he may be physically, and as little as he seeks worldly matters, he has well arranged his household and suffers lack of neither cattle nor food, which he accepts as a blessing from the hand of His heavenly Father with much humility and praise.

I visited the Berenberg woman and found that, although she is a bit apprehensive now because she is new here, she likes our arrangements, in particular our divine services and the ample opportunities for edification, as had been promised to her by Senior Urlsperger. She was in service in N. [Ulm] and told many sad things she had observed among the wicked young people in church. I told her some instances of the Lord's help that we have received in and after our many tribulations, and which had so advanced us that I did not think that she would hear anyone complaining of the decision to come here. She knows the Crause woman, who comes from the same jurisdiction as she, and I told her that she should look upon her as an example of what the Lord's blessing can bring about for people whose first desire is the kingdom of the Lord. Not only have she and her husband been furthered in their Christianity, but within a little more than three years they have obtained for themselves a household so well furnished with many things that they would not have achieved one like it in many more years in Germany.

This Berenberg woman would much like to be able to read and has time to spare for learning it; she as well as another woman will soon be helped in this respect. She remarked that it hurts her to see others in church sing from their hymnals, while she has to sit with her hands in her lap. She praised Gschwandl, in whose house she lives, as well as his wife and his children for their industry in reading, praying, and singing, which I much liked to hear. I visited another woman in the neighborhood who told me that this Berenberg woman had been quite restless about having come here, but that she and her husband had so movingly reassured her from God's word and their own experience that I was much pleased by her way of putting things. For this woman had previously been without much understanding and so full of prejudice that she now marvels and is shocked by her former blindness and the depth of her perdition, which the Lord has made her realize. She praises His mercy above all. Thus the Berenberg woman is in good company and with good neighbors, which is fortunate in view of her special needs.

Because I had a most important meeting with the men from the community yesterday afternoon, for which reason the hour set for private assembly in my house had to be cancelled, the hungry souls came today to present to the Lord that which had been omitted yesterday. God made me right useful to them; and I pray that my good and comfortable quarters, which will be fully finished this week, may be dedicated entirely to His praise and to the edification of our dear listeners. My dear colleague left for Savannah this morning, partly to deliver our letters and partly to fetch the money which the merciful and loving Lord has seen fit to provide for his house and for the orphanage. The storehouse manager, to whom Mr. Oglethorpe had forwarded it several weeks ago, had not been in Savannah for several weeks, and this caused the long delay in our receipt of these sums. In the meantime, we have expressed our deep-felt gratitude for these gifts in letters both to the Honorable Trustees and to the praiseworthy Society, and we also have given some news concerning the blessing with which the Lord has until now dignified our office. May God let everything redound to the glory of His name! Oh Father, Thy name be hallowed!

Wednesday, the 11th of July. Last Sunday, Gschwandl and another man relieved the herdsman of the other herd so that he could, as is usual, attend church with his family. He told me that out there where the cattle are kept there had been such a terrible thunderstorm accompanied by such heavy rains that he could only marvel at it, having not seen the like of it before. Everything had turned so dark and black that they could not see the cattle before them, which refused to budge but started milling around in confusion. This made him think of the events in Egypt. I reminded him of the future of Christ in judgment, where the faithful, disregarding all horrible happenings, shall look upward and lift their heads to their Immanuel, whereas the enemies shall wish and pray that mountains and hills should cover them. We had heavy rains here, too, but not nearly as heavy as out there. No bridge can be constructed there.

Two Indians visited my rooms today; and I again had occasion to observe a trait I had recently observed in some others: i.e. what is given to one of them, particularly the oldest, he shares in equal parts so that each may have a share, and this custom is observed for every little thing as long as it can at all be divided up. This particularly impressed me; no greed, egoism, or jealousy is noticeable in these people, but everyone wants his comrade to have as much as he himself wishes for.

Thursday, the 12th of July. I was much fortified by the report from a married couple that God had blessed in them the story from Judges, chapter 13, concerning Samson's conception, childhood, and youth; this although I have felt myself much too thin in substance and not very edifying in most of the recent prayer meetings. Due to some difficulty in my throat [for which Mr. Thilo knows no medication] I have much trouble speaking. Praised be God, who has begun to strengthen me again yesterday and today, so that I no longer notice the aforesaid affliction. May He render me grateful and bless all my limbs and strength for the glory of His service and His honor.

My dear colleague brought the news that Mr. Oglethorpe is in Savannah and truly intends to travel up to the Indians at the beginning of next week. Therefore, he will probably inspect our community and bring the Honorable Trustees' presents for the orphanage. There has been some conflict and misunderstanding in Savannah among those whom the Lord Trustees have commissioned to pay out the money both for my dear colleague's house and for the orphanage; therefore, out of kindness to us, Mr. Oglethorpe is willing to pay said sums from his own money,[7] and he already made arrangements for my dear colleague to receive the money for his house while he was in Savannah. No doubt the Lord, who has intended for us to be blessed with these gifts, will maintain and magnify him.

Today Simon Steiner's wife delivered a very premature child. Since it had all human limbs and appearances and was alive, I did not hesitate to baptize it nonetheless in the name of the triune God. It died soon afterward and was buried toward evening. This woman has already aborted several times, so that she and her husband were recently admonished to observe all precautions that are required for a person in her special condition. They seem to have followed these admonitions, but the loss of the child seems not to have been preventable.

[Friday, the 13th of July.] We are now treating of the 14th chapter of the Book of Judges, which contains so many beautiful lessons for parents, children, and those who wish to get married, that I hope that they will be well noted and practiced by all. We are careful to treat each point at some length and to apply it to our circumstances so that everything among us may be done right honestly and properly and everyone may recognize that it is not a matter of stubbornness on our part when we do not always follow customs practiced in Germany but instead wish to prevent not only all that is bad but also that which could offer an opportunity for evil and cause offense.

In our private assembly, in addition to the last part of chapter 14 of the Gospel of St. John, we used special points of the beautiful narration that we received in our letters from Halle concerning the state of religion in Germany and other countries. We then thanked the Lord for His kindness, which is governing us, and prayed for ourselves and others that we and they might use the precious jewel of the gospel and a free exercise of religion well and that the Lord might hold back His judgment, which ungrateful Evangelical Christians have called upon themselves.

Saturday, the 14th of July. Praise the Lord! We have received more peaches in our garden than others in the community. The late frost had killed all blossoms on the new trees, but some survived on the old ones, such as ours. We were much surprised to find that the best kind of peaches, which are easily detached from the stone and have a pleasant taste like wine, do have a stone or hard shell inside, but no kernel,[8] so that we will not be able to plant this pleasant species this year. The lesser ones, which are called wild or Indian peaches and which cannot be detached from the stone, on the other hand, have a fresh sound stone.[9] This latter kind has a somewhat harder flesh, but they are nonetheless full of juice and of pleasant taste once they are fully ripe. The bursting of many of the peaches may be due to the heavy rains; and because of it they tend to rot quickly. We do not yet have apples, pears, or other cultivated fruit at our place; and the vines we planted are not bearing yet this year.

General Oglethorpe gave my colleague a full, fairly ripe bunch of grapes that had been grown in Savannah. I was much amazed at the size of the bunch and of the individual grapes, which indicate that this must be beautiful wine country indeed. Those grapes on our wild vines which gave us such hope of a good harvest in the spring have all fallen off. Mr. Oglethorpe advises our people to grow grapes and then to dry the grapes and use them only as raisins, since at this stage of our settlement, when the people have to look out for their sustenance, making wine would be too complicated and demanding a task for beginners.

Sunday, the 15th of July. An Englishman from Old Ebenezer addressed a letter to me in which he takes great pains to make strong excuses for a German family there whose disorderly ways we cannot consider acceptable. However, I pay little heed to such intercessions and apologies, as the disorderly mind of these people is obvious and they only try to disentangle themselves with lies and representations, which are merely a sign that they do not wish to repent. I hear that N. [Bach], who only advances such disorder and is no longer recognized as a member of our congregation, is intending to present his case to Mr. Oglethorpe and request to be reinstated as one of the inhabitants here. Mr. Oglethorpe will not accede to this, as he knows only too well how necessary it is to check evil people early and before there have been too many and too serious offenses and that it is better to cut off the rotten limbs than to let the healthy ones perish too.

We discussed a text from Luke 6:36 ff. today which is well suited for this point. As the words of the Savior in this *pericopa*[10] as well as other passages of the gospel are often seriously misused by wicked people who dislike being counselled and punished, I used Leviticus 19:17 as an exordium and treated of the text dealing with love for our neighbors. Among other things, I showed that this not only involves real acts of beneficence and proofs of a positive good, but also all that which serves to further the physical and spiritual well-being of our neighbors. It is incumbent upon those in authority in all walks of life, as well as upon every Christian, to work toward this goal and to act from a merciful love to relieve the need of our neighbors, even if, in consideration of the circumstances, this includes serious measures. These do not then reflect a lack of love or a stubbornness, but the will of the Lord, as is shown in verse 42, as well as in Matthew 18:15 and Luke 17:3, cf. Psalms 141:5 and Proverbs 27:6.

Monday, the 16th of July. This morning I married two couples, that is, Ulich the shoemaker to Margarethe Egger, and the Austrian Pletter to Elisabeth Wassermann. For the ceremony, I used the text in Matthew 18:20 and dealt with the previous promise of Jesus to those who come together in His name. In the application, I showed that our assembly for this ceremony should not take place from mere habit but in the name of Jesus if a blessing is to follow and the marriage itself to be well performed. I said that it should be right comforting to them that the act now being performed was done in the name, upon the order, and by the strength of the Lord Jesus, cf. verse 18; also, that to be married in the Christian way, whereby two people are joined in marriage, was not displeasing to the Lord but most joyful, cf. John 2:2 and Genesis 2:18. Christian people who commence and continue their married state in His name can always take comfort in the precious promise that Jesus is not only among them but within them and lives there in His merciful and strong presence as within a sanctuary and temple. Here they were instructed, together with several others, to become of one mind in the conduct of their marriage and to agree among themselves, as prescribed in verse 19. For the benefit therefrom is obvious and will be theirs.

The marriage ceremony was performed in my room, which is quite spacious and in fact dedicated to the service of the congregation and the execution of my office, in that the members of my family have their own parlor and bedroom for their lodging and their household business. With the exception of the glass windows, everything is well finished now; I shall postpone the purchase of the windows, however, since the house has already cost much more than I had believed and guessed and more than the old and experienced carpenter had estimated. Even before beginning construction I had requested glass for the windows from Court Chaplain Ziegenhagen, who will surely do his best with the Honorable Society and the Lord Trustees to obtain some contribution to the construction costs. The Lord, who has directed the Lord Trustees to reimburse my dear colleague for the £30 sterling expended and thus to make him a gift of a total of £40 for his house is still alive and can easily direct them or other dear benefactors to make some contribution toward my house too, which, with His help, is to be the actual parsonage. For it is truly a great benefit that, as a result of the £30 sterling received, my dear colleague has been enabled to return to me the £14 sterling which the esteemed Court Chaplain Ziegenhagen and Senior Urlsperger lent for the construction of a parsonage or even intended as a gift if the Lord Trustees were not to see their way to bear the costs. With this repaid sum of money I shall be able to satisfy for some time at least my construction workers, who have much patience with me and are quite contented.

I also consider it a great benefaction that the manager of the storehouse, an honest man and our dear friend, has received permission from Mr. Oglethorpe to advance as much from the storehouse as I have felt I could request in nails and food supplies for the builders. Also, the funds expended on this building have remained in the community, among our dear listeners, who are glad and grateful to the Lord that they were thus able to earn some money toward their clothing and other needs, while not neglecting any of their planting and field work. For it is true that, as reported previously in connection with the building of the orphanage and my dear colleague's house, they thank the Lord for every opportunity to earn some money in our town as much as if the money earned by their labors were given them as a gift. This is particularly true this year, since the Lord has preserved their bodies from fever and other accidents that have occurred previously and has noticeably strengthened them physically.

As for the high expenses we have incurred, I am comforted among other things by the thought that, after I was led to undertake this building despite much hesitation and almost against my own will, there have since been many signs that the Lord, the almighty Creator of heaven and earth and their King, has indeed given His consent to this undertaking. I also find strong and faithful intercession in those who come to me eagerly and often for their edification, and in others. Since God grants what is asked by those who fear Him, He will surely let the time come that this request will be heard and my house will be paid for. Everyone in the community is glad that my house has turned out so well and that it has been built so sturdily, durably, and comfortably that, in the opinion of knowledgeable people, little will have to be repaired or improved for some hundred years.[11] Thus, my successors as well will praise the Lord in this house for a comfortable lodging, as I and my family have much reason to praise Him after having spent some years learning how it feels to live in a hut. *Er hat es alles wohl bedacht, und alles, alles recht gemacht, gebt unserm Gott die Ehre!* [12]

Tuesday, the 17th of July. This morning, I married Mr. Thilo to Mrs. Helfenstein's daughter. For the sermon, I used the first part of the Sermon on the Mount, Matthew 5:1–12, from which the Lord granted me (and I hope others) much edification.

There are some Englishmen with horses in our town who have orders to await Mr. Oglethorpe here and accompany him to Old Ebenezer and thence to Palachocolas. Our dear Salzburgers are greatly pleased at the prospect of having this dear benefactor among us, for we have not had this honor so far. May God turn his arrival to the benefit and the best of our congregation and the orphanage, for which we shall pray to Him.

Wednesday, the 18th of July. The Berenberg woman is much upset and shows much fear; and therefore good friends and we ourselves are doing our utmost to quiet her. It has been arranged for her to go to school and improve her reading, a task to which she is much inclined. However, she has had an attack of fever today and must first get well. Hans Floerel is a pious, knowledgeable, and skillful man who knows how to deal with people in a true Christian manner and to make people accept his advice; and he wishes and is willing to give his time to the service of his neighbor and for the glory of the Lord, without any self-interest. We have made him the schoolmaster for the Berenberg woman and other adults who wish to learn how to read; and, for his pains, we will let him have some of the gifts that God has provided for the orphanage. For, as much as we would wish, our office and our strength do not permit our taking over this new task. May God look pleasantly upon this task in Christ.

We assume that Mr. Oglethorpe arrived in Purysburg today; and, since his boatsmen know neither the road to our town nor the sandbanks and other obstacles in the river, our Salzburgers wished to set out and meet this dear benefactor in Purysburg. I joined them in the boat toward five o'clock in the afternoon, and we had the pleasure of meeting him halfway, accompanied by his entourage of Englishmen and Indians. He asked me to join him in his boat, which I accepted as a sign of his affection. This afforded me the opportunity to present him with the largest part of the matters that I intended to discuss with him and submit for his resolution. Since it soon turned dark and the Englishmen did not know this part of the river, our Salzburgers were able to offer their services to good avail, which much pleased Mr. Oglethorpe. We arrived here at eight o'clock in the evening, and both my dear colleague and some other Salzburgers were waiting at the landing to receive Mr. Oglethorpe and light his path up the hill with torches. The first thing that much pleased Mr. Oglethorpe was my house, and he even decided to have a similar structure built in Palachocolas; he even summoned our carpenters to him that very evening to discuss the matter. However, the beginning of this work will have to be postponed until after his return from the Indian nations, and we are quite content with this, as the people do not only have to tend to their crops but have to build several things for the congregation, such as a threshing floor and a barn for the orphanage.

Thursday, the 19th of July. [Ortmann, the schoolmaster, and his wife have caused our dear Mr. Oglethorpe much displeasure and trouble this morning, thus depriving him of the time to take a good look at our town and its arrangements. He has again prepared a lengthy and miserably executed written presentation which is in fact directed against me but does not fail to include my dear colleague as well. In it, he defends to the last his wife as a poor innocent lamb, as he calls her, and makes me out as the most insufferable tyrant, ascribing to me the name of Nero to prove his point. As this is now the seventh time that he

has importuned Mr. Oglethorpe with his letters and accusations, that gentleman took the pains to examine every point
most carefully, to question witnesses extensively, and to give a
judicial opinion. Notwithstanding, and as it could not be otherwise, all ended badly for Ortmann and his wife. And, since their
offenses are quite undeniable, it has been made quite clear to
them what they should expect from the worldly powers with
regard to their misdeeds and in view of their ugly and obviously
unjust accusations, were it not for the fact that they were to be
spared out of pity.[13]

[When she could not prevail, Mrs. Ortmann conducted herself so impertinently and outrageously before Mr. Oglethorpe's
very face that her wicked heart became clear for everyone to
see, and Mr. Oglethorpe saw ample evidence of how she tends
to behave toward me. Both he and she have revealed themselves
in all their true nature and offensive manners before everyone
present, and it could not have been more embarrassing.

[Among other things, Ortmann complained that I had expelled him from the English classes and thus deprived him of
his living. However, his written presentation had turned out so
poorly that Mr. Oglethorpe showed it to the other gentlemen so
that they might judge whether a man who writes such rambling
and corrupted English is fit to be a schoolteacher. He then declared him entirely unsuited for this task and requested me to
inform the Lord Trustees and the Honorable Society of his lack
of skill and his ill manners and conduct. That I should have
done long ago if I had not felt sorry for this old man, now that
he has been living here for some time. Mr. Oglethorpe himself
intends to report on the entire matter, which has been carefully
investigated. Mrs. Ortmann was so forward as to loudly declare
the judgment for invalid and unjust, to impugn the honesty and
conscience of the witnesses, and to pretend that my standing among the members of the congregation was such that I
could twist them around my finger and persuade them to do
anything.

[With regard to this and the other annoying occurrences, we
could not but admire the patience and most generous disposition and composure of Mr. Oglethorpe. As Mrs. Ortmann had
taken in her servants[14] on her own decision, she must now keep

them and provide for them in sickness and health, in return for which they owe her their labor. Therefore I must return these people to her house from the orphanage, where they were accepted a fortnight ago as sick and rejected paupers. Ortmann claimed that Dr. Gerdes would pay for them and that he had written to him in this respect. At about noon, this unpleasant business was concluded whereupon] Mr. Oglethorpe visited our orphanage and was much pleased by all our arrangements, both there and in the rest of the town. He had the gift of the Lord Trustees for the orphanage disbursed to me and requested me to inform the Lord Trustees that, despite their commission, two magistrates had refused to sign the notes from London, so that he was obliged to return them and advance from his own funds the money for the orphanage and also for the house built for my dear colleague, as we could not do without it any longer. May the Lord be praised for this! Mr. Oglethorpe also lent me another £10 for my house costs and added the promise that he himself would write to the Lord Trustees that he thought my house was cheap enough. He is also willing to extend money for a water-driven flour mill; and, when he saw our present hand-operated mill, he declared that he wished to have two of this kind built for the people in Frederica as soon as he can obtain millstones.

Upon my repeated requests, he is also willing to let our people share the same benefits with regard to their present crops and on the same conditions as the people in Savannah so that, in addition to the normal price, he will add a bonus of two shillings sterling for each bushel that they do not need for themselves and can deliver to the storehouse. He cannot allow the full provisions formerly given to the Salzburgers to the new people who came over with Sanftleben, since the Lord Trustees did not send any instructions in this respect. However, he will assign to them the same amounts as allowed the new arrivals in Frederica, which is said to be little. I shall soon learn the exact amount in Savannah, and whether it is to be a present or advanced on credit. I understood from his words that the Lord Trustees will probably not send or support any more colonists on the old footing, rather they will have to pay their passage or work it off here. I would have much liked to persuade him to pay for the linen sent long ago by Mr. Schlatter in St. Gall, which I had turned over to Mr. Causton. However, he referred me to the accounts in Savannah which are still being examined and put in order; he assured me that, nonetheless, I would receive the money after all, if not from Mr. Causton then from the funds of the Lord Trustees.

After dinner Mr. Oglethorpe and his entourage rode off to Old Ebenezer and left a quantity of sugar and wine in my house as a present. Because the Salzburgers had assembled in front of my house in the big square to witness the departure of this dear benefactor, I had the men come in and offered them some of the wine. I took this occasion to tell them to their great joy of the good advantages that I had secured from Mr. Oglethorpe and how pleased and well disposed he had shown himself to us. [The men were not at all content that, by their annoying complaints, Ortmann and his wife had prevented Mr. Oglethorpe from taking a good look at our town and its institutions; and, as these poor people have already often invited the displeasure of the community and have now aggravated this situation, we would be much pleased if they were to leave us once and for all and fulfill their threats to sell their belongings here and move to Charleston. Mr. Oglethorpe ordered them to recognize their offenses for what they are and to make public apologies. I have been charged with observing their conduct carefully and reporting on it. If there is no improvement, punishment by the authorities is sure to follow.]

I had an occasion in Mr. Oglethorpe's presence to purchase fifteen cows and their calves for the community and five oxen for the orphanage, all of which will have to be brought here. He was much pleased that the Salzburgers guard their money and use it to buy cattle, whereas others in this country make frivolous and ill advised use of their funds. The people have been rendered able to make this purchase, and somewhat more well off, by their work on my house.

Mrs. N. [Ortmann] had accused N. [Rauner] of hiding rum in his house, and Mr. Oglethorpe immediately dispatched some men to search it from top to bottom. Nothing was found there, but instead Mrs. N. [Ortmann] was shown guilty of this offense, exposing herself to rigorous punishment if one had wished to proceed *secundum rigorem legis*.[15] Mr. Oglethorpe used this occasion to invest four tithings-men, who are to act against all offenses and therefore against the import of rum and who will assist me in all respects. He had this order executed on my and their behalf under his hand and seal.

Since there are now many Germans in Frederica and its surroundings who are in need of a minister, Mr. Oglethorpe expressed the desire to have one sent from Germany. I offered my services to write about securing a well-qualified candidate from Halle, if he could give me written orders and a power of attorney for this.[16]

Friday, the 20th of July. Yesterday, the Salzburgers agreed to undertake the joint construction of a shelter in the woods for the cattle so that they might be better protected during rainy weather. Today, they all went out; but in the meantime the wind, or some cows and horses, upset a length of fencing in the big field and the cows and hogs caused much damage, particularly since no one but a few women and one or two men were available to chase the cattle off. The corn is quite high everywhere and therefore one or the other hog may still be hiding in it, continuing and increasing the damage. The deer have left few of the beans untouched this year. As this summer has brought more rain than previous years, the summer is very pleasant and bearable.

A Salzburger woman told me in the praise of the Lord that her soul was feeling very well this Friday, for she was savoring the peace of the Lord. She said that it was most useful to get up right early and pray to the Lord for a blessing to last the whole day. She had done just that today; when she had heard the alarm ring at four in the morning in the orphanage (in whose vicinity she lives), she had encouraged her husband to rise and to fortify himself and her with prayer before starting on the business of the day. She told me of N. [Floerel] and his wife, and of the blessed marriage they were leading as an example for all married people. She is in and out of their house so as to assist the sick lying-in woman [Mrs. Floerel] and thus has an opportunity to learn much that has edified her from the Christian, humble, quiet, and contented manner of this couple. She used many good words to describe them. I am much pleased when people use to their good advantage the living examples of God's children, for this is implied in the verse: "Let your good works so shine before men, that they may see," etc.

Today, the private assembly in my room was attended only by some pious women, but it was nonetheless most edifying for me. One woman prayed for herself and others and in particular for our benefactors in a most earnest and moving manner and praised our Father in Christ so heartily for all previously bestowed benefits that it was most enjoyable for all of us who prayed with her.

Saturday, the 21st of July. Instead of the conference, today we held a praise, prayer, and thanksgiving meeting in the orphanage, which was attended by both old and young. I again informed my audience of the immense benefits that the Lord has bestowed upon us through what was sent by the Lord Trustees and paid out by Mr. Oglethorpe, as well as all other gifts that have recently flowed to the orphanage; and therefore much praise and thanks were owed to Him from all and everyone who finds his sustenance here. I admonished both adults and children to the diligent use of prayer, intercession on behalf of our benefactors, and a childlike praise of the Lord, as well as to the observance of Christian order and obedience toward the manager of the orphanage. We then fell on our knees before the throne of our Father reconciled in Christ, praised Him, and asked for us and others that which we need for our bodies and souls.

N. [Johann Christ] has been restless again for a few days now, and as late as yesterday he wished to leave the orphanage when he could not get his will in some matters. This would surely throw him into great need. This afternoon I admonished two pious Salzburgers to whom he tends to come first because they are old neighbors of his, to work on him with proper admonitions and remonstrations and make him stay in the orphanage, where he can find a pleasant life, for his salvation. God so blessed this undertaking that one of them brought him back to me. He begged me to forgive him for his haste and offensive conduct and promised to again observe the order imposed on him. He is treated like a child there, and he is burdened with neither work nor other matters; yet he will not refrain from being hardheaded. He is quite unhealthy and will probably live only a little longer. If he were only to prepare himself well!

[We have heard that Mrs. Ortmann has sold her cows and therefore is really about to carry out her threats and move away with her husband, perhaps even to return to London. There is not the slightest sign of a true conversion or improvement in either him or her; and now that they have fared so poorly with the proof of their right shameless accusations and charges, they will probably calumniate and malign me even more than they have done so far both publicly and secretly, regardless of how much we were prepared to serve them in all ways, even if not as they wished. We could not make five an even number or look through our fingers at their disorderly and offensive conduct. We are also afraid of an additional annoyance with regard to the sale of their cattle; yet it will be impossible to prevent it, for Mr. Oglethorpe has given orders that no one who moves away from here can take along the cattle given by the Lord Trustees but must turn them over to the orphanage. Since they have received a fat cow in addition to pigs and poultry, it will be difficult to persuade them to accept this arrangement. They can address Mr. Oglethorpe in this respect; if he is willing to make an exception in their case, we shall have no objections. I now recall that among many other unproven charges which Ortmann and his wife have brought against me, but of which I have learned only a few this time, there was one in the presentation to Mr. Oglethorpe that accused me of having driven away Mr. von Reck, Mr. Vat, and Mr. Zwiffler. This is an impertinent lie,[17] which Mr. Oglethorpe found easy to refute from his own better knowledge without having to call on me for proof.]

Three of the German servants from Old Ebenezer have called on me and told me that Mr. Oglethorpe spent hardly an hour there but almost immediately left for Palachocolas. It is not known whether or not he approved of the mill there. I have learned that many boards are being cut there now, but nobody knows what to do with them. I have done my best to intercede with Mr. Oglethorpe on behalf of these three servants, who are faithful in their work but held in little regard by their masters, and he was prepared to lend an ear to their request. Now, much will depend on the administrator of the storehouse and the present stock of supplies there[18] if they are to be helped in accordance with their wishes.

Sunday, the 22nd of July. In today's gospel, Luke 5:1 ff., we dealt with a matter well suited for our congregation and which I commend to the Lord for His blessing. In the exordium, I dealt with the noteworthy judgment of the wise King Solomon on the work of natural unconverted people, Ecclesiastes 2:22–23, and the great difference between converted and unconverted workers was demonstrated by comparing it with 2 Chronicles 15:7. From this text I preached the best refreshment of the disciples and followers of Christ in their heavy work and the restlessness of this life. The dear Lord has ordained that our inhabitants, who are working in the sweat of their brow, continue to find refreshment in and from the benevolent word of the Lord. The more they taste it, the more willingly and eagerly they crowd to it, and they are kept away neither by their tiredness after their work nor by the long way from their plantations nor by any other obstacle that might prevent them from the eager attendance of the preaching of the Lord's word. Nonetheless, they need to be encouraged ever more strongly by examples and evangelical admonition. Those who are indolent and neglectful are put to shame by the examples in the text and by living examples.

It is truly a refreshment for blessed workers in all the labor of this life that they can work in their calling with the word of Jesus and entrust the results of their labors to Him. And, if the profit and reward of their work is not as hoped and wished for, it is enough reward to have done one's work with His word and thus in God; and it will yet be rewarded in its time, when it will be said from the Savior's mouth, "Well done, thou good and faithful servant: thou hast been faithful," etc. Here, two verses were read which mean the same thing, and their strong and evangelical expressions were applied to those listeners who are not seeking profit in their work but are of an honest, simple mind, i.e. Ephesians 6:5–8 and Colossians 3:22–24. In both it is said, "Knowing," and thus also in today's text, 1 Peter 3, "Knowing that ye are thereunto called," etc. Oh, may we only know this well and note and retain it.

Monday, the 23rd of July. Inasmuch as one of us will be traveling to Savannah on behalf of the German people, I am writing a few letters which may yet be forwarded with the recently delivered packet. It is necessary to inform Court Chaplain Ziegenhagen of a certain matter [which we do not wish to mention in this diary]. At the same time I am writing to the esteemed Mr. Vernon[19] to inform him that my house is now fully completed, that the expenses therefor are high and getting higher than we have expected, but that it is of a most durable construction and most serviceable for my purposes. I am therefore asking him to recommend this matter highly to the Lord Trustees so that they might enable me to return with gratitude what Mr. Oglethorpe has advanced from the storehouse for payment of the building costs. In my letter to him I also mention that Mr. Oglethorpe has been here and has shown much affection for the Salzburgers and in particular for our orphanage; also, that out of his own pocket he paid the £40 sterling which was to have been paid to me for the orphanage at the Trustees' order by two gentlemen in Savannah, who refused, however, to endorse the required promissory notes, which must therefore be returned to the Trustees as nonnegotiable. And, as Mr. Oglethorpe has instructed me to report the offensive conduct of some people [Schoolmaster Ortmann and his wife] to the Lord Trustees and the Society, I have made some mention in this respect in my letter to Mr. Vernon, for he, as a member of both the Society and the Lord Trustees, will be best placed to use this knowledge with both. May the Lord accompany everything with His blessing. We are also inclined to enclose the continuation of this diary, for much has happened since our last mailing that our Fathers should be aware of. [As soon as the long awaited crates have arrived, we expect to write more with God's help.]

Tuesday, the 24th of July. [Ortmann and his wife have sold their cows and delivered them to the buyer for possession and use. Now they have regretted this deal, and last night they attempted to seize the cows by force. However, the owner was too strong for them and refused them in a right strict manner. They importuned me last night just before the prayer meeting, but I told them to wait until today. As is his custom, Ortmann again drew up a presentation which is so full of lies that they as good as jumped in one's face. All his arguments are intended to show that the sale is to be declared void and the cows should be returned to him. But, as everything had been transacted in a most orderly fashion in the presence of a witness and a formal deal had been arranged, including the delivery of the cows and their use for three days, the sale had to stand and the present owner must keep the cows and the Ortmanns the purchase money. However, there is a reservation concerning the cow which was given by the Lord Trustees, pending Mr. Oglethorpe's opinion.

[These people see nothing wrong in lies and tricks while all the time invoking their conscience and the all-knowing Lord. I fear that their judgment is drawing closer and closer. It has become known in Purysburg that Mr. Oglethorpe did not react favorably to their unconscionable accusations, and they have heard from three of their creditors from whom they had bought articles without which they could well have survived. They have right good crops in their fields; but, as they do not know how to economize but lead a wasteful life, that will not be enough.]

At the bedside of his sick wife a man told me today of the many gifts the Lord had bestowed on them in his illness; he had received much help in his spirit but had suffered no harm in his body. For, although he had been kept from his work for a long time and incurred many debts, God had now kept him in good health for so long and had given him the opportunity to earn some money so that he was now relieved of his debts. He complained of his bashfulness which prevented him from doing as others do, namely, from presenting his plight and that of other Christians in the prayer meeting at my house in his own words; and therefore he desired to become right simple and sincere toward the others, which would bring much blessing.

Wednesday, the 25th of July. The weather this year has been quite different from our previous experience. We have always had cool days so that the people could use almost all daylight hours for their work. True, it is becoming warmer now, but it is still quite bearable and very beneficial for the crops. The nights have been as cool as in spring and fall. On the plantations, the people are said to be much plagued by gnats during their work and at night, but we have none of that here. In a newly cleared

forest there are always new difficulties. The fever is now attacking some of the people, particularly the recent arrivals; and at
this time of the year it is almost always more noticeable than at
others, but it tends to pass quickly for some and is not nearly as
strong as in the first and second years.

[Ulich, the shoemaker, and his wife also suffer from the
fever; I visited them and learned that Spielbiegler, who lives
close by, had been involved in an ugly fight with his mother. I
therefore went to his house and reminded him of the Fourth
Commandment[20] and of his duty, likewise of what we shall hear
in next Sunday's text from the mouth of the Savior: "Whosoever is angry with his brother (let alone his mother) shall be in
danger of the judgment," etc. He could not deny his offense,
but insisted on having been in the right, since the burden of
housekeeping rested on him; and his mother, who is weak and
almost childish, tended to do damage here and there. Then he
would be seized by rage, but shortly would come back to his
senses, etc. He is a poor, unbroken man who, like his mother,
cannot be convinced of the need for a change of heart. They
also attend the prayer meeting and the sermons only infre-
quently and can always give a heap of excuses when they are
admonished.]

Thursday, the 26th of July. [The people in Old Ebenezer like
to play tricks upon us whenever they can; but they rarely succeed, for the Lord will not let them. Last week, they abducted
our horse, which has rendered such good service to the community. For this reason I wrote them a serious letter yesterday, and
today the horse was returned, although in bad condition, by an
Englishman. We are always ready to fulfill reasonable requests,
so that they may have no reason to become embittered against
us.] It is a great pleasure that, when we need people to do some
work for us, they[21] always carry out their tasks honestly and
faithfully, nor do they demand the wages that are customary in
this country. Our community is well provided with carpenters,
tailor, shoemaker, and locksmith; and, once we have some flax,
we will also not be wanting for weavers. God may even one day
present us with a smith, who would have his hands full here, for
the locksmith has neither the skill nor the strength to do a
smith's work. Some time ago we had an opportunity to have a

German smith from Carolina come here, but he moved to Purysburg because we could not arrange for his redemption. His and his wife's conduct, we have learned, is not much better than that of N. [Mrs. Rheinlaender], who used to live here; and therefore I am well pleased that I have had nothing to do with their moving here.

N.N. [Mrs. Rheinlaender] contacted Mr. Oglethorpe's secretary on the occasion of his visit in Purysburg to complain of me and sought his help in being permitted to return here. However, I acquainted the secretary with her character, and at dinner I found occasion to mention her before Mr. Oglethorpe and the entire company; and I could well see that Mr. Oglethorpe does not like to hear about this type of people. He seems glad when they leave the country. [Her conduct in Purysburg is so offensive that we hear nothing but complaints about her and against her; her neighbors and all those who have become acquainted with her would be glad to see her go. It is said that through a false oath and contemptible hypocrisy she has moved the governor of Carolina to give her several hundred acres of land and also some money for provisions, as well as a house lot in Purysburg.]

Friday, the 27th of July. As the Salzburgers already own more than 250 head of cattle and again are about to buy some more from the Carolina area with the money they have earned so far, they are now busy making hay to provide fodder for the winter. They do not really have any meadows yet, but on fertilized ground some kind of sweet long grass grows so abundantly that they can cut it several times a year. They also break off the green leaves from the Indian corn at this time and on several other occasions throughout the year and dry them; this is better than the best hay for cows and horses, and probably also for sheep if we had them here. These leaves are to be found in plenty, and the corn is not damaged if the lower leaves are cut first and then the uppermost leaves and the head once the corn has become fully ripe and bent. Since there are no horses and wagons or well cut roads, they must carry the fodder home, which they do not mind doing as they are richly rewarded for their troubles later with milk and butter. The fodder is supplemented by plenty of straw from the rice, oats, and barley (the latter, though, was planted only by a few), and the cattle also seem to like the shells of the beans.

As time goes on, our dear people keep improving their arrangements, and everything goes more easily. We have no place in the orphanage to store fruit and crops or fodder, so we are compelled to build new barns for threshing the rice and storing the harvest; these are now under way. The threshing floor will also benefit those who help in its construction, and none are excluded who think that they may need it. True, this will cause new expenses; but, since this construction is quite indispensable, we trust in the Lord that, as in previous times, He will make the well of His grace flow on us.

N.N.'s [Simon Steiner's] wife is still in bed after her miscarriage, but she is out of danger and has regained most of her strength. She told me that she counts this sickness among the blessings of the Lord and that it would not be good for her if the Lord were not to attack her thus. As she cannot work now, I admonished her to perform the necessary work on her soul, that is, to industrious prayer, so that she might thereby gather strength to prove more faithful in the future in her Christianity and her housekeeping. It was probably due to a lack of vigil and prayer that there had been several unpleasant things that upset them, too: now that she could not work, she would let the dear Lord work on her soul all the more strongly and then she would experience the most unspeakable benefit.

She told me that during the evening prayer meeting, when her husband was at church, she suffered from much temptation, great fear, and all sorts of fantasies that made her hear and see horrible things; but these disappeared when her husband returned. This gave me an occasion to point out to her the great blessing of the married state, wherein God has joined man and wife and given the woman, as the weakest tool that is subject to so many accidents, her husband as an advisor, protector, and helper. They should just take care that Satan might not pervert the Lord's wise providence. I also showed her what a blessing it is to have a good conscience purified by Christ's blood. For, if we are in good standing with the Lord as one's father, then we need fear neither the devil nor anyone else, for no hair on our head can be harmed without the Father's will and permission. And, because she had to admit that it was her bad conscience that arose in such circumstances, I admonished her to relieve herself thereof by living in the order of the Lord, of which the Lord Himself reminded her and to which He was goading her. I read her several pertinent verses.

Saturday, the 28th of July. My dear colleague, Mr. Boltzius, left for Savannah last evening; may the Lord strengthen him so that he may preach the gospel with much benefit. In the first days of last week, until Thursday, we did not know whether either of us could travel, since I have had several attacks of the fever and did not know whether it would decrease or become more virulent. On Thursday, however, the dear Lord so strengthened me even during the last attack of the fever that I believed my dear colleague would be able to make the journey. And the dear Lord has indeed shown how He can help, for today the fever did not return and I felt so well that I could hold the prayer meeting, which I had not felt capable of last night when my dear brother departed. May the Lord be praised for all His love and kindness which He has shown me during this small illness, in that it has served me to much good. May he also help me so that from now on I may use my time and my strength more fruitfully in His praise.

Sunday, the 29th of July. The dear Lord has strengthened me today to preach His gospel and to repeat that which I taught this morning in the afternoon and to support it with several verses. The proper text for the 6th Sunday after Trinity dealt with the one right way to heaven and to salvation. For the exordium, I took Isaiah 30:21, "This is the way, walk ye in it when ye turn to the right hand, and when ye turn to the left." May the Lord be praised for the blessing which He has bestowed on my soul by this, and may He also bless it in the others. Last night I visited the shoemaker, Ulich, during his fever, which has attacked him together with his wife. I repeated some of the truths we had heard about, and he could not marvel enough at the fact that the Lord Jesus had so far descended to man as to become his path. He made some further remarks that I shall apply for my own good with the grace of the Lord. May the Lord God strengthen this dear man again!

Monday, the 30th of July. I have visited Master Ulich a full three times today, but I could not talk to him, although it seemed that he had understood some of my words during the first visit.

I also visited N.N. [Bacher] who until now has just idled along and been content with good motions and fancies. Now the Lord is starting work on him through His spirit in earnest, so that he has realized that he is not yet well off. The sins of his youth oppress him, and he wishes for nothing more than to become truly repentant; and he is very sad that he cannot repent as strongly as he would wish. I showed him what a great mercy of the Lord it was to bring him to such recognition, and how He now wished him to turn toward Him with all the abominable sins he has committed, for else he will not be rid of them. It was such souls that the Lord Jesus desired, and he was not to wait until he recognized his sins in such and such a manner. It was enough for him to recognize them truly so that he would wish to be relieved of them and would ask for nothing more than a drop of His mercy, even if he were to forego everything else. He should just turn to the redeemer of all sins, the Lord Jesus, for He would make him so beautiful that the Father would not find a single sin upon him. And, since God was working on him now in earnest, he should not relent until he had persevered, for else he would find it harder and harder to convert to the Lord.

Tuesday, the 31st of July. Last night before the prayer meeting I returned, God be praised, in good health; and I found both my dear colleague and my family better off physically than I had left them. The faithful Lord be humbly praised for all the good He has shown to me and to them. The German servants in Savannah whom I visited in the performance of my office are mostly ill from the fever; and, since the weather was quite stormy both on Saturday and Sunday, few came in from the plantations. I treated the proper text for the 6th Sunday after Trinity, i.e. concerning the appearance and the power of a godly life, which I repeated briefly in the afternoon. I also read and applied the song, *Du sagst, ich bin ein Christ*, etc. May God lead these poor people to the proper recognition of themselves, so that they may see that they are still lacking the true essence of

Christianity and that those who have achieved it once are most blessed. Some of the masters do not give permission for their servants and maids to come to church for fear they might reveal to the authorities their poverty, great want, and pitiable circumstances. I again heard much of their harsh and right barbarian treatment, and I felt obliged to make written and oral presentations to the authorities so that these poor people might not be completely ruined and driven to the utmost. For, when the masters treat them so cruelly and a maid or a servant commits an offense as a result, they turn matters around and claim that it was that very offense that led to the harsh and cruel treatment. For the greatest part the masters themselves have not much to eat and they want to have people who will do their work; but they give them neither food nor clothing so as to maintain their strength. Because the authorities know of the treatment of their servants by most masters, I was asked to return to Savannah next week, when masters and servants are to appear before them. I could not well refuse this request, as there is no one else to take up the cause of these poor people.

Mr. N. [Whitefield] has written to his very trusted friend N.N. [the schoolmaster, Mr. Habersham]; and in his letter he mentioned our letter to him and wrote that he had in fact received it. We had sent a large packet to Charleston at the same time, which has therefore been correctly delivered. These letters were from November and December of last year. Mr. N. [Whitefield] is now expected in Savannah every day on Captain Thomson's ship. The present preacher in Savannah, Mr. Norris, showed me two letters from the Lord Trustees wherein he is asked to take on the office of minister in Frederica and thus make room for another [Mr. Whitefield], whom the Lord Trustees had appointed regular preacher in Savannah for a number of weighty reasons. He is not content with this arrangement, though, and intends to return to place a complaint with the Bishop of London. This good man imagines the Bishop to have greater power in this colony than the Lord Trustees have granted him, for they do not wish to relinquish the right to accept such chaplains or court preachers as please them and send them here—a privilege also enjoyed by other Lords in England. None of the provinces in America, with the exception of Carolina, acknowl-edges the power of the Bishop in ecclesiastical matters, as is shown by the fact that he has a *commissarius* nowhere else but in Charleston, who acts in his name and corresponds with him.

On Sunday it became known that a Spanish spy had made his way to Savannah by way of Purysburg and had been arrested that very evening with two servants.[22] He was examined in the house of Mr. Jones, the storehouse manager, where we have the habit of staying when in Savannah; and both from him as well as from his two servants, who are right shiftless and prepared to shrink at no evil trick, the interrogators learned a number of quite suspicious things. The man's face was of a black-brown color as if he were Indian, he spoke broken English, and he had a glib tongue; he was quite audacious and managed to give a good explanation for any contradiction he might be caught in. He produced a number of letters purporting, among other things, to show that he was an honest man practicing medicine and surgery who, in the course of his profession, had spent sev-eral years in a variety of places. He calls himself Anton Masig, but in his letters he went by a quite different name.

He first sought the acquaintance of the Jews in Savannah and pretended to be Jewish himself; but, when they saw him smoke tobacco in the inn on the Sabbath, they became suspicious. Later, he denied all this and said he was a Christian born in Cologne on the Rhine; however, it was established soon enough that he was born in Old Spain. He had looked around in South and North Carolina and now was on his way to the camp at Frederica, on the pretense of seeking work as a medical man and surgeon. As his intent became clear prematurely, he had his things brought to a secretly hired boat at night and was about to return to Purysburg when he was apprehended and carefully examined. He was put in jail at once during the night from Sunday to Monday, where he will be kept until Mr. Oglethorpe's return.

Yesterday, after my arrival, I was called to shoemaker Ulich, who was already in his last throes and could neither talk nor hear a word. I prayed with his young wife by the side of his deathbed and tried to comfort her. He died between nine and ten and was buried tonight. In him we have lost a pious man, who was most useful and skilled in his profession; and his loss is much regretted by the entire community. The Lord has given, the Lord has taken, the name of the Lord be praised. Last week he was only suffering from the tertian fever and on good days was quite able to perform his work. When I saw him last week and found his wife in the paroxysm of the fever, I talked much about how a person afflicted with the fever, particularly in this country, should conduct himself, both as regards perspiring and diet. I told him how I had observed these rules in this very hut wherein I had long lain ill of the fever with my wife, and that God had blessed this regimen in me until my full recovery, whereas others, including my wife, who had failed to maintain a constant steady sweat or a light perspiration, had retained a hard swelling like a stone[23] in their side. He understood all this well and agreed, so that I do not know what caused the fever to turn and why he died so quickly. He could not take the final medication prescribed by Mr. Thilo. He had lost consciousness on Saturday, but then recovered slightly on Sunday.

[One of Count Zinzendorff's missionaries, Mr. Schulius, died a week ago in Purysburg of a high fever. Mr. Thilo had been called to his side the previous Saturday, but the medicine he ordered had no effect. Mr. Boehler as well is afflicted by the fever and is bedridden in Purysburg.[24]

[A young Salzburger had accompanied me to Savannah in order to settle his marriage to a woman there with her parents and herself. The family is Reformed and the Salzburger had above all made the condition that the daughter he is to marry would have to promise before God and witnesses to confess the Evangelical-Lutheran religion, for else he would not consent to this marriage. Both daughter and parents know us well and are aware of what we teach from the Lord's word. However, they did not wish to yield on this point but remained in the old faith, and therefore the marriage will not take place.] A [another] young Salzburger wished to marry a German servant girl who is employed by a German Jew[25] and behaves well. He is prepared to pay the costs of her ocean travel, but the Jew does not wish to let her go and cannot be made to do so by law.

AUGUST

Wednesday, the 1st of August. Ruprecht Steiner is building a sturdy and spacious house for himself on his plantation and is being aided in this task by six helpers. He asked me to come out during the week and pray with the workers. We both went out and had much pleasure in the company of these people. After the prayer, I applied the beautiful words of the apostle from Romans 8:1 to good use. Because of the lasting rains, the paths are quite bad; and, since I have been inconvenienced for some time now with internal heat and physical weakness, I was so tired from this trip back and forth that I was quite useless for any work all afternoon. Once the people live out there, it will be necessary for us to acquire a horse so as to visit them more often, for which purpose the Lord can easily provide the necessary funds.

Mr. Oglethorpe seemed inclined upon my request to have a flour mill built for us, and I was to inquire for this purpose into the availability of some millstones which are lying in the open air in Purysburg. They belong to the merchant Purry in Savannah,[1] a son of the deceased Mr. Purry. This man is usually quite reasonable in his transactions so that I was all the more surprised that he asked £60 sterling for these two stones. He wants to be rid of them, for he has no use for them; but who would be willing to pay such a large sum of money for them?

Thursday, the 2nd of August. We have had much rain this summer, so that until now it has been as agreeably cool both night and day as is customary here in the fall and the spring. Consequently, the weather has not bothered the people in their work. [The young Zuebli came to see me today and complained that the hogs have invaded his corn and other crops. He demanded that I should speak to the people, in particular Gschwandl, whose pig is doing most of the damage, to get rid of the hogs and remove them.[2] When I could not agree to this request, he was at first very upset. He has not built a fence and we therefore have long feared some unpleasantness like this. I am afraid of much harsh judgment and loveless criticism if the people will not agree to do as he wishes and pen in the hogs both day and night, which they can hardly be expected to do. The brother in Purysburg must have received good letters, so that he now conducts himself towards his brothers, who are living here, more kindly than formerly. This young Zuebli was on his plantation in Purysburg last week and is clearly hoping for some material benefits.]

Friday, the 3rd of August. Lackner's sister, who recently arrived here with Sanftleben, is in bed in Gruber's house with the fever; she usually stays with her brother on his plantation, where she would have little care in her present circumstances, and therefore she has done well to take lodging here. She is quite well cared for here, for she is not only being helped in all ways that affect her physical well-being, but is being edified as well with God's word and prayer. She recalled with much pleasure yesterday's prayer meeting, of which Mrs. Gruber had told her. The latter had said, among other things, that she was now faring as we did in the beginning and the Savior was calling to her, too, "What I do thou knowest not now; but thou shalt know hereafter," from which I gathered that Mrs. Gruber had predicted for her from her own experience much of the spiritual benefit that honest souls have garnered from their long illness. In the beginning her brother had also suffered from a long and severe illness, which the Lord blessed in his soul, and I have recently impressed her mind with this.

Saturday, the 4th of August. N.N. [Mrs. Ortmann] was ill in bed throughout this week; and, when I went to her house today, I told her and him about the true intent of the Lord in attacking man with physical afflictions, i.e. that they might all the better be reminded of their mortality and learn to pray with all salvation-happy souls. "So teach us to number our days, that we may apply our hearts to wisdom," which spiritual wisdom consists in becoming certain of God's grace in Christ and thus dying in joy. In this connection I briefly presented to them the whole order of salvation and showed them how to go about partaking of the grace of the Lord in Christ if they truly wished it. Imagined piety, self-assured comfort, and other human things will not suffice, etc. They outwardly agreed with my words, but I shortly thereafter noticed from the words of both that they lack the inclination and the desire to do true penance but feel that it has already been done. May God open their eyes!

[There have been some misunderstandings and errors with regard to the leather which was given to the deceased shoe-maker, Ulich, by the Lord Trustees; and we used all the prudence at our disposal to prevent the young widow from becoming prejudiced against us. Sanftleben and she both say that the leather had been given to the late Ulich as a gift on the condition that he would make as many pairs of shoes for the orphanage at half price as there are people living there; for the rest, he was to use the leather as he wished. However, Mr. Verelst had put the matter in his letter of 2 April 1739 as follows: "At the Request of the Shoemaker, the Trustees have supplied him with Leather & Wax to the Amount of £10:19:10 Sterling, which he chose himself, & has the Possession of; in consideration whereof he has agreed to make shoes for your Orphan House to be delivered at half Price to that Amount, the Leather being thus pay'd for." I do not wish to interpret these words myself, although they are quite clear and imply much more than Sanftleben and Mrs. Ulich claim. Rather, I will inquire with our superiors in Savannah and in particular with Mr. Oglethorpe into the precise meaning of these expressions, so that we may be certain on all counts. I also will take this occasion to inquire what is to be done with the leather, of which there is a plentiful amount of good quality, now that the shoemaker has died and cannot fulfill the above condition. In the meantime, the young widow is receiving all the money, without the slightest deduction, for all shoes that her deceased husband has made for the community from this leather. The remaining leather will be kept in a safe place. It is a difficult and weighty matter to be judge in *propria causa*,[3] wherein we must include our orphanage; and we would wish to have a knowledgeable man in our community to whom we could entrust the arrangement of all material affairs.]

Sunday, the 5th of August. A few days ago I suffered an attack of jaundice; and, since I am taking medication, I was prevented from holding the sermon this morning. My dear colleague assumed this labor in the name of the Lord and, as I learned from a pious Salzburger, it was crowned with the blessing of the Lord. Instead of the repetition hour, I continued in contemplating the text in Judges 16, where it is told what happened to Samson, who had run into a labyrinth of misery because of his sins, both in prison and during the idolatrous thanksgiving and pleasure feast of the Philistines. I showed how this judgment on Samson was tempered with much mercy by the Lord, for he could as easily have lost his head as the hair on it. Which means: "The Lord hath patience with us and doth not wish for anyone to be lost, but that everyone repent," etc., which he doubtless did during his imprisonment, as can be seen from the following circumstances. The quick and extraordinary growth of his hair was to show him that the Lord regarded his repentance, like that of the greatest sinner, Manassis, with grace because of the Messiah and had again accepted him as a Nazarene, confederate, and a child of God. In this connection I recalled the expression of the late Dr. Anton: "The miraculous Lord uses many a way to assure the repentant sinner of His grace, even where sometimes it takes the form of a *testimonium paupertatis*."[4] The example of Mrs. Krueger's servant girl in Halle, who converted to the Lord, which is recounted in the *Contributions to the Building of the Kingdom of God*,[5] belongs here. A pious Salzburger told me that he had formerly heard people make fun of the story of Samson and treat it frivolously, and only now did he appreciate its importance.

Monday, the 6th of August. My dear colleague told me of N.N.'s [Hans Floerel's] wife that she was not only sick in her body but much depressed in her spirit because of her many sins committed in former times and the weaknesses still clinging to her. Even if a drop of comfort penetrates her heart now and then, it does not last long, but the deep recognition of her misery seems to her to render her undeserving and incapable of any comfort. May God bless all encouragement that she receives from His word. She has a very honest husband who is well experienced in Christian matters and has learned to pray in the school of the Holy Ghost; and he is faithfully assisting her with this gift. I have heard from others that, when other women came to her who were dejected and upset by their sins and complained to her of their situation, she was always able to comfort them strongly with words from the gospel and to direct them to the straight path; she herself, in contrast, finds it difficult to apply the grace of the Lord in Christ to herself. She considers herself below all Christians and the most miserable sinner, in whom there is much wickedness and whose repentance is not yet the truth.

Tuesday, the 7th of August. N.N. [Burgsteiner] had some business with Mr. Thilo because of his weak health and called on me to receive an admonition from the Lord's word. He praised the merciful Lord for having extracted him from the many temptations which he suffered some years ago in Germany and in which he had become ever more embroiled, and for having brought him to the true recognition of the path to salvation. He well remembers the time when the dear Lord started to bless His word in him, whereas previously it had gone in one ear and out of the other and he had remained blind all the time. I just then had before me the *Sixth Contribution*[6] and therein the beautiful example of the recently mentioned ignorant servant who was converted to the Lord (p. 655); I read this to him in a simple manner, as he too was brought up blindly and in ignorance, and then prayed with him. We cannot yet bring all our listeners to the point that they visit us diligently in our house, but we must instead visit them in their huts if we are to find an occasion for their edification. Those who come often well notice the benefit. May the Lord finally relieve me of my physical weakness and of the many material matters which force us to travel to Savannah often, and may He, for the sake of Christ, not make me account for the omissions which are occasioned thereby.

Wednesday, the 8th of August. Last night a couple of our friends from Savannah visited us so as to inspect our town and its arrangements, and for this purpose we had sent our little boat down last Monday. One of them was the schoolmaster and the other a merchant from Savannah[7] [both very close friends of Pastor Whitefield, who is being expected any day now]. They were both quite happy here and joined us in thanking the Lord on our knees for all the good that He has done to us and them in His miraculous kindness. They are both God-fearing men and regard that which the Lord has done here with quite different eyes than natural people do. They were much pleased by the work of the Salzburgers, their harmoniousness, their economy, their fairness in demanding wages for their work, our orphanage and all other things that they found. They will surely use all that they have seen with their own eyes to good purpose. May God be praised, who still secures for us benefactors and well-wishers even in this country, and men who seek our best by intercession, good advice, and even through letters to other benefactors and friends.

Thursday, the 9th of August. To be sure, I had promised the authorities to be in Savannah yesterday or today so that some help and relief could be provided for the poor German servants there by my intercession. However, the physician does not advise travel in view of my still pending recovery, and therefore my dear colleague has gone down with our two friends. He will advise the authorities of my inability to travel and also take care of the provisions for the new arrivals and for Mr. Thilo, who has until now hardly claimed any of his provisions but who now seems to need them.

To this end, the large boat has been sent down. I only worry that there may not be as much provisions in the storehouse as the boat can carry. It is a great blessing of the Lord that our Salzburgers have now been able to eat their own bread for a year; for, if they had had to rely on Savannah for their food, the supplies would have been quite meager, as there have been many shortages in Savannah and no money has been available to purchase new provisions. True, Parliament has set aside £20,000 sterling for this colony, but this money must be spent in part on Mr. Oglethorpe's regiment and in part for the payment of old debts, so that little will be left for new expenditures. The closer the harvest has come, the more our people have felt a lack of supplies, but they have managed as best they could. Now they are eating new corn already, and the giver of such blessings is being offered heartfelt praise by all honest souls. The rain has not done the damage to the corn which disbelief and reason have feared, rather it is more bountiful everywhere than in any previous year. There will be few beans, since the deer have caused much damage at night; but with God's help the rice and potatoes will amply make up for the shortage in beans.

Friday, the 10th of August. The wife of the servant[8] in the orphanage has been ill for some time now and in some respects causes much inconvenience to the others there. The house is provided with separate rooms for the manager and the children, as well as with separate quarters for both sexes; and in this initial period we have not been able to undertake any extensive planning, as we will eventually have to do for the best of the orphanage; and consequently there are no quarters for caring for the sick. However, occasionally there are several sick people whom, like this woman, we would wish to care for in a separate room so that the healthy will not be disturbed in their work, their meals, and their sleep. This is not possible now, though, in particular as the crops we have been blessed with in the fields urgently require the construction of a barn and threshing floor, for which the ground will be prepared next week with God's help. It may well be that it will please the Lord to bestow on us, sooner or later, a new blessing of funds with which to pay for this barn and construct a sick room.

I visited some of the women whom Sanftleben has brought here. They all have the fever and do not yet know how to conduct themselves in their illness, and therefore they much need personal advice on the diet to be observed during a fever, particularly in this country. In particular I talked with them regarding the well known verse: "Come unto me all ye who . . ." and attempted to instruct them to recognize the burden of sin on their hearts and the kindness of the Lord Jesus towards repentant sinners, with regard to which their knowledge is still sadly lacking. Inasmuch as one of them [Sanftleben's sister] has much prejudice against the truth and always uses her simplicity as an excuse, I recommended to her brother to read her the edifying example of Pastor Kusens and the ignorant servant girl who was nevertheless converted to God, of which we made recent mention, so that she could see that, however simple and ignorant these people might have been, they nonetheless became most knowledgeable and understanding in the work of salvation because they left room for the Holy Spirit in their soul through the word. I admonished the brother [Sanftleben] to show much seriousness and application in his Christianity, for his example would then by the grace of God all the more surely convince her that the honest exercise of the Christian faith is not only necessary but also possible.

Saturday, the 11th of August. My dear colleague returned from Savannah already this afternoon, although they did not travel on the big boat. The people, who had wished to return quickly because of their work, had travelled by night, in particular as this is more pleasant than during the day because of the heat. Only a portion of the desired provisions have arrived, since there was not much left in the storehouse. I now have hope that the money for the linen which the Swiss merchant, Mr. Schlatter,[9] had sent to Mr. Causton for sale may indeed be paid shortly. The Lord Trustees have appointed three commissaries who are to examine all bills and debts of the storehouse incurred under Mr. Causton and make a report to them, so that later all debts found sound and justified can be paid.

The last few days have been veritable summer days, as they usually are here in this country, and they have been most beneficial for the ripening corn as well as the beans and other crops. May the Lord provide that this beautiful harvest may be received and enjoyed with a believing and thankful heart on the part of all, so that it may in fact be a true blessing!

Sunday, the 12th of August. Today we again had several listeners from Purysburg, who, together with others in the congregation, announced publicly their intention to go to the Lord's Table next Sunday. Regarding the regular text for this Sunday, Matthew 7 : 15 ff., we presented a matter which is most necessary especially for these people from Purysburg and is exactly what I treated for the German people in Savannah concerning Matthew 5 : 20 ff. a fortnight ago, that is, the semblance and power of Christianity.[10] In the afternoon, it was up to my dear colleague to treat of the dear truths that lie in the 5th Petition, wherein the fatherly intent of the Lord is most beautifully revealed to us through Christ His Son, for the comfort of all dejected sinners.

After the afternoon service Mr. Thilo was called to Old Ebenezer to care for a German servant of the Lord Trustees, who is said to lie gravely ill with colic. The people there derive much benefit from our town, and it is to be desired that they should be grateful therefor to God and men.

Monday, the 13th of August. Today the carpenters and other Salzburgers have made a start with preparing the wood for the barn of the orphanage, for which may the Lord bless them and assist them. To be sure, some of the people in the community were prepared to join in this labor without pay so as to have some claim to the use of the threshing floor later on, but it has been found to be better to have it built entirely at the expense of the orphanage so that the orphanage will have sole right of disposal. As circumstances permit, we will surely be willing and able to provide services for others, as has happened before with a number of things, but it should not be so much a right as a privilege and charitable service. Also, each of them needs his time badly these days, and if they can spare a day or two from their work, they should not be begrudged the little money they can earn in this construction. In the manner of the well kept and durable barns in the Salzburg area, this barn will be constructed entirely of solid wooden planks.

The threshing floor itself will be located in the middle and consist of thick and wide split and planed planks. On each side of the floor will be two large receptacles for corn, rice, beans and other crops, which are floored with thick boards, as in this country the high humidity forces us to store all grain and other produce fairly high off the ground. On the top we will store hay and other things necessary for housekeeping and farming. May the loving and merciful Lord let us feel His blessing in this construction, as in our other undertakings. The manager of the orphanage is full of faith and good hope and is constantly presenting, together with his family, this undertaking to the almighty and merciful Lord in his prayers.

A Salzburger woman had been late for our private edification and prayer meeting because of her sickly child; since this had happened on several occasions, she cried bitterly and told us of the great damage she suffered from her inability to attend services and prayer meetings as diligently as before. She also had less strength and fervor in her prayers, etc. I comforted her, especially with a beautiful saying from the *Treasure Chest*,[11] which fitted her circumstances well. I also advised her how to provide for her child in the future if she wished to come to my room Mondays and Fridays for prayer. In this meeting, I read aloud a most beautiful letter from the *Contribution to the Building of the Kingdom of God*,[12] wherein the writer shows, in an incomparably beautiful manner and based on his own experience, how we can reach the power of Christian belief and grow and flourish therein.

Tuesday, the 14th of August. [Rauner again pretends to many good intentions and is attempting to persuade me that I should admit him and his wife to Holy Communion. However, I am admonishing him to take time for a thorough preparation. Ortmann and his wife carry many grudges against him, although they themselves are not much better. He agreed to ask forgiveness for all his insults to them, but both refused to listen to him and showed him the door, and even threatened him with a beating. Mrs. Ortmann pretends sickness as an excuse for missing all services, yet she was nonetheless able to travel as far as Purysburg with the people from Old Ebenezer. He does not leave the house either but pretends a state of dizziness, for which reason the small children are made to come to his house for instruction. There is little hope with these people, who approve of the truth only to the extent that it is not applied to them and their circumstances. Sometimes, they accuse themselves of being the poorest and most forlorn sinners; but if one goes into detail with them, they think themselves so holy that there are few to compare with them.]

There was a quantity of flour on the petiaguer[13] that brought Sanftleben and his people from Charleston to Savannah which had been sent by the Lord Trustees for the welfare of the colony. However, as there was much and heavy rain at the time, the flour has started to smell and is now almost beyond use. The storekeeper told me that it had been examined by the three commissaries and found to be unfit for human consumption. Since a barrel containing about 300 pounds is being sold for as little as five shillings, our Salzburgers have fetched a boatload of it and will travel to Savannah as long as there is some flour left at this low price. This flour, which would have been used in Savannah to feed the hogs, is a true blessing for our people; these poor folk are not choosy but know how to put everything to good use, even this flour, especially since they are now harvesting new corn.

Wednesday, the 15th of August. The merchant from Savannah who visited us last week with the schoolmaster borrowed our English translation of the book by the blessed Arndt on the true nature of Christianity. While still here, he had already found much pleasure in the preface by the late Boehme[14] as well as in the book itself. Now our schoolmaster from Savannah writes us, among other news, that the dear Arndt is his and the merchant's daily companion and is giving them as much comfort as any honest soul is bound to find therein who has a true taste for the right kind of riches. May God place His mercy on the reading of this beautiful book. [Zettler has again shown his displeasure at not being permitted to go to the Lord's Table until his previous misconduct has been made up for; he refuses, however, to recognize its sinfulness, and much less is he willing to submit to discipline. He is a coarse unbroken man and he much needs someone to rough up his mind, for nothing is being achieved with kindness. The cowherd, Nett, and his wife are also unbroken people who do not know even the beginning of conversion.]

Thursday, the 16th of August. This morning after school I had something to discuss with the carpenters and other workers who are preparing the wood for the orphanage out in the forest. Because we were together in one place, we prayed together, as I found the people most ready and eager to do. We may well hope again for the Lord's blessing on this construction, for the work is being done in God's order. As often as they commence or end work, they first pray to the Lord and praise Him for His assistance.

The stories in the 18th and 19th chapters of Judges have been written as instruction and as warning to us, as we now recognize with the Lord's help in our scheduled readings during the prayer meetings. Oh how much we need, like those others who came to a new land and enjoyed much material good under the Lord's providence, to watch ourselves so that we may not forsake the living source after receiving all the blessings, but instead dig wells here and there which are full of holes and hold no water. It is easy for the heart to become sluggish and luke-warm after a while, to deviate from the Lord, and instead cling to the created world; as in the case of the Israelites and thousands of others in evangelical Christendom, this becomes so habitual that they are led to idolatry and do not even believe that it is so wicked. With God's help, we have attempted to warn each other against idolatry in matters spiritual and of the sin of habit in matters material and in religious affairs; and we have learned from God's word that leaving God and becoming faithless toward the blessings bestowed are the cause and reason for many a spiritual and physical judgment, as can be seen from the context of the 18th and 19th chapters. Cf. Romans 1:21–32.

Friday, the 17th of August. Last night saw the death of Held's wife, who had been sick for some time, first of the fever and then of a tumor. She and her husband were among the last German servants to come here, and they had initially been given by Mr. Oglethorpe to an Englishman in Savannah. However, they were ill provided for there; and, upon their urgent request, they were taken into the service of the orphanage. The man told me at the funeral that she had had a special urge to come to America and had always been sad when he showed no real desire. When God had arranged for their arrival at our town, she had thanked Him many times from the bottom of her heart for having brought her to the pure word of the gospel and having so richly refreshed her with it, as would never have been possible in her homeland, where things are said to go quite badly. She much loved hearing the Lord's word, and she assured me repeatedly that it had led her to the recognition of her sins and the faith in the Lord Jesus. On her deathbed, she highly praised her Jesus and His sweetness to her, and she looked forward to redemption. As we had assumed that she had not yet truly recognized the horror of sin and the great perdition of the heart and may have secretly comforted herself with her previous good conduct, eager prayers, etc., we bore much witness against self-justice and wrong comfort, and repeatedly pointed out to her that the Lord Jesus called to Himself and accepted only the poor, naked, and miserable sinners, and that self-made comfort would not serve her well on that final day. The manager of the orphanage and his wife give her a good testimony.

Toward evening the Englishman from Carolina brought the cows and oxen we had purchased a month ago.[15] On his way he lost a few, partly in the water and partly in the forest, but he is nonetheless willing to bring us cattle as often as we demand, for here he receives his money in cash, whereas in Purysburg and in other places he is obliged to give credit for long periods of time, which causes him many losses. He has acted honestly and, in accordance with his promise, has brought our people cattle that are as good as they could wish for, yet not so expensive as in previous times. Our people have managed their money well and hope that the dear Lord will give them the occasion to earn some more. Cattle are indispensable to them in their house-keeping. May God be praised for this benefaction as well!

Saturday, the 18th of August. This afternoon eight people arrived from Purysburg to join the congregation tomorrow, if it pleases God, in Holy Communion. I prepared them in my room prior to the public act of repentance and confession, and I hope from the bottom of my heart that all may be led to a recognition of the truth and to the realization of the honest way that is in Christ, wherein most of them are still lacking. Those people who live in dissension and annoying discord with their neighbors have not come up with them, although they had intended to do so a week ago. We do not long for them, since they will not accept admonitions to be repentant. When people who have not yet been really converted to the Lord in truth push themselves to the Lord's Table, we have much trouble with them.

A man from Old Ebenezer had his wife register him for Communion and did not come to see me, although I had asked him to. I spoke to him after confession and patiently admonished him for his cursing, which I myself had heard in Savannah. I asked him to repent this and all other sins. As a former soldier, he seems to think little of his cursing, but excuses it with his impatience, which was abetted by his difficult circumstances. Therefore he is far removed from conversion, and I asked him to abstain from the Lord's Table until he should be in a better prepared state. He did not say anything to this and stayed away; may God give me wisdom, love, and seriousness to maintain the proper conduct with our listeners in the use of the means of salvation, so that forward and unconverted people may be kept away, but the weak not be rendered timid and scared away and so that no one will become embittered. Those who feel the burden of our office in regard to this point may well desire from the bottom of their heart to be rid of it, if possible. Oh, could I but give it to another, and care for my own soul only, how happy I would be!

Sunday, the 19th of August. In the morning we dealt with the example of the unjust householder, Luke 16:1 ff., as showing the love of the flesh as the true and main idol of the children of this world. In the prayer meetings last week the dear Lord had let us hear some necessary lessons from this material in the text of Judges, chapters 18 and 19; and, since He has thus prepared the minds of our listeners for today's sermon, I am sure of some benefit in our dear listeners, who in large part have not known this idol in its full repulsiveness. In particular the Purysburg people need to be told what the love of the flesh is and that one cannot be saved while under its power and dominance. These people came to my room at night and let me read them an example of a carnally-minded man of the world and mammon who came to a sad ending, and therefore horribly experienced the fraud of sin in all eternity. In the repetition hour, the time went so quickly that I could not read it then, which is a shame, since it confirmed and clearly illustrated the preceding text.

Monday, the 20th of August. [I found the Berenberger woman much aggrieved and full of ill will against Sanftleben and the others in the community, although the reason for her displeasure is of little or no importance. I have asked her several times to come to me for advice and am fully prepared to make everything as easy as possible for her and to assist her wherever I can; however, so far she has not availed herself of this offer. She does not seem to have the best of dispositions. She told me of some instances of her masters and of the evil treatment she had received both in the bleachery in Ulm and in Augsburg, and in particular that she had been forced to work right hard, etc., which is not a good sign. In the presence of Mrs. Gschwandl, in whose house she is living, I sought earnestly to admonish her and to encourage her anew, in which the aforesaid honest woman is supporting me.]

Simon Steiner is complaining of his bashfulness, which is preventing him from praying aloud in our private meetings and from presenting the agony of his heart to the Lord before his brethren, as the others do. He is much edified, he said, by their unity, simplicity, and heartfelt conduct; and he is only worried that others might not turn their hearts to him and believe his prayers to be honest. He fears that they might remember, and still be offended by, some of the actions he took with his wife a year and even longer ago, when she had been most unreasonable and in need of serious discipline and admonishment. We had met in a right pleasant little group and prayed for ourselves and others most heartily in great poverty of spirit but nonetheless with much praise of the Lord, who is so merciful and kind in Christ. I take this as a sign that the Lord has blessed the reading of His word and the use of the Holy Supper.

N. [Leitner], who has until now been lazy and grouchy in all matters, as well as having been ill recently, finally recognizes better than ever before, by God's grace, that he is lacking in the true and unpretending conversion to God. He has resolved to tackle matters seriously for once so that he might become a child of the Lord. Today, he came to our meeting for the first time.

[Mrs. Helfenstein is experiencing much unrest over her oldest son, which we would like to be able to relieve if at all possible. She had first placed him with the shoemaker of the Herrnhuters in Savannah; but, as he was used only for field and housework there, she took him away and believed to have found a better place for him with a German shoemaker in Purysburg, where she hoped he would learn the profession thoroughly. This man, too, however, uses him only for field work and some housework and provides him with nothing but his food, whereas the mother must provide his clothing. Now there is even the chance that this shoemaker, as many in Purysburg have done, may return to Germany; and therefore the boy will not learn his trade. On the other hand, he has forgotten all that he had learned here in school and has seen and heard many disorderly happenings, so she is forced to take him back here and use him for work in the fields. She also will make a trial to see whether she and he can undertake her husband's profession, which was tanning both brown and white leather, so that they can support themselves.

[In this country children are not well provided for by their masters, and I would advise no one to place his child in Purysburg or Savannah; it is as if they were to be sacrificed to Moloch. The widow in question acted without my advice in this regard. At the time, we could not approve of her intentions with regard to her oldest daughter, and therefore she was much inclined against me. However, she has now learned that we are of honest intent toward her and try to seek the best material and spiritual arrangements for her and her children.]

Tuesday, the 21st of August. Last night I learned that N.'s [Floerel's] wife is sick with quartan fever [which is quite common this year] and was thus prevented from coming to the Lord's Table last Sunday. She is in need of evangelical comfort; and for this reason I visited her today and found her dejected and unhappy. When I asked her whether she was gaining more hope in her dear Savior and therefore finding comfort in Him, she put her head in her hands and cried for a long time. I gave her a number of comforting verses to contemplate, such as: "I will bring her into the wilderness, and speak comfortably to her," likewise: "Oh thou afflicted and not comforted," etc. I opened her *Treasure Chest*,[16] page 130, "Lord, turn our captivity," where the divine answer is also given from Isaiah 49:8–9, regarding which I said only a few words according to the circumstances of her weakened spirit so that I might encourage her to find the Father reconciled in Christ. Finally she complained with a few words, which she let fall with many tears, concerning the great perdition of her heart which she felt less than the pains of her body; likewise concerning her impatience, whereupon I showed her that all this should not drive her away from, but towards, Christ, the Savior of the world. Moses and his law afforded her no peace, and she could hardly fare better, for this honor was Christ's, who had extended His arms wide on the cross so as to grasp in them all sinners, as shown by the example of the great sinner, the thief. Finally, I prayed with her and left with the resolution to commend her to the Lord's care in my private prayers and to visit her again soon.

[Those who must deal with Ernst still have much trouble with him, and we ourselves cannot get along with him. With regard to his material subsistance, we have tried to intercede on his behalf in Savannah, and we have also made an advance to him; but this only causes us to be calumniated all the more. I shall again mention him in Savannah, as I have been asked to by some in the community. He has a very fine plantation; and, since others have taken in a man and shared with him the profits from the good land, he should have done likewise, for such a man would have been able to help him build a fence. Others have had their land fenced in for a long time now, but he still has not done it, thus endangering his neighbors' crops. He has often been asked to build his share of the fence, but he has always found an excuse and has become spiteful and argumentative. Now I will have to hear in Savannah what can be done in the case of such bad neighbors. His wife, who is not worth much either, is afraid to move out to the plantation; it seems he has threatened her to kill her or to beat her to a pulp and then to run away. And, since there is no one in the vicinity, she would have nowhere to beat a retreat. He also threatens others (as he has done me), and therefore nobody wishes to be his neighbor. Perhaps we shall be rid of him one day. He and his wife are both willfully blind and quite obdurate.]

Wednesday, the 22nd of August. N. [Grimmiger], whom I today admonished in my rooms to yield his heart to the dear and pious Lord, told me that N.N. [Ruprecht Steiner], whose plantation adjoins his, has given him much good instruction, particularly with regard to prayer, which had caused much good fruit in him. He was much ashamed; and he complained that he had prayed little or not at all in previous times and is now praising the Lord for not tearing him away in the state of sin. He is already noticing the benefit of prayer, which he no longer puts in mere recitation of prayer formulas but offers in his own words according to his own circumstances. I wish that R.S. [Ruprecht Steiner] would soon move out to his plantation, which would be most useful to this man, who cannot read and has little understanding.

I have again purchased a horse so that I may visit our listeners on the plantations several times weekly. Whenever I go out there on foot, my present poor physical state so tires and weakens me that I am not fit for my duties either here or out there. I hope that by and by several people will move out, as they have wished, so that we can then arrange for meetings during the week and on Sundays. Now, the few families who live there come in on Sundays; but this is most inconvenient for them because of their housework and the occasionally bad weather. May the dear Lord only see fit in His fatherly intent to strengthen my constitution, for I have been feeling quite sickly for some time now and have been hindered in the constant and eager exercise of my work. Perhaps the dear Lord will bless the exercise in us if we should visit our dear listeners frequently on horseback.

Thursday, the 23rd of August. It has not hurt at all that I have kept N.N. [Ruprecht Zittrauer] and his wife from taking Holy Communion. Rather it has even had a good effect on him, since we have continued, in God's mercy, to show him our devotion and love. If we can visit him often on his plantations, we hope that good effects will follow. He does not yet have his neighbors, who are good people, out there; and, since neither he nor she can read and both are constitutionally incapable of grasping what they are told in church, they are badly off in their solitude, where they must also forego the daily prayer meeting.

The German man from Old Ebenezer whom I recently could not admit to the Lord's Table because of the state of his mind misbehaved so grievously last night that he was brought to us today and will have to be sent to Savannah to face the authorities at the first opportunity. In a rage, he inflicted such a terrible wound on a most useful horse of the Lord Trustees that it is now lame in one foot and may well have been rendered unfit permanently. He is not admitting to the deed, but the circumstances are so evident that no one can be the evildoer except him and his wife.

Friday, the 24th of August. N. [Brandner] and his wife visited our private assembly, and I noticed in him that he is gaining beautifully in the blessing and the recognition of our dear Savior. I was much moved by his prayer, wherein he most touchingly recalled our dear benefactors in Europe and in this country. The Lord is showing us much mercy, both in the public services and in these hours which we spend before His face, for which we are praising and honoring Him.

In tonight's prayer meeting we finished the Book of Judges with divine help, and we shall shortly set out to read the Book of Ruth. God be humbly praised for all His assistance and for the blessing He has bestowed on me and others in this reading, and may He let us find many fruits from the spiritual seed sown before His throne in blessed eternity. We have been able to gather, both from reports and from the prayers of our dear listeners, that the texts read and discussed heretofore have made a great impression in many instances. In the last chapter we were most seriously impressed, as in a mirror, with human perdition as first caused by the Fall of Adam. Here we referred to the 2nd and 41st chapters of book I of the blessed Arndt's *True Christianity*.

If God pleases, I shall travel tomorrow to Savannah on official business, while my dear colleague will continue to read the New Testament in the evening prayer meetings, for which may the Lord bestow strength and wisdom on him.

Saturday, the 25th of August. The old N. [Bacher] continues on in the blessing of salvation. His heart is turning right soft, tender, and broken; he cries like a child and regrets that he did not obey his Lord earlier. "Oh," he said today, "how good would it have been if I had left room and place in my heart for the mercy of the Lord as soon as I came to Ebenezer." I showed him, however, that there was still time and that he was still welcome to the Lord, for He had reached His hands out to him. He should but be confident, for He would have mercy on him as there is much forgiveness in Him.

Sunday, the 26th of August. In today's text for the 10th Sunday after Trinity the Lord Jesus has been presented to us as one who on this our day is attempting to seek all who are still lost in Ebenezer and to save them. Oh how great is the kindness of our Jesus! He wishes to let no one perish in his misery, nor will He abandon the sinner however much he might deserve it, but goes right close to his heart so that he might feel it clearly.

This day has seemed to me a special day of visitation by the Lord's mercy, and I have tried to present it as such to our dear listeners, so as to see if they all would let themselves be won over once and for all. The Lord be praised for His help which He has shown to this poor worm, and may He bless it in His great mercy.

Monday, the 27th of August. Under God's protection, I returned tonight from Savannah, arriving just when the people were in the prayer meeting. I am glad to be back home among our listeners and with my dear colleague, where I am much quieter and happier than in other places. In other places [in Savannah and Purysburg] one hears and sees almost nothing but unpleasant and sad stories; and, since one cannot help, one would rather stay home than be there. [In Savannah, there is much discord among those who are appointed as authorities above the people, and it has led to several annoying legal proceedings. If the authority of Mr. Oglethorpe, who is still among the Indians, cannot settle these matters, it will go from bad to worse.]

Among the German people, to whom I again preached the word of the Lord both morning and afternoon, there is nothing but envy, hatred, persecution, faithlessness, and voluptuousness, drunkenness, and rowdiness, and they consider none of these as sins, although we show them from clear passages of the Scriptures that they are indeed sinning. [The Reformed in particular are mainly very wicked people who bitterly hate those who belong to our church.] Things look quite pitiful, and the judgment of obstinacy seems to have been pronounced on the people there. As our office has accomplished little or nothing with them, we are longing to remain with our congregation at all times rather than preach there. They now prefer the English preacher for their baptisms and marriages, because we will not permit them their drinking, dancing, and other disorder. Also some [of the members of the government and some Englishmen] would rather not see us come to Savannah too often, since the servants, who are treated right harshly, bring their complaints to us and we have to speak for them to the authorities. They argue that every time their servants come into town, they are made rebellious; and one of them was so forward as to impute to me in front of several others that I had twice incited his servants to leave their masters and move to Ebenezer. I urged him to have the people fetched from the plantation, and when he pretended sickness and inability to travel on their part, I myself took steps to have one he had named brought before him: when he examined him in my presence, he heard the very opposite and was put to shame with his accusations.

In large part, the man and woman servants are treated right barbarously, against the will and intentions of the Lord Trustees; but then this may well be a judgment on these people, the majority of whom are entirely godless and impertinent. Those in the service of the Lord Trustees are well treated, but are mainly dishonest and selfish, so that the Lords suffer many losses in their affairs. It may well be that this was the last sermon I will preach for them. I preached to them on "The Punished Ingratitude for the Precious Offer of God's Grace," and as an exordium I took Deuteronomy 32:6, "Do ye thus requite the Lord," etc. Also, our people are now beginning to make arrangements to have services held on the plantations; therefore our presence here will be necessary in any event.

Sunday afternoon letters arrived from the governor of New York and from a colonel from Charleston to the effect that 200 Frenchmen had joined forces with 500 Indians in the area of the Mississippi river and attacked a certain Indian nation who trade with the English in Carolina and Georgia and are friends of the English.[17] It seems that they wished to vanquish these Indians and then invade the adjoining territory. It is being assumed that they are the Cherokee Indians, who have until now been feuding with the Creeks; Mr. Oglethorpe is exercising his utmost effort to reconcile these two tribes, for in these letters it is also mentioned that the Frenchman whom Mr. Oglethorpe had saved and ransomed from the Indians who were about to burn him alive as a French prisoner is now one of this troop and among their leaders.[18] Just as this report had been sent express to Purysburg and Savannah, Mr. Oglethorpe was also informed from Charleston by messengers on horseback; it is assumed that he knows of the designs of the French long before the news reaches New York and Charleston.

Tuesday, the 28th of August. I learned here that the rains had been unusually heavy in our area last Saturday, while Savannah was not affected. In some of the low-lying spots, the water has risen so high that the herdsman could not assemble the cattle in the woods, and therefore almost half of the herd had been dispersed. Today, somebody has been sent out on horseback to drive them back together.

[A Reformed shoemaker from Purysburg let me know that he would like to move to our town so as to carry on his trade here if we would have him. The Reformed in Savannah are quite obstinate and contentious; and, although his neighbors have given this man a good testimony, it is difficult to agree to his request. True, we urgently need a shoemaker, for nothing much can be accomplished with Zettler, who has only half learned the trade. Maybe we will get somebody from Europe. We know of no opportunity of sending mail to England, so we will not be able to write and give news of Ulich's death until Captain Thomson, who is expected every day now, has arrived.]

Wednesday, the 29th of August. I inquired of Mrs. N. [Floerel] how she was faring both in body and soul. Her reply was: "God is now fully uncovering my perdition to me; I am learning to understand fully the 2nd chapter of book I of Johann Arndt's *Of True Christianity*; and I see ever more clearly why the Lord has seen fit to bring me to Ebenezer." I talked to her partly about what I wish to present in connection with the 1st chapter of the Book of Ruth, and partly about the beautiful words of Zacharias in Luke 1:78–79—"Through the tender mercy of our God, whereby the dayspring from on high has visited us, to give light to them," etc.—which are a great blessing not only for the blind among Jews and heathen, but also for those souls who wish to recognize their perdition and consider themselves the most miserable and pitiful people worth only eternal darkness. For the Savior intervenes for these and shows that He is the light coming into the world so as to lighten the path of the darkest sinners, to refresh them and to make them blessed. There is salvation under the wings of this sun of grace.

[My dear colleague has talked to old Mrs. Spielbiegler and tried to relieve her of her erroneous assumptions concerning her faith and her salvation; however, as has happened to me on another occasion, he was ill received in that she not only offered all sorts of excuses and prevarications, but responded quite rudely and, after his departure, directed her wicked and rough temper against another in the most shameful manner. Her son had some business with me, and I told him of the conduct of his mother against the Lord's word and against His servants and asked him to seek an occasion to impress this on her in love. I sent him on his way with the verse: "Obey and follow your ministers"[19] and without complaining. He is as bad as she is, but I had to tell him the truth for once.]

I hear that the water in Old Ebenezer has risen so high that it has almost destroyed the milldam and the sawmill itself, so that there cannot be any attempt at repairing and restoring. This work costs a great sum of money, and therefore the Lord Trustees are again suffering a great loss. It is said that the servants there will be moved to another place, since the mill can no longer be maintained where it is. When we still lived there, we once had quite a heavy flood too, but it seems not to have been quite as bad as they are describing the present one to be.

The widow Arnsdorf has for quite some time now intended to take her two girls out of the orphanage, and today she brought them home. In today's meeting, the two children were lovingly admonished in their mother's presence to let that be accomplished in them that their dear Lord has intended through all the physical and spiritual benefits granted to them. In the end, we prayed with them and the others. It seems that the mother no longer needs to have her children in the orphanage, and we are not at all opposed to their making room for others. They have both conducted themselves well in the orphanage and have given us hope that they may one day become useful to the Lord and to men, provided that they continue to accept Christian discipline and admonitions.

Thursday, the 30th of August. Last night during the prayer meeting the man whom I had taken in as a servant for my household about eight months ago died against his and our expectations. His name was Peter Heinrich and he came from Württemberg. He had long been ill with the fever and used all the medical prescriptions faithfully; in the end, he suffered from swelling, which caused him much suffering, although he always remained patient and content. He was not only a right faithful worker, but has let himself be brought to the recognition of himself and of the Lord Jesus, his Savior, through the word of the gospel. Therefore he accepted with much gratitude our comfort from the Lord's word and our words about the paths to salvation. He can therefore be said to have come to rest after what must have been much unrest. Since the swelling had receded from his arms and he had been able to breathe more freely, he had believed as late as yesterday that there was still hope for improvement, but in the evening he went as quickly as a snuffed-out light. His wife had died in Savannah a year ago from a similar swelling. He leaves three daughters in our town:[20] the middle one is going to marry a carpenter after the harvest; the oldest is quite weak and has often been ill with epilepsy and other symptoms, but is working in my house as much as her strength allows, all the while preparing herself for eternity and accepting good advice from us; the youngest is maid with one of the Salzburgers and is a faithful and industrious little thing. Apart from these children, there are a grown son and a daughter of the deceased in Savannah-Town, where they are in the service of an English merchant. We have not heard anything of them except for what this very merchant once told me.

Friday, the 31st of August. God is giving us such dry and beautiful weather that we could not wish for any better for the harvest. We have cool air now both at night and in the morning and evening, and it is not too hot during the day for workers. In yesterday's prayer meeting we heard the beautiful expression of Ruth. Naomi had heard that the Lord had visited His people and given them bread, which will remind us of our duty to consider the present rich harvest as a merciful visitation of the Lord and to use it to better purpose than did the Jews, of whom the Lord Christ in the recently read gospel had to say, with tears in His eyes, that they had not known the time when they were visited, whereupon a terrible tribulation of rage had to be visited upon them. As the Lord in His wisdom has seen fit to report on this occurrence of Naomi and Ruth at such length, we shall use all of it to our advantage with His merciful help; and we can only marvel that in previous times we did not seek and find in this book that which the Lord has now revealed to us.

In today's and yesterday's prayer meeting we received much edification and food for thought from the deep love between this mother-in-law and her daughter-in-law, their willingness to render service to each other, their warm talk to each other on their journey, her edifying words when she took leave and her blessings, the good name which the Israelites gained by Naomi's honest conduct with these two young widows and probably also with others—verse 10—as well as Naomi's wise prudence with regard to the resolutions of the two daughters-in-law, the inconstancy and the dominant worldly mind and fear of the cross on the part of Orpah, and the deepfelt honesty and right holy resolution of Ruth. We also learned from Naomi's wish and prayer, verses 8–9, which God did not let fall on the earth nor leave unfulfilled in Ruth (as shown in the following story), what a great benefaction it is that so many honest and faithful servants and children of the Lord wish us and ask for all the good in body and spirit before the Lord's face, which wishes and prayers shall only benefit those, however, who, like Ruth, acquiesce in the divine order, whereas Orpah was left with empty hands because of her guilt.

SEPTEMBER

Saturday, the 1st of September. Yesterday between ten and eleven in the evening four gentlemen from Savannah arrived here and stayed with me, because they were acquainted with me and my dear colleague. They were Colonel Stephens, the storehouse manager Mr. Jones, and Mr. Oglethorpe's secretary, Mr. Moore, who is also Adjutant-General of Mr. Oglethorpe's regiment, and a doctor whom we did not know. They had received news that the flooding water had made the sawmill in Old Ebenezer entirely unusable, which great damage they wished to see with their own eyes and report to both Mr. Oglethorpe and the Trustees. They returned at about noon and travelled back to Savannah after lunch. They were pleased by everything they saw at our place and in the orphanage.

In Ebenezer[1] several oxen have been trained to pull, which have been used until now at the sawmill. Now that the sawmill has become unusable and can hardly be repaired, I have asked the storehouse manager for one or two oxen for a few weeks, because we in the orphanage are intending to train a pair of young oxen for the same purpose, and this is to be granted to us very shortly. The gentlemen can well see that, even if the sawmill had remained in a usable condition, the Lord Trustees would have had very little use from it. If we, who are the nearest neighbors, were to fetch our boards from there, they would cost more than if we had them sawn by a couple of people at our place.

Sunday, the 2nd of September. It rained a great deal yesterday and especially today, and this has caused some discomfort for our people who come in from the plantations to divine service. We treated today's gospel for the 9th Sunday after Trinity, which was the same material we had treated on the 6th and 8th Sundays after Trinity, namely, "Appearance and power of Godliness."[2] In the exordium we applied it to the first two brothers (Genesis 4) and in the tractation to the example of the pharisee and the poor publican. Oh, how necessary it is for this teaching to be taught diligently so that the people will be aroused from their sleep of complacency and self-deceit. In the catechization my dear colleague began the fourth major article of the catechism concerning baptism, and in the prayer meeting in the orphanage he read something about the treasure of baptism from Statius' *Treasure Chamber*.[3] May the Lord let children and adults highly value the grace that has come to them already in their tenderest childhood, without their deserving it or being worthy of it, yea, without their asking for it.

Monday, the 3rd of September. After the hour in which several members of the congregation had assembled in my house for prayers, a woman remained behind and complained to me with many tears about her sins and the plight of her soul. She is faring just as David confesses in the 38th Psalm, and she wishes to go with her sins to the Lord Jesus but cannot do it. She is finding no comfort and strength in her prayers; but the more she prays the more sins she remembers and the greater they become. However, she is somewhat comforted by hearing that many righteous people and children of God in this congregation are thinking of her in their prayers also, which God will surely look upon with mercy for the sake of Christ, even if her own prayer is not worthy of being heard. Among other things, I told her that penitent and humbled sinners could be comforted by the fact that the prayer of the poor publican, who was so low in his own eyes and also despised by the world, was cited by Christ himself as being a prayer heard by God, for otherwise it is written in the troubleladen hearts of penitent people: "God heareth no sinners." God did not let her pray so far in vain, I added, for she should look upon her recognition of her deep perdition as an especial blessing of God. She should merely continue: the Lord would surely let His time and hour come when He would refresh her.

At the same time I explained to her the important word "faith" as found in Romans 4 in the example of Abraham, the father of all children of faith. I told her that, through the grace of God, she would have to practice following Him in trusting hope, since (according to reason) there is nothing to hope for. To be sure, it is hard to believe that God would be able and willing to show mercy to such a vile and wicked sinner as she acknowledges herself to be and would save her from her sins and bring her to salvation; yet He has promised this, and one must learn to trust. She had to admit that what Jesus says is true: "Thou hast wearied me with thine iniquities"; yet she cannot believe the subsequent verse: "I shall blot out thy transgressions for mine own sake," etc., which is joined to the foregoing and should not be separated from it. Because she is being tormented by some special sins and hopes to find rest only after certain conditions have been fulfilled, I cited a couple of Bible verses for her use and warned her against the error of not wishing to come to Christ before she has somewhat compensated for her wicked deed.

Mrs. N. was exceedingly pleased that I visited her. If we do not call on her for some time, she thinks we have something against her and therefore has less heart to visit us in our homes for private edification. It is a shortcoming of several of our parishioners that they refrain from coming to us and making use of our council and instruction either out of shyness or because they know how busy we are. We seldom find their husbands at home, and therefore such visits would be very useful to them. Because N. has planted a bit on his plantation and therefore must remain out there most of the week, his wife is much hindered by their small and always sickly child from coming to the prayer meeting. This causes her much worry and disquiet, which I tried to dispel by speaking to her. When I asked about her husband, she answered that his lack of faith showed itself rather clearly when want and trials occurred, but that he has been proving for some time to be much better than formerly; and I was very pleased to hear in what a loving, thorough, and scriptural way she is correcting him and reminding him of his Christian duty.

Tuesday, the 4th of September. The children who are being prepared for Holy Communion have not been worked on entirely in vain, rather they have revealed some of the good that the Lord has effected in them through His word. However, we have not wished to be too hasty in confirming them and letting them go to Holy Communion, but have given them many opportunities to prepare themselves better and better through a true conversion for this important undertaking. Today I learned that the little girls sometimes gather to pray together; and, because they have done it in the fields among the corn, I advised them to do it in a hut, even if it were only in a stall, so that they would be nearer to people.

I visited the widow N., who has been sick for some weeks with quartan fever and has hardly gone out because of it. I had occasion to discuss many edifying things with her and hope it will prove useful. God has prepared her spirit nicely to apply His word to the proper purpose; and for some time now we have observed she has more confidence in us than in former times. Because she is poor and has a heap of children,[4] we try to help her in every way. When she is healthy and can work, she receives orders for spinning and knitting from the orphanage, especially since cold weather is gradually approaching.

Wednesday, the 5th of September. Mrs. N. visited me to tell me something about the state of her soul and to ask for advice. Her conversation and prayer truly strengthened my heart and caused me a new and very special awakening. She knows how to extol the mercy of God in Christ, which she has received for her conversion and continues to receive anew every day; and her heart and mouth are full of God's praise. She bears in her heart all Christendom, especially our benefactors and benefactresses and also the condition of our congregation and orphanage; and in her conversations and prayers she wishes nothing more than for all people to be helped and brought to feel the dear mercy of Christ. She also prays diligently for those who have helped us to come to this place as ministers and to be maintained without any hardship to the congregation. The blessing of the ministry is very dear to her. Her children are very dear to her heart; and in her prayers she struggles right earnestly for their salvation. Not long ago it occurred to her with great clarity and to her unutterable joy that God would certainly have mercy on her children and bring them to salvation. She lives her entire Christianity in constant struggle and praise of God. She is a true jewel in the congregation.[5]

I had the men of the congregation in my room to discuss with them several things, which concern chiefly their cattle and some arrangements.

Those people who are brought into this colony as indentured servants behave very badly for the most part and cause all sorts of disorder when they have the chance. Some time ago we accepted a man and his family at our place purely out of compassion, and they have all been well provided for; yet their hypocrisy and laziness are becoming more and more apparent. Of these same German people we took someone into the orphanage at his fervent request but he has now become a burden to the manager and his wife.[6] May the Lord let this and that person be impressed by the beautiful example of Ruth and Naomi, whom we are now treating in chapter 2. They were both quiet in their great poverty, content with the guidance of God, and not a burden on their wealthy friends; but they trusted in *Elschadai* that He would let His hour of help come and would let them find mercy and favor in someone's eyes when it was useful for them. Ruth, as a new proselyte, was tested as to whether her departure from her country was done solely for the sake of God and her salvation; and she stood the test and thus gave a beautiful example of love and respect for her in-laws and of sincere humility and diligence, nor was she ashamed of the lowly task of gleaning. For this she was deemed worthy of divine providence and guidance, so that it is written of them: "Thou shalt guide me with thy counsel, and afterward receive me to glory."

Thursday, the 6th of September. This morning I walked to Old Ebenezer for the exercise and at the same time visited four sick men of the German indentured servants, to whom I gave God's counsel for their salvation according to the nature of their circumstances; and the well ones listened too. Like many others, these men hope for salvation for the mere reason that they are baptized Christians, pray with their mouths, and are, in their minds, sorry for their sins; and therefore we must show them publicly and privately that God demands of those who wish to be saved not only the name of Christian, the use of the means of salvation, and civil righteousness, but a true change of mind, in which I was well served, among other things, by the two verses in Matthew 7, "Not everyone who saith," etc. and Hebrews 3:12–13, "Take heed, brethren, lest there be," etc., compared with Ezechiel 36, "A new heart also will I give you," etc., and likewise, "Create in me a clean heart, O God," etc.

Friday, the 7th of September. I unexpectedly came upon the biography of the late minister's wife, Mrs. Majer in Halle, which I do not think I am reading only by chance but rather I believe that our dear Lord has been keeping the edification in it for me and my family for this particular period, in which we need it because of our domestic situation. This afternoon I read a bit from this edifying biography to the people who had assembled for private edification; I intend to continue with it at our next gathering, and I promise the Lord's blessing from it for me and others. What simply edifies me in private, is doubly edifying when I use it again in a sermon or at a gathering. This can be attributed to the promise of the Lord Jesus, who says, "For where two or three are gathered together in my name, there am I (the God of blessing, from whom power emanates) in the midst of them." The dear Pastor Majer is often in my mind with the last conversation I had with him upon receiving my vocation; and for all his sincere affection and love I wish him thousandfold blessings from the Lord for the conduct of his office and the management of his house. I consider it an especial benefaction that he let me preach in his affiliated church at the time he went away for a few weeks; for our marvelous God mercifully wished to prepare me then for my present station.

Saturday, the 8th of September. We have had rainy weather for several days and hope that the Lord, who holdeth all things in His hand, will give us dry weather again in His time, since we need it greatly for this harvest. We have had a great deal of rain all summer, because of which the grass has, to be sure, remained green and continued to grow; but it is said to have become sour and very harmful for the cattle, for which reason several large calves have died. Also, a Salzburger found that a young cow he had slaughtered had the dropsy. The wet summer would not have hurt the beans on dry soil if they had not been devoured by the deer. Those people who wish to save their beans must watch them at night and scare away the game with shooting and shouting.

I inspected this and that in the orphanage and found everything in good order. The dear Lord is giving Kalcher and his wife grace to get along loyally and thriftily with the blessing that He has granted for maintaining His work; and they know how to make everything useful for their economy. The food is, to be sure, simple and common fare, but so well and purely prepared that no one could ask for anything better; and for this Mrs. Kalcher has a beautiful talent. They both are most careful not to let the least thing spoil so that it would be thrown away, or not to use everything faithfully; they observe the established order in every detail and earnestly pray the Lord for mercy and prudence in the execution of their task, wherein they find honest assistance and support in Mrs. N., that woman who knows how to pray so strongly and believingly.[7] And though they fully merit anything used for their own welfare and sustenance by their unremitting, faithful, and industrious work, they consider themselves quite unworthy of any benefits that they may enjoy in the orphanage and thank the dear Lord from their heart that He has let them come to this house and provided for them in His fatherly fashion both in their spirits and their bodies. I wish I were in a position to recompense them somewhat for all their honesty and faithfulness, but the Lord can be trusted to do this in His time.

Sunday, the 9th of September. In the evening a young Salzburger called on me and told me, to my great pleasure, about the *magnalia Dei*[8] that he has experienced today and at other times. In his conversion, God opened his eyes; and he cannot marvel enough at his former blindness and lack of understanding, which he himself could not believe. Even though it is still bitter for him in his daily struggle, God is nevertheless granting him much refreshment and comfort so that the word of God, which he hears on Sundays and workdays, is becoming ever sweeter and dearer. He pities his relatives who are still in Germany; for he rightfully assumes that they will be satisfied with the external appearance of Christianity and thus lose their salvation. He told me of several serious obstacles lying in the way of him and others in Germany so that he could not achieve any true change of heart, and this made no little impression on me.

May God give His servants and children wisdom to act correctly with the Salzburgers, in whom He has done great things by powerfully and miraculously saving them from Babel, so that their emigration will not consist in external matters but rather that they will all be delivered like little lambs into the loving arms of the Lord Jesus. May He be praised in that (as is written in today's gospel) He has separated us from the people and has already begun His work in many; He shall also carry it to a glorious conclusion. This reminded me of the beautiful words of Hosea 2, "I will bring her into the wilderness, and speak comfortably to her." The song *Mein Schöpffer bilde mich*, etc. was very impressive and comforting for me during today's sermon while I was treating our reformation through Christ; and therefore I also recommended it to the listeners in the repetition hour.

A Reformed woman from Old Ebenezer requested for herself and her husband an Arndt's *True Christianity*, which I had recently recommended to them as a very useful book when I visited them. These are the people whom Sanftleben recommended to Court Chaplain Ziegenhagen and whose redemption from the Lord Trustees' service he requested. They depend upon external honesty and consider themselves better than other people. I recently tried to demonstrate to them their perdition and the inadequacy of civil righteousness and of a virtuous and quiet life and consequently of the inevitable necessity of a true conversion, all of which they will find even more clearly and thoroughly in the book I have given them, provided they read it without prejudice, as they have promised.

Monday, the 10th of September. Yesterday I received written permission from Savannah to fetch a yoke of oxen for the use of the orphanage for some time. This permission I had requested because necessity demanded it. They were brought here to-day and will be used tomorrow for bringing in the timber for construction, at which time two young oxen will be trained in drayage for the orphanage. That is a new blessing for the orphanage, for it would be very difficult for us to haul up the heavy lumber for building the barn, since there is only one horse in the community.

In today's evening prayer meeting we repeated the sermon from yesterday morning, because the time was too short for it yesterday. Through the grace of God we are attentive to lay, for ourselves and for those who hear us, a firm foundation in the recognition of the deep perdition of human nature and to show the way a man can be saved from it and be renewed in the image of God and finally be brought back to the salvation he forfeited; this was the chief content of yesterday's sermon. As long as man is blind in the recognition of himself, so long he will refuse to humble himself before God and have no real yearning for the Physician Christ and His dear medication.

Tuesday, the 11th of September. The community's cattle have increased well in the past few years, since various Salzburgers have bought an occasional head with the money they have earned here. Because the pasturage is now becoming too scarce and the herdsmen are not proving truly loyal, the men decided today in my room to drive those cows into the woods that are not giving milk and will be of no immediate use, and then to seek them at a convenient time and bring them back. They will all be well marked with a brand and a cut in the ear and also on the horns[9] so that we can distinguish them from the Trustees' cattle and whatever else roams around in the forest. This practice is, to be sure, subject to many difficulties and to the danger of losing a few head; but, for the previously mentioned reasons, we know of no other solution.

Because the Lord Trustees have several hundred head in Old Ebenezer, our pasturage is very restricted; and Mr. Oglethorpe gives no permission to drive the cattle across Ebenezer Creek, because the land is supposed to belong to the Indians, even though the Englishmen in Old Ebenezer let their horses and draft-oxen graze across the creek. If the cattle that have been driven off are to be found again in the spring, or whenever it is necessary, we will need horses, for which, however, there is no money on hand. I hope to find some man in Carolina who is willing to give the people perhaps a half year's credit for some horses. Meanwhile the dear Lord will grant a physical blessing. It would have been good for the cattle's pasture if a village commons had been surveyed for the town, but the Lord Trustees' plan did not allow for that. The still unoccupied plantations must serve the present colonists as pasture; and, when the land is fully occupied, everyone will have to graze his cattle on his own land, for which purpose forty-eight acres (since two acres are for the garden by the town) are rather small, to say nothing of the fact that there are no pastures or grassy areas at all in many places.

I came into a hut where the husband had just informed his wife that they had suffered the loss of a young cow, which had lost its calf and afterwards its milk, because it had run away from the herd. Although these people are very poor and the loss is consequently very great for them, their spirits remained composed, and they applied their loss to their greater faith. They complained about their hearts, which were revealing themselves as wicked and treacherous in their tribulations, and they lament to God in all simplicity. The wife asked about the song she had heard sung yesterday in the private gathering, which had impressed her and whose beginning she did not know. It was, *Wie Gott mich führt, so will ich gehen*, etc. I read it to her and her husband to their great refreshment and edification.

Wednesday, the 12th of September. I was told that two people had gotten into an angry altercation about some external matter, from which strife and discord had arisen. When I visited them today, I found them both sick. I mentioned the discord that had recently occurred between them and admonished them to penitence. They both lack a true recognition of their innate misery; so, when they speak of sins, they understand only external outbursts and, when they are not particularly aware of these, they consider themselves to be pious. However, if they misbehave coarsely, as previously mentioned, they call it an overhasty and human weakness, for which one must ask God's pardon. One of the two has more recognition than the other and is more easily convinced, whereas the other is ignorant and has fancied her faith and comfort in Christ's merits so firmly that she will live and die therein. In addition to being blind and ignorant, she is also lazy, does not come regularly to church, and will not visit us in our homes so that we can instruct her.

I spoke to another person, who is just as blind as she, and persists therein despite all the efforts we apply, in order to see whether I could reach her heart with the word of God. However, she began as usual to talk partly of external matters and partly of her diligent prayer, also of the great tribulations she had suffered all her life. I interrupted her, however, and cited the verse, "It is appointed that man will die, and after that the judgment"; I told her that she had more reason than other people to think diligently of both points: she could not avoid either of them; and, since she had to stand in judgment after death, she should reflect whether she would stand the test and be able to hear the joyful voice: "Come ye blessed of my Father." Answer: "I pray diligently; and, because the Lord Jesus died for all men, He will take me as a poor sinner into heaven." I then asked whether Jesus had not died for all men and all sinners and whether she thought that everyone would be saved. Answer: "Not all, because they do not believe." She, however, did believe, and therefore she would be saved, for it is written, "He that believeth"; and, besides, she prayed diligently. I showed her that no one is saved through prayer, as she thinks, but rather we are directed to be brave and to pray, N.B., so that we may become worthy or come to a state of grace that pleases the Lord.

I asked her further whether she had not read that the devils also believe and thus tremble, as impudent Christians, who are frivolous and full of self-imagined comfort, do not even do. There are, accordingly, two kinds of faith, namely an historical, and at the same time self-made faith, which is found in all unconverted people who are Christian in name only, and also a true faith which God infuses into a penitent and contrite heart and which purifies the heart and makes pious and holy those who receive it. Since she made fun of saints and the holy life (and used improper words about them before my very ears), whereas faith makes sinners and Godless men into saints and pious people, as it was the purpose of the passion and death of the Lord Jesus that we might not only be saved in time and eternity but be reborn sanctified and in the image of God (John 17:17); and furthermore, as I said, since she knew nothing of all that, but did know about many outbursts of sin and about her frivolity, she should not hold it against me if I had to tell her from God's word and my own recognition that her faith, which she imagined, was nothing but unbelief and that, if she remained in this condition, she would come to no good.

When she became disturbed by this, I asked her (1) whether she believed that I, as minister of this congregation, understood the way to heaven through Holy Scripture as well as she and others, (2) whether I meant well with her and their souls and would like to lead them to heaven, (3) whether I could not test the condition of my parishioners better than they themselves, etc. When she did not doubt this, I asked her to believe what I had told her from God's word about her dangerous condition. Because of her prejudices and strong belief in her long-continued faith, I said, she could not believe that she had no faith and was consequently in an accursed condition; and therefore, among other prayers, she should begin to pray zealously as follows: "Dear God, my minister has told me that my faith is a conceit and unbelief and I cannot be saved in this condition. I do not yet recognize myself to be that way. I may well be blind in my self-recognition and in my recognition of the way to salvation. Oh, have mercy upon me so that I shall not deceive myself!" She promised to do this.

A Salzburger woman told me that the word of God in a sermon had so penetrated her heart that she could not stop weeping. The above-mentioned N. had been standing next to her outside of church and asked her why she was weeping, assuming she must be ill. When she answered that she had good grounds to weep, because she heard from God's word that our Lord had suffered so greatly to redeem us and that she was still so wicked, frivolous, and ungrateful, the other woman thereupon said, "I won't bother to cry about that. Our Lord has a broad back and can bear much," and these dreadful and frivolous words caused her even more distress and sighs, whereupon she remembered the verse, "Then cometh the devil, and taketh away the word out of their hearts," etc. May God have mercy on the miserable woman! After our exchange she called my attention to what had occurred recently between her and my dear colleague and confessed that it had vexed her greatly when he recited especially for her, and applied to her, the verse, "Many sorrows shall be to the wicked." Thereupon I reminded her earnestly of her rude and disgraceful behavior toward him and admonished her to recognition and penitent remorse for this grave sin, too, and also recited this verse for her again, "Obey your ministers," etc. "and not with grief: for that is unprofitable for you."

Thursday, the 13th of September. In yesterday's evening prayer meeting we learned that, as indicated by time and circumstances, Boas had entertained his workers during and after the winnowing of the crops he had harvested, and had given them a feast of joy and thanksgiving. However, this feast has degenerated in Christendom, especially among the rural population, into great abuse and disorder, as is known to me especially in my native land of Lower Lusatia. Of the pious Boas, it is written that, when he had eaten and drunk, his heart was (according to the Hebrew) good and merry, and (as the Jews themselves interpret it) he, as housefather, praised the Lord his God for this good land and rich harvest as an example and encouragement for the others;[10] and we applied this and other things to our circumstances during this harvest season, as we have received many good housekeeping and harvest rules from this good book. The manager of the orphanage was still in my room after the prayer meeting and requested me to praise the Lord with him and the people of the orphanage in a special ceremony after they have brought in the crops which the Lord has granted the orphanage, and to awaken ourselves to a truly grateful and God-pleasing use of those gifts; and this shall be done with God's help.

The oxen we borrowed from Old Ebenezer to help in hauling wood are being sent back today because they are too old and incapable of pulling, although they are trained. In this country, people undertake many things wrongly, and the people who are employed by the Lord Trustees in their business seek nothing but their monthly wages and their regular provisions. Therefore the desired purpose is achieved in few things. The yokes and whatever else pertain to drayage are so clumsy that the oxen suffer great harm and are hindered in their work. One of our carpenters is making us a yoke like those used in the Salzburg area, which the oxen carry not on their necks but on their horns. We hope to accomplish more in one day with our young oxen, which are very tame, than in several days with theirs; and with theirs you have to use a horse in front of them because they are trained not to take a step or to pull anything without a horse.

Friday, the 14th of September. A woman called on me and accused herself greatly because of her lack of faith in her Christianity. She complained of herself and the sloth and wickedness of her heart, but also of her sorrow and heartbreak because of her family, who are so little concerned with their Christianity. Her husband is often powerfully moved, and she sees that he prays and acts as if he wishes to be saved; but, as soon as he leaves his prayers, he becomes vexed and angry over any little thing, and that is a sign that his prayer has helped him but little. I read something to her and my family from Arndt's *True Christianity* and prayed with her.

Another man thanked me, in the presence of other people, for the little book or sermon by the late Professor Francke, which had been given to him. It is called *Concerning the True Essence of Christianity* (Trinity Sunday, John 3).[11] It showed him the way to heaven, he said, and did him much good; so he respects it highly. He complained that he and his family lack a zealous and serious prayer, otherwise things would go better for them. I told him where many people go wrong in their prayers: (1) They do not seek a silent place and do not turn inward, but are either too busy with other people or lost in distractions. (2) Their prayer is not truly penetrating and forceful, and it is generally looked upon as a part of the divine service one must perform, or else one would not be a Christian, whereas it should be used as a means to receive the grace of God from the abundance of Christ. Most people who pray do not truly recognize their lack and do not hunger for the means of salvation. (3) Even if they have prayed earnestly and their hearts have been warmed by it, they do not remain right before the Lord like David; and in doing their business they do not wait for the gift they have prayed for but distract their senses again and do not reflect that prayer must be connected to vigil. He who prays earnestly will find some obstacle in his path that wishes to rob him of the strength and blessing of his prayer. But if they remained right still before God, then they would remember their requests and afterwards run up quickly and thank God for it. That is the way, I said, that He will show us His salvation.

Saturday, the 15th of September. I kindly showed N. that she had no recognition of herself and of her lack and of the danger to her soul, which are more easily recognized in her by others who have begun to tread the narrow path to heaven than by herself. Therefore she should, I said, gladly accept and learn to believe what others tell her about her salvation. It costs more to be saved than people usually imagine; and therefore it shall come to pass that (as the Savior Himself assures us in Matthew 7 and Luke 13) many will be deceived on that day of judgment and find themselves at a very unblessed place, as we can see in the example of the rich man whose eyes were opened only too late.[12] If anyone had told him during his life that he was on the broad way and would be lost, he would have taken it badly in his blindness, just as people, and also she, are doing. She had no grounds (I added) to be disquieted because she did not have such heavy work now as in N.N., for it will soon come. God is now giving her time to care all the better for her soul. And, since she is lacking greatly in recognition, I offered myself to instruct her if only she wished to come to me (however, she has no desire for this, or to learn to read, although she had begun to learn to read in N.).

I warned her against acquaintanceship with wicked people, instead I advised her to become acquainted with honest women who will tell her what the Lord has done for their souls in this wilderness and how He has brought them to recognition of their previous blindness, disbelief, etc. These women thank God sincerely for bringing them here; and this is the way it will gradually go with her too, finally, if she will only accept good advice and become another person through the grace of God. Because she will not come to me herself, I shall visit her often and undertake something with her for the salvation of her soul. She is very ignorant and needs instruction. Because of her fever she has come to church and prayer meeting only occasionally so far. To be sure, she is pleased with our divine service, but not with this place and this strange country, because she cannot be with as many people as she was accustomed to since childhood. She does not wish to continue learning to read, which she began in N.

We are finishing the fourth and last chapter of the book of Ruth; and I thank God on my part for all the dear truths that He, in His great mercy, has let me recognize in contemplating this story. God has so gloriously blessed the sermons in some of those with whom I have had a chance to speak recently that I hope we will again find a joyful fruit from it in blessed eternity. This evening during the last part of this story several verses became very clear and living for us, such as "Thou shalt guide me with thy counsel, and afterward receive me to glory," etc. Before this it is written, "My son, give me thine heart, and let thine eyes observe my ways," etc., which verses were excellently illustrated by the example of Ruth, likewise Psalms 113:5–9. With what expressions our dear David must actually have looked upon his dear great-grandmother! This cannot be other than comforting for bowed souls who have been humbled under God's hand. Concerning Boas we heard that he was not only a wealthy man but also kindhearted with his wealth (chapter 3:7); and therefore he applied his temporal wealth to the good of widows, orphans, and miserable people and does not belong among the rich of whom the Lord says, "How hard it is for a rich man to enter the kingdom of heaven," etc.

Ruth, although a Moabite and a stranger to the people of Israel, achieved the honor of being an ancestress of the Lord Jesus; and Christ says in Matthew 12, "Whosoever doeth the will of my Father in heaven, he is my mother," etc., to which is added the verse, "If any man will come after me, let him deny himself (like Ruth) and take up his cross every day (like Ruth) and follow me" (as Ruth did too, chapter 2:12). In this order one will become a servant and even a mother, brother, and sister of the Lord Jesus. Oh, great honor! It can be clearly recognized that the behavior of present-day Christians at weddings, baptisms, and other public gatherings differs greatly from that which is described in this chapter; and we admonished them of what is most important in this matter.

Sunday, the 16th of September. Last week during my visits to the people in the congregation I noticed that some of them, both men and women, persist in their obstinate ignorance, which stems from their carelessness and laziness, since we give them opportunity enough to reach a recognition of the truth. There are people of both sexes in the congregation who have advanced not only in the literal but also in the spiritually salutary recognition of the truths of the law and of the gospel. To-day's gospel, Luke 10:23 ff., gave me an opportunity to direct my sermon to this[13] frame of mind in some of my parishioners, which is so odious to me. The exordium was from 2 Timothy 3:7 (cf. verse 15). Because the hearts of such frivolous people are filled partly with desires and partly with theoretical and practical errors, none of the divine and salutary truths can enter in or stick to them.

The sermon itself treated of the recognition of truth for godliness, (1) that the divine truth and recognition of it are a great and dear blessing of God, and (2) that they must be applied for a practice of godliness. During the sermon I had to pour forth my sorrow at the people's willful ignorance; and I did this again during the repetition hour, revealing not only its causes but also its danger and pointing out means to escape from it. I also had to indicate that I was planning to examine the people about the basic truths of Christianity and would not allow the willfully ignorant to take Holy Communion. For the clarification and confirmation of my sermon during the repetition hour I was served excellently by the beautiful example of Henning Kusen, who was at first ignorant but was later taught by God. I read this example as far as time would allow, after having briefly repeated the chief themes of the sermon. May our gracious Lord grant His blessing to our imperfect efforts! Because good examples make strong impressions on the spirit and reveal not only the necessity but also the possibility of an active Christianity, I referred in the repetition hour to the beautiful conduct of some Salzburgers in Prussia,[14] some of whom have learned to read in their old age and have come to a beautiful recognition.

Monday, the 17th of September. This morning I found several men at a very necessary communal task, which I had, to be sure, recommended at the end of last week but had not expected them to accomplish so quickly. Because there is so much to do now during the harvest season, I look upon this willingness as a fruit of the word of God that was preached yesterday; and I thank God for it in my heart, just as we once saw in the example of the prophetess Deborah (Judges 5:2).

N. received one of the best plantations by lot; and people have hoped from the beginning that he would share it with someone who lacked good land, since he could not use so much good land anyway. Therefore he is voluntarily sharing with N.; and he considers it more of a blessing than an obligation to divide his plantation. In exchange he is receiving half of N.'s plantation near the city, which, to be sure, has no good land but all the more good timber. N. had not wished to take up farming, and therefore he selected a plantation that lay nearby and had a quantity of timber for himself and his profession. However, when he saw that most of the congregation are supplied with good land along Abercorn Creek, he developed a desire for some too; and I am pleased that he has been able to be provided for in a good manner. I and my dear colleague still have no plantations, otherwise ours would have been at his disposal. No one suits this neighborhood better than N.; for he is always compliant, never gets angry, and has courage to resist public wickedness and impudence. He called on me yesterday; and I must admit, to the praise of God, that I received much edification from him. He is earnestly seeking the salvation of his soul.

In our private gathering we had a right hearty refreshment together from the extremely beautiful song *Herr Jesu Christ mein Fleisch und Blut*, which was first read aloud to our hearts and then sung; and by it we were again reminded of the virtues and righteousness of the pious Ruth. In both parts of our hymnal there is such a treasure of old and new hymns that it can only be regretted that they are so little known among Christians. Therefore it might be wished that people would become familiar with them for their own and other people's edification and apply them to the proper purpose before they make up new hymns, through which the old strength-giving hymns fall into oblivion for those people who like novelty and change. It has pleased the dear Lord to afflict me for the last half year with a soreness in my mouth and throat that hinders me in singing, although not in speaking. Consequently, our singing practice has been interrupted. If the dear Lord who liveth among the praise of Israel should strengthen me, I should give our listeners continued opportunity to further this lovely and edifying undertaking.

After the prayer a woman remained with me and told me with tears that God had again let her hear many edifying things yesterday that had penetrated to her heart and that she was greatly worried because she could not yet apply to herself the treasures that Christ had merited and offered in the gospels to the faithful. She is still thoroughly worthless, she said; she must begin all over if she is ever to know how she can come to an understanding of the mercy of God and the forgiveness of sins. Last week she had spoken about Christianity with a pious man who had told her it was easier to deny the whole world than one's self. This drove her, as soon as she reached home, to pray to God to give her recognition of herself so that she would not deceive herself: perhaps her lack of self-denial was the reason she could not come to any strength and experience in her Christianity. She noticed that she had previously regretted her sins only out of fear of hell and not out of sincere love for God and had let herself thus be deterred from doing evil. That was, she said, impure. Yesterday in church during the reading of the second chapter of the prophet Daniel, she had heard that, in answer to his prayer, God revealed to Daniel the things hidden in King Nebuchadnezzar's heart that had appeared to him at night in a dream: I should now ask God on her behalf to reveal to me the reason she cannot break through[15] and achieve the taste of God's grace.

This woman is honest at heart and has great poverty of spirit; and, because she loaded a great mass of sins on her conscience in her youth and has also inclined greatly toward frivolity, pride, etc., the Lord is leading her on ways that are hard on the flesh in order to lead her all the better to a recognition of her corruption. However, at His own time, He does not leave her without comfort and hope of grace, which, nevertheless, disappear again to her humiliation and further deep brooding. I made a distinction between having God's grace and feeling it, and I showed her that such divine guidance as she was experiencing is salutary and necessary. However, it behooves her not to be so embarrassed before the Lord Jesus, who looks out for lowly and miserable people, and not to consider the grace of God, which she experiences from time to time, to be slight or herself to be incapable of it. I asked her what she thought of some other women with whom she consorts and prays; and, when I learned that she recognized a great measure of grace in them, whereas they felt themselves, in their great humility and lowliness, to be the greatest sinners, I showed her that where grace is, there are humility and poverty of spirit too and that, as long as a man continues on this path full of hunger and thirst, he is going surely, straight, and well, etc.

Tuesday, the 18th of September. For a rather long time the Lackner woman has had a series of attacks of quotidian fever and has been greatly weakened by them. She has proved herself in this sickness as a Christian should; and today I received much edification from her behavior and words. She herself recognizes that God means well with her in these external sufferings and that she has had no loss but only gain for her soul from them. Now she is worried (but surely without need) that, if her sickness should last longer and her strength decrease and her pains increase, she might become impatient and thus sin against God. However, the honest Mrs. Gruber (in whose hut she is lying sick and in whom she has a true spiritual and physical foster-mother) comforted her in this with a verse, "But God is faithful, who will not suffer you to be tempted," etc. I directed her to James 1:17. This very Mrs. Gruber and her husband often tell her that, soon after our arrival in this country, it pleased God to test them like others and pour out manifold physical woe for us, but that He had so blessed it in their souls that they still thank Him for it. They now understand from experience the verse, "Now no chastening for the present seemeth to be joyous," etc.

In this connection I told her again of the paths of trial and humiliation on which God led Ruth soon after her arrival in the land of Israel, which paths, however, had finally led to such a splendid and blessed end. I also repeated what we had heard in yesterday's prayer meeting about the godly Hannah in 1 Samuel 1, who had both inner and outer pain, dragged herself around with it for a while, had nothing but disquiet as a reward, and finally, at her husband's urging, reflected about it and went with her problem to the right door, poured out her trouble-laden heart before God, and found relief and, finally, the complete hearing of her prayer. Therefore, according to this example, the following admonition is salutary: "Cast thy burden upon the Lord, and he shall sustain thee," etc., likewise, "And call upon me in the day of trouble," etc. "This poor man cried, and the Lord heard him," etc.

I also visited Elisabeth Wassermann, who is married to Pletter. I noticed that the dear Lord is working on her powerfully through her long-lasting sickness. Her husband is honest and encourages her sincerely from God's word. He is very zealous in hearing God's word and feels its worth abundantly. He says that not a prayer meeting passes without his gaining something from it for his heart. In the presence of a single woman another man praised our dear Lord for the good opportunity He gives him in the prayer meeting to learn to understand His word better. He looks forward to the stories in the first part of the book of Samuel in a right childish way and wishes that he and others could be right grateful to the dear Lord for them.

Wednesday, the 19th of September. Before dawn today Mrs. Schneider, whose child was baptized yesterday, died unexpectedly. She has had fever up to now and got it again yesterday evening, but after the heat was gone she changed suddenly, lost understanding and speech, and lay that way until this morning. With the approval of the doctor, the child, who is also very weak, was given to Mrs. Landfelder to bring up.

For a long time Eischberger has had a withered arm; and, since none of the medicines he used internally and externally would help, someone has lent him a strap of human skin, which he has tied around his very thin arm, and he has already noted a marked improvement because of it. Previously we have considered such a cure as superstition, and I shall see how it eventually turns out. He also has holes on his chest and shoulders, which are now healing better than formerly. He has borne his cross so far with patience and has always believed that the hour of help, which is ordained by God, will finally come; and it is his resolution never to forget what the Lord has done for him.

I found N.N. at home alone and asked about his wife's Christianity, of which he could not approve. He said that she does, indeed, recognize herself as sinful and worthless; but she uses no seriousness to become better. He could not persuade her to ask him about God's word or about the sermon, even though he wished so very much to edify himself simply with her. He wishes to send her to me in the lesson that is to be scheduled for the ignorant and negligent. I also admonished N. and his wife to visit this lesson; and, because the man is irregular in visiting the prayer hour and both of them are in discord in their marriage, I told them from yesterday's prayer hour that Elkana had gone with his family from his city as far as Silo and attended divine services diligently and had tried to control the discord and disunity in his family through good means, particularly by bringing peace offerings. He himself was no quarreler and blusterer but knew how to bear Hannah's weakness with patience and love.

N. accused herself bitterly because of her sloth and said that God was working on her husband powerfully in His mercy, as she had noticed in him several times. However, because he was not keeping vigil, he soon loses his reawakening and good resolutions again. She could not persuade him to visit the prayer meetings in my house with her. He claims that the people who know that he is not yet righteous would think that he is not sincere and that it is merely hypocrisy.

Thursday, the 20th of September. This morning I again visited N. in order to give her a friendly invitation to visit the instruction in my house. She was sick and lying in bed. I asked her whether she had carried out what I had recently told her from God's word for her salvation, and she affirmed it. In order to remind her of what I had recently said and to confirm her in it even more, I read her the 8th chapter from book I of Arndt's *True Christianity*, in which is clearly and thoroughly shown that there can be no comfort from Christ's merits in an impenitent life, but rather that all who wish to have a share in Christ must convert themselves and hate and renounce sin, by which the order of salvation is demonstrated beautifully. Several points, which are especially necessary for her to note, I read out with short additions and explanations. She approved of all this, thanked me for my efforts, and promised to reflect further; and she also had me mark down the chapter.

I had scheduled the hour from one to two for giving instruction to the parishioners for the literal and spiritual recognition of the truth; and it gave me much pleasure that they overfilled my room, were very eager, and answered simply, freely, and sincerely to the questions I posed. At the beginning of the hour I had a part of the catechism recited several times so that they could gradually grasp it verbally or retain it better. However, I actually laid the so-called interrogatory parts at the end of the catechism as a basis for the catechization, because I intend to prepare the ignorant parishioners for Holy Communion. Yet the questions give me very beautiful material for instructing them in various important articles of the Christian religion: e.g., in the first question we cover the article of the state of innocence and the image of God, and after *de lapsu & peccato*;[16] likewise in question 2 concerning the law and how we should use it, in question 3 concerning penitence, etc., and in the following one concerning God and especially concerning Christ our Savior. Even though some necessary articles in our interrogatory part are not mentioned at all, the connection that the articles of faith have with one another leads me to the point that I hope, with divine assistance, to acquaint my listeners with the most necessary articles of Christian dogma. May God be pleased by this mean effort on behalf of Christ and bless it!

Friday, the 21st of September. The weather is still dry and therefore convenient for bringing in the crops, and this encourages us to praise the Lord. The rice is becoming ever riper; and, whereas in previous years it was damaged and devoured by a great multitude of little birds, we have been left in peace in this regard. On the other hand, the deer have been all the more harmful to the beans at night. They hardly turn any more when we shout and sound our clappers, and we do not accomplish much at night by shooting between the cornstalks. We are also lacking powder. Now, since our loving God has given our Salzburgers enough bread and foodstuffs this year, He will know how to provide for their clothes too, of which some of them have a right great need. Today, during our communal prayer in my room, a pious man mentioned in particular those blessings that should long since have been dispatched and at sea. May God keep everything from harm and give us joy by their early arrival. We need some winter clothing for our orphans and other workers in the orphanage but have postponed buying them until we receive a blessing from the Lord, who clothes the flowers in the field and gives each animal his hide, hair, and wool as a cover, but who has granted us men His Son and, with Him, has promised to bestow all things.

Saturday, the 22nd of September. Kalcher has been very busy this week with some helpers in hauling up the lumber for the barn, and two oxen have been trained for drayage. To be sure, it cost a great deal of effort and trouble; but, because many men from the congregation have voluntarily lent their hands and strength, everything has proceeded without harm; and the oxen, especially one of them, have not been able to balk or shake off the yoke. In putting on the yoke our people have a very good method, which is bearable for the oxen and which I have never seen before and is not customary in this country. When several join together with counsel and deed, everything is made easier and the purpose is achieved all the sooner. May God grant whatever is required for this construction! His rivers have an abundance of water, well for us if we trust in it and persevere!

This morning my dear colleague travelled to Savannah to preach the word of God to the people there, and for this we wish him divine aid and blessing.

At three o'clock in the afternoon we had the pleasure of seeing General Oglethorpe at our place. He came down the river in a trading boat with his retinue and remained for a few hours in my house, which again pleased him very much. He was delighted with our arrangements and with the industry of the Salzburgers; and, because he has received letters that the Lord Trustees are inclined to accept more Salzburgers and other persecuted Protestants, arrangements will be made to lodge them here according to their needs. The Lord Trustees no longer plan to maintain a storehouse and therefore he is pleased that our people have such a rich harvest and will gradually have oxen and hogs for slaughtering. He left six muskets and some

powder and lead here; because a number of Negroes or Moorish slaves in Carolina have taken up arms, plundered and
burned many houses, and slain the people, it is feared that they
may cross the Savannah River into this colony.[17] Since we have
no midwives and I could recommend a German woman in Savannah, he will send her up in Mr. Gronau's boat for the service
of the congregation; I consider this a very great benefaction.[18]

Mr. Oglethorpe told me with what great honor and joy he
had been received by the Indian nations and how peace had
been instituted between some of them who had long been wag-
ing war against each other. The remote nations had sent deputies to him to renew their friendship with the English and to
help them in every way in case the land they received from the
Indians should be disputed.[19] He does not believe (as rumor
now has it) that the Spaniards will try to accomplish anything
against this colony; for they have more to fear from us than we
from them, unless the Lord has ordained some misfortune for
us. He departed from us at five o'clock and assured us of his
continued affection. May God accompany him!

Sunday, the 23rd of September. N.'s wife, whom he brought
from N.,[20] is now coming to a better recognition of the truth
and is striving, with God's grace, to become what she has not yet
been, namely a true Christian, and today she used some very
fine expressions about this.

This afternoon I briefly repeated the morning's sermon on
the faith of the Samaritan as a model for us; and afterwards I
catechized concerning the keys to the kingdom, which follow in
order in the catechism. Now that Holy Communion is again approaching, we are occupied with some disobedient and impenitent persons, who have once again heard the evangelical dogma
in regard to church discipline; and at the same time they were
shown that it is more of a blessing than a punishment if we do
not allow them to go to Holy Communion in their impenitent
condition, but rather work in advance for their improvement
with love and seriousness. And, since the keys to the kingdom,
the spiritual power to forgive or retain sins, has been granted by
Christ to the entire church, then the congregation should not
leave everything up to the ministers but should do their best not
only to refuse to participate in the conduct of disorderly people,

but also to help work on them. On the other hand, it is a great mistake if impenitent people not only harden themselves against evangelical church discipline and become angry but also seek refuge in other parishioners and become strengthened in their wickedness and disobedience, which merely makes it more difficult for the servants of the church to perform their office.

Tuesday, the 25th of September. Yesterday evening, just as the prayer meeting was to be held, the dear Lord brought me back to Ebenezer. We were ready to depart from Savannah on Sunday evening; but, when I heard from Colonel Stephens that his maid was to be given to us as midwife, I postponed the journey until yesterday morning. However, she could not leave because she was tending a woman in a hard and long-lasting labor. My dear colleague travelled to Savannah last night in order to discuss various matters with Mr. Oglethorpe, who will not remain there for long; and we hope he will bring her back, if the Lord has destined her for us. Colonel Stephens has great need of her as a maid in his house, yet he is gladly giving her to us because Mr. Oglethorpe has asked him to and because he can thereby show us his kindness and affection. From this we can see how the dear Lord is still inclining the hearts of the authorities to us so that they are zealous on such occasions to show us their affection. May the Lord repay them for this! This time, using the Gospel of St. Luke 17:11 ff., I preached to the Germans in Savannah on "The Lord Jesus as the free and open well-spring against sin and impurity." All of them, even the greatest sinners, were invited to be made right beautiful and glorious, if only they would let themselves be brought into divine order.

In the afternoon I preached on the so glorious and comforting dogma of holy baptism; and I asked them to convert themselves with the prodigal son and to renew their baptismal covenant so that they would again be so blessed as when they were lifted from their baptism, and thus they would be able to gain much for themselves from holy baptism. The Lord be praised for all His aid, and may He bless everything for the sake of His kindness!

Wednesday, the 26th of September. This morning a person was in my house because of some external business, and at her departure I read her something from page 17 of the *Treasure Chest*.[21] When I visited someone in her house this afternoon, I had to recite the last words for her a couple of times so she could note them well and also recite them to her husband. She had wished to do it at noon, but she had not been able to remember the words during her work. They are: "If all together turn against me, Thou art my salvation. Who will damn me? Love hath accepted me." She was full of joy and also said these words: "They are dwelling on earth and living in heaven," also, "They are tasting of peace despite all confusion." Even though she cannot read, she takes note of such special expressions. She remembered her former legalistic condition, when she had always wished to feel an emotion; for, as long as she felt that she was happy; but, if she could not feel it anymore, then everything seemed over. My dear colleague had called on her, she said, and had encouraged her; and she had felt good during his encouragement, but afterwards she had lost everything. When she acted very frightened because of it, a Christian man had asked her about the cause of such anxious behavior; and, when he heard this, he said she should just be comforted; when things get very bad, then the time of help is not far, as he himself had experienced.

During the period of her legalistic condition[22] she had always thought, whenever the sermon in church did not go to her heart so that she had to weep because of it, then it was nothing and she had gained nothing from the preaching of the divine word. She had been in such a condition for a long time; but now she was, to put it briefly, in a condition of rest, as her expression was. She had not yet told anyone about it because she was afraid she might lose it again. She cannot praise the dear Lord enough for bringing her into this land and not somewhere else. She is looking forward with pleasure to Holy Communion, which will be held soon; and she could not marvel enough at the precious food and drink that the Lord Jesus would bestow on her. Her desire was that the Lord Jesus might prepare her properly for them. She said other things, but not everything can be written down.

Thursday, the 27th of September. This afternoon I returned from Savannah, and we have reason to thank the Lord for again giving His blessing to this trip. This time I was able to talk with Mr. Oglethorpe in more detail and to present the congregation's circumstances orally and in writing better than at other times. He will now earnestly see to it that the Lord Trustees pay the merchant in St. Gall[23] for the linen that was sent to the storehouse. In the spring he promised the people of Savannah to reward them for their industry in the field with two shillings per bushel of corn and beans; but (as he said this time) he did not wish to extend this beyond Savannah. However, when he learned that the community would be satisfied with one shilling per bushel, he allowed himself to be persuaded to grant us such a benefaction too.[24] Previously there was the condition that all the corn and beans that our people could spare had to be delivered to the storehouse, and then they would be paid the reward for their industry in addition to the going price that year; but now the people can keep their corn and can sell it how and where they wish, and they will still receive one shilling sterling for all the corn and beans they harvest. God be thanked for this!

Pichler asked through me whether he might utilize the land that he had obtained in Carolina, not far from us, through his marriage; but Mr. Oglethorpe would rather let him move away than to consent to this, because it would be prejudicial for our community.[25] It might also be a matter of consequence, so it is probably good that the judgment went that way. Among the benefactions that the Lord is now showing to my family and the congregation through Mr. Oglethorpe, I rightfully count the widow whom he has given to me as a maid and to the community as a midwife. The last time he was here and happened to hear something about my helpmeet's dangerous circumstances and to learn that we were not provided in our village with a midwife or any other woman experienced in these matters, he offered to take care of the matter in earnest. Because I could suggest an honest German woman, who had long yearned for Ebenezer, he promised to send her here, which he has now done with the consent of her recent master. Our Father in heaven knoweth what His children need.

My previous maid,[26] who has been very loyal (something that is very rare in this country), is going to marry a Salzburger. Her righteous and very industrious father, who was a servant in my home, died here a short time ago. The servant Bischof, who was sent from London five years ago for my service, will receive his freedom after the present harvest and, with Mr. Oglethorpe's approval, he will begin his own household.[27] We two are now often sick and could not do without help; and now the Lord has ordained for us to receive so useful and skillful a person in our house.

Mr. Oglethorpe showed me a letter written in French, which Mr. N. had written to him on behalf of the Salzburgers. It was dated in April of this year. Its contents were very pleasing for Mr. Oglethorpe, since he holds Mr. N. in great esteem; and recently at dinner at our place he used very fine words before his travelling companions about his important office and his praiseworthy efforts to extend the kingdom of Christ. Praise be to the Lord, who still grants to this His dear servant wisdom and strength to take care of us and the congregation before God and man!

A warship has arrived and explained why Captain Thomson's long-expected ship has remained away for so long. The reason is that the King of England is going to declare war on the King of Spain, before which it should be announced to all his Majesty's subjects in America so that they can arm themselves, take precautions, and take revenge at sea, which they have not been able to do yet after suffering so many losses. In order that the planned declaration of war might not be made known to the Spaniards by merchant vessels before it is known to the English, an embargo, or general prohibition against going to sea, has been placed on all ships ready to sail until the warship that has been dispatched has arrived in the American colonies. The Lord Trustees are said to have made the effort to obtain a license from the King for Captain Thomson, and therefore he is expected any day.[28]

Friday, the 28th of September. My dear colleague travelled to Old Ebenezer today to speak with a woman who had let her husband register her with me for Holy Communion. She is expecting to give birth shortly and therefore wishes, as she expressed it, to reconcile herself with God in Holy Communion beforehand. I showed her that she would have to prepare herself first through a true conversion if she wished to partake of Holy Communion to her profit rather than to her harm. So far, she has not been at all regular at our divine services, for which she gives excuses. In Savannah we got to know her and her family as very wicked and godless people.

A man brought the news that the Negroes or Moorish slaves are not yet pacified but are roaming around in gangs in the Carolina forests and that ten of them had come as far as the border of this country just two days ago. In answer to the request of the inhabitants of Savannah to use Moorish slaves for their work, the Lord Trustees have given the simple negative answer that they will never permit a single Black to come into the country, for which they have sufficient grounds that aim at happiness of the subjects. Mr. Oglethorpe told us here that the misfortune with the Negro rebellion had begun on the day of the Lord, which these slaves must desecrate with work and in other ways at the desire, command, and compulsion of their masters and that we could recognize a *jus talionis* in it.[29] I, however, ponder the fact that the mill in Old Ebenezer was also ruined by a flood on Sunday and that the work that was done then through necessity by the servants did no good.

Saturday, the 29th of September. N.'s wife was hesitant to go to Holy Communion because she has not learned the catechism completely with questions and answers. To be sure, she does not have its exact words in her memory, but she has its content in her heart. God has let her recognize the entire order of salvation from earlier sermons, and she can find herself in them; and therefore I could not let her remain behind because of the above-mentioned reason, even though we usually insist upon the learning and repeating of the catechism. I also gave her the advice, since she herself cannot read, to let her husband or her little girl read to her every day, and then she will gradually grasp it better, which is necessary and useful. She requested an ABC book and will try to see whether she can still learn to read. Grown people who have delayed and have a poor memory are advised to learn only those words in the first five main parts of the catechism that are taken from the Bible. When they have finished with them, they can acquaint themselves with the explanation of each of the main parts and of the twenty questions for those who wish to go to Holy Communion.

During this week I was prevented by my trip and by bodily weakness from continuing with the catechism lessons and from speaking diligently with the people who wish to go to Holy Communion. Those who still lack recognition and proper preparation I advised to wait until next time, and they have agreed. In Savannah we have not been able to hold Holy Communion with the German people there for a long time because they have shown no real improvement. As often as we go there we hear people complain not only that most of them are disloyal to their masters but also very disunited among themselves. They quarrel, fight, and make themselves unworthy of this feast.

Sunday, the 30th of September. Last week my dear colleague had to hold the prayer meeting and the preparation for Holy Communion, and today he had to preach for me, because I was prevented from it by a certain painful eruption on my body. With God's help I was able to speak again during the prayer meeting with our dear listeners, who had again gathered in a large number. Today there were forty at the Lord's Table, and I hope that all of them came here as penitent and grace-hungry sinners and were refreshed by Christ.

OCTOBER

Monday, the 1st of October. In my home prayer meeting today I began, in the name of God, the reading of the New Testament; and we are planning in this way to read through one gospel after the other and then the following books for our common edification. We read one verse after the other slowly and clearly, pausing a bit after a significant verse or expression or else reading it out again; and at the end of each lesson, which is constituted by a connected story or sermon, we mention for their edification something concerning the *dicta classica*[1] of what we have read. I am planning in the future to have the listeners read little pericopes, since this will greatly increase their attention. I will also let them recite the verses they already know so that the others will be stimulated to make the effort to learn them too. In our prayers we often hear our pious listeners praise the dear Lord for the blessing in the fields which He has granted and which is almost harvested. They also ask grace to use it as a blessing for the blessing and salvation of their souls, which, of course, no man can do through his own efforts.

N. had some business with me because of his sick child; and on this occasion I asked whether he was in harmony with his wife, etc. He had to admit that there was trouble sometimes, but that things were going better with her ever since I gave her some admonitions about two weeks ago.

Tuesday, the 2nd of October. N. N. is proving to be a righteous housefather, who not only sincerely allows the grace of God to work on his own soul but also applies the received grace for the edification and improvement of his family. The catechism has again become a cherished book for him; and, as is demanded in the name of God by the blessed Luther before each main part, he reads and teaches it simply to his wife and maid and thus does not leave it all up the minister. We notice his spiritual growth in all things.

Because of her continuous fever the Lackner woman became very weak yesterday, but today she recovered somewhat. She knows for certain that she is sick through the will of God her Father and does not ascribe it to the country or to other grounds or *causis secundis*;[2] and therefore she is very calm and wishes only that the Lord's will be done with regard to getting well or dying. She is certain of the forgiveness of sins in Christ, her dear Savior, and knows that she has God as a friend, indeed as a Father. She is worried because she is so weak and cannot pray, but I assured her from God's word that our loving and reconciled God demands no more from His children than He gives and that He does not look so much at the words as at the heart and that He also hears the desires of the miserable. Mrs. Gruber, in whose house she is, shows her more than motherly and sisterly loyalty and loyally shares with her those things from the prayer meeting and sermons that have been blessed in her own heart. She and her husband thank God a thousand times for having brought them out of Salzburg and out of the teeth of the enemy, just as He did the Children of Israel out of Egypt, even though they had little opportunity to pray to Him or ask Him to do so.

Rainy weather began yesterday and has continued rather hard today. It is just the time for gathering the beans, of which the people have already harvested a good part. Our heavenly Father knows what we need and will give us dry weather again at the proper time.

Wednesday, the 3rd of October. At my question a woman told me how she felt after taking Holy Communion. She said that during the preparation on Saturday she had become so very fearful that she almost left the church, but the dear Savior had later granted her so much grace that she had gone to the Lord's Table with noticeable spiritual profit and will have reason to praise Him as long as she lives. Yesterday another woman said that her spirits were not very good at first, but a young Salzburger had read to her, among other things, the verse "The sacrifices of God are a broken spirit," etc.; and this had made her heart light and full of sweet confidence. I also learned that Mrs. N. is now beginning to recognize better how well God has meant it with her journey to America and Ebenezer and that she did not wish to return, etc.

This afternoon Mr. Thilo unexpectedly sent me a book for which we had been waiting for a long time. It was B. Hartmann's *Pastorale Evangelicum*,[3] which had been given to him in Halle to bring to us but which, as he said, he had forgotten among his books. Oh, how dear this book is to us, and how much advantage we could have had from it in all sorts of circumstances, in which we needed good advice, if only it had come to our hands sooner. Dear N. had reported to us long ago in a letter that it was to be sent to us from Halle. May God let us use it with much blessing for the spiritual good of our dear congregation. In its notes it refers often to *Consilia Latina B. Speneri*,[4] which we would like to have if God grants the means and opportunity. At our departure we could take only the German counsels with us; the Latin ones were not available at the bookstore of the Orphanage, and, as far as I could remember, not to be had elsewhere.

Thursday, the 4th of October. Mrs. N., the wife of N. who

came from London,[5] came to my room after the prayer hour and wished to say a few things to justify herself for her annoying behavior; and these were partly foolish and partly painful for chaste ears. She thought she had edified herself from the example of the pious Hannah, the mother of Samuel, and clearly seemed to be comparing herself with her, whereas it would have been better for her to pay attention to everything that was preached in today's prayer hour concerning the two undutiful sons of Eli and their vexing behavior. The listeners were admonished not to accept the things they were told by them but rather to recognize God's holy judgments incurred by those who had rejected the good opportunity and proffered grace for a thorough conversion; for God punishes sin with sin, and the people gradually become callous and incapable of believing. By comparing the pious Samuel with these children of Belial I could clarify the verse, "For whosoever hath, to him shall be given, but whosoever hath not," etc. I also recommended, for later reading, the late Arndt's *True Christianity*, book I, chapter 7, especially its last part, which shows how one should judge the wicked behavior of people in Christendom. All mouth-Christians and hypocrites, who, even among us, are satisfied with external respectability, civil righteousness,[6] and the external use of the means of salvation, and who time and time again suppress and smother the good emotions and chastisements of the spirit of God, were loyally warned against these spiritual judgments.

Friday, the 5th of October. No matter how much we need the barn, the people do not have the time to erect it, even though all the boards are lying at the construction site. The dear Lord has given us dry weather again since yesterday; and therefore everyone who has any strength for working, from the smallest to the largest, is busy in the fields harvesting the beans and, in part, the rice. We must also interrupt school for a couple of weeks, since the parents need their children for the harvest. Even the little children are used for something, even if they merely rock the babies, since the mothers are in the field or doing some other necessary work. The parents send their children to church and prayer hours regularly, and therefore they always have an opportunity to hear something good.

Saturday, the 6th of October. We hear from Charleston in South Carolina that almost a fourth of the inhabitants of this populous city have died of spotted fever in a few weeks; and it is also said that most of those who fled there from our colony have perished miserably, some from lack of food and some from this epidemic. Many have moved from Savannah and other newly established towns in this colony to Carolina and Charleston because they do not wish to work and be satisfied with little; but there, too, they have not received something for nothing.

Today I wrote a couple of English letters to London; and on Monday we shall have an opportunity to forward them to Colonel Stephens in Savannah, who, as secretary of the Lord Trustees, often corresponds with London and has the letters forwarded very safely via Charleston. One of them is to Mr. Verelst,[7] in which I report at Mr. Oglethorpe's command that the shoemaker Ulich died of a fever five weeks after his arrival and two weeks after his marriage with Margaret Egger and that he has left most of the leather that the Lord Trustees had sent with him. He, or his widow, has been completely paid for all the shoes he made for the congregation; but for the orphanage he did not make more than two pairs at half price. Since we now need shoes against the winter for the orphanage and since the orphanage owns a large share of the leather at the order of the Lord Trustees, I have asked Mr. Oglethorpe what we should do; and he gave me permission to have shoes made from the leather and to report it to the Lord Trustees in order to learn what to do with the remaining leather. Zettler is not capable of making really useful shoes, so we are hiring a shoemaker for a few weeks and giving him a certain sum for each pair.[8]

The other point in the letter concerns Mr. Schlatter's linen, for which Mr. Oglethorpe cannot pay here but has referred me to the Lord Trustees. Both he and the storehouse manager, Mr. Jones, will recommend strongly that it be paid for soon so the merchant will not be hindered any longer in his business and so there will be no evil talk. I enclosed a letter to Mr. Schlatter's correspondents, Messrs. Norris and Drewett in London, and advised them that Mr. Oglethorpe has given me good hope that the Lord Trustees will pay for the linen and that they should turn to them.[9] We wish to send our diary shortly, just as soon as the long-awaited things and letters have arrived (we hope with the next ship).

Sunday, the 7th of October. A young Salzburger read to a married couple who cannot read those chapters of Arndt's *True Christianity* that are prescribed for today's gospel. When I came up, the woman said, pointing to the book, "That is a treasure. With it God led us out of Salzburg, and Moshammer (a Salzburger who died a blessed death) was His instrument." Our parishioners make use of the late Arndt's writings loyally and carefully; and there is probably not a family where one could not find his books on *True Christianity*, along with the dear Bible and the catechism. They have the praiseworthy custom of reading the chapter prescribed for each Sunday. Today we contemplated the gospel for the 16th Sunday after Trinity, "The Office and Work of our Dear Savior," which, according to the introduction to the text, consists of (1) "He comforts those who suffer," (2) "He makes the dead alive," and (3) "He fills the heart of man with His blessed recognition." My dear colleague concluded the fifth main point concerning the sacrament of Holy Communion. May the Lord bless everything!

Monday, the 8th of October. The Berenberger woman has hired herself out as milkmaid to the orphanage and moved in today. Her fever returned yesterday, and she was afraid that we might not take her now that she was sick; but I sent her word that she was dear to us in both well and sick days, she might bring her things in at any time and enjoy sick care, as God may grant it. I am pleased for several reasons that she has moved into the orphanage, especially because she is now working regularly and has her livelihood from it and will be less likely to live intemperately or to regret her voyage to America. Kalcher and his wife have learned to have patience, and therefore she is provided for here both physically and spiritually. Now all the women whom Sanftleben brought here have been provided for until the dear Lord shall provide further for those who are still unmarried. Until now we have been unable to get anything from the storehouse for the new arrivals except some Indian corn and rice, because the Lord Trustees have sent no orders to this effect. No doubt it was assumed that the women would find an opportunity to marry soon after their arrival. The Lackner woman and the Egger woman, who was the late Ulich's help-meet, have been sick from the very beginning and still are.

Before our private prayer meeting I was informed by two men that the Lord had blessed His word in them yesterday. One of them had achieved a true recognition of his sins and felt great disquiet and worry because of them; but the other had come to a confident trust in God in Christ. I gave both of them instruction according to their circumstances. Instead of the regular chapter of the New Testament that follows, I read to the gathering a piece from the late Prof. Francke's sermon about the very dear lesson from the epistles we had yesterday, in which it is shown very emphatically and in detail that a zealously maintained prayer is the nearest and most certain way to growth and increase in Christianity, and what great harm and hindrance can arise if a man does not say his prayers seriously, even though he uses other good means diligently. It also shows very wisely the cunning of the devil and the deceit of the heart that can creep in during prayer. Afterwards a woman said that it was a beautiful lesson, which applied to her in all points: her prayers fared just as it is written here, etc.

Tuesday, the 9th of October. Schartner, who was received some time ago into the orphanage as the community's cowherd, is receiving a good testimony from Kalcher, who says he is not only more regular in his work than formerly but that he also prays more diligently and accepts good advice for practicing an active Christianity. It is no little blessing for the community that the orphanage is providing its own herdsman with clothes, food, and other necessities. Because there are many people there, we require, to be sure, much for their maintenance; but so far the dear Lord has not let us suffer lack in anything. He openeth His generous hand and satisfieth the desire of every living thing, and He will not forget the orphanage.

I found the Lackner woman a little stronger today than last Sunday. The violence of the fever and the constant vomiting are letting up, she is beginning to rest better, and she has more appetite for eating. She thanks the Lord for strengthening her enough so that she can collect herself and pray, and she remembers with pleasure the physical and spiritual good that the Lord granted her in N. and especially in N.'s house.

Wednesday, the 10th of October. Last week we proposed to several people in the community to accept work with the schoolmaster[10] in Savannah. Some of them had an inclination to do so, but they soon thought differently and decided to remain here rather than disperse themselves. Today one of them reported this to me in the name of the others so that I might write it to the schoolmaster. The reasons the man gave that he and the others would rather remain here than accept work elsewhere pleased me very much and have good grounds. Among other things he said that the Trustees had spent so much on them to enable them to settle here and cultivate the land, and that they would not be able to do this if they scattered themselves in the land to earn money. They had stuck together in times of trial and want, had kept to God's word, and had awaited the time of help; and therefore it would be improper and sinful to remove themselves now from the good opportunity and edification, since necessity demanded it less now than formerly. One could also see in the case of those who took work elsewhere that they got no blessing from it and that they now had less than the others. They had received such good land from God's providence, he said, and they had promised to clear the plantations communally so that no neighbor would suffer; but this could not happen if some of them went to another place for several months.

The chief thing was the edification of their souls, and they would have to do without it at such a distance. Also, their families needed their help, which they would not be able to give them. To be sure, some of them lacked necessary clothing; but they hoped with time to find some work here and thus earn some money, as they have done before, which they could do easily without neglecting their own households. In answer I told this Salzburger that we do not begrudge our people any service, but they must check to see whether or not it is advantageous to them. Their reflection and decision pleased me, because I would prefer to have the congregation together rather than dispersed.

In a Salzburger's house I found the catechism lying open; and, when I asked him whether he and his wife were studying it diligently, he used very fine expressions from this little book and its contents and complained that he had previously used it so little and had not found in it what he was now finding. I recited for them the verse "Except ye become converted, and become as little children," etc.

Thursday, the 11th of October. This morning during my stroll in the fields I heard a voice behind the rice praying fervently; and, when I came closer, I saw two married people on their knees, a man with his previously frivolous but now better behaved wife. Even though I could not understand the words, I received a most edifying impression from the man's sincere and imploring prayer, and from their humble gestures, since their eyes and hands were raised toward heaven; and this aroused me to the praise of God. Oh, if only everyone would learn to pray to God in spirit and in truth and would raise holy hands and hearts everywhere.

Recently I invited N. in a friendly way to visit the catechism lesson in my house, since she needs this practice because of her ignorance. Because she had remained away, I admonished her again this morning, and she promised to come; but she remained absent again today. A man complained to me that he could not persuade her to attend the evening prayer meeting because she considered church-going at night to be an innovation in our town, which is (according to her knowledge) not customary in the Lutheran Church in Germany. A certain man told her from his own experience of the utility of the Bible stories that are contemplated in the prayer meetings, and he told her again this morning that God had especially blessed the story of Jacob's undutiful sons and their sinful behavior by letting him recognize his misery[11] and had gradually brought him to conversion. I, too, spoke to her movingly and tried to convince her that she is in a dangerous condition, which she cannot believe or recognize because she has no eye-salve.

Yesterday, during the story in which Samuel thought the voice of the Lord, who had called him, was a human voice, I showed that this error could be forgiven in the case of Samuel, as it is actually forgiven in verse 7 by the Holy Spirit, and that such an error had occurred for Eli's sake. However, it is not to be forgiven in the case of blind Christians who make thousands of kinds of errors and do not wish to recognize God's call: e.g., when God's word is emphatically laid on their conscience, then self-assured and carnal people act as if it does not concern them. If the conscience is awakened and the Holy Ghost chastises them through the word so that they become disquieted, then they probably consider it an emotional disturbance and think that their sadness and disquiet come from a bad blood condition and forebodes a misfortune, or they ascribe God's touch to some Satanic temptation. Especially when ministers perform their office individually and privately on an unconverted person and show him his cursed condition, then in his blindness he does not consider it the voice of God but of a partial person or of their enemy, etc. Thus we and others fare who mean well with their parishioners' souls.

Friday, the 12th of October. Like several others in the community, Hertzog has had quartan fever until now; but our loyal God has meanwhile worked very powerfully on his heart. He considers it a great blessing that he is being used as a servant in the orphanage and, without any trouble on his part, receives his maintenance and such good opportunity to edify his soul. I visited him and gave him some necessary admonishments.

After the prayer hour in my house a woman complained of the distress she felt because she was sometimes too pressed to remember a single verse to give her encouragement and comfort, even though she had learned many of them by heart with God's blessing and assistance. That depressed her even more and was a sign of the hardness of her heart, etc. During a certain task in her house, she said, she had remembered again the gross sins of her youth and, because of them, she had fallen into great pain and embarrassment before the holy majesty of God. The example of the great sinner Zachai, who had performed such great feats of penitence, still lay in her mind; and she wished to hear reports concerning some sins she had committed in Germany and had reported there by letter, so that she might be freed of her disquiet in this case too. She wished to be disgraced before all men and to subject herself to the worst punishment, for it was worth it. She could hardly marvel enough, she said, at the uncommonly great patience of God, with which He had put up with her for thirty-seven years. She requested from me a passion story extracted from all four gospels in order to read through it with prayer and pleading, to see whether it might bring her to a salutary remorse for her great sins and to a faith in the Lord Jesus, etc.

Another woman spoke from a similar poverty of the spirit and could not sufficiently lament and bewail her blindness, disloyalty, and sloth. I referred her to the beginning of Christ's sermon on the mount, in which the Lord Jesus does not deny, but rather attributes, blessedness to those who are nothing in their own eyes, who mourn, and who yearn for help. Her sincere and humble prayer stood me in good stead and encouraged me to further earnestness.

Saturday, the 13th of October. So far God has granted us such beautiful weather for harvesting that we could not wish anything better. The beans are ripening completely and can be gathered dry; and therefore our people are getting as many this year, and a bit more, than in the last years, when, to be sure, the deer did not do as much damage but when most beans were spoiled by the rain. In addition to the beans they are bringing in the rice, which has right large and beautiful grains this year. Everything has turned out well and the good hand of the Lord has protected everything from harm; and he must be a very fortunate man who would refuse the good Giver a humble word of praise for it. We admonish against this diligently in our sermons and prayer meetings and humbly implore the Father of all Mercies for grace to use these and all other gifts with proper gratitude.

N. is not a little bit distressed that her sick and still very young child so often prevents her on weekdays and Sundays from visiting public services and the opportunity for edification in my house. Until now her husband has had much work on their plantation; and, when he is at home, he too likes to hear something again for his spiritual profit. From time to time she leaves her little child with her neighbor and comes to my house for prayer and instruction. However, her spiritual hunger is not satisfied by that, rather she would like to enjoy this good all the time. She thinks that this unavoidable obstacle is the reason that her prayer is so weak and fragile, as a result of which her spirit is so depressed that she would almost like to stop praying, because through it she is just sinning against our holy God.

I warned her, however, not to listen to such temptation from Satan and her flesh; and I showed her from God's word, especially from Psalms 34:19, that our dear Lord is pleased, for the sake of Christ, by a struggling prayer that is difficult for the one who prays and displeases him because of the defects that adhere to it. If only she would continue to struggle and pray, I said, she would soon feel an advantage from it. In this way she would resist the devil, and he would flee from her. I made an appointment with her in order to read her some of this important material and to underline some basic and strength-giving verses for her. Her husband was happy that God had not let that occur which some people in Salzburg had wished and hoped for, namely that the archbishop and the clergy would allow the Protestants there to have Protestant ministers and thus be prevented from emigrating. For then, as this man thought, because of the many offenses, sinful customs, wicked acquaintances and comradeships God would not have achieved His purpose as He is doing in this wilderness.

Sunday, the 14th of October. Toward evening yesterday we had the pleasure of receiving a rather large packet of letters from our patrons and friends in Europe, for which both of us bent our knees before the throne of God, who has been reconciled by Christ and is exceedingly merciful, and thanked Him for this new blessing. Captain Thomson brought the letters along with the long-expected chests; and he sent the letters to Savannah, because he has sailed with his ship to Mr. Oglethorpe's regiment at Frederica. Praised be the Lord our God for having preserved our reverend Fathers and friends in life and health so far and for having again inclined their hearts to send us spiritual and physical benefactions such a long way over the sea. May He bless in us all the edifying letters, which always suit our circumstances so well, as well as the physical gifts in the chests, which are presumably still in the ship; and may He let them serve for His eternal praise and our true well-being!

Several members of the community have been cheered by little letters; especially the penitent and sorrow-laden N. thought that what our dear Mr. N. included on her behalf in his letter was a balm on her head, and she listened to it with many tears of joy. Oh, how she will praise God day and night on her knees for

letting things fare better so far with her and her former transgressions than she had thought possible. She told me in great
humility and childish joy that God had beautifully blessed, for
the strengthening of her faith, a certain circumstance in the
story of the Passion, which she had begun to review word by
word for her private edification. From this I can see that she is
like a hungry little dove that finds a small grain where others
would fly away.

Our good and pious God has provided so abundantly for the
orphanage this time that the barn we have begun can be paid
for and other necessary expenses be covered; and this will
strengthen to no little degree our faith in the unshortened arm
of our living God. If He will but teach us to believe more and
more, then we will see His glory both during and after our tribulations. I must also recognize with particular thanks that our
worthy Mr. N. has dared in his faith to send a considerable sum
to pay the building costs for the parsonage and for constructing
the church. May God make us grateful! We do not doubt that
our merciful Father in heaven has destined much fine blessing
for us and our congregation from the letters we have received,
since once again their main content is to be publicly known. May
the Lord reward both our most worthy Mr. N. as well as all our
dear reverend Fathers and patrons for the especial love and
affection they have shown us and our congregation particularly,
through their communal and very sincere and moving letters.

This evening during the prayer hour we made simple use of
the precious letter that some servants of Christ wrote jointly to
our congregation; and together we praised the Lord for all the
good we experienced from it, invoked Him to give us obedient
hearts to follow all admonitions loyally, and prayed for God's
abundant blessing as a recompense for this benefaction. I do
not doubt that, through the grace of God, the forceful evangelical expressions of this letter, along with our admonitions, will
encourage the members of the congregation to a new seriousness in their Christianity and to a renewed sincere praise of God
for having brought them out of the turmoil of the world and
into this tranquility and solitude and for having awakened so
many pious ministers and other pious Christians to care for
them as for their own children, brothers, and sisters and to

work for their improvement. Out of the letters of dear Mr. N. we read publicly those points that were aimed at the congregation also or at least could give occasion for good admonitions.

It pains us and our honest listeners in our souls to hear that many Salzburg exiles are imitating the world and going the way of perdition. May God awaken the dead and strengthen those who wish to die. The damnation of such people will be manifold, as can be seen in the prefiguration of the judgments of the Israelites in the wilderness. May our Father in heaven reward the worthy Mr. N., our dear father in Christ, with thousandfold spiritual and physical blessings, as well as the worthy Lady von N.[12] and all our benefactors and friends for their especially hearty and constant love, their sincere blessings, intercessions, loving efforts, and all the kindness we have experienced so far from their faithful service. It is our new covenant with the Lord to struggle and pray for them all, as if for ourselves, before the throne of God so that we all may be given entry into the glorious kingdom of our Lord and Savior Jesus Christ and that we will one day be placed guiltless and joyful before the countenance of His splendor.

Monday, the 15th of October. This morning N. called on me and told me with much emotion and many tears how much God had blessed yesterday's reading in him. To be sure, things are going worse for him now than for other Salzburgers; yet he thanks God so heartily for His marvelous and good guidance in having led him in this wilderness to a recognition of his misery, that I am most delighted about it. In N. he was as well off materially as anyone was before him or could be now; and it pleases me all the more that his heart and mouth are full of praise and thanks for God's wise and merciful guidance, even though he is now worse off than formerly with regard to physical provisions.

We omitted the *Lectionem cursoriam N. T.*[13] at our home prayer meeting this time, and I read a very edifying letter from dear Professor Francke and the two letters from Mr. Berein, which he wrote to us in the name of Court Chaplain Ziegenhagen. All three were, God be praised, very refreshing for us and gave us much matter for the praise of God and for Christian intercession. Because the printed continuation of the Ebenezer reports has again reminded Prof. Francke of the paths on which God led us for our good in the years 1736 and 1737, I promised the congregation assembled for prayer that in the future, when these printed reports come into our hands, I will use them for this purpose here, too, according to the example of God, who let his servants remind the People of Israel of the old paths again and again for a very salutary purpose. He has helped us gloriously out of much hardship and tribulation and has often put our disbelief to shame; and He has also given us courage to trust further in His goodness in all fearful circumstances, and therefore in the hovering danger of war.

For our comfort Mr. Berein pointed out to us the 46th Psalm, and especially the words: "The Lord of hosts is with us; the God of Jacob is our refuge. Selah." At the same time, to strengthen myself and those present, I mentioned what we had heard on the occasion of 1 Samuel 1 : 3 about the beautiful name of God, when He calls Himself the Lord Zebaoth, which name appears to have arisen in Samuel's time and, indeed, at Ebenezer, where the Israelites first suffered greatly because of their sins but later defeated their enemies because of their penitence and Samuel's prayer. They will have said, "Our army is indeed very thin and we have become few, whereas the enemy are very mighty and numerous; but we have on our side the Lord Zebaoth (the Lord of hosts, at whose command everything in heaven and earth must stand). He can help through wind, thunder and lightning," as it came to pass, chapter 7 : 10–12.

I read the beautiful 46th Psalm in its entirety, and it greatly refreshed me in this connection. We sang the song *Ich hab in Gottes Hertz und Sinn mein Hertz und Sinn ergeben*, etc. Yesterday the 5th verse of the song *Wie ist es möglich höchstes Gut*, etc. gave me a necessary admonition: "Thou art loyal, I unjust, Thou art pious, I am a wicked servant and must truly be ashamed that I, in such an evil condition, should receive any good from Thy generous and fatherly hand." And this time our exceedingly merciful God is giving us so much. Because, to our comfort and joy, the letters we have received so often mention that servants and children of God in no small number are praying for us zealously, we remembered our duty to do the same for them with devotion and zeal in place of any repayment, as we have been requested to do several times in letters. And because (God be praised!) this has been done by so many honest souls in my room and because we have often mentioned the dear benefactress of our congregation, the worthy Lady von N.,[14] before the throne of our merciful and reconciled Father, we hope that our poor prayer, which, however, is based on Christ's merits and intercession, will be applied by Him to help her in the former unpleasant circumstances that were mentioned in a letter and that He will superabundantly bless her and her husband and entire family for her continued benefactions.

Tuesday, the 16th of October. Yesterday toward evening I visited the sick Lackner woman and told her during the conversation that Mr. N. was still thinking of her in right fatherly love and was commending her very kindly to our spiritual care and concern, etc. Because she herself could tell me how people prayed both day and night for Ebenezer in this dear father's house and because I could confirm this from the letters we had just received, I applied this to her comfort and to the strengthening of her faith and said she should be comforted in her physical weakness because, as a member of our congregation, she lay in the heart and mouth of this dear man and other saints on earth, and the heavenly Father will surely let the hour come that He will bless her and their prayers for her recovery, provided it is pleasing to Him and useful to her. She considered herself entirely unworthy of this remembrance and intercession, and also of the benefactions she had enjoyed in Mr. N.'s house; and she wished them all physical and spiritual blessings from God in return. She lies there like a quiet lamb and says, "If only I go to heaven and remain unseparated from Christ, then I am content." Because she considers herself a miserable person, I reminded her of the lovely verse, "I will look upon him who is miserable and him who is of broken spirit," etc.,[15] likewise, "The sacrifices of God are a broken spirit," etc., and also, "The Lord hath said, I will not abandon you," etc.

Christian Riedelsperger asked me for advice as to what he should do. He said he had already written three letters to his two sisters and to three close blood-relatives in Lindau, but had still received no answer. In them he had reported, to the praise of God, how much good he was enjoying here in physical and spiritual things and that their assumption had not proved true that he would never find things better for his soul and body than he had had in Lindau. Because of his love for their souls he would like to have them all here in Ebenezer, and he did not doubt that, if they once broke through all prejudices and came here, they would not only be pleased with all the arrangements here but would also praise God with him for the grace that He shows here. I advised him to continue earnestly with his intercession for his relatives and to write on their behalf to Master Risch, who would soon learn whether they had received the letters and how things stood otherwise with the state of their souls. This Riedelsperger has such an honest love for his countrymen that he would like to bring all of them out from the chance of temptation and tell them what the Lord has done for him and how much it cost Him to save him from his blindness and his own selfmade piety. He is also a very useful and serviceable man in external matters.

N. requested that he and his wife might alternate in visiting the catechism hour in my house, since their little child and household conditions do not allow both of them to come at the same time. He regrets that so many of his countrymen and acquaintances are letting themselves be overcome by bad examples in Germany; and he believes for sure it would not have gone better with him if he had remained there, even though the ministers there apply every effort and work on the Salzburgers. His heart has been very touched by dear Mr. N.'s expression: "I am pleased to hear that so many Salzburgers recognize why God has led them to Georgia. They will all recognize it." His eyes filled with tears at this and he thanked God, who had brought him here; and he wished that he would not resist the spirit of God that is working on his heart through the word, etc. This N. is a very useful man in the congregation and will be even more useful when God has completed the work of conversion in him. For some time he has had quartan fever, in which our loyal God is tugging on him loyally.

I was visited by an Indian who had four letters from Savannah with him, which he must take back and forth among the Lord Trustees' officers who are with the Indian nations. The letters were numbered with I, II, III, IV so that he could deliver them one after the other at the proper place without confusion.

He is, as he let me understand, being sent up to the Cherokee Indians by Mr. Oglethorpe, who is still in Savannah, in order to bring down a number of them against the Spaniards for the good of our colony. A couple of weeks ago two Englishmen rode up to the Indian nation with a commission from General Oglethorpe for this same purpose.

After the catechism practice a German man from Old Ebenezer asked me to baptize a child there, for whose sake I rode there immediately; and because of that I was prevented from holding the prayer meeting because I returned too late. My dear colleague, who holds prayer meetings in my stead when obstacles arise, had journeyed to Savannah early yesterday with three Salzburgers because of the chests that have arrived.

Wednesday, the 17th of October. My dear colleague returned hale and hearty yesterday from Savannah; but he had travelled in vain because Captain Thomson had sailed directly to Frederica with his ship and had sent nothing but letters and a few indispensable things to the storehouse. It is assumed that he will come to Savannah with his ship in three weeks, and therefore we will have to be patient about the chests until then. Mr. Oglethorpe mentioned to my dear colleague that he wished to help bring a new transport of Salzburgers here, if only our Salzburgers would deliberate as to how much money each new colonist would have to have for maintenance in the first year. The Lord Trustees would rather give money than provisions, and this would be very useful for the people and for our entire community.

In the evening prayer meeting today we concluded the sad, but very important, story in 1 Samuel 4, which we had begun last week. At its conclusion we were reminded to pray diligently and zealously for our dear Germany, from whence so many charitable gifts have flowed to us in previous times and this time too, and to ask that God's mercy might hold back the spiritual and physical judgments that the people, like those in Silo, bring on their heads through their ingratitude for the treasure of the gospel. We also prayed that the Lord would arm with strength from on high His servants, whom He has arrayed from time to time, so that they might step before the abyss and awaken the sleeping sinners through their sentry cry.

Because there was still some time, I read briefly what Mr. Berein had extracted from Mr. N.'s letter of 7 July 1739 and sent to us at the request of our dear Court Chaplain Ziegenhagen. They were pure testimonies of a constant fatherly love, with which he most tenderly embraces us unworthy ones and our congregation, especially the pious ones, and assures us all of his prayers and those of many servants and children of God in N. and elsewhere. God be praised for this! The intercession of so many righteous ministers and pious Christians is such a dear blessing that we do not know how to value it highly enough; and the pious among us praise the Lord for it with mouth and heart. My dear colleague had an especial pleasure in hearing the inspirational and strength-giving letters, and therefore I did not wish to continue with them in his absence. In the coming prayer meetings I shall read the remaining ones; and I know in advance from previous experience and from the grace of God that much edification, joy, and praise of God will arise from them. If I had not been kept from the meeting in the orphanage at noon today by a severe attack of fever, which held me in bed for four hours, I would have read Mr. N.'s beautiful letter to the elders and children in the orphanage, from which I hope for the blessing of the Lord.

Thursday, the 18th of October. Our parishioners of both sexes gather in my room for the catechism hour in such numbers that they have no room; and therefore I shall be required to divide the sexes so that the women come on Tuesdays and Thursdays, while the men come on Wednesdays and Saturdays, but I shall teach them the same material so they can repeat it all the better at home. In this way one of them can always remain at home and perform the household chores while the other is at the lesson. The dear people cause me uncommon pleasure through their desire for the truths of the catechism and their simple conduct during the questions and answers.

At the beginning of the lesson a small assignment from the catechism is repeated *verbotenus*,[16] and the Bible verses we have had the last time are recited loudly and clearly so that they can be gradually learned through constant hearing even by those who do not know them. Next I pose some questions about the divine truths that have been preached last and continue in order with questions and answers, in accordance with the twenty questions appended to the catechism. May God bless all this to His glory and to the salvation of the congregation! If there are not too many present, then we can arrange everything all the more simply with questions and answers, since some of them show more bashfulness in a large crowd, and thus this division will be useful in various ways. Sanftleben's sister has now joined us on two occasions; may God grant that she be constant and eager![17]

In the evening prayer meeting I read two very edifying letters from Prof. Francke, and God granted us much edification from them. Through them we were reminded of the especial ways and guidance of God in the year 1738, and we were shown how many advantages our congregation has over many thousands in Christendom, which we must, of course, apply loyally and gratefully if we do not wish to lose these splendid advantages. It was also lovingly suggested to our listeners that, when they gradually move out to their plantations and cannot have such rich spiritual refreshment in the regular prayer meetings as they have had so far, they should arrange their home devotions and spiritual practices and especially their prayers, following the example of others who are already doing it here and there. All this was impressed on them emphatically.

Among other things I reminded the listeners of the story from Genesis 41, which tells of the seven fat and the seven lean years. Had our pious God, who loves living things, not granted Joseph wisdom in his heart to gather supplies during the rich and inexpensive years for the lean years, how miserably things would have looked for everyone, even in his own father's house. God had let us live together so, I said, for almost six years, during which we have had fat years in spiritual things and much opportunity to lay in stores. Who knows what kind of times are coming? Therefore, if anyone is frivolous and does not accept God's grace for a thorough conversion, things will probably look bad for him when he no longer has such rich refreshment and perhaps will be removed from our particular supervision. To confirm the warning against disloyalty toward such excellent grace, I admonished my listeners from the story of the city of Silo, where divine services were held for a long time but, because the people did not use this advantage properly, God cast the candelabrum from its stand, etc. In their unconverted and godless nature, they were helped as little by their physical trust in the Ark of the Covenant as the Jews were by their trust in the temple and other advantages (Jeremiah 7). Nothing counts before God but a new creature, and for this all advantages must be applied.

Because the love and care of Prof. Francke and other dear benefactors in Germany shine remarkably in our eyes, I have publicly offered to compose a letter of gratitude to the Salzburgers' known and unknown benefactors in the name of the entire congregation, if only they will give me the opportunity by expressing their opinion. I already know in advance that they will all be very pleased with it, but I prefer for them to initiate it themselves and express their grateful spirit. Several have already asked us to write something for them. May God reward everyone abundantly!

Friday, the 19th of October. This morning I had our little flock in the orphanage before me, twenty souls in number, sang with them the song of praise *Man lobt dich in der*, etc., and invoked God's blessing for our undertaking. Next I read the right fatherly and most enjoyable letter of Mr. N., which he had addressed to the father, mother, and children of the orphanage; and at every point I added the necessary application to remind them of the many marvelous ways of God they had experienced in this house in order to awaken them to His praise and to encourage them to gratitude. When reading the beautiful superscription of Psalms 146:9,[18] I remembered the beautiful song *Lobe den Herrn, O meine Seele, ich will ihn loben*, etc., which was based on this psalm. We do not yet know the melody; but, as soon as we can find some time, we will familiarize ourselves with the melody and with the exceedingly beautiful content, which well suits our orphanage and reminds us of our duty in all happen-stances and also points out the well of comfort in times of want and tribulation.

Children and adults both listened to the content of the letter and the accompanying admonitions with many tears. At last we fell on our knees, praised the Lord for all His kindness, and prayed for our worthy Mr. N. and all benefactors of the orphanage and the community. After the prayer I asked what winter clothing I should buy for the children and adults from the money which dear Mr. N. has donated to the orphanage, trusting in the living God, and which I should borrow on a note according to the good advice of our worthy Court Chaplain Ziegenhagen.

What we might need to cover the building costs for the barn and what might be required for other expenses will be provided by the almighty Creator of heaven and earth, who has hitherto shown that the orphanage is His work. The five cowherds receive all their clothing from foot to head from the orphanage, and this is a great benefaction for the poor in the community. If God grants something for the poor-box, as has occurred again this time, then the orphanage receives a hand from it in case of emergency, if perhaps a leak must be stopped here or there; and this is not at all against the intent of the dear benefactors, as we see from Senior Urlsperger's letter. Oh how good it is when both young and old among us are reminded also from afar what great advantages they have over many others in Christendom, as was done particularly yesterday and today in the letters we read. It makes a great impression. The difference between us and others in this colony is apparent, for the poor in no other place are so well provided for and no other people enjoy such special care in spiritual and physical matters as in dear Ebenezer. The Lord hath done it, and it is His work. Halleluiah!

The Lackner woman has been very weak again for several days, now that the vomiting has begun again. Both my dear colleague and I visited her yesterday and today and spoke with her from the holy gospel about the preparation for a blessed departure, at which time she always proves very edifying and prays sincerely with us. During her last weakness, when the vomiting subsided, I had already offered her Holy Communion; however, because she had begun to recover, she hoped to enjoy it with the congregation. Because I found her very weak yesterday, as I reported to Mr. Thilo, our doctor, I let Mrs. N.[19] ask her after my departure whether she would like to take Holy Communion before her anticipated demise. I had my reasons for letting her be asked by this person, who does her many kind services in both spiritual and physical ways. Today I learned that she longs for this spiritual medication right sincerely and will expect me in the evening, when the fever and vomiting have passed. At first, after asking her a few questions about Holy Communion, I recited the gospel verse "Come unto me all ye that are laden," etc., which she herself slowly repeated; and she eagerly heard its gospel content from me. After a humble prayer in which I humbly presented to the true Savior these and other glorious promises, such as "And I, if I be lifted up from the earth," etc., and "They that are whole need not a physician, but," etc., I administered Holy Communion to her according to Christ's institution, fell on my knees with two Christian women who were there, and thanked Him for this dear gift and blessing that had been granted to Elisabeth Lackner. Twice she opened her arms and then closed them again as if she wished to embrace the Savior, and said, "The Lord Jesus is with me." I prayed for her the beautiful words, *Ich habe Jesu Fleisch gegessen, sein Blut hab ich getrunken hier. Nun wird er meiner*, etc.,[20] which she herself repeated very movingly. I told her that, God willing, I was going to travel to Savannah tomorrow and could therefore not visit her for a few days, whereupon she wished me much good on the way.

Saturday, the 20th of October. Yesterday in the evening prayer meeting my dear colleague, Mr. Boltzius, read publicly the joint letter that was written to us by some servants of the Lord in Germany, partly because there are so many beautiful and edifying things in it and partly because it contains much about the importance of the ministerial office and clarifies what was said last Sunday, from the catechism and in conjunction with the *Haus-Tafel*,[21] of the ministerial office. The letter shows that the names Holy Scripture gives to ministers were aimed only at the good of the congregation: e.g., when they are called "watchmen," it is a great blessing that ministers look after their flock and ask about them. Therefore everyone should be pleased when we perform our office on him in this way and not say, "Who told on me?" when we ask about this or that person. Likewise, when they are called "father," by whom spiritual children are begotten, one can see the purpose of the ministerial office, namely a new birth; for in Christ Jesus nothing counts but a new creature, and therefore everyone should let this purpose of God be achieved, etc.

When it is written that our desert is being threatened by the enemy with an even greater devastation, then they are thinking about what they fear most, namely, the bad examples here in this country, and they hope that the dear Lord in his mercy will keep our congregation from being spiritually devastated by them. May He also make come true what is written at the end of the letter: "And we wish you for the future the strength of the resurrection of Jesus so that, despite all suffering, you will be comforted and that you will be blessed by and rejoice in the conversion, strengthening, fortifying, and preserving of the souls entrusted to you." We consider it a great blessing when we are so greatly awakened from afar. May the dear Lord repay such love a thousandfold.

Our spirits often sag, but we are comforted again by having a Jesus who gave Himself for the sake of our sins and was resurrected for our justification; and that gives us strength and joy to proceed with comfort in the suffering connected with our ministerial office, to struggle, to fight, not to step back, to persevere, and to overcome, as is indeed demanded of a minister in the above-mentioned letter, if the demanded loyalty is in fact to be crowned. The more a minister recognizes in a living way the death of reconciliation of Jesus Christ and the strength of His resurrection, the more he is put in a position to perform his office with blessing. I was very much struck by what I had as an exordium last Sunday from 2 Corinthians 4:13–14, "We having the same spirit of faith, according as it is written, I believed, and therefore have spoken; we also believe, and therefore speak; knowing that He which raised up the Lord Jesus shall raise us up also by Jesus, and shall present us with you." For this purpose may the Lord place His blessing on our office for our people and on the offices of these worthy ministers for theirs! What is written in their worthy letter can give us hope that we will have in our resurrected Savior a loyal, mighty, and kind Lord, who liveth from eternity to eternity. etc.

A couple of years ago, to wit on 26 August 1737, Court Chaplain Lau, who ordained us, sent us a special letter that is so dear to me that I often read it for fresh encouragement. Because it is so very edifying, I shall incorporate it in this diary, particularly the four noteworthy points that are presented in it:

"I treasure the wealth of the mercy of God in Christ that the heavenly Father has let flow to you so far in so many hardships. Oh, if only we could properly value and sufficiently praise the fact that our God did not consider His own Son too dear but sent Him to us for our sins and healed our wounds through His wounds. Yes, that is the way it is. We must never forget that the Father has led us through living faith to a common possession of, and participation in, the death of Jesus Christ. Soul, do not forget it! Whenever my heart wishes to vacillate and despond, God gives me grace to remember earnestly that His Son is mine, and in this contemplation I always find my rest and refreshment. May the Lord not let a single day, not even an hour pass by in our life that we do not think of the death of Christ and of its glorious strength. This first occurred to me during the sighs with which I prayed to God to give me what I should write to you. We can rightly look upon it as our chief pastoral care to let Christ's death, blood, and wounds become fresh and new every hour in our hearts and to renew in our hearts, through a reaffirmation of faith, the assurance that we are the children of God and fellow heirs of the glory of Jesus Christ.

"(2) Through the contemplation of what the Father has granted us in and with the Son, we wish to encourage ourselves sincerely not to tire in our work but to run with patience into the battle that has been ordained for us. Running and at the same time fighting is, to be sure, something difficult, especially when enough inner and outer enemies are there who try to interrupt both and to exhaust us. I speak from personal experience when I say that there are a thousand snares that Satan sets for us. Especially our own heart, because of its own natural heaviness, always sinks again to the earth and to its cold and lukewarm nature so we must keep watch over ourselves at all times and, as it were, wind up the clockwork of the heart time and time again if we do not wish eventually to die in ourselves and forfeit the crown. But I have found nothing more proved and more serviceable than a constant *anazopurein*[22] of the evangelical grace that is in us. A heart that swims in the blood of

Jesus Christ like a little fish in water, and a pastor who firmly holds his element in the dear treasure of grace of the glorious gospel does not die but ever gains new strength to be loyal and cheerful with patience in the office for which God has chosen him. The superabundance of the inner well of grace is the best food for our parishioners and best hits the goal for which we should always aim in our office. Dear Father, transfigure Thy child Christ Himself in our souls so that we will rightly know what we have in Him and how graciously Thou hast blessed us in Him.

"(3) I find something very special in prayer and learn to understand better what an unlimited mercy of God it is that we are free to step before His countenance and to speak as with a reconciled father with Him before whom all Seraphim hide themselves. Yesterday someone told me that, if he could not pray any more, then he would not wish to live another minute. However salutary prayer is for us, the devil tries just as hard to keep us from it. One can often be so preoccupied with the operation of one's business (to say nothing of other snares) and be so intoxicated in spirit that, without noticing it, one becomes involved in a great activity without having discussed it properly with the Father in heaven. From this, I have noticed, come disquiet and suspicion and, if the work does not turn out well, despondence. Or, if it succeeds, pride and self-confidence. On the other hand, if, before undertaking a project, we step before God with the smallest things as well as with the gravest and speak with Him about it until our hearts are warmed and we come into a cheerful calm, and if even during our occupation we sigh to the Lord who rules all things, then I have found this advantage, that we can be calm, thoughtful, sober in our spirits, and full of confidence. When the work has been completed, our hearts can remain humble if it turns out well and yet remain full of faith even if the work seems to have turned out badly. Lord, teach us to pray!

"(4) I have found that the devil tries to tire the soul through external difficulties. So many things occur here and there and even from outside that seem to run directly counter to the Kingdom of Jesus Christ. Then it costs much to keep on guard so that we will not be beguiled. Often worries arise and bring us into great agitation. Sometimes we are depressed and would rather throw everything away than remain standing at our post. In such instances, I have experienced that it is very useful for us not to believe that we understand the way in which the Kingdom of God is to be built but to allow God, who has promised His Son in order to give us all the ends of the world as a heritage, to take entire charge of how this is to be brought about. One should be a *spectator precans*[23] of His miracle and wait patiently for what will come. One's courage must not sink, above all one's spirit should not become enmeshed in earthly worries. Just sweeping out a house in faith is an accomplishment that pleases God in heaven.[24] There is always someone, perhaps just a child, to whom we can tell something about the Lord Jesus. If we have been true and patient in small things for some time, then God will come before we expect it and clear the road further, and advance the gospel through our better service. Oh what a great thing a wise and loyal housekeeper is!"

Mrs. Schweighofer came to me this morning and brought two little letters that were written to Senior Urlsperger, one of them by her oldest daughter and the other by one of the orphans. She told me how, yesterday evening before they had written the letters, they had prayed together that God would give His blessing to their writing. This morning her daughter had read the letter to her, at which she (the mother) could not hold back her tears. This Mrs. Schweighofer wishes for nothing more than for her children to devote themselves honestly to the Lord; and she would have the greatest joy in the world if this should happen. She remembered her former condition when she had gone around bent and bowed and could find no comfort and could not trust herself to obtain it. I asked her when she had come to a complete breakthrough, and she answered, "In the orphanage."

Sunday, the 21st of October. Today there was a strong wind and it was also very cold, yet the congregation attended in a large number to hear the preaching of the divine word. I preached to them on the gospel for the 18th Sunday after Trinity: "The living recognition of Jesus Christ and the good that is in Him, as the chief thing that a man should seek in this world." This was first clarified in detail, and then I showed "for what a man is made fit through this," namely, to love God with all his heart, etc., and his neighbor as himself. Christ was contemplated especially with regard to His person and His office as intercessor; and I showed the good that we have from it. I also demonstrated in detail, with the aid of the Holy Ghost, that this is the important thing that the listeners should not only grasp according to the letter but especially learn on their knees so that they might immediately lay a firm foundation for their Christianity and then continue to work further on it.

The exordium was taken from the Epistle to Philemon, verses 4–6; and, because so much, if not all, depends upon this matter, it was repeated during the afternoon. In the evening I read to some people who had gathered in my room, both adults and children, the useful applications of the 110th Psalm from Frisch's *David's Harp*.[25] May the Lord in His mercy place some blessing on all this work for Christ's sake! May He open my eyes better and better so that I will learn to know Christ better and so that all my sermons will aim at nothing but to lead my dear listeners with the aid of the Holy Ghost to a living recognition of Him and to show how they can take from that all their strength for an active Christianity. The Lord has greatly blessed in my soul the late Prof. Francke's *Paraeneses* concerning the epistles to Titus and to the Hebrews.[26] I read them while I could not hold school because the children were being used for harvesting the crops. Since, God willing, I shall begin school again tomorrow, I beg our dear Lord to give me grace to use what I have garnered through His blessing and to apply it to His glory.

Monday, the 22nd of October. During a visit I spoke with a person who told me how she was faring. Sometimes she savors the grace of God in such a way that she is moved to many tears by it, because she considers herself entirely unworthy of it. At other times, however, she is wholly depressed, namely, when she thinks back on her previous life and can find no comfort and help. Yesterday, she said, she could not go to church but had to remain warm in bed at the doctor's orders because of an illness. She was greatly troubled because she kept being overcome by sleep and could not pray so earnestly as she wished to. This reminded her of another person who, even when she was just as weak, still showed such great earnestness in prayer that she forgot about eating and everything else because of it. This increased her worry, and therefore she could not be content; and today things were not getting any better. She was praying, to be sure; but she was finding no strength.

At this point I showed her what was lacking, namely, the living recognition of Jesus Christ; she imagines Him and the heavenly Father quite different from the way He has revealed Himself in His word. To be sure, when recognizing her sloth she should not become frivolous; but she should not lose courage either, or she will lose everything. Instead, she should lay aside the sin that is clinging to her and making her slothful; she should advance with patience into the struggle that is ordained for her and, at the same time, learn better and better to set her eyes upon Jesus, the Beginning and End of all faith. She should use the reading of Holy Scripture and the practice of prayer with the aid of the Holy Ghost in order better to recognize Jesus Christ's dear work of redemption and the father-heart of God that has been reconciled by it. This would give her the greatest strength for remaining serene and comforted in her Christianity despite all feeling of her remaining defects and shortcomings. May the Holy Ghost itself transfigure Christ in her and lead her in all truth!

Various matters detained me in Savannah, so that I arrived home again only today at noon, hale and with God's blessing, praise the Lord! On Sunday I preached to the German people for the last time, because our circumstances will not allow us to divide ourselves any longer and be absent from our congregation several days every four weeks for the sake of these people. Also, we see little or no advantage from our work because, despite all public and private admonition, the people continue in their profane and, in part, frankly godless behavior. Also, they have wished to use us as advocates and intercessors in their physical distress, which oppresses them in their physical work because of their sins, more than they have wished for us to tend to their souls and their children's souls. When it turns out that we cannot agree with their requests or if our intercession has no effect, then they cast the blame on us.

In the sermon that I held for them on the regular text for the 19th Sunday after Trinity, I presented them with "Three Main Obstacles to a True Conversion to God": (1) disloyalty toward the convincing truth of God's word, (2) self-deception, (3) un-yielding ignorance. The words of the exordium were from Paul's farewell sermon in Acts 20:26–27, which, as usual, was repeated in the afternoon and further applied. Now these German servants are resuming their complaints. Previously they have received provisions of meat, corn, flour, and butter; but now, because the Trustees' storehouse is closing and no more foodstuffs can be bought, those who work are receiving, instead of provisions and clothes, a certain sum of money, which does not please them as well as the previous provisions, with which they had formerly found much fault.

Mr. Oglethorpe was still in Savannah and I had two opportunities to settle several matters for the congregation. The letter I had recently written to Mr. Verelst was still in Savannah; and, because I learned from my dear colleague that Mr. Oglethorpe had changed his mind about the Swiss linen,[27] I communicated the letter to him. He approved of everything in it and wished every precaution to be taken to have it carefully forwarded in the Lord Trustees' packet. He again mentioned the reception of a number of German people at our place, for whose passage and support in the first year the Trustees would pay, but the colonists would have to pay it back in a few years. This would not, however, be appropriate for the Salzburgers.

He again requested me to write to Prof. Francke for a preacher for the German people in and near Frederica. He would pay his salary, but he will have to know how to suffer some and renounce comfort for the sake of the Kingdom of God. I requested a written plenipotentiary power for this with his signature, and thus it stands for the present.[28]

Here in Savannah, right in the middle of the street between the city hall where church is now held and the churchyard, I found the grave of the Indian King Tomochichi, around which a square fence of thin boards has been made and on which a stone epitaph is to be erected in the future.[29] He had been sick for a long time, and finally died, in his house on Pipemaker's Bluff, where a few Indians live together; Mr. Oglethorpe had a coffin made for him and had him brought to Savannah by water. He was received at the landing by several citizens of the city and carried to his place of burial. During the procession Mr.

Oglethorpe and five of the senior officers of his regiment held the pall, the coffin was accompanied by the queen and two Indians who were always with him to manage his affairs, and by Mrs. Musgrove and a great multitude of people. The citizens stood at arms and fired three salvos, and the cannons were fired too. He himself had requested to be buried among the white people, because he counted himself among the Englishmen and the king's subjects.

Mr. Oglethorpe misses him very much because he always sided loyally with the English and always served their best interest. There is no colony except ours in which the Indians have not killed many white people, especially at the beginning. Whenever angry Indians here have wished to do so, this Tomochichi always stepped in between them and soothed them through clever words and said that, before they could kill any others, they would have to begin with him, since he was an Englishman too.

Usually, the Indians are accustomed either to burn or else to bury what the deceased has left behind in the way of household effects, provisions, and other things, by which they wish to prevent a wife from being tempted to murder her husband through greed for her husband's goods. Through that she would gain nothing, because everything he possessed is burned, and what won't burn is buried. One of the Salzburgers found something in the woods that looked like a grave, and on it he found a pewter spoon, which he is still using. I was told that every Indian contracts with his wife at their marriage that he will supply her with meat but that she will provide him with corn and with the preparation of the food (they do not need any laundry); and therefore the men do no work but go hunting and see to the meat and skins, while the women plant corn, beans, and gourds.

Mr. Oglethorpe communicated to me what had occurred and been agreed between him and the Creek Indians, to whom he had travelled a couple of months ago. Written on a document to which the names of sworn witnesses were attached, this was looked upon as a renewal of the treaty between the Indians and the English. The document, which was confirmed with the names and seals of the sworn witnesses, had the following content: On 11 August 1739 the chiefs and warriors and also representatives of all the towns of the so-called Creek Indians gathered first in Cowetas and afterwards in Cusitas, where Mr. Oglethorpe held a speech through an interpreter to all estates on a large square. Before the deputies proposed anything in reply, they drank to each other with their black drink (made of a certain kind of tea that grows here) according to ancient custom, through which they obligate themselves to loyalty and faith. Otherwise, if they do not keep their promises truly, they wish and believe that this water will have a harmful effect.

In their speech the deputies assured, as if with one mouth: (1) That they were still steadfastly persisting in their old love for the King of Great Britain and were still holding firmly to the treaty they had made with the Lord Trustees in 1733, of which they had given each and every town a copy at that time, which the deputies still had and showed. (2) That all the land between the Savannah River and the St. Johns (not far from St. Augustine), and all the islands lying between them, and from the sea to the mountains belonged to the Creeks through ancient right, which they had maintained against all usurpers; they could still show the heaps of skeletons of their enemies whom they had slain in defending this their right. (3) That they had enjoyed the protection of the kings and queens of England from olden times, and that neither the Spaniards nor anyone else had a right to this land and that they would not allow anyone to settle on this land except those whom the Lord Trustees recommended. They continued to recognize that they have ceded to the Trustees all the land from the Savannah River to the Ogeechee River and all the land on the sea to the St. John's River and upland as far as the ebb and flood reach, also all the islands as far as this river stretches,[30] especially Frederica, Cumberland, and Amelia, which names they have given to these islands out of gratitude to the royal family. Yet they let it be known that all the land from Pipemaker's Bluff, which lies four miles above the city of Savannah (where a few Indian houses are standing and where the deceased king Tomochichi lived), to the city of Savannah, also the islands of St. Catherine's, Ossebaw, and Sapelo were reserved for the communal use of the Creek Nation. Mr. Oglethorpe promised them solemnly through a charter he issued to leave this stipulated land to them and to protect them in their rights against all usurpers. This was drawn up as a treaty and contract, signed, and supplied with the Trustees' seal in the city of Coweta on 21 August 1739.

In Savannah I had planned to borrow on a note the money which had been intended for our orphanage by Senior Urlsperger, Court Chaplain Ziegenhagen, and other benefactors, and also what was destined for my house; but money is now so rare that no merchant could help me in this.

Captain Thomson is still in Frederica and is not expected in Savannah until Mr. Oglethorpe himself has arrived, whither he plans to journey in a few days. Mr. Oglethorpe wished to have some English orphans taken into our orphanage, but their mother would not consent to this because she wishes to be with her children. A German widow asked me to accept her daughter and take care of her here; and I promised to do so upon the intercession of a pious merchant, who had redeemed her through pure mercy from the hard treatment she was getting from her present master. The girl is generally hardworking, but occasionally she has an attack as if she were not in her right mind; and, because her master and mistress cannot get used to her weakness but beat her severely and rage at her, she runs away and hides for many days under the houses until extreme hunger and thirst drive her out again. Then, when her master catches her again, he hangs her up and cruelly whips her, and the wounds are washed with salt water, which is truly a right Turkish treatment. I would have taken the little girl in the boat with me, if only she could have been found.

Six other German children of the Evangelical faith at Fort Argyle on the Ogeechee River have lost their father and mother and a couple of siblings one after the other through death; and, because most of them are still small and not yet reared, the two largest sons, of whom the oldest may be sixteen years old, asked me to have mercy on them and bring them to Ebenezer, otherwise there was no one in their place who could help them. Mr. Oglethorpe does not wish to let them go, but my intercession did avail in having them taken to Savannah and sheltered there.[31]

Another German man, who also suffers a very harsh treatment, offered to serve me with his wife and two sons for eight years if only I would take him to Ebenezer. But I do not covet my neighbor's man servant nor maid servant but am devoting myself more and more to retrenching my household. Meanwhile I have reported his justifiable complaint to the authorities, for which the masters look askance at me but can do me no harm. There are some well-intentioned people in Savannah, on whom the money would be well applied if one could advance them some money for their redemption, for otherwise they may well perish or lose their health. But this is entirely beyond our means. I have been assured by one of the authorities that the Lord Trustees will send a plenipotentiary who will hear all the complaints of the servants and their masters and pass judgment. Most of the servants are very wicked, disloyal, and treacherous people, who give an evil name to the others who are perhaps better or would like to become so.

Thursday, the 25th of October. A blanket from the orphanage was given to N. N. for his bed, and for this he and his pious wife greatly praised and thanked God. He was able to tell me several things about the providence of God that has ruled over him in physical and spiritual matters so far, and I applied this to make him be patient toward his wife, who cannot give him much help because of a natural defect and also because of a small child. She prays all the more often and zealously and performs all her limited activities in faith and in the fear of the Lord, which brings more blessing into his house than much human strength and skill. I also told him how highly I value Mrs. N. because of her righteous behavior and zealous prayer in the orphanage, even though she cannot work because of her physical infirmity. Her faithful prayer does more than can be accomplished through physical work, which is recognized, to be sure, not by her (for she lives in great poverty of the spirit and considers herself an *inutile terrae pondus*)[32] but by those who have spiritual eyes with which to see. I often speak with him in favor of his wife, because there is no lack of people who make comparisons between his wife and others who can work, which have probably done him harm. He is beginning to judge his domestic situation not according to reason, but according to the rules of Christianity.

Today I could not speak with Miss Lackner, because she had entirely veiled herself and lay either in sleep or in extreme weakness. In recent days she had recovered a little, but this did not last; and for several days her breath has been so bad that the people who tend her must practice great patience and abnegation. Her brother has necessary work on his plantation and can probably not get away because of his cattle; but from now on it will probably be necessary for him to take care of her. The fever stopped; and, because she then got worse, this is surely not a good sign. The Lord has her in His hands; He will continue to carry out the good work that He has begun in her until the day of His epiphany.

Friday, the 26th of October. N. N. caused me a heartfelt joy yesterday after the evening prayer hour by his encouragement. He told me, to the praise of God, how his eyes were opening more and more to recognize his misery, to which his selfmade justification and piety belong, and to come ever closer to the grace in Christ that is so richly offered to all sinners. Last Sunday God granted him a great blessing in my dear colleague's sermon; and he also noticed in the case of others in church that the gospel is a power that moves hearts, as he could recognize from outer symptoms (of which he cited some special examples). It pleased me to hear that he now recognizes better than previously the many advantages that our community has over many others; and he praises God for all His goodness. He can hardly marvel enough at his previous blindness, but even more at God's patience, which has put up with him for so long. He also recognizes the grace in others of the congregation, and he knows how to make good use of everything he hears from God's word in the sermons and prayer meetings.

In the evening prayer meeting we learned from the story in the 6th chapter of 1 Samuel that the Philistines asked their priests for advice as to what they should do with the Ark of the Covenant, which for them was an odor of death toward death (as the gospel is for many people in Christendom). They advised them as well as they could in their blindness as idolatrous priests, related the story of the obstinacy of the Egyptians and of their plagues, and chastized the Philistines and their princes for their obstinacy. And we do not read that they resented it, as many blind Christians do, some of whom desire no advice as to how to flee the judgments of God and to come to peace with God, and some of whom scorn the advice and become angry at the necessary chastisement and remonstrances about their sins. But, if the heathens profited from the stories that occurred in ancient times among the Israelites, and our marvelous God, who desires the salvation of all men, let the report of them come to the most remote and blind nations for this purpose, it is indeed a great blindness if Christians have no respect for these stories. And, in order that these people, and others like them, might be shamed and corrected in their blindness, I showed that Christ and His apostles (1 Corinthians 10 being read as a special example) cited and applied the stories of the Old Testament in their sermons. It is written twice expressly, *loc. cit.*, why our merciful God let them be written down and preserved for posterity.

Saturday, the 27th of October. While I was visiting the very sick Lackner woman, a Salzburger woman told me how good it is when one does not postpone one's penitence until the sickbed; for then one has enough to do with one's sickness and more than a few days is needed for the important change of heart. Some time ago, she said, she was violently sick with fever, at which time she prayed to the dear Lord to grant her a bit longer period of grace, even if it were only for two weeks, to prepare for the great change between time and eternity. He had heard her, yet it was still going badly with her. She had once heard, she said, that the Lord Jesus, at the right hand of the Father, is still concerned with our souls and is loyally tugging at them and working on them. Then she thought that, even if He had nothing else to do, He still had enough work with her, since her heart was so wicked, etc. Still, she was full of good trust in her good Savior, He would complete the work He had begun in her and her husband.

Sunday, the 28th of October. This morning Lackner brought me the news that his sister had passed away yesterday evening while we were at the prayer meeting. At the end she had not been able to say anything but "yes" and "no" and could scarcely hear, and one had to shout into her ear what he wished to say to her. She had taken no food, drink, or refreshment, or else she vomited it all up again. Her face had wasted away during her sickness, and her lips had swollen greatly, so that she was the very image of misery and could teach us what man has become through sin.[33] Tomorrow, if it pleases God, plans will be made for her burial. If wishes could help, we would gladly have kept this honest person with us longer; she would have made a good helpmeet for a pious Salzburger; but she wanted nothing more than for the Lord's will to be done, and therefore we must be, and wish to be, content. Her brother resigns himself to this and makes the best use of this death. From today's very beautiful gospel for the 20th Sunday after Trinity we took a comforting image of our perfect and eternal redemption through Christ and investigated in the examples before and in the text: (1) how ugly and misformed we appear without Christ and His redemption; (2) how glorious and blessed we can become in Christ and through His redemption. As an exordium we had the extremely precious words of Hebrews 9:12, "But by his own blood he entered," etc. May the pious Savior be praised for the blessing which He again granted me from His sweet gospel; may He make us all use right loyally the grace we have received!

Monday, the 29th of October. The good harvesting weather has lasted uninterrupted for many weeks; and our workers have been able to garner their blessings from their fields dry, which is to be recognized with proper gratitude. Our desire for the gifts in the four chests that were intended for us long ago is very great, especially since most people have great need of the linen and other things that were sent. Now that the harvest is over, some of the people wish to go all the way to Captain Thomson's ship at Frederica and fetch the things; but one of us would have to go along and we would have to have a good guide, because one can easily get lost on the water in the many rivers and creeks. Because of this and other difficulties such a long journey will probably not take place. We shall be unable to send our diary and the letters from us and the congregation until we receive the chests and the letters contained in them, which Sanftleben was to bring.

This evening after the prayer meeting several men and a couple of women again gathered in my room to have me read them the letter of admonition and exhortation that is being written to their compatriots, acquaintances, and friends, as well as the thank-you letters. They too had pleasure in them. Mrs. Gruber remained behind and asked me to send thanks in her name to Mr. N. and his dear wife for all the good that she, and especially her late husband, Moshammer had experienced on the occasion of their marriage and that had been wished for them with cordial love, and to report that none of their cordial good wishes had fallen on the ground, previously in the case of her late husband or now in the case of her, but that all had been abundantly fulfilled. He had overcome, and now she too was certain of the mercy of God in Christ. She had long wished to send her thanks, she said, but she had had to postpone doing so until now because she could not yet have said of herself with such certainty and joy what she can now say through the pure mercy of God. Today a Salzburger remembered the loving efforts of Mrs. N. when the last transport was dispatched; he marveled greatly at them and wished to be grateful for them, if only he could.

Tuesday, the 30th of October. This morning Paul Zittrauer was married to Anna Maria Heinrich,[34] who has served for almost a year in my house. During the meal the Salzburgers in attendance remembered Burgomaster Morel in Augsburg and could not find words to express how much good this distinguished benefactor had shown them. They requested me to send him their most obedient thanks for all the benefactions and much work he had undertaken so willingly both day and night as if they had been his own children. I hope the worthy Senior will give this dear benefactor our thanks in place of a letter from us, since time and our activities will not allow us to write to him. Since letters are more likely to go astray during this time of war than previously, we desire to write more often and to submit smaller diaries.

The recently received letters from Europe, which brought special blessings to me and others, caused me to read some of the first reports of the Salzburgers who came here to Ebenezer with us and after us; and, when considering the ways that God has gone with us from the beginning, I was not a little ashamed that at first I was disquieted by the fact that such reports had become known through publication. I thought they might have been harmful for our parishioners and other people, because some things did not rhyme well with the tribulations we had at the time; and I thought we might be misjudged in our office because of it, since people are accustomed to look upon external tribulations as something harmful and not to look through them at the salutary purpose of God and at the sweet fruit that finally follows them if one only persists. Now that the Lord has helped us through so gloriously and has treated us better than we deserve, or than we could have imagined, I am pleased with such printed reports; and I do not doubt that the Lord will bless in some souls the work which He has undertaken among us and which has been made public in this way. When we think back on these five years or more that we have been with the congregation, we must be ashamed of our many frailties, ignorance, and offenses and therefore humble ourselves before God. May He deign to illuminate us through His spirit so that we may henceforth perform our office with divine wisdom and strength and be useful to God and to men both near and far. They continue to work on us through letters and know that, through the grace of God, their words find a good place here and that in this way their work also is not fruitless in the Lord.

Our letters, which are to be taken to Savannah tomorrow or the day after tomorrow and forwarded to England via Charleston, are partly by us and partly by the parishioners. We have written to Court Chaplain Ziegenhagen, Senior Urlsperger, and Professor Francke, also to several ministers in Germany who sent a joint letter to us. The congregation is sending a letter of thanks to all benefactors in Europe, which we have accompanied with a postscript.[35] Likewise some Salzburgers and others are sending a letter of admonition and exhortation to their compatriots, friends, and acquaintances. The orphanage is thanking Mr. N. and other benefactors for all their love and cordial care in a little letter. May God bless it all!

Wednesday, the 31st of October. If another transport should ever be sent here (to which the Lord Trustees are not disinclined, but at present do not have the means), then they will probably send along some shoemaker who wishes to support himself among us in a Christian manner.[36] Now that the Lord Trustees are no longer maintaining a storehouse for provisions and supplies, if a new transport is sent here, the provisioning of the new colonists must be properly arranged in advance in England; for, if the Lord Trustees do not issue express orders for it, then nothing will be given here and it will take far too long if one must first write back to London concerning it.

NOVEMBER

Thursday, the 1st of November. This morning my dear colleague went to Savannah with our letters and diary all packed together; and he will give them to the secretary of the Lord Trustees, Mr. Stephens, for forwarding. Rainy weather began already yesterday and has continued heavy today; and therefore he will have a very unpleasant journey. May God strengthen him and his travelling companions!

I now hold the catechism practice in the hour from eleven to twelve; because the time immediately after eating is difficult for me, and speaking then is bad for my health. I also hear that this time is almost more convenient for the people than the former one. They still attend in large numbers and are very sincere in reciting the main parts of the catechism and answering the questions I pose; so I promise myself, with divine assistance, much blessing from this lesson. After the lesson Mrs. Schweighofer remained behind and complained that her prayer was without strength or savor and that she no longer felt any comfort or assurance of God's grace. She felt nothing, she said, but outright perdition and a very wicked heart, etc.; she would gladly bear all this and gladly fight against her enemies, if only God would not reject her, etc. I spoke to her sincerely and said that in Christianity there is a condition known as the condition of temptation, in which one must have faith without feeling and always simply go on praying, and in which one must pay no heed to all the clapper that the devil makes nor to all the objections of one's body, etc. It is a good sign, I told her, that she hates, as much as Satan himself, all sins and all the wicked things that occur to her even while praying. She is still in Jesus Christ, and therefore there is nothing damnable in her, etc. I especially found for her the comforting words of God in Isaiah 49:13–16, "For the Lord hath comforted his people, and will have mercy upon his afflicted. But Zion said," etc.; and I let her take them home with her.

Friday, the 2nd of November. The carpenters have been prevented from building the orphanage barn partly through sickness and partly by their work of harvesting in the fields. Kalcher has now taken care of his harvested crops; and, for threshing his rice, he knows of a good place instead of the threshing floor. Therefore we have postponed this construction until some future time, and we have stored away the lumber and shingles safely so that they can be used in the future. The wood and roof shingles cost £19 9s 9d, which must be paid from the last physical blessings from Augsburg and London. Since we can get along this year without the barn, it is better for us not to incur any debts until we learn what the Lord is planning for us. The most necessary thing now is to lay a firm floor of sawn boards in the orphanage and to side the walls with boards so that this winter the adults and children will not be so uncomfortable and hindered in good works as last winter. Boards are now being cut for that purpose. If God grants enough to buy a stove and set it up in the house, it will be a great blessing for both the well and the sick. The carpenters assure me that the orphanage will last much longer if it is sided with boards so that the rain can no longer rot the wood by getting into the grooves into which the shingles or clapboards are fitted. If it is the Lord's will for our little institution to grow and we are required to construct another building, then the present house could be used for all sorts of housekeeping purposes.

Saturday, the 3rd of November. My dear colleague returned to us yesterday evening from Savannah healthy and well preserved after delivering our packet carefully, so we hope it will go to London with some safe opportunity. He also brought with him the little German girl whom we have already mentioned and whom Mr. Flerel[1] has taken under his and his wife's supervision. Because of her weakmindedness she does not get along in a crowd, otherwise we would have put her in the orphanage. To be sure, she has a poor but pious mother in Savannah, whom God has brought, in this new world, to the recognition of her sins and of the Redeemer of the world. Mr. Oglethorpe is still in Savannah and is waiting for the Indians who are to be used against the Spaniards. He has been heard to say that he wishes to write a letter to Prof. Francke and request him to send a minister trained in self-denial for the German people in Frederica, of which he is still expecting many more from the Palatinate.[2] He has also promised something to the theological student Zoberbiller, who has been preaching to the Reformed people on Sundays since his father's death in Purysburg, if he will take charge of the people at Palachocolas who have moved there from New Windsor (the city that is to be built near Savannah-Town); and we should help him with good advice and give a testimony of his behavior and diligence.

Sunday, the 4th of November. N. N. announced that he and his wife wished to take Holy Communion next Sunday; and on this occasion he told me something from which I could recognize his increase in goodness. To be sure, he is having a rather hard time in a physical way, since he is old and is just starting his plantation; yet he is very content with God's guidance and praises Him for bringing him not only out of Salzburg but also out of the Empire and for bringing him closer to His word in tranquility and to a concern for the salvation of his soul. He is humble at heart and considers himself (as his expression was) not worth the least little grain of rice; and he is working on his wife with great simplicity and earnestness.

N. told me that he will remember today, Sunday, as long as he lives; for God showed him great mercy two years ago in the repetition hour through the gospel for the 20th Sunday after Trinity, which we had today, and that he is still enjoying its fruit. He is no longer the Old Adam but has learned to know himself; he denies his personal justification and self-made piety, and only seeks his rest and salvation as a poor sinner in Christ and His eternal redemption. His mouth was full of the praise of God for the many spiritual and physical benefactions He has shown us here.

Monday, the 5th of November. Both last Saturday and also in this evening's prayer meeting the story from 1 Samuel 7 reminded us, to the praise of God, that our loving God has already let us experience many Ebenezers[3] in both spiritual and physical things. He has let us live together for almost six years now and has shown us so much kindness on the voyage, in Old

Ebenezer, and now at this place that we have good grounds to remind each other of them diligently and awaken each other to the praise of God. It was also shown by the example of the penitent Israelites what we must do if we wish to have God on our side and as a furtherer of our work, namely, we must convert ourselves to Him in our hearts and bring the fruits of penitence. Then, according to God's promise, we will not lack any good thing that we need for our life either here or beyond.

N. spoke with me about his intention of going to Holy Communion, and I found his words very edifying. He is otherwise very simple and has few natural gifts; yet he could tell me so much good out of yesterday's sermon and even out of the Bible stories we have contemplated so far that I was truly joyful. Whatever he hears, he includes in his prayers; and for this purpose he locks himself in his hut so that no one will disturb him. He was not very pleased with those who run into his yard to draw water from the well right after church on Sunday, since the first thing they should do is to reflect about what they have heard and to pray about it.

Last week, when the congregation's thank-you letter was to be sent to all the benefactors in Europe, he came to me several times and expressed his pleasure with it and wished me to send his greeting to these and those benefactors who had been kind to him, especially in Augsburg, Ulm, Memmingen, etc., some of whom he could call by name; and he wished me to assure them of his grateful remembrance of their benefactions. Among others he particularly remembered Lord and Lady von N.;[4] but he was afraid that they might be displeased that his name was given among the signers, because he was such a bad person, etc. I set him right concerning this, however, since it is apparent that they are not ashamed of poor and simple people who are members of Christ, etc.

Yesterday in the repetition hour it was stated that people who wish to be saved should not hide the sins of their youth but must do true penance for them if they wish to win the mercy of God, the forgiveness of sins, and salvation. Sins that are past but not regretted are not forgotten by God, as by frivolous people; and it is not enough for one to have been punished by men and afterwards to have improved in his worldly life, etc.

Tuesday, the 6th of November. God is showing us great mercy this year not only by granting us a very rich harvest in every way but also by constantly giving us such good weather that everything can be brought in dry to the very end. Also, there has been no frost yet either, so the pumpkins and sweet potatoes can still grow. Most people have received so much produce that storage space has become too limited and they must think seriously about new buildings. In the orphanage also we have received so beautiful a blessing in corn, beans, rice, sweet potatoes, pumpkins, etc. that we can rightly praise the name of our God for them. Kalcher told me that he can well feel that the Lord is with the work in the orphanage. Mrs. Kalcher said that if Mrs. Urlsperger, who observes the ways of the Lord in her housekeeping, should see this blessing with her own eyes, she would not be able to hold back tears of joy. We shall not forget to praise together the loving Giver of all good gifts as soon as the sweet potatoes are harvested. Wherever our pious people go, we hear them praising God; and they consider themselves unworthy of such gifts.

Wednesday, the 7th of November. A Salzburger woman who registered for Holy Communion gave me great pleasure through the testimony she made of the grace of God in Christ which she had experienced so far and which she had comprehended in faith; and this encouraged me to a new seriousness in the Christian struggle in which she had proved so loyal and had triumphed so gloriously even here against her enemies, to the praise and renown of her merciful God. She wishes nothing more than for her husband, on whom God is working with loyalty and profit, to achieve a complete certainty of his state of grace, for which purpose she encourages him very evangelically from her own experience. Her expressions concerning the nature of faith and its various struggles and victories were right exceptional and gave me material about which I plan to preach next Sunday, God willing. Our dear parishioners are often our best reminders concerning this or that text to be preached, and in many instances we have thought of this or that consideration simply by looking at them and recalling the state of their minds during our lectures. Usually, the wonderful Lord lets me find a good place to apply these thoughts.

I experienced a good example of this just this morning; in the last repetition hour God directed my mind to some material that made an impression on several people, as they revealed to each other during their work. The above-mentioned Salzburger woman carries around with her the verse, "Good and upright is the Lord; therefore will he teach sinners in the way," etc. She says that this verse applies well to us Salzburgers: the Lord has well instructed us on our way and is still doing so. What a blessing it is, she said, that He let things be hard for them in Salzburg. Had it been a little bit easier and more bearable for them, then she and others with her would have remained there; and from that it could be seen that the cross, which seems disagreeable at the beginning, is very useful, etc. Ebenezer, so far the Lord has helped us,[5] and she praised the Lord that Ebenezer was the city of her spiritual birth and of many others.

A pious single Salzburger asked me to examine him as to whether he could go to Holy Communion in accordance with the present desire of his heart. To be sure, it is written, "But let a man examine himself," etc.; yet, in order to deceive oneself all the less, it is necessary to subject oneself to the examination of one's ministers. In order to come to my point, I asked whether he is still consorting diligently with his neighbor, who would also like to be saved but is still so weak; and I learned that he had had a useful conversation with him and another man at work just yesterday. Another man, whom he did not name to me, had asked him what it meant when it was constantly emphasized that one should free oneself from one's former sins, and the man had become quiet when he explained it to him. He knew that a newly converted Christian, even if he is still just a beginner, is subjected to being ensnared by the devil in spiritual and physical arrogance until he makes a big thing of the good received and scorns his neighbors, and that this is the most direct way to separation. However, if one penetrates as a woe-begone sinner into the poverty of the spirit, tries to be justified through Christ alone, and lives holy and piously for this reason and remembers how long God has put up with him, then he is acting humbly. A man who imagines himself holy and pious without justification is a miserable and dangerous person, etc.

Thursday, the 8th of November. N., who spoke to me about his state of mind and his Christianity when he came today to register for Holy Communion, pleased me so much that, from the depth of my heart, I had to praise our loving God, who means well with all poor sinners, for the grace He has shown him. For some time he has felt many kinds of physical infirmities, which he looks upon as forebodings of his approaching death. His sins, which he can well feel, cause him much worry; and sometimes it seems to him as if he has been too sinful and has already missed his time of grace. However, since God has imbued him with a disgust and loathing for all sins and because he now feels more strength than previously to resist enticements to sin and other disturbing emotions, he accepts all this simply and as a good sign. He also said that this made him hope that God will not reject and damn him; because, if He had wished to, He could have done it long ago. Now He has shown him so much mercy, and is still doing so, that it will not have been done in vain.

Among his chief blessings he counts the fact that he had come to a partial recognition of the truth already in Salzburg and that he had been led out of his dark and superstitious fatherland. He had grown up in blindness, he said, and was already grown when a Protestant servant had lent him a little book to read, and in it he found more beautiful things than he could remember ever having read. His desire for the evangelical truth and for the unmutilated use of Holy Communion was so great that he could not rest until he reached a Protestant country. His greatest wish and desire now was to praise God evermore for all His work and benefactions; and he related some special items that he is accustomed to introduce into his praise of God, which concerned the three main articles of the Christian faith in general and, particularly, what He had shown him in his fatherland, after his departure, here in Ebenezer, and especially in the orphanage. He also told me how he prays for his own and other people's needs, all of which was in accord with the image of salutary dogma and the thoughts of a true Christian. At his departure he asked me not to become tired of him at the orphanage, especially since he cannot work much because of his infirmities. The abundant care he enjoys there in soul and body he attributes chiefly to God and thanks Him for it; yet he should thank me too, etc. He now recognizes better than previously what a jewel the orphanage has in N. and N.;[6] and he was not at all pleased with N. and two other people, whom they were never able to satisfy.

In yesterday's prayer meeting we heard, from the example of the Israelites in 1 Samuel 8, what self-will and carnal thoughts desire and what a burden they bring down on one's neck, this being something that people do not believe at first but afterwards have to experience to their own harm and sometimes too late.

This evening before the prayer meeting a Salzburger woman called on me to receive instruction about some things that occasionally transpire between her and her husband. Her husband is somewhat careless, does not pay attention to the housekeeping as she would like, and becomes irritable and angry if she says anything to him. At the same time he is not practicing his Christianity as seriously as he should. As examples she related several special things that had caused anger, disquiet, and trouble; and from this I could see that the husband is not in the right but has proved obstinate and defiant and has sinned through harsh words. However, I could also not approve of her behavior toward him, her contradiction, urging, comparison with other husbands, reproaches, etc. I showed her from the *Haus-Tafel*,[7] and especially from 1 Peter 3:1 ff., what her duty was according to God's commandments, namely, not to command, reproach, contradict, but rather to subject herself in all things (provided they do not run counter to God's word and her conscience). According to verse 4 she must, I said, show a meek and quiet spirit through the grace of God and speak with her husband in such a way as to tell him in a loving and humble way what she sees differently, but otherwise be obedient, even if her suggestion and advice do not please him. At the same time she would sigh and pray sincerely for herself and her husband and loyally perform her work as her husband wishes it. If any ill effect were to occur in the housekeeping when she had done her part in this way, then she would not be to blame; but through the providence and grace of God and through her prayers her husband would become wiser because of it and would learn to reflect so that he might well be won, according to verse 1, through her quiet, humble, and obedient spirit, and in the absence of words. I assured her that I had told her husband, like her, several times what his duties were and how he should behave toward her. She was well pleased with all this and desired nothing more than to be instructed how to behave properly.

Friday, the 9th of November. Today, instead of the prayer meeting in my house, I held the catechism practice with the women, since I had been kept from it last Tuesday because of blood-letting; but I still wished for them to keep up with the men in regard to the truths of the catechism. Our good and pious God lets me clearly feel His merciful presence in this simple yet very necessary work, of which grace I consider myself entirely unworthy. The people of both sexes always attend in large numbers and willingly, are gladly catechized, learn one major part after the other with its explanation, and comprehend the basic truths of the Christian religion correctly, as can be seen from the examination questions always posed at the beginning of the lesson. And, what is most important, their hearts are deeply touched so that they sometimes shed tears.

N. N. must have received a blow to her conscience; for not only did I see her before me with weeping eyes, but she also remained behind and complained to me that she had allowed herself to be tempted to very serious things in her country, for which she must still do penance. To be sure, they are not known here to anyone except N.; but God in Heaven knows them well, and she wished to reveal them to me too. I told her that she had sinned grievously; and I also held up to her the verse in 1 Corinthians 6:9 ff., from which she could learn how far she could come if only she would convert honestly to Christ: His blood makes all penitent sinners clean of all sin, etc.

A pious Salzburger was reminded very emphatically of the sins of his youth and thought it necessary to confess them to me, as he would gladly do, since he had not been punished by men. However, from his very first words I understood what he was aiming at and instructed him that it was not absolutely necessary to confess to his minister everything that had occurred in his youth, if no one had been vexed by it, unless his conscience left him no rest and he needed advice, instruction, and aid. Otherwise it is written, "Against thee, thee only, have I sinned," etc.; and therefore it was only necessary for the sinner to settle the matter with God, whom he has insulted, through the intercessor Jesus Christ and to find mercy and forgiveness, which will take place richly and superabundantly if one crawls to the cross as a penitent and grace-hungry man. In sins against one's neighbor, especially with regard to the Seventh Commandment,[8] it is another matter, since God demands a release through restitution, which will occur if the penance is of the right kind. The man was very pleased with this explanation, and I asked him to call on me often.

There are several sinners in the congregation of whose serious sins from earlier times we learn from other people, or else we can almost notice by looking at them that they have a secret muck upon them. Now, because such sins did not happen among us and we may not reproach them with them and yet they must still be brought to recognize and regret such abominations and finally do penance for them if they are ever to be serious in their Christianity, we must attack their consciences with the law and bring to light the matter they have kept concealed. To be sure, this first touches others who are serious about their salvation and causes them to remember their former sins; but God also blesses this method with those whom we in fact meant to address, as can be seen in the recent example of a certain person.

Saturday, the 10th of November. General Oglethorpe has written a letter to me in which he requests a righteous theological student from Halle as a preacher for the German people in Frederica, of which still more are expected from Germany; we should ask Professor Francke for him at the first opportunity.[9] He promises to give him £40 sterling per year for his maintenance. Before this letter reaches Halle, may almighty God choose and prepare a theology student who will be able to accomplish something useful here for the praise of His Glory and for the salvation of souls. Mr. Oglethorpe would be most pleased if it were to be someone who would enter into good understanding, brotherly love, and intimate correspondence with us and would persist in it steadfastly, for he himself knows from much experience in this country the advantages of such material, let alone spiritual, unity. While dining in his room with many of his colleagues he attributed the blessings he had seen in our community in part to the good policy that the members of the congregation are directed along only one path and follow these directions simply. We shall invoke the Lord of the Harvest to incline the hearts of our dear Fathers, who so far have always made common cause regarding our office, to an individual who will especially fit these circumstances. Perhaps we will think of one whom we have known as a loyal fellow-worker before the Lord in the Orphanage, whom, other things being equal, we could recommend.

Today a married couple was revealed to me because of their discord, neglect of communal prayer, etc., so I reminded them of their duty by reading from the *Haus-Tafel* and other works and exhorted them strongly. The man had tried as hard as possible to conceal his thoughts and he answered my questions right ambiguously and with mental reservations just so he might be admitted to Holy Communion; and for this reason I had to admonish him all the more seriously afterwards. During the prayer tears flowed often from his eyes; and from his subsequent humble behavior I could see that they were not from anger or wickedness. At his departure I reminded him of something that had made a great impression on him several years ago; and I hope the Lord will bless this in him again.

Sunday, the 11th of November. On this day of the Lord forty-five persons among us were fed at the grace-laden table of our dear Savior in Holy Communion; and may He bless this in all of us for the sake of His great and sincere love.

A woman from a plantation near Purysburg had come to us to take Holy Communion with us. Along with other listeners she heard much good from the word of the Lord, and may He bless it in her and us all. Today my dear colleague began to ask the first part of the catechism questions, after having completed the *Haus-Tafel*. We utilized the beautiful gospel John 4:47 ff. by treating it partly with regard to the nature and quality of faith and partly with regard to its growth and increase, these being the two most important items for being saved. God blessed this abundantly in me and, as I noticed, in some others too. Today there was a very strong wind, which will not suffer any light to burn in the old church hut, so instead of a repetition hour we gathered partly in my house and partly in that of my dear colleague, where we had our repetition and prayers. In the same way we gathered together yesterday evening in my room.

Last night we had heard that two couples, one of whom wished to take Holy Communion, were at odds; so this morning before church they were heard and reconciled by my dear colleague. This time we would also have confirmed some children who have been in preparation until now (not without advantage, God be praised!) and let them take Holy Communion, if their parents or guardians had gone this time too. Therefore it has been postponed until next time (May God let it be to their greater blessing!). The parents are not urging us to admit them soon but are fully satisfied with our decision. May God make us useful to old and young!

Monday, the 12th of November. Our church hut stands, as it were, upon weak feet; and last Sunday we were afraid the very strong wind might blow it down over our heads. Because God has allowed us to detect, in the last letters, a trace of His providence, which guards us in this matter too, we intend to make plans to build a church in His name as soon as the carpenters and other helpers are finished with their other construction. The wood that was cut at the expense of the orphanage suits the needs of this construction very well, according to the judgment of the carpenters; and therefore it will probably be used for that purpose. May God let us consult with Him in all things and begin with faith, and then it will succeed.

Tuesday, the 13th of November. We have again received news that the merchants in Savannah cannot lend money on personal notes. Because money is required by the congregation for buying winter clothing and other necessities and we would like to pay the debts for the orphanage, my construction, and other things, we have found it necessary for my dear colleague to travel to Port Royal or, if our note is not accepted there, all the way to Charleston, for which purpose people in our congregation have volunteered to row him there and back in our large boat. Consequently, he departed this afternoon in the name of the Lord after holding public prayers; and he hopes to find a good guide in Purysburg or Savannah.

Because there are safe and fast opportunities for forwarding from Charleston to London, we have transmitted a copy of the letter Mr. Oglethorpe sent me concerning the preacher desired in Frederica to Court Chaplain Ziegenhagen, together with an enclosed note concerning the circumstances of the German people at Frederica; also a few lines to Secretary Newman and an extract from the new and very brief diary to Professor Francke. May the Lord accompany my dear colleague and the letters he is taking with His blessing, and may He let us see him soon again in health. Both we and the orphanage, like several in the congregation, need various things which are not to be had at all in Savannah or are very expensive, but which we will probably be able to get from Charleston in this way.

To the praise of God a pious woman told me that she had been blessed last Sunday and during the previous preparation for Holy Communion with much edification but that she was now being depressed by her disloyalty and sloth, etc. But in truth she is such an honest soul as our good and pious God has before Him in Isaiah 54:4–17, and therefore I read this passage to her slowly and let her read it with me. I had to underline all this for her with red ink so that she might frequently remember these comforts of the Lord.

Wednesday, the 14th of November. We have now had two hard night frosts in a row, which were the first of this year. The Lord has granted our people many sweet potatoes and given them time to ripen and be harvested. The acorns have also turned out especially well, and the people gather them in quantity. One kind in this country is larger than is found in Germany; and, since the people have many other kinds of feed too, they would be able to raise many hogs this year, if only the bears in our region did not do so much harm. They swim across the Savannah River from Carolina to our side, as the Salzburgers have often seen while travelling in their boat. There are also a large number of walnuts, but the ones in this country have too thick a shell and not as much meat as in Germany; but they do have just as sweet a taste.

Old Ebenezer is now becoming entirely empty of people, since the Lord Trustees' German servants, who were used at the mill, have been called back to work at Savannah. The mill has been taken apart; and, because the wooden and iron parts that were sent here from England may have cost very much, they do not wish to waste them but rather have them carried back to Savannah, which will again cause much expense. Bringing something from Old Ebenezer to Savannah requires much effort, time, and expense. Now there is only one German family left there, who must guard the wood and iron parts of the dismantled mill so that the Indians who pass through Old Ebenezer on their way to Savannah will not burn or destroy them. There is also an English family who are in charge of the Trustees' cattle there.[10] The Trustees profit from the cattle there, which have good pasture in the entire forest; and they would have even more profit if only they had experienced and loyal people in their service. They receive none of the butter or cheese; the little that is made is used by the Englishmen. Their actual profit is the increase in the cattle, since the cows are left with the calves and grow up all year in the forest without care or supervision; and thus the herd of cows gets larger every year, whereas the oxen are slaughtered when they are old and fat enough and are applied to the Trustees' use. Therefore nothing will become of Old Ebenezer, and it is a shame that so much money was spent on it.

Thursday, the 15th of November. Soon after the catechism lesson we baptized twins, with which Ruprecht Eischberger's wife was couched this morning. Until now the woman has had fever and a growth all over her abdomen, but God has mercifully helped her through.

After the catechism lesson a pious widow remained behind and said that God had greatly refreshed her with His word and that she would like me to underline the verse in Ezechiel 33, "As I live, saith the Lord," etc. We treated the fifth question, "Do you hope to be saved?", etc. and showed what it means to be saved, namely, to be saved from the unblessed condition of sinners and placed into the blessed state of the children of God. The first thought and the first question that occur to truly penitent people when feeling their sins and the punishment they have merited from them should be, I said, whether any mercy can be hoped for by such great and abominable sinners and whether even they can be saved. This was affirmed and proved partly from unambiguous Bible verses and partly from the fact that God not only wishes lovingly (as lovingly as the most loving person) the salvation of all men and gladly furthers it, but also is love itself; from which incomprehensibly high love He gave His Son as a Savior for the entire world and also clearly revealed the order of salvation, namely, conversion and rebirth, and ordained the means for salvation: the word of God, prayer, and sacraments, so that we might be led by them in the order of salvation and be preserved in it, provided, N.B., that we use them rightly. Within this order one can be sure of his salvation, without it there is no hope. God does not lead us to trust our salvation to feeling and savoring, but only to this order, etc.

Friday, the 16th of November. Among the last gifts, our dear Lady N. N. in N.[11] remembered our lying-in women with a gift of money, which, to be sure, we do not yet have in hand because we have not yet been able to borrow any money on a note. However, in anticipation of it we can already help such suffering people, as we are now doing for poor Mrs. Eischberger. May God repay her and all her illustrious family with interest in all their circumstances for this benefaction. Eischberger and she have been visited by a long-lasting domestic affliction in that he has suffered very serious attacks on both arms and chest and is still dragging himself around with them, whereas she has had fever and other severe bodily conditions for a long time. They have well used their little strength during the summer and also harvested a little for their needs through divine blessing, from which they will be able to eke out an existence until the next harvest. However, since the husband has been incapable of earning any money for clothing and other necessities, they need the help of kind people, especially now in the circumstance of her lying-in.

I am very impressed by the detailed instructions concerning the benefactions for our congregation and orphanage as they are specified in worthy Mr. N's letter. We shall make even better use of them for the praise of God, the strengthening of our faith, and the intercession for such dear benefactors when we thank our dear God for the richly granted harvest at a special gathering in the orphanage, which is to be held with God's help at the beginning of next week. In the story from 1 Samuel 10, which we are to contemplate now, we find the noteworthy circumstance that, on his return from Samuel, Saul was met in the name of the Lord by three men who greeted him in a friendly way and gave him two loaves of bread according to Samuel's prophetic words; and in this we must marvel at God's power to incline hearts. Here in Ebenezer we have received material enough for such holy and edifying admiration of the miraculous providence and government of God, according to which He has inclined the hearts of entirely unknown people in love and affection for us. God will continue to make good all want in the orphanage and congregation! He has everything in His hands. God is loyal if one turns to Him; if He begins well, He intercedes and accomplishes.

Saturday, the 17th of November. Our dear Father in heaven has granted me a great blessing in my house, which is very useful in performing several official duties. I have now dedicated one room entirely to the service of the congregation, especially since the place for our public gathering is very uncomfortable. Baptisms and marriages are performed here, and I am especially pleased that I can hold school here in the absence of my dear colleague and hold meetings with the adults of the congregation, namely, on Tuesdays and Thursdays with the women and on Wednesdays and Saturdays with the men, in addition to the prayer hour, which is held on Mondays and Fridays. It is a very fine thing that I can instruct the sexes separately in the catechism, since they show less bashfulness and more confidence, sincerity, and simplicity in the questions and answers. The meetings where we practice the catechism, wherein all principles of the faith and ancillary duties of our Christian religion are presented in order, are as dear to the people as any other opportunity for edification; and God dignifies us in this with His blessing. We detect a clear sign of God's providence in the fact that He is once more letting us lead the entire congregation into the catechism and instruct them in the basic dogmas of Christianity before the people move to their plantations, where it would be less possible to do so.

One of Eischberger's twins died this morning and was buried in the afternoon. The Salzburgers have long seen that the thin dwelling huts, in which they feel every change of weather, not only cause great discomfort in winter and summer but also cause harm to health; but so far they have been unable to do anything about it because they have had to apply their time to other necessary work to win their bread and to earn something for their needs. Also, they have had to do a lot of work in vain both in Old Ebenezer and here because they lacked their own land. This winter they are beginning new construction work on their plantations, and they will do everything they can to see that they get firm and well protected houses.

It is too bad that we have so few carpenters, otherwise the constructions would proceed much faster. In this matter also God has, for our good, disposed the Salzburgers to decline, with good reasons, the call to work on the orphanage in Savannah and whatever else is to be built there.[12] Mr. Oglethorpe was agreeable to this, although he had formerly wished to employ them here or there after he himself had seen the skillful and inexpensive construction of my house (for it is cheap compared to building costs in this land, even though in Germany it would be reckoned expensive). From now on he will not expect any outside work from them. At first we considered the offer from Mr. Oglethorpe and the schoolmaster in Savannah to be a blessing, but God knew and ordained it better. Oh, if only we would let Him lead and guide us in all things! The surveyor[13] has not yet completed his work on the plantations; and, even though Mr. Oglethorpe gave him definite orders for this in my presence and even had his pay for work already done held back until its completion, he still does not come. However, this does not do the congregation as much harm as in earlier times. Meanwhile, we can see from this that this gentleman cannot always achieve his purpose at once, even with his authority and all the means he uses.

Sunday, the 18th of November. We received news from Savannah that my dear colleague found the desired guide to Charleston and departed from Savannah very early last Thursday. The merchant Montaigut, who usually accepts our personal notes, died recently; and apparently his widow will not get involved in any complicated business, all of which helps confirm the fact for us that this distant and difficult journey was necessary. May God stand by him and his travelling companions in every way! Such a separation for a short time teaches me what a blessing of the Lord our comradely friendship and work is. May He let us enjoy it for a long time in accordance with His mercy!

Monday, the 19th of November. We know of a Salzburger in the congregation named Hans Floerel who is a true fruit of God and has right fine qualities for a Salzburger schoolmaster. He has a beautiful gift in getting on with children, is loved in the entire community, is content with little, and thus useful to God and man. Perhaps God will incline his mind to accept the call to become schoolmaster; and we hope the praiseworthy Society will not refuse to allow him Ortmann's salary, namely £10 sterling. It will please them that we ourselves, with God's blessing, have trained a schoolmaster who suits the community and that they can thus save the cost of sending another one across the sea. The younger Zuebli would also accept the position gladly. Perhaps, if he lets himself be still better prepared through the grace of God, we can someday use him for some other purpose. The English youth, Bishop, whom I freed a short time ago and who is now beginning his own household, will gradually also qualify as a schoolmaster, provided he continues to accept good instruction and to grow in his initial goodness. He now holds the English school and receives £5 sterling from Mr. Oglethorpe.

Because the dear Lord has granted the orphanage a great physical blessing in the harvest they have gathered and has let much other good flow from the well of His goodness so far, we promised several weeks ago to thank Him publicly for all His kindness and benefactions at a time set aside for it; and this took place at about noon today with much edification for all of us. I had mentioned this plan last Saturday at the prayer meeting; and this had the good effect that the three front rooms of the orphanage were filled with men, women, and children, who showed through their presence and the hymnals and Bibles they brought with them that they had just as much reason as the orphanage to praise our merciful God with us for His kindness; and this impressed me greatly. Through the beautiful song *Ich singe dir mit Hertz*, etc., which was sung first, our spirits were already awakened to a grateful remembrance of the abundant benefactions we have enjoyed so far; and this was done even more afterwards through the presentation and clarification of the impressive verse in Joel 2:21, "Fear not, o land," etc. This right golden verse was sent to our congregation with the last letters, together with a gift of money, by our dear Deacon Hildebrand in Augsburg; and, because it suited us well in our present circumstances, we made common use of it.

We have experienced many proofs that the Lord is doing great things in our dear Ebenezer, and these were cited individually for the praise of God. Therefore all those among us who become obedient to the voice of the Lord can be assured that they shall continue to experience the *Magnalia Dei* in their souls and bodies and that even our temporal enemies will not be able to harm us, no matter how great they might be. Therefore we compared the last words of the above-mentioned verse with Isaiah 37:24 ff. and especially with Psalms 76:11. Through the last words of the psalm our marvelous God had sowed a good seed into my heart through dear Mr. Hildebrand's sermon in the *Collegium Biblicum* at Professor Francke's house, a fact which he perhaps does not know.

We recognize well enough from the above-mentioned verse and from other items that were read from Senior Urlsperger's list of the last gifts, in which the names of some of the benefactors are written, that pious people in Europe recognize the great deeds God has performed and is still performing for us in this corner of America, just as He formerly did for His people in that corner of Asia; and we recognize that they are pleased by them, praise God, and contribute everything possible for the glorification of God's glorious name. This has aroused us to open our eyes rightly too, so that we will not overlook any of God's miracles and fail to praise Him. After the prayer we sang the beautiful song *Lobe den Herrn, o meine Seele*, etc., which is based on the 146th Psalm and which had been assigned to the children to memorize. From now on they will also learn the psalm word by word, which might be, and might be called, the widows', orphans', and other needy people's own psalm.

Several days ago, while we were discussing this public thanksgiving, Mrs. Kalcher reminded us that we had promised to praise the Lord together also for the orphanage's well, which is a right great blessing of the Lord; and she said that it had gone with us as it had with Jacob in Genesis 35, who had to be reminded again by God of his almost forgotten promise. Therefore we included this blessing too in our humble thanksgiving prayer, which was based on Christ's sacrifice of reconciliation. May God be well pleased with such practice in Christ and let it bear much good fruit!

According to the above-mentioned letter of Senior Urlsperger, many in the congregation will be refreshed by the charitable gifts to be received: e.g., the poor according to their circumstances, and particularly the sick lying-in women, by the gift of the House of N. and N.; the last seven colonists (who are still subject to some physical ailments) by the Evangelical Body in Regensburg; the colonists from Memmingen, twenty-six in number, by the praiseworthy magistrate there; our poor, sick, and impaired by the late Mr. Hüntzelmann through Schauer's balm, linen, and money; and in part the entire community and in part our orphanage by worthy Mr. N., Inspector N., Pastor N., Mr. N., Mr. N., Privy Counselor N., Mrs. N., Mr. N., Mr. N., and Mr. N. Oh, may our loving God repay them all in time and eternity and write their names in the Book of Life! And since our loyal High Priest has so richly blessed us through the hands of these and many other spiritual priests, we can say from Ecclesiasticus 50: "Thank all ye God, who doeth great things on all ends of the earth," etc.; He gives us all good. May He give you and us a joyful heart, and grant us eternal peace and ordain that His grace remain forever with you and us. And may He redeem us as long as we live.

I utilized the three noteworthy signs that the prophet Samuel made to Saul in the name of the Lord in chapter 10 in this way: whoever remembers his mortality rightly is satisfied with little through the grace of God, even if it were only a piece of dry bread. If God, as He has promised, fills his needs, then this should bring him to the multitude of spiritual prophets and priests to say humble thanks in their company (but also in his closet) for all His kindness and all good guidance of the Lord and to ask Him for grace to be and to remain loyal. How much more that should be the case if God grants us more than our basic needs. God has always placed a great blessing on common prayer and praise of God.

Toward evening in my room it was revealed to me that two people, a man and a woman, had received much blessed edification through God from the meetings in the orphanage. Among other things the woman said with tears that God had already blessed the edification and the orphanage prayer meetings in her often and right amazingly, and today too He had again granted her something that was necessary for her. He had revealed to her in conscience that she had previously insulted God and her neighbor so much, yet He was doing more good for her than for others; He had saved her from Salzburg like a tinder from the fire and was following her with great patience and mercy. However, her frivolity and disloyalty were so great, she said (then her tears flowed so richly that she did not hear my encouragement the first time).

To comfort this sorrowful soul, I told her from yesterday's gospel that it is a good sign if the dear Lord drags us before the judgment throne of our conscience during the period of grace and holds everything up to us to our shame and humiliation. He is only doing it to prepare the poor sinner properly for the mercy and forgiveness which He has already prepared. I also reminded her of the comforting little verse that was so sweet for us yesterday, Hebrews 7, "Our merciful High Priest is also able to save them to the uttermost that come unto God by him," etc., and therefore this evening hour too is a time for being saved, etc. Yesterday, from the gospel for the 22nd Sunday after Trinity, God proclaimed to us both mercy and wrath, mercy to the penitent and the humble and mercilessness and wrath to the impenitent and the wicked.

In the afternoon we heard something about the questions in the interrogative parts of the catechism concerning our loyal intercessor Jesus Christ; and we learned that His office as intercessor, the reconciliation He has instituted, and the goods of salvation He has obtained apply to all, even to the greatest sinners, of which we receive the most certain promises in the gospel, in the words of the sacrament, and through the dear pledge of His body and blood in Holy Communion.

Tuesday, the 20th of November. The economy of the orphanage required us to build a durable s. h. pig sty of heavy wood.[14] It is so arranged that a rather large number of hogs have room in it, and separate appended stalls have been made for fattening them. Over it is a good attic for storing and threshing rice, which we have greatly needed. Even though it is only a sty, the construction costs have amounted to £6 sterling. But it is so firm and durable that the orphanage will derive benefit from it for many years. In the beginning the Salzburgers built stables and other buildings only of planks, which were built quickly and with little expense; but there was no profit in this because they had to repair them every year and rebuild them very soon.

Wednesday, the 21st of November. After the troubles I had yesterday, our kind Savior refreshed me again abundantly in the catechism hour as well as through the visit and encouragement of some pious men. Oh, how the dear people thank God for revealing to them their imagined and self-made, but entirely inadequate, piety and righteousness through the light of His word, which also sets aright what is concealed in the heart. They have learned to believe that it costs more to be saved than is generally thought and that there is a great difference between one who has come close to the kingdom of God and one who has actually broken into it through an earnest struggle of penitence and faith and who seizes the kingdom of heaven with force.[15] They heartily wish that they could tell all their compatriots, especially their near of kin who are partly in the German Empire and partly in Prussia,[16] that, to a large extent, they had previously been caught in self-deception and had never truly experienced penitence and faith; and they wished to warn against this dangerous snare of the devil. One of them had asked me several times already, and again today, to write a letter to his righteous brother, whose attitude he had formerly been entirely unable to accept and also to inform his other brothers and sisters, who were not so righteous, what the Lord had done to his soul; and for this purpose he himself dictated the material to me.

Another praised the kindness of the Lord, who had powerfully inclined his heart, which had been against the voyage to

America, through the entirely open and free advice and prayer of our dear Senior Urlsperger, to accept the call. And there are several here who will thank him before the throne of God in blessed eternity for his fatherly love and concern for their true salvation. Another gave me pleasure by inquiring carefully after the merciful will of God and how to please Him in certain secular circumstances and he shared my pleasure greatly when we found something in the word of God that serves his purpose. God granted him a beautiful blessing last Sunday and during the communal thanksgiving for the blessed harvest. The little verse Joel 2:21, which we had as a text, had served him and his wife very well previously in certain difficult circumstances.

Thursday, the 22nd of November. Last night our gracious God showed me and my wife great mercy by giving us the joy of seeing a young and well-formed little son, who was baptized this morning.[17] The words in Joel 2 "The Lord will do great things," as well as in the song *Wirds aber sich befinden, dass du ihm treu verbleibst, so wird er dich entbinden*, etc. have become right alive for me through this new experience of God's help. He receives the name of Gotthilf Israel, the first name as a constant and grateful reminder of the especially experienced help of God, the second as testimony of my brotherly love and respect for my dear colleague and brother-in-law, Mr. Israel Christian Gronau.[18] May God let him be a true Israel in the future, as he has now become through holy baptism, and thus be useful to Him and his neighbor. While preaching about the inestimable grace of God in last Sunday's gospel, the 130th Psalm became for me a right golden jewel; it tells of the long desired and awaited help of God and promises and offers Israel much splendor, and it tells how it is finally received and enjoyed.

Friday, the 23rd of November. Yesterday and last night there was a rather harsh cold, which is very frightening for the poor who lack clothes. God will help; for many will be refreshed when my dear colleague returns from Charleston and we have received the long-expected gifts from Captain Thomson's ship. From the orphanage we give the poor as much as we can and as much as God grants us the ability to do. Last week I had already written to the storehouse manager in Savannah for a bolt of woolen cloth on credit, but he had had so much to do when an express boat arrived from General Oglethorpe that he missed the opportunity to send anything. If we wish to accomplish something, then we must travel down ourselves often, which, however, is not possible now because of my dear colleague's absence. The boards have been cut for covering the outer walls of the orphanage, and the carpenters began yesterday to put them up; and this is a blessing not only for the occupants of the house but also for the house itself, because the rain will be less able to damage it and penetrate through the cracks and joints. The name of the Lord will be praised by the pious people there for this benefaction too, as has already been done today in our private prayer meeting. The Lord will also provide for a pair of oxen and some glass for windows.

Saturday, the 24th of November. At about noon an Englishman brought me two Indian chiefs who wish to go to General Oglethorpe, and I was requested to send them down to Savannah without delay. We would surely like to be spared from such commissions before Sunday, if it were only possible. The Indians whom Mr. Oglethorpe wants against the Spaniards are hunting in the forest; and these two wish to get oral and written orders to call up the Indians for service. Once they have his word, it will mean as much as if the King of England had said it. Smallpox is said to be still raging among the Cherokees, and this is one of the reasons that the men would rather be in the forests than at home.

The surveyor has assured me in a letter that he wishes to be here shortly and finish his work. He also promises me a drawing of our plantations and all the land that belongs to our town which will please me and all our patrons in Europe. I had requested this from General Oglethorpe; and therefore this offer of the surveyor is a result of the order he received from Mr. Oglethorpe.[19] This man had secretly informed Mr. Oglethorpe that the Salzburgers were not going to let the 200 feet on each side of Abercorn Creek lie vacant for the common use of the colony, as is the express order of the Lord Trustees in the entire country, but use it as their own property. I advised this gentleman that the opposite was true, namely, that they had, to be sure, cut down the trees along the creek but did not therefore consider the land their own, although in the beginning they would plant it (in order to eradicate the bushes and shrubbery).[20]

He was satisfied with this, yet he demanded that all the trees within 200 feet of the river on both sides should remain standing, because it was very convenient to have wood near the water. I spoke about this with the leaders of the community and learned that, if the wood had to be left standing, they would suffer a very great loss from it. The high trees would cast much shade, in which corn and beans will not grow in this country; and thus a large piece of land as far the shade reached, would be useless. Also, wild and harmful animals, vermin, and wicked people would hide in such a forest on both sides of the river and cause the people great damage in their huts during their absence. Moreover, across the river, where the good plantations actually are, there is low land that is flooded several times during the year; and therefore houses or stables cannot be built there but must be built on this side where there is high land. Now, if the trees should remain standing on either side for a depth of 200 feet, the people would lose all view of their fields; they already have a long way from their houses to their cleared and planted land, which is very inconvenient both for work and for harvesting their crops. Both men and women go to work; and damage will occur if they cannot see their huts.

We know from experience that, as long as trees stand near the dwellings, the people cannot keep chickens and other fowl or even pigs. What a great hardship this would be. Also, a certain kind of quadruped that the English call raccoons and possums hide in the trees and often dig up the planted corn from the ground and devour and destroy entire ears. In addition, in some years we have had an extraordinary multitude of birds that do great damage to the corn and especially to the rice; and no amount of watching and scaring off can help if there are trees nearby. There may be even more reasons why these trees cannot stand, but they are not known to me. Because the trees are more harmful than useful, I hope our people will not be burdened with having to let them stand. Enough wood remains standing near the river that could easily be brought to the river, if it should be needed, once the people have gained a bit of strength.

Abercorn Creek is so very shallow, narrow, and crooked that timber rafts cannot possibly be made in it, or it would cause uncommonly great expense. There is enough wood all along the Savannah River, even if it should remain standing on our plantations as far as the 200 feet go. Through this order they perhaps wished to prevent trees from being felled into the river, through which the river might be made, if not unusable, at least difficult of passage. However, this is not to be feared in Abercorn Creek, for self-interest will keep everyone from letting trees fall into the water, because the present clearing of the river is costing much work.

Sunday, the 25th of November. According to the old calendar we have only twenty-three Sundays after Trinity, and today we concluded the church year. We encouraged each other through the words of Ecclesiasticus 50:24–26 to the praise of God for the spiritual and physical blessings we have enjoyed so far; and we took from the gospel several necessary admonitions for examining and awakening ourselves. May the Lord bless this in all of us so that we will reject everything that has run counter to salutary dogma in our congregation and so that it can also be said of us: "Old things are passed away; behold, all things are become new." In the afternoon we finished the last questions from the interrogative part of the catechism; and in the new church year we are to take up the regular Sunday and feast day epistles for the edification of the congregation. Today I was still alone, and therefore the repetition could not be held. The cold was very great and, if my domestic situation and strength had allowed me to join with the parishioners in the warm room, several (and many, if I had given the signal) would have attended. Only one room has a stove; and steps will be taken in the future so that the other can also be used in winter. Several children were present at my home prayer meeting.

Tuesday, the 27th of November. Yesterday the dear Lord let my dear colleague and his travelling companions return here hale and with His blessing to my and the parishioners' joy; and he, as well as we here, has cause to praise the goodness of the Lord, who doeth great things in all places. He let him succeed in everything on the journey and in Charlestown even better than he had expected, for which may His holy name be praised! Our

dear Lord wonderfully ordained for my dear colleague to become acquainted with a couple of honest, kind, and helpful
merchants in Charlestown who deal together and who accepted
our note without hesitation and will accept others in the future
and be ready to serve us in all ways. Their names are Messrs.
Wragg and Lambton.[21] If there should be a lack of safe mail
from this province to London, our letters would be forwarded
most safely and swiftly if we can first get them safely to Charleston; for our last and small packet is to be sent with the next ship,
and our large packet, which we addressed to the Lord Trustees'
secretary in Savannah, is said to have already been forwarded
via Charleston.

In Charleston many people have died of hemorrhages and
spotted fever; they infect each other and often are carried away
suddenly. Now everyone is healthy again and doing well physically. As recently reported, they have brought a Spanish sloop
into Charleston, in which they found only letters at first but
finally found gold and silver in the water cask. Nothing is heard
of any hostilities from Frederica or the Spanish coast except
that three Scotch Highlanders, who went into the woods un-
armed, are presumed to have been murdered by hostile Indians. Two of them were found dead without a skull or male
organs, and the third may have been dragged off and burned
alive. For the Indians treat their prisoners very barbarously.[22]

Wednesday, the 28th of November. Since the 19th question
from the interrogative part of the catechism was treated last
Saturday, I read to the congregation what our blessed Luther
had written so impressively in his preface to his catechism on
page 10 about scorn for, and scorners of, Holy Communion.

On Monday I was asked by Pichler,[23] in his and others' names,
to attend the thanksgiving ceremony they wished to hold some
day next week in grateful remembrance of all the blessings they
have received from God as well as for the good harvest they
have had. He was delighted with the devotional service we had
had in the orphanage for that purpose, which he would have
liked to attend, for (he said weeping) it had once appeared that
he would receive little or no grain but that the Lord had now
blessed him abundantly.

This morning I went to this Pichler's plantation; and I was

agreeably impressed that the people there, both men and women, were awaiting me eagerly and had made good arrangements for joint edification. A nice crowd had gathered and I preached to them as I had done recently in the orphanage, using the beautiful words of Joel 2 : 21 as a basis for our edification. In conclusion we knelt and thanked our loving God for all the blessings He had shown us, especially in Old Ebenezer and here, and encouraged each other to pay careful attention to His ways and works, which are always great both in the realms of nature and grace, and to find greater pleasure in them. I came home so late that the usual catechism hour could not be held this time. What a great and excellent blessing the dear Lord has shown the Salzburgers with the land on Ebenezer Creek is now known to everyone; but it will be really revealed only when they have cultivated it in the fear of the Lord and have enjoyed its fruits. If they should wish to ask for anything better they would be sinning against the good Giver. The only inconvenience with it is that the path from here to there is rather difficult to walk when it rains; but this can be corrected gradually through joint work.

Thursday, the 29th of November. Now that God has given them a good harvest, and especially much corn, our people often speak of a grist mill, which they would like to build on a good place they have found on Abercorn Creek if there were some money for it. Grinding with our hand mill is hard and slow; and, because it is used daily, it is often unreliable. Since it is driven by two strong people, or by several if they have a lot to grind, they have to work hard for the meal, which is indispensable for them. It is especially difficult for the people on the plantations, who have to carry their corn here and their meal back again on their backs. Mr. Oglethorpe once offered to help us with a mill; and therefore I shall write to him soon and inform him of our carpenters' plan to build a mill on Abercorn Creek.

For a long time Rottenberger has had quartan fever, which is greatly consuming his strength. We need him very much as a skillful carpenter; but God knows better what is good for him and us, and He is working mightily on his soul and trying to free him better and better from all impurities. He complains that he cannot visit the evening prayer meetings even on good days because the wind penetrates the church hut and causes drafts that do him much harm. The construction of a church should be the first thing for which our loving God, in His good time, will provide the costs, as He has begun to do, if only we had more carpenters. Our carpenters do not wish to neglect their farming, and this should not be advised, so one thing must be done after the other.

Friday, the 30th of November. To the new colonists who came here with Sanftleben we have distributed the viaticum they received from the Evangelical Body.[24] Ulich has died; and his widow, the Egger woman, has received his share. The Lackner woman had received more clothes in Augsburg than she would have received from this money, and her brother is heir to all her things. Senior Urlsperger writes that, because she is poor, the 2 florins 50 kreutzers spent for her in Augsburg should be considered a present; and now this will fall to her brother if Senior Urlsperger consents, otherwise he will give it back. We request his opinion in this matter. Ulich's young widow will marry Lackner, who has already announced it to me. His sister had recommended this woman to him on her deathbed, for already during the voyage she saw that she suited him. In him she is receiving a pious Christian and an industrious worker as a husband and will therefore be provided for in body and soul.

DECEMBER

Saturday, the 1st of December. This week we made use of various circumstances from the 11th chapter of 1 Samuel, which were related to the circumstances of the times in which we live through the grace of God, now that we have come so close to the new church year and to the solemn contemplation of Christ's incarnation. God touched the hearts of the Israelites and filled them with His fear, so that they gathered unto their anointed and proclaimed king. The joyful news of their approaching aid and redemption was sent to the hard pressed citizens of Jabes in Gilead, who well recognized their great need, danger, and misery; and this aid actually followed. Also, Saul's enemies and opponents experienced the mercy and forgiveness of their king, who did not wish to avenge himself but rather to forgive and forget the insult, after their hearts had been won and brought to *metanoia*.[1]

Yesterday evening we had the first part of the 12th chapter, from which we superintendents and ministers of the congregation could learn good lessons at the conclusion of the church year. This evening we learned what mercy the Lord had shown the Israelites and their ancestors in physical and spiritual things and how their behavior had been toward their Allhighest Benefactor: they forgot Him, substituted Him, and rejected Him and chose in His stead vain and transitory things, etc., for which, however, they had to feel His heavy hand. He sold them as evil-doers to strange and tyrannical masters, just as the English are accustomed to send criminals into slavery in America; yet, when they called out to Him in their need, He looked with mercy upon their impure prayer, which had been forced out by their plight, and let His help and salvation fall upon them, but with bad results on the part of the Israelites, etc.

Just as this serves us to examine ourselves at the end of this week, of this month, and this church year, we should also let the following admonition of Samuel serve to awaken us, namely, the admonition to fear the Lord our God, to serve Him, to obey His voice, and not to be disobedient to His mouth; then He will grant us more and more grace and strength to follow Him. Indeed, He Himself will lead us with His hands and eyes and go before us to clear the path; otherwise things would go no better with us than with the Israelites. God be blessed for this beautiful text, which He has surely been keeping for us until this noteworthy change in time! Our loyal God, who blessed this text in me, will also bless it in other people and let us enter this new church year with such a resolution that beginning, middle, and end will be, and will remain, good.

Sunday, the 2nd of December. On this first Sunday of the church year God has brought salvation in Christ very near to us; and our sincere wish in our prayers is for everyone to accept it and be saved. This year my dear colleague is using the regular Sunday readings as a basis for the catechization, after having gone through Luther's *Small Catechism* last year, and from it the five main parts and likewise the dogma of the keys to the kingdom, the *Haus-Tafel*, and the interrogative parts. This year I am again presenting the Gospels, the contents of which I present briefly without a special exordium, and from which I take something for the main instruction to elucidate, confirm with Bible verses, and apply as is required by salutary dogma and the circumstances of our parishioners. Today the main instruction was this: our chief care in this church year and in our entire lives should be to learn to recognize and love Jesus Christ our Savior rightly through the Holy Ghost.

I have announced to the congregation that I shall not let myself be kept from the repetition hour this year by anything (unless by sickness or unavoidable travel), because its value is very apparent and I wish this year to further the dear parishioners' recognition of truth to godliness in every possible way. If strong wind and rainy weather make our meeting hut uncomfortable for holding the repetition hour, we will come together in the orphanage. Perhaps our heavenly Father will soon help us to a regular house in which we can gather for the glory of God and our own edification. Yesterday and today we have had rainy weather, which made the sermon very difficult for me because the rain was violent in the morning. For we can hear every drop that falls on the roof; and we must speak all the louder if the listeners are to hear anything.

Monday, the 3rd of December. N.'s wife was confused about a matter that had occurred to her before her departure from Germany, so I visited her today and spoke to her and her husband about it; and this was so fruitful that she could understand everything better than a few days ago and was content in her heart. When such people let themselves be corrected, it is useful to them and pleasing to us. It is very good when they just speak out their thoughts, for we are glad to set them aright through God's help and blessing. Both of them are now very contented and know how to get along with each other better than at the beginning of their marriage.

Instead of the house prayers today I held the catechism lesson with the men, since I had had to cancel it once last week because of my trip to the plantations. I hear that the men are beginning their work on the plantations and therefore are pleased if the catechism lesson is held with them on Mondays and Saturdays, because then they need not miss any of them even if they are out there all through the week. I was glad to hear that they do not wish to miss a lesson, because through the grace of God they feel its value. Toward Christmas I hope to be finished with all articles of the Christian religion. May God continue to give me strength and the parishioners willingness and diligence to contemplate the word that is preached and to transform it into life!

Tuesday, the 4th of December. Yesterday evening we utilized that part of the Bible story from 1 Samuel 12:5 and 16–18 by warning each other against scorning the word preached in the name of the Lord, since God is showing us the mercy of letting us hear it this year too for our salvation. The prophet had emphatically and movingly reminded his listeners of their sins and especially their obstinate and perverted request for a king (whom they had first chosen unbendingly and firmly in their hearts and then requested, verse 14). However, he could well see from their eyes that they were little moved by his remonstrances but, in the manner of frivolous parishioners, had considered their sins to be slight and perhaps thought, "Samuel is treating such trivialities as sins; his office requires him to preach a sharp sermon. He may be angry with us because we do not wish to have him and his sons as our regents. Let him say what he will, and let us believe what we wish," etc. They probably blessed themselves in their hearts and judged their behavior not according to divine law but according to God's providence: because they had succeeded against the Ammonites under the leadership of their king, they underrated all the more their sin of abandoning their Lord of the Covenant and King of Grace and of trusting in carnal power.

Therefore, at Samuel's prayer, God had to show by the weather that not human words but His word was being preached to them and that Samuel had not made their behavior into sin but that it was in itself a great evil and wickedness before the Lord, which not only was a sign for the Israelites of what God could have done to them before the judgment throne because of their wickedness, but also serves us as an example of what will come to all disobedient and recalcitrant parishioners, even among us, if they reject His grace this year too. This was shown to us clearly from Psalms 7:12–14, and in Psalms 11:6 and elsewhere. And, as we see in Samuel's example what a trusting prayer can obtain from God, a zealous practice of prayer should be desired this year by the hearts of all, even of those who are indebted to, and ruled by, sin and are therefore frivolous at heart. For, although Samuel as a prophet had the exceptional advantage of being able to perform miracles through his prayer, penitent people who pray with belief still have in common with him that their prayers are pleasing to the Lord and that He hears them according to His will and for their salvation. We are not a little bit disturbed that some people in the congregation are not improving, even though the will of God is being revealed to them with much effort from week to week, indeed, almost daily. And, since the Lord is blessing it in some of our people and they are experiencing the power of the word for a spiritual conversion, the blame must just lie in the disloyalty of the former kind of people.

N. is penitently confessing his sins during his physical tribulations, and he told me several things that revealed a sinful condition to him some time ago during a sermon, as well as quite recently. His spirit was very mellow, and his eyes flowed over as he told of his spiritual misery and the unmerited mercy and patience of God. Through the catechism and what was preached with it God touched his heart mightily; and, like other people who yearn for salvation, he considers this hour a great blessing of the Lord. Because he can now seldom visit the prayer meetings and did not visit the one yesterday, I told him of its main contents and opened the Bible for him to the two verses from the 7th and 11th Psalms and admonished him to use the present period of grace in such a way that he might come not only to a penitent recognition of his sins but also to a trusting seizure of the merciful forgiveness of sins and to a certainty of the state of grace.

Wednesday, the 5th of December. Captain Thomson, who has our chests in his ship, has not yet come to Savannah because (as they say) he was not allowed to unload the things that are destined for Frederica and Mr. Oglethorpe's regiment until Mr. Oglethorpe himself had come to Frederica, and this was greatly delayed.

Simon Reiter announced that he had resolved with God to

marry one of the serving girls[2] who were brought to our place last year by General Oglethorpe and to declare his bans publicly next Sunday. He fears God with all his heart; the maid has a good testimony from the honest Ruprecht Steiner, in whose service she has been so far, that she has not only performed her work quietly and loyally but has also accepted good instruction and proved diligent and serious in prayer and in attending church. He brought her along to my study (as must always occur before the bans are published) so that I could discuss necessary things with them both and pray with them.

Thursday, the 6th of December. Two women spend much time with each other and remember the good that is told them from the word of God. For their spiritual awakening I told them of the edifying transformation and hopeful departure of the late Mrs. Gschwandel, by whose childlike nature and patient lamblike behavior I am still impressed. She knew about true conversion and rebirth and how much struggle is required for a serious practice of Christianity, but at the same time she experienced until her death the love and assistance of the Lord Jesus. Mrs. N. told me that God was continuing the work He had begun in her and that she was now experiencing what she had once heard a year ago in a sermon, namely, that when one comes to a recognition of sin and penance, neither food nor sleep tastes good, etc. The devil plagues her very much at night too, whereupon she becomes very frightened; but she gets up and prays, and then things go better.

In today's catechism lesson another woman had heard the verse, "Give diligence to make your calling and election sure"; and she said to me, "No one likes to do anything in the world in uncertainty. Why shouldn't we gladly try to reach certainty in the work of our salvation?" In today's evening prayer hour, on the occasion of the 13th chapter of 1 Samuel, we treated this necessary matter, namely, coming to a correct firmness of heart in our conversion and rebirth. Saul allowed himself to lack this, to his great harm; and therefore he failed the test that Samuel set for him in the name of the Lord and was repudiated because of his side-stepping and disobedience toward the will of God, which he wished to conceal behind some external divine service. From the judgments of God that were visited upon the Israelites we learn in general what sin causes, since they could have fared very well with their king if they had obeyed the sermons of the prophet and had chosen the good and correct path that he had shown them, for God was accustomed to reward their piety abundantly with temporal happiness too. All this, together with the other circumstances in the Bible story, gives us very salutary instruction at the beginning of the church year.

Friday, the 7th of December. Rather late this evening the younger Zoberbiller[3] of Purysburg came to me and brought a German captain and judge from there with him.[4] He had with him a letter to me from General Oglethorpe that announced that Mr. Oglethorpe wished to settle his barony near Palacho-colas, which lies in Carolina near Georgia above Purysburg, with a few families of Swiss from New Windsor and North Carolina, and that the said Swiss had petitioned him for Mr. Zoberbiller as their reader and preacher and that he had appointed him for this purpose. Because Zoberbiller had requested a recommen-dation from him to us, Mr. Oglethorpe wished to make it at this time and to request our friendship, good counsel, etc. for him. We accepted Zoberbiller with love. However, because it was al-ready late at night and he wished to travel further at daybreak, we did not have much opportunity to discuss with him all that might be necessary.

Saturday, the 8th of December. A servant of the Trustees, who had worked in Old Ebenezer with his wife, asked me to help him get permission to move to our place and take up land here. He wishes to redeem himself, provided the Trustees will give him credit for three years, for which the clockmaker Mueller will be answerable and give several clocks as a pledge.[5] The congregation will consider what should be done about this. We would like to help German people of our confession to live among us, but we need caution in this so that we will not admit all sorts of people.

Gabriel Maurer wishes to marry Held's daughter,[6] one of the girls sent here, and requests that the bans be posted tomorrow; and therefore there will be three couples to marry in the com-ing week. May God make them all into right Christian spouses who will conduct their married life for His glory, the edification of the congregation, and their own salvation.

Sunday, the 9th of December. All day long we had a very cold and strong wind, which inconvenienced us no little bit in our meeting hut. For that reason the repetition hour had to be held in the orphanage, which is now well protected on all sides and therefore rather warm, even though we still have no stove or fireplace in it. When more of our parishioners have moved to the plantations and divine services are held out there on Sundays too, we plan to gather on Sundays and for the prayer meetings here in my house, for which we do not now have room if all the congregation are together. Nothing will come of the church construction until God bestows some means for it and our people have first established themselves on their plantations. Until then they will have no time to help with the construction of the church.

Monday, the 10th of December. This morning I married two couples, namely, Simon Reiter to Magdalene Gebhart (whose father is in Frederica)[7] and Martin Lackner to Ulich's widow, the Egger woman. They are all honest people and, we hope, will lead their just-confirmed marriage state in the fear of the Lord and to their own salvation. At the wedding they were reminded of the words of 1 John 2:17, "And the world passeth away, and the lust thereof," etc.

This evening there was no prayer meeting because of the great cold, so the gifts that were sent for the people from Memmingen were distributed to them. Because of our lack of small money this distribution had had to be postponed until now. Each of them received one florin or, according to the English money, 2 shillings 2½ pence. This benefaction is new evidence of the heart-guiding power of God and should rightfully arouse us to His praise and to trust in His further help.

Tuesday, the 11th of December. This morning I married the third couple, namely, Gabriel Maurer and Elisabeth Held, whose father[8] is a servant in the orphanage. I likewise expounded for them, and for their friends who had gathered in my house for the marriage ceremony, the important words from 1 John 2:17, which may God bless in them. Because necessity requires the people to begin their regular work on the plantations, the young men are looking around for loyal helpmeets; but there is a lack of them among us, and those who are not provided for must wait for what divine providence might allot to them sooner or later.

Saturday, the 15th of December.[9] Mrs. N.[10] is approaching her confinement; and, because she would have no help from knowledgeable women on the plantation and would lack other necessary care, her husband requested us to provide her with a little room in the orphanage for a few weeks. The orphanage is there only in order to give help to needy people in the congregation in all sorts of ways as far as it is possible. We have now finished everything that had to be built because of the winter both in the house and in the kitchen, down to a few window sills and the installation of the glass. To be sure, this cannot be paid for now; but the workers will be patient until God grants something again, and they do not suffer any want because of it.

Sunday, the 16th of December. Yesterday toward evening I was in N.'s dwelling to settle and put to rights a disagreement in which they were quite involved with someone concerning external matters. In this I found N.'s spirit more composed and more inclined to compliance and reconciliation than ever before in the past. After that was done, I informed them of how I intended to dispose in the congregation of the matters by which they had caused vexation and to receive them again into the community of the Christian church; and they were both fully satisfied with this.

This morning after the sermon and church prayer, I read the following to the congregation: "I must announce to the Christian community that, through the grace and mercy of God, N. and N. have come to a recognition of their sins, through which they have caused offense in the community and have distressed both us ministers and also other pious Christians and that they have assured me before God that it is true that they have recognized and regretted their sins. As penitent sinners they hope, for the sake of Christ's merit, to receive forgiveness from their heavenly Father for all their sins and for the vexation they have caused; and they have earnestly resolved, through the power and aid of the Holy Ghost, to live from now on such a life as suits a Christian. And therefore they request the Christian community to forgive and forget all the wrong they have caused until now for the sake of God's love, with which He loves even the greatest sinners, and at the same time to pray for them sincerely that God may continue to grant them His grace to carry out, with His help, the resolution they have made before Him.

"If anyone in the community should hold anything against them, he is asked to tell it to them with an open heart. They are willing and ready to settle everything in a Christian manner and thus to reconcile themselves with God and man. And, since there are still some present in the community who are not looked upon as members of the congregation because of their apparent impenitence, to which probably external vexations have been added, and who must be repelled from the table of the Lord until they show a true internal and external improvement, these are admonished and requested on this occasion, for the sake of their own salvation, not to sin even longer and even more through persistent impenitence and not to esteem church penance lightly, to their dreadful judgment, but to ask God likewise to let them penitently recognize their godless nature and to grant them grace to bring forth fruits of penitence so that they too can be recognized again in the same way as members of the congregation and so that the name of the Lord can be praised through their reception into the communion of the Christian Church.

"Moreover, they might well reflect on what the Apostle Paul says in Galatians 6, 'Be not deceived; God is not mocked: for whatever a man soweth,' etc., and likewise Hebrews 13, 'Obey your ministers, and submit to them,' etc.[11] If any among the pretended or lip-Christians in the congregation should be so bold as to reproach these or any other persons in similar circumstances for these matters which have been disposed of and forgiven, or who consider this kind of church penance to be a degrading thing and calumniate it, he is in darkness. But may God, who has pleasure in penitence and in the life of the poor sinner, bless in all our congregation, for their eternal salvation, the office of the gospel and at the same time the lawful use of the key of binding and loosing as a benefaction which Christ has granted His church. I shall close for the instruction of you all with the words of the blessed Luther from our *Small Catechism*: 'What is the office,' etc., pages 66–68."

On this day we again had much rain; and, because it con-

tinued in the evening also, we gathered together in the orphanage for the repetition hour. God be praised for all the
blessing that He granted me again from His word. May He let
all of it serve to fill me and my dear colleague rightly with His
dear grace for this edifying period before the Holy Days, so that
we will be capable of imparting it properly to our dear congregation too. Oh, how much is demanded of a preacher of the
gospel! Oh, how little one thinks of it when accepting His calling! May God just help us through!

Monday, the 17th of December. Because we shall go to the
Table of the Lord next Sunday, several members of the congregation came to me this morning to speak with me about the
state of their souls; and they caused me great joy with their
openhearted confession. I notice how God is ever better revealing their perdition to them, at which they sigh, despair of themselves, and seek all their salvation in Christ alone. Others are
increasing in grace and are becoming ever more cautious and
ever more aware of what manifold tricks the devil uses to en-
snare their souls and to make them slothful and careless on
their path to blessedness.

On this occasion it becomes apparent that the Lord richly
blesses His word that is proclaimed in the prayer meetings and
on Sundays. He blesses it for chastisement, instruction, admonition, and comfort; and this gives us new courage to continue
working with hope in the name of the Lord. Yet there is no lack
of those who have gone to Holy Communion several times but
have not improved and whose dangerous condition will have to
be held up to them again this time; my trail was blazed for this
purpose by what we noted today about Saul in chapter 14 of 1
Samuel. In his many transgressions this king was not told the
truth by anyone except by Samuel, whom he could not bear
because of it, just as he could not bear the priests of Silo. This
was, however, a very great misfortune for him, as it is for all
from whom the truth is suppressed. And on this occasion I said
I regretted that there were several in the congregation who did
not like it and proclaimed it to be hostility, if we said in affec-
tionate terms that they could not pass thus into the *foro divino*[12]
and are not worthy to go to the Lord's Supper. And now the
test will come whether they will be able to bear the truth this

time when they register for Holy Communion, or whether they will bring forth the old bald excuses, evasions, and exculpations (which were also announced today).

Tuesday, the 18th of December. I have heard that the public acceptance of N. and N. into the community of the Christian Church has made a deep impression on some of the congregation; and, because some of them have implored God for their conversion, they have great joy at this beginning and praise the Lord. To the praise of God a married couple told how useful they have found the catechism that has been expounded so far and the divine truths that have been preached with it, for they have begun to understand everything in the sermons better than previously and to relate all the truths together in a correct manner. In church they only listened, they said; but here they themselves were asked and, if they answered awkwardly and were corrected, this left a lasting impression. Regarding the catechism, God has often been praised by the mouths and hearts of the pious listeners.

God is working very powerfully on Mrs. N., as others, too, have noticed in her. However, she is still very bashful and does not consider herself worthy of joining us on such occasions when we gather together. However, as often as she has dared to do so and has broken through her shyness, she said, the Lord has always granted her great edification, which she repeats to her husband, to his and her joy. Many are bashful, to the harm of the Kingdom of Christ and to their own spiritual harm, and one is afraid of and flees from the other. Therefore we make an effort to bring honest souls together under our supervision, even if they are only beginners, so that they may get to know each other properly in the Lord and will be able to profit from each other's gifts and grace. We are beginning our song hour again, in so far as it can take place without harm to my health and other activities. Perhaps this is also a good way to flow together in a Christian manner for mutual advancement in the good. This evening we learned the song, *O grosse Freude*, etc., which is composed incomparably beautifully both in text and tone, and also *Die güldene Sonne*, etc.; and, although very few in number, we were especially refreshed by them.

Wednesday, the 19th of December. At the beginning of this

week N. requested me to remonstrate with a certain person about the sin of wrath, through which she was doing herself much harm, and today I had a right welcome opportunity to do so. She had been with someone because of some business, in which someone wished to burden her with some unpleasant and mendacious matter, which was said to have been hatched by Mrs. N. As soon as she came home, her anger revealed itself by sharp censures against N., and the agitation would have continued for a while on both sides if we had not arrived unexpectedly and reproved her from God's word. When she began to reflect, she was amazed at the special providence of God, who had (1) let something befall her through which her wicked heart was again revealed so that she might recognize how little foundation it has, and (2) let me arrive so that I would know it too and could see, from a clear example, what overhastiness and quick temper was in her and so that I had been given such a good opportunity to work on her according to necessity and the nature of the situation and also to prevent her from confusing herself even further and hindering herself in her preparation for the holy days.

I told her that a Christian must be indifferent in all external matters, calumnies, and gossip and act as if he does not hear them; if one wishes to fight everything through and always have the last word and to convince wicked and slanderous people of one's innocence, one will speak many words in vain and finally have nothing but disquiet from it. I particularly reminded her of the verse in Colossians 3:12 ff. and spoke of the sinfulness and harm of her emotions. In today's prayer meeting we heard that God often ordains all sorts of things for men and lets them get into all sorts of vile situations only to reveal their hearts for their and other people's good; e.g., both the unchanged and unbroken heart of King Saul and also the good foundation of Jonathan in similar circumstances (chapter 14) were revealed. So far we have recognized abundantly from many special cases what a miserable creature an unconverted and worldly-minded man is and how troublesome he is for other people. And even now, if one were to describe the life of an unconverted man, as the Holy Ghost did in the case of Saul, one would likewise discover nothing but foolish, stupid, and pitiable things; but such blind people do not wish to recognize this in themselves but think themselves very clever.

The Lord is working very powerfully on N., and I was greatly pleased by his humble confession of this and by the great humility of his heart at his disloyalty and many shortcomings. He has a very loyal helper for his Christianity in his wife and he well recognizes the excellent grace that God has given her, and he profits from her. He wept when he talked about the disquiet and distraction that he has caused himself because of his plantation and he will ask God for grace to comply with the little verse that was said to him at his marriage: "But seek ye first the kingdom of God," etc. This man and other similar very simple and previously ignorant people are a living witness that grace can set all men aright, even foolish and silly ones, if only they do not wish to persist wantonly in their ignorance. Therefore we cannot be content with those who cite their age, weak memory, negligence in their youth, etc. as the reason why they are, and remain, so ignorant. It is merely sloth and disloyalty.

N. and N. have been such people until now. For some time we have had to repel them from Holy Communion for that reason, and this has had a good effect. Today I spoke with them very stirringly and instructed them as to how they could discover their blind and very corrupted hearts. N. was so disquieted at this that she could not accept the gifts that were given her because of her poverty and she could not speak a word for pain and weeping; and, when she came to me in the afternoon, she gave me a good reason for this. Now they are both very desirous of being instructed and are happy that N. is going to move into their dwelling on the plantation and remain until he himself can build something and that he will help them in their undertaking with reading and praying, as he has also promised me to do. It truly pleases me that they are so desirous for Holy Communin and would rather do and suffer anything than to be kept from it so long.

Thursday, the 20th of December. N. N. is also registering to go to Holy Communion this time. At first she was very restless and needed instruction, and therefore it was good for her to postpone the taking of Holy Communion until she is better prepared. As long as she has been a servant girl in the orphanage she has not only been very calm and contented but has also been worked on so powerfully by the dear Lord through His word that she sincerely regrets and deplores her previous sinfulness and unconverted condition and has resolved to become a different person. Oh, how she thanks the Lord who brought her here and even led her into the orphanage. Although someone tried to turn her against Mrs. N.,[13] she finds the exact opposite and asks her to treat her more severely and more seriously and not be so lenient with her, because she needs discipline. God is showing especial mercy to Mrs. N. and is properly preparing her through His gospel to be a useful instrument to help her neighbor in spiritual and physical ways.

Mrs. N. came to me this morning with her girl, and both of them caused me much pleasure with good resolutions they revealed to me. The girl is following a good path; and I hope, not without reason, that she will become a wise virgin.[14] They have united themselves in a fine way, and I gave them some admonitions with regard to their Christianity, the use of the means of salvation, and some external physical circumstances. How good it makes me feel when those whom I have helped prepare for taking their first Holy Communion take firm root and reflect in themselves the life of Christ. Oh, if all would recognize that Christianity is not a fearful work but a royal banquet and gives nothing but royal prerogatives!

Friday, the 21st of December. A mother told me that she had more joy and contentment from her seven-year-old son than from the others. When he comes home from school he generally brings her a precept or a good little verse and also says his prayers in childish simplicity. Once, when he came into the room with a little book and was asked by his older brother what he had prayed, he answered, "You shan't know, for only the dear Lord and I know." However, because they persisted in finding out, he said that he had called upon the dear Lord for another heart that would be better than his old one. Now he is happy that my dear colleague has given the children freedom to come to him for prayer and Christian preparation next Monday, since no school will be held because of the feast day that falls on Tuesday.

From the orphanage we received the joyful news that God

gave the children a great awakening yesterday and that now almost all are serious in turning their hearts to the Lord Jesus, and this has made a deep impression on the adults. Some of them have requested me to let them attend the song hour in my room too, and I permitted this under the condition that they would bring not only their mouth but also a devout heart that was ready for the praise of God, which they must request from heaven above; and they promised to do this. In this practice I do not wish anyone but those who are concerned with edifying their hearts and who would like to become more closely acquainted with other salvation-hungry people through an edifying conversation, prayer, and praise of God. May God bless and hallow all this to His glory!

All through yesterday's evening prayer meeting our loving God especially revealed Himself in order to prepare the members of the congregation for the approaching partaking of Holy Communion. Satan has also been right active in hindering this blessing and in instigating harm, as I discovered in the case of a couple of families. They perceived the depth and artifices of Satan, let themselves be reprimanded, wept bitterly, and promised to humble themselves properly before God, who had revealed their hearts to them in such confusion, and to apply this case to their recovery and caution.

Saturday, the 22nd of December. This day has, to be sure, been a day of much restlessness in my office, but also of much spiritual refreshment. Several people have had to be repelled from Holy Communion, among whom are N. and also N. Indeed, we have no pleasure in this but only great trouble, but it is better to be severe when the circumstances require it than to become guilty of alien sins through permissiveness.[15] Despite all seriousness and warning, some still go to Holy Communion without showing any improvement afterwards. However, we cannot prevent this when such people conform to all external order and church discipline, pretend that God has worked grace in their souls, and promise improvement. God will help us perform our office for the salvation even of those who so often deceive us, and most of all themselves.

During the catechism lesson, in which the dogma of Holy Communion was treated today, God brought one of them to a recognition of his unworthiness when he heard that faith is not ignited (as in Holy Baptism) but is strengthened in Holy Communion; and therefore it is absurd and most punishable if anyone comes to it without faith and spiritual life. Likewise, if anyone receives the body and blood of Christ under their visible signs with only the mouth of his body and not with that of his faith, he is sinning grievously, whereas penitent and believing communicants achieve manifold profit. He therefore remained behind this time and will let himself be properly prepared. Another honest man, who had heard the words of 2 Corinthians 13, "Examine yourselves, whether ye be in the faith . . . except ye be reprobates," would have remained behind too if I had not advised him against it because he felt himself to be full of perdition. He reveals the symptoms of a worthy communicant.

Three girls from the orphanage were with me yesterday evening also and told me that God had let them fully recognize their perdition and that they had resolved to convert themselves righteously to God. I reminded them of what they had promised previously when they had felt the many tugs of God's grace. Because of that I was afraid, I said, they would not remain serious for long, so I recalled several verses to them. However, they assured me that, through the grace of God, they were and would remain serious, etc.; and they asked my pardon for previous naughtiness, etc. We are planning to let two of these orphans partake of the Lord's Supper. I had discussed this previously with Kalcher and his wife, who hope with us that this confirmation of the baptismal covenant will make an impression and bring a blessing, especially as their spirits are still very soft and pliable. I also discussed what was necessary with the parents of the other three children who are to be admitted for the first time.

Today we came to the end of the catechism and the Christian dogmas, after these had been introduced and contemplated with men and women weekly for four hours in my house; and I must rightfully praise and thank our merciful God for having strengthened me so far and having shown me so many traces of His blessing. May He further grant His prosperity to all that is planted and watered so that among both adults and children

many, and if possible all, will be prepared for His praise as trees
of righteousness and plants.

Sunday, the 23rd of December. This time we had fifty-five
communicants, including the four girls and one boy who were
admitted today for the first time. The names of these hopeful
children are Peter Arnsdorf, Agnes Elisabeth Mueller, Maria
Christina Helfenstein, Maria Schweighofer, and Magdalena
Haberfehner, whose parents are living or else died here some
time ago. They have been in their preparation for a long time
and, with divine aid, have attained a fundamental recognition
of the basic and main truths of the Christian faith, about which
they were examined publicly this morning. The grace of God
has shown itself very powerfully in them, especially in the recent
past, of which not only we, but also the parents and those serving in place of parents have given testimony. For this reason we
can present them to the congregation with joy and good hope
and perform the act of confirmation on them. This has again
made a great impression on these children and on the adults, as
was sufficiently indicated by the many tears that were shed. All
in all, this day has been a very edifying day of preparation for
the approaching holy day; and for this may the Lord's name be
praised.

We cannot remember whether we have ever incorporated
into this diary the manner in which the act of confirmation is
customarily held among us; and therefore we will do it on this
occasion in keeping with our duty to account to our Fathers for
all our official acts. (1) It is announced to the congregation one
or two days in advance that some children are going to be
confirmed, and this important undertaking is recommended
for communal prayer. (2) Instead of the regular sermon, the
children are examined publicly about several important articles
of faith; and they must verify all the points with chosen verses of
scripture, without referring to the Bible. Time does not usually
allow the catechism to be recited, but this is not really necessary,
because generally they recite it in the afternoon on Sundays between the first and second song. The entire examination is arranged for the edification of the entire congregation.

(3) The examined children step up to the altar and are ad-

dressed as follows: "Dearly beloved children in Christ, you are planning to go to Holy Communion today with the congregation for the first time, for which reason you have been instructed from the divine word according to the grace that God has granted and have been prepared for this important undertaking with many earnest admonitions and hearty prayer. In the examination that has just been held you have given a sample of the content of the Christian dogma that has been taught you so far from God's word for the recognition of your salvation and the practice of true godliness. From this the Christian community has been able to perceive that you have been directed not to human teachings and fables but to the unfailing word of God in order to found your faith upon it and to learn the path to salvation from it. It remains to remind you briefly of what God has undertaken with you already in your tender youth and what grace He has shown you in Holy Baptism and what you in return have agreed to and promised Him through your godparents and witnesses.

1. "First of all, you should know and believe with certainty that in your tender childhood you truly received Holy Baptism according to Christ's institution and entered through this door into the communion of the Christian Church and all the blessings merited through Christ. That you are really baptized is not only proved by your name, but also your parents and sponsors, if they are still alive and present, will assure you of this most certainly. You should doubt their assurance and witness all the less, since your parents must account for you on the day of judgment as the children entrusted to them. In order for you to have a sure and certain proof of your baptism after the death of your parents even in this strange land, we will register in our regular church book your name, the day of your birth, and baptism from the baptismal certificate you have brought or other certain and unquestioned assurances, and from this you will always and under all circumstances be certain of what we are now saying.[16]

2. "As said, you are to be reminded of what great mercy God showed you in your tender childhood shortly after your physical birth. The Lord Jesus, who instituted Holy Baptism as a means of grace and salvation, has let you be truly reborn in His

blood of reconciliation, in which the water, although true water, is not something simple but a water composed at God's command and united with God's word. He has cleansed you of all your sins and has clothed you, as with a beautiful garment, with His innocence and with His righteousness, which is valid before God. And, as it is so beautifully written in the catechism, He has poured the Holy Ghost upon you abundantly so that you might become heirs of eternal life through the grace of the Holy Ghost and as reborn children of God. God has promised and given you these and similar blessings so that you will learn to know His love, to value His grace, and to flee and avoid everything that is repugnant to this holy God as your great benefactor. This you have promised through your sponsors who represented you at your baptism: namely, you have renounced the devil and all his works and all his essence and have devoted yourselves to the triune God—Father, Son, and Holy Ghost—in childlike obedience and sincere faith and have promised not to seek your salvation and bliss in any other than in the triune God, in whose name you were baptised.

"You have promised to love Him above all things and to serve Him with an unblemished conscience and also to carry your cross patiently behind Christ your dear Savior and to prove yourselves steadfastly as good soldiers of Jesus Christ. Now have faith in the first point: you should not doubt in what the triune God has granted you in baptism; for Christ says expressly that the Kingdom of God belongs to those children that are brought to Him, and consequently all the blessings that are in the Kingdom of God are theirs. To confirm this He also says in Mark 16, 'He that believeth and is baptized, he,' etc., Now you are baptized, and you have also received the true faith through baptism, which is a bath of rebirth and renewal of the Holy Ghost; and thus, according to the content of this pronouncement of Christ, you are saved and have been placed into the blessed state of grace as children of God, which is indeed an uncommon and praiseworthy blessing of God.

"The second point, however, which concerns your promise to God, requires more examination because daily experience unfortunately proves that men do not keep to what they have promised so holy and firmly in baptism, whereby they invalidate

their baptism as long as they continue as breakers of their covenant and draw down on their heads the judgment of eternal
damnation. Now you too have promised the dear Lord in baptism to have nothing to do with the devil, his works, and his
nature, but rather, according to your baptismal covenant, to live
a godly life until your end. Have you not promised this? Answer: 'Yes.' But have you kept what you promised? Answer, unfortunately: 'No'; and therefore you have again forfeited the
once-offered grace of baptism, and God would have had cause
to drag you away as perjurers and oath-breakers and cast you
into perdition. However, he has waited until now for your penitence and the renewal of your baptismal covenant and has given
you sufficient means and opportunity for it.

"Now it all depends upon your examining and testing yourselves as to how your hearts now stand. Whether, through the
grace of God, you have learned to recognize and regret your
scandalous disloyalty, covenant-breaking, and forfeiture of
God's grace, as well as the many sins you have committed from
youth on? Whether you are now tired of the yoke of sin and
wish nothing more than to renew your baptismal covenant and,
instead of children of wrath and damned and lost sinners, to
again become children of God? If you sincerely recognize and
regret your sins and your relapse from your baptismal covenant
and yearn as penitent sinners for the forgiveness of your sins
and the grace of God in Christ, then confess it publicly with
your mouths too. Answer: 'Yes.' Then I herewith renew the
baptismal oath of each of you before the congregation, etc. I,
N. N., herewith renew, etc. I believe in God the Father, etc.

"Let us next pray sincerely to God as follows: 'Merciful and
ever gracious God, we thank Thee sincerely not only for in-
stituting holy baptism through Christ Thy dear Son our Lord
and Savior but also for letting all of us, and therefore also these
children, partake of it in their tenderest youth and for pouring
the Holy Ghost over them abundantly and letting them be truly
reborn through it and be made children of God and inheritors
of eternal life, instead of children of wrath. Oh Lord, we and
they are far too unworthy of all the mercy and loyalty Thou hast
shown us. Oh, if we had kept faith and a good conscience and

had remained loyal and steadfast in Thy covenant: but now our conscience tells us that we have broken our baptismal covenant through willful sins and have therefore buried the baptismal grace we have received; and thus we have returned to such an unblessed condition that we would have long since been thrust into the abyss of hell and damnation if Thou hadst wished to reward and punish us according to our sins. Have then sincere praise and thanks, oh Father of all mercies, for Thy patience and forbearance that Thou hast had with us to this very minute.

"These children must also confess this sin of transgressing their baptismal covenant, and they humbly confess herewith their sins and implore mercy. Oh Father, spare them, do not punish them as they deserve, think not on the sins of their youth and their transgressions but remember them according to Thy great mercy for Thy goodness' sake. Send them divine remorse and sorrow and the earnest resolution to persist loyally, through Thy grace, to persevere in the baptismal covenant that they are now reestablishing with Thee in the name of Jesus Christ and through the Holy Ghost and to guard themselves all their lives long so that they will not acquiesce in any sin or act contrary to Thy commandments. Remind them diligently of what has been said to them now publicly from Thy word and according to Thy will.

"Print Thy word of truth, in which they have been instructed until now, into their tender souls and do not let them become liars and disloyal people in regard to what they have again promised Thee, but rather arouse them to seek strength from the wounds of the Savior through constant and sincere prayer to lead a holy life that accords with their promise and is pleasing to Thee so that they may achieve the goal of their faith, namely the salvation of their soul. Hear this, oh dear God for the sake of Christ and in the power of the Holy Ghost. Amen! 'Our Father, who art in heaven, etc.' Fill this Thy child, oh Lord, with Thy Holy Spirit and with all the treasures of grace and salvation that Thy dear Son has won for us so that he will be Thy own and live with Thee in Thy kingdom and serve Thee in eternal righteousness, innocence, and bliss until it finally reaches the place of everlasting joy and glory! Amen! May the Lord bless you all, and guard you, etc. May the Lord, the triune God, bless your goings out and your comings in from now until eternity. Amen!"

This time the wisdom of God marvelously ordained that all the young people who have previously been confirmed in the congregation were present at the ceremony today, three such children having come from Purysburg. Because some of them had become unfaithful or at least lukewarm toward our dear God, their spiritual circumstances required me to remind them of what great mercy God had previously shown them and what they had promised Him in return when reinstituting their baptismal covenant and how necessary it was for them to set out again on the path of peace they had once walked. We hope this will not be without a blessing.

Monday, the 24th of December. Mrs. Pichler is in childbed in the orphanage, where we have given a little place to her at the request of her husband and out of love for their souls. God has shown Himself very merciful and helpful in regard to her labor, as her husband told me with tears in his eyes. How much we would like to show kindness to everyone, especially to those in the congregation, if only we had the means. We hope that the fountain which has flowed so abundantly so far will continue to flow to this little institution so that many more poor, widows, orphans, sick, strangers, etc. can be refreshed by it. He has granted us His Son and transfigured Him in various souls in the orphanage, and He is beginning to transfigure Him again. How could He not grant us everything with Him?

N., whom we have recently accepted again, is accommodating himself to all good order and is content and grateful for everything that God is doing for him without his merit. He is again feeling strongly the pull of the Father to the Son.

Kieffer of Purysburg, who formerly had two daughters in the orphanage, is again requesting us to accept three of his children into the orphanage and school; and he promises to repay everything that is spent for them. So far he has not been able to pay back all of what was previously paid out for maintenance and some clothing; but we are overlooking this and not pushing him, because the money is not there.

This evening we had the gospel scheduled for yesterday, John

1 : 19 ff., as a basis of the preparation for the Christmas celebration, and the dear Lord let it be a blessing for me and others. The main dogma that flowed from the gospel was that it is God's serious wish for all men, even the worst and most perverted[17] sinners, to come to His Son and to the enjoyment of His grace, and this was expounded from the gospel and from comforting scriptural passages. Yesterday the gospel could not be treated because of the examination of the five children.

Tuesday and Wednesday, the 25th and 26th of December were the feast of Holy Christmas. Our merciful God has shown us much grace in these days and made His word of the comforting Birth of our Savior right sweet and savory for us; it has proven itself a vivifying word in several souls and as one that is entirely worthy of being received. In the evening after the repetition hour many people gathered, and we learned some beautiful Christmas songs for the praise of God and prayed together. It was as if we were already in heaven. We sang the two songs, *O grosse Freude*, etc. and *Wie kündlich gross sind doch die Wercke*, etc. publicly in all four voices, and this brought much joy and edification. Mr. Thilo has a fine bass voice, can read music very well, and is therefore very useful to us in this celebration of edifying music. God be praised for this blessing, too!

For the past two weeks we have had the most pleasant weather, warm both day and night, but without rain; and therefore the weather did not cause us the least discomfort during the holy days.

Thursday, the 27th of December. Nearly all the men have gone out to the plantations, partly to build huts and partly to work in the fields; and during my visits I found only women and children at home. Because it was rainy or windy toward evening, we did not hold the prayer meeting but came together in my house, where I posed some questions on the Christmas material and read the 72nd Psalm. The remainder of the evening we spent in learning the song, *Uns ist geboren Gottes Kind*, etc. and with prayer.

Friday, the 28th of December. The surveyor has finally returned here and wishes to complete his work; but he is returning entirely empty-handed as previously and is demanding provisions for himself and several people as assistants in his work. I asked General Oglethorpe to give him orders requiring him to provide for provisions and fellow workers himself, and I don't know why it is that he is again a burden to us. The Salzburgers are now fully occupied in preparing their land for planting, for which much work is again necessary because the land is uncommonly overgrown and entirely filled with thick trees, thorns, cane, and all sorts of thick bushes. Therefore we cannot presume upon them to go around with the surveyor and to lose their time.[18] Also, they are very poor in the shoes and clothes that they must have when surveying the land and that are quickly torn. To be sure, the expenses previously incurred for the surveyor should have been made good from the storehouse in Savannah, but this has not yet happened, and I would not dare to request Mr. Oglethorpe to pay back what is now to be spent. Also, we are not now in a position to pay something like this ourselves unless the congregation can and will find men who wish to help the surveyor; in that case, we would provide for this man's food, drink, lodgings, and laundry, which will amount to more than five shillings per week. Our people, who do not understand English and prefer to perform their work in quiet, do not suit this man's work. This very same surveyor surveyed Mr. Oglethorpe's barony near Palachocolas a few weeks ago and received people and provisions for this work; therefore, those who are moving there from Purysburg and elsewhere have no more difficulties.

Saturday, the 29th of December. This evening we began the story of David, the beloved servant of God (which his name means and which his deeds prove), with the 16th chapter of 1 Samuel; and hardly any other story so well suits the conditions of our time. May God let everything that is preached from it be blessed in the young and the old for a recognition of truth for bliss, so that they will not merely stop at hearing and enjoying these remarkable stories. Rather, may the purpose that God is seeking through them be achieved in them all; and may we, through His grace, avoid the footsteps of sin but instead accept, and be blessed in so doing, the grace that others have accepted and thereby been made children, servants, and handmaidens of the Lord. We warned each other against disobedience to the enticements of God's spirit through the gospel, since we learned in the last story how ill Saul fared because of his disobedience. If disobedience against the divine law is so great a sin, what will disobedience against the gospel be, as St. Paul concludes in Hebrews 2 : 2 ff.? After the prayer meeting a room full of eager people again assembled in my house, where we again learned a song, in the company of my dear colleague and Mr. Thilo, and finally prayed.

Sunday, the 30th of December. We utilized today's gospel, Luke 2 : 33, in such a way as to direct our thoughts, as far as can be done wisely and in good order, to the simple and edifying intercourse of the first believers of the New Testament; and we were able to learn much from it for our awakening and imitation. We experience and well know the blessings of such unaffected and wisely arranged intercourse between souls in regard to themselves and others. Therefore we would much like for the bond of upright Christian love and edifying intercourse to be tied ever tighter and for the weak, complacent, legalistic, and other such people to be attracted to it. The Lord has already done great things in us, and He will surely let it come about that both great and small will serve Him, the Lord, with childish spirits publicly and privately, and that we shall all become right ardent in our love for God and for one another.

After the sermon we sang chorally the exceedingly beautiful song *Uns ist geboren Gottes Kind*, etc. Since the repetition hour could not be held in the miserable hut because of the rainy weather and because, for several reasons, there is no place in the orphanage either, we again gathered in my room and learned with four voices the glorious song *Singt dem Herrn, nah und fern*, etc., which Senior Urlsperger had given to the third transport to take with them. Next we prayed together that God would give us grace to close this old year well and to receive the new one with blessing. Oh, if only everything in Ebenezer, in London, in Halle, in Augsburg, and everywhere could be filled with the glory of the Lord, which is bearable and lovely in Christ.

Monday, the 31st of December. For several days, and again today, we have had rain, and it has been very cold. The path to the plantations is very bad, yet our people have to walk it because of business and divine services. In one region they are planning to build bridges over a little river that flows into the

Savannah River and across a couple of swamps so that we can pass back and forth all the more easily, as this will be necessary in a short time because many of the people are moving to their plantations. They would like to have one or two prayer meetings each week; and, because even now many cannot attend the prayer meetings all week long and do not come to town until Saturday, we were asked to hold a longer prayer meeting for the workers on Saturdays than is ordinarily held. They do not wish to miss the Bible stories, especially now that they are treating of David, for the Lord has laid such great blessing on it, of which certain particulars were cited.

At the same time I learned that the new songs, which have been sung chorally in church several times, have made a deep and pleasant impression on one and all, and this inspires us to continue this good practice. A woman told me she heard a neighboring woman praying on her knees with many tears in a place, while her husband and others were occupied with external matters. She had been made sincerely happy by this and had hoped that this woman would someday see the truth, but she dropped it all again and went her old ways. As the first was pleasing for her, so the second was depressing. To be sure, even the naughtiest among us are mightily awakened by the word; but it is always our complaint that, because of their disloyalty, it does not take them far, and old acquaintances do each other much harm. They all love the good and hold fast to good practices, and they may well be convinced that they are not yet in a condition pleasing to their God, but for many of them it does not progress beyond this. May the eternally loyal and merciful God, who has helped us so far and has let us perceive many traces of His grace in the execution of our office and in our Christianity and also in our external domestic affairs during this past year, be humbly praised for all His goodness, aid, help, and care! May He grant that in this newly beginning year 1740 we will be something for the praise of His Glory both in and outside of the community, and may He let us and those who hear us come ever nearer to the jewel which the heavenly vocation in Christ holds out to us!

Soli DEO Gloria! [19]

Appendix I

Index of Hymns sung in 1739

Hymns followed by F-T with volume and page number are reproduced in Albert Friedrich Fischer and W. Tümpel, *Das deutsche evangelische Kirchenlied des 17. Jahrhunderts* (Gütersloh, 1916; reprint, Hildesheim: Olms, 1964). Authors followed by asterisk are identified in Albert Friedrich Fischer, *Kirchenlieder-Lexikon* (Gotha, 1878; reprint, Hildesheim: Olms, 1967).

Befiehl du aber deine Wege ("Commend Thy ways"), by Paul Gerhardt,* p. 288. F-T III, 435.

Die güldene Sonne bringt Leben und Wonne ("The golden Sun brings life and joy"), by Paul Gerhardt,* p. 305. F-T II, 308 (F-T attributes this hymn to Philipp von Zesen).

Du sagst, ich bin ein Christ ("You say I am a Christian"), by Johann Adam Haslocher,* p. 169.

Eins Christen Hertz sehnt sich nach hohen Dingen ("A Christian's heart doth yearn for lofty things"), by Maria Magdalena Böhmer,* p. 102.

Gott hat alles wohl bedacht ("God hath considered all things well"), by Gustav von Mengden,* pp. 62, 154. F-T IV, 576.

Herr Jesu Christ mein Fleisch und Blut (Lord Jesus Christ my flesh and blood), p. 4. This is probably the same as *Herr Jesu Christ, mein Trost und Licht*, by Johann Rist.* (Cf. *Fleisch und Bluht* in strophe 6, v. 1.)

Ich habe Jesu Fleisch gegessen ("I have eaten Jesus' flesh"), p. 249. Unidentified.

Ich hab in Gottes Hertz und Sinn mein Hertz und Sinn ergeben ("My heart and mind I've yielded to the heart and mind of God"), by Paul Gerhardt,* p. 241. F-T III, 393.

Ich singe dir mit Hertz und Mund ("I sing to Thee with heart and mouth"), by Paul Gerhardt,* p. 284. F-T III, 420.

Jehova ist mein Hirt und Hüter ("Jehovah is my shepherd and keeper"), by Johann Anastasius Freylinghausen,* p. 105.

Kein grösser Trost kan seyn im Schmertz ("No greater comfort can there be in pain"), by Johann Heermann,* p. 30. F-T I, 328.

Lobe den Herrn, O meine Seele ("Praise the Lord, O my soul"), by Johann Daniel Herrnschmidt,* pp. 247, 284. F-T I, 275 (F-T attributes this hymn to Martin Alther).

Man lobt dich in der Stille ("We praise Thee in quiet"), anonymous, p. 247. (Often attributed to Joachim Neanders, based on a hymn by Johannes Rist.*)

Mein Heyland nimmt die Sünder an ("My Savior doth receive all sinners"), by Leopold Franz Friedrich Lehr,* p. 145.

Mein Jesu, dem die Seraphinem ("My Jesus, whom the Seraphim"), by Wolfgang Christoph Dessler, p. 30. F-T V, 392.

Mein Schöpfer bilde mich dein Werk nach deinem Willen ("Create me, Lord, according to Thy will"), anonymous, p. 204. Found in Freylinghausen's songbook.

O grosse Freude, die auf der Weide ("O great delight that on the meadow"), anonymous, pp. 305, 317. Found in Freylinghausen's songbook.

Schwing dich auf zu deinem Gott, du betrübte Seele ("Soar aloft unto thy God, thou troubled soul"), by Paul Gerhardt,* p. 105. F-T III, 445.

Singt dem Herrn, nah und fern ("Sing unto the Lord, both near and far"), by Johann Daniel Herrnschmidt,* p. 319.

Solt ich meinem Gott nicht singen? ("Should I not sing unto my God?"), by Paul Gerhardt,* p. 50. F-T III, 416.

Uns ist geboren Gottes Kind ("To us is born the child of God"), by Bartholomäus Crasselius,* pp. 317, 319.

Wenn dein hertzliebster Sohn, o Gott, nicht wär ("If Thy dearly beloved Son, O Lord, were not"), by Johann Heermann, p. 29.

Wer ist wohl, wie du, Jesu ("Who can be like Thee, Jesus?"), by J. A. Freylinghausen, p. 129.

Wie Gott mich führt, so will ich gehen ("As God doth lead me, I wish to go"), by Lambertus Gedicke,* p. 206.

Wie ist es möglich, höchstes Gut ("How can it be, my highest Good?"), p. 241. F-T III, 491 reproduces a hymn beginning *Wie ist es möglich, höchstes Licht*, by Paul Gerhardt.*

Wie kündlich gross sind doch die Wercke ("How great and manifest are all Thy works"), anonymous, p. 317.

Wirds aber sich befinden, dass Du ihm treu verbleibst ("Should it come to pass that thou art true to Him"), by Paul Gerhardt,* p. 288.

Appendix II

Signers of the letter of gratitude sent on 26 October 1739 to the Salzburgers' benefactors in Germany. This is one of the few documents giving the names of the Salzburgers' wives, and the only one giving their maiden names.[1]

Ebenezer in Georgia
26 October 1739, old style

Matthias Brandner
Maria Brandner, née Herlin
Thomas Bacher
Maria Bacher, née Schweiger
Ruprecht Kalcher
Margaretha Kalcher, née
   Günter
Ruprecht Eischberger
Maria Eischberger, née
   Riedelsberger
Hans Maurer
Catharina Maurer, née Mayr
Georg Kogler
Barbara Kogler, née
   Rossbacher
Veit Lemmenhoffer
Maria Lemmenhoffer, née
   Halbenthaler
Simon Steiner
Gertraud Steiner, née
   Schoppacher
Georg Bruckner
Anna Margaretha Bruckner,
   née Müller
Thomas Pichler
Hans Flörel
Anna Maria Flörel, née
   Höpflinger
Hans Schmidt
Catharina Schmidt, née
   Zehetner

Hans Cornberger
Gertraud Cornberger, née
   Einecker
Thomas Gschwandel
Sibylla Gschwandel, née Schwab
Bartholomäus Rieser
Maria Rieser, née Zugeisen
Michael Rieser
Balthaser Rieser
Georg Rieser
Friedrich Wilhelm Müller
Christina Müller
Johann Paul Müller, their son
Anna Maria Magdalena Müller
Ruprecht Zittrauer
Anna Zittrauer, née Leihoffer
Carl Flörel
Simon Reiter
Peter Reiter
Barthol. Zant
Martin Herzog
Leonhard Crause
Barbara Crause, née Einecker
Peter Gruber
Maria Gruber, née Kroehr
Veit Landfelder
Ursula Landfelder, née
   Wassermann
Johann Pletter
Elisabeth Pletter, née
   Wassermann

{ Georg Schweiger
  Eva Regina Schweiger, née
    Unselt
{ Ruprecht Steiner
  Maria Steiner, née Winter
{ Frantz Hernberger
  Anna Justina Hernberger, née
    Unselt
{ Matthias Burgsteiner
  Agatha Burgsteiner
Gertraud Boltzius, née Kroehr
Gabriel Maurer
Christian Riedelsperger
Christian Leimberger
Paul Zittrauer

Leonard Rauner
Christian Hessler
Martin Lackner
Georg Sanftleben
Margaretha Schweighoffer
Catharina Holtzer
Joseph Leitner
Ruprecht Zimmermann
Carl Siegmund Ott
Andreas Grimmenger[2]
{ Stephan Rothenberger
  Catharina Rothenberger, née
    Piedler
Catharina Gronau, née Kroehr

Appendix III

Reliable report of the Inhabitants still Living at New Ebenezer, as well as of those who have Deceased since the year 1734, as they were Compiled and Transmitted by the two Pastors on 19 May 1739.[3]

We have been requested to send back, in letters or in our diary, a report of our parishioners who are still living. Because at this time, since we are hoping for a new transport, it is especially necessary to know how many inhabitants are still alive at Ebenezer, we wish to add to our diary a catalogue of both the living and the deceased persons of our congregation. Many are still wanting, if the number of 300 Salzburgers, which the Praiseworthy Society has resolved to receive, is to be filled.

I. Inhabitants of Ebenezer who were still living when this report was sent.

First Transport

1. Johann Martin Boltzius.
   Gertraud, his helpmeet.
   Samuel Leberecht, son of 2 and 1/4 years.
2. Israel Christian Gronau.
   Catharina, his helpmeet.
   Hanna Elisabetha, little daughter of 8 months.
3. Peter Gruber.
   Maria, widow Mosshammer, his wife.
4. Thomas Gschwandel.
   Sibylla, widow Resch, his wife.
   Margaretha, daughter of 7 years.
5. Leonard Rauner.
   Maria Magdalena, his wife.
   Matthias, son of 14 years.
   Maria, daughter of 7 years.

6. Georg Schweiger.
   Eva Regina, his wife.
   Catharina, daughter of 6 weeks.
7. Margaretha Schweighofer, widow.
   Maria, daughter of 13 years.
   Thomas, son of 11 years.
   Ursula, daughter of 11 years.
8. Martin Hertzog.
9. Christian Leimberger.
10. Simon Reiter.
    Margaretha Huber, orphan girl.
11. Christoph Ortmann, schoolmaster.
    Juliana, his wife.

Total 28

Second Transport

12. Simon Steiner.
    Gertraud, his wife.

13. Ruprecht Kalcher.
    Margaretha, his wife.
    Ursula, daughter of 3 and 1/2
      years.
    Maria, daughter of 5 months.
14. Thomas Pichler.
    Margaretha, his wife.
    Maria, daughter of 4 years.
15. Stephen Rottenberger.
    Catharina, his wife.
    Susanna, daughter of 1 and 1/4
      years.
16. Matthias Burgsteiner.
    Agatha, his wife.
    Ruprecht, son of 4 years.
17. Ruprecht Steiner.
    Maria, his wife.
    Christian, son of 1 and 1/2
      years.
18. Ruprecht Eischberger.
    Maria, his wife.
    Catharina, daughter of 2 and
      1/2 years.
19. Matthias Brandner.
    Maria, his wife.
    Maria, daughter of 4 years.
20. Veit Lemmenhofer.
    Maria, his wife.
21. Bartholomäus Rieser.
    Maria, his wife.
    Michael, son of 18 years.
    Balthasar, son of 15 years.
    Georg, son of 13 years.
22. Veit Landfelder.
    Ursula, his wife.
    Agatha, daughter of 7 years.
23. Hans Maurer.
    Catharina, his wife.
    Elisabetha, daughter of 1 and
      1/4 years.
24. Thomas Bacher.
    Maria, his wife.
    Maria, daughter of 12 years.
    Apollonia, daughter of 10 years.
25. Georg Kogler.
    Barbara, his wife.
    Maria, daughter of 5 months.
26. Ruprecht Riedelsperger.
    Anna, his wife.

Johannes, son of 6 months.
27. Christian Riedelsperger.
28. Georg Sanftleben.
29. Gabriel Bach.
30. Gabriel Maurer.
31. Bartholomäus Zant.
32. Christian Hessler.
33. Jacob Schartner.
34. Georg Brückner.
35. Ruprecht Zimmermann.
36. Paul Zittrauer.
37. Carl Sigismund Ott.
38. Heinrich Bischof, an English
      boy in the pastor's service.

                              Total 59

Third Transport

39. Hans Schmidt.
    Catharina, his wife.
    Barbara, daughter of 8 months.
40. Hans Flörel.
    Anna Maria, his wife.
41. Johann Spielbiegler.
    Rosina, his mother.
42. Johann Cronberger.
    Gertraud, his wife.
    Anna Maria, daughter of 5
      months.
43. Leonhard Crause.
    Barbara, his wife.
44. Michael Rieser.
    Anna Maria, widow Steiger, his
      wife.
    Gottlieb, son of 4 years.
45. Joseph Ernst.
    Maria, his wife.
    Susanna, daughter of 7 years.
    Johann Ludwig, son of 4
      months.
46. Dorothea Helfenstein, widow.
    Maria Friederica, daughter of 18
      years.
    Johann Friedrich, son of 16
      years.
    Maria Christina, daughter of 14
      years.
    Johann Jacob, son of 12 years.
    Jeremias, son of 10 years.
    Johannes, son of 6 years.

47. Friedrich Müller.
    Anna Christina, his wife.
    Johann Paul, son of 18 years.
    Margaretha, daughter of 15
      years.
    Elisabeth, daughter of 13 years.
    Maria Magdalena, daughter of 6
      years.
48. Dorothea Arnsdorf, widow.
    Peter, son of 16 years.
    Sophia, daughter of 14 years.
    Margaretha, daughter of 12
      years.
    Dorothea, daughter of 9 years.
49. Andreas Grimmiger.
    Catharina, daughter of 3 and
      1/2 years.

50. Frantz Hernberger.
    Justina, his wife.
51. Karl Flörel.
52. Peter Reiter.
53. Martin Lackner.
54. Matthias Zettler.
55. Josef Leitner.
56. Gottlieb Christ.
57. Johann Pletter.
58. Barbara Maurer, single.
59. Susanna Haberfehner, an
      orphan of 17 years.
    Magdalena Haberfehner, an
      orphan of 15 years.
    Catharina Holtzer, an orphan of
      15 years.

Total 52

The following persons have joined the congregation:

Ambrosius Züblin ⎱ two brothers from St. Gall.
Jacob Züblin ⎰
Mr. Thilo, doctor.
Johann Robinson, an English boy as servant of the orphanage.
Five families of German people, 6 girls, and an old widow have come from
  Savannah to the congregation as servants.

Total 21

The entire number is 160.

II. Deceased Persons of the Salzburger Congregation in Ebenezer from our Arrival in 1734 until the Present Time.

A. ADULTS

In the year 1734

1. Tobias Lackner	40	years
2. Matthias Mittensteiner	41	”
3. Balthasar Fleiss	27	”
4. Lorentz Huber	54	”
5. Maria, his wife	52	”
6. Maria Reiter	27	”
7. Matthias Braumberger	31	”
8. Hans Gruber	45	”

In the year 1735

9. Christian Steiner	30	”
10. Sebastian Glanz	43	”

11. Margaretha Gschwandel	23	years
12. Anna Schweiger	26	”
13. Ruprecht Schoppacher	49	”
14. Johann Madereiter	49	”
15. Hans Mosshammer	36	”
16. Simon Reuschgott	24	”
17. Barbara Kraher	39	”
18. Christian Schweigert	24	”

In the year 1736

19. Sabina Grimmiger	26	”
20. Paul Schweighofer	44	”
21. Andreas Bauer	24	”

22. Frantz Haberfehner   40 years
23. Thomas Ossenecker   30   ”
24. Georg Felser   50   ”
25. Anna Regina Zwifler   44   ”
26. Joh. Jac. Helfenstein   57   ”
27. Maria Haberfehner   40   ”
28. Nicol. Riedelsperger   48   ”
29. Adam Riedelsperger   38   ”

In the year 1737

30. Andr. Lorentz Arnsdorf
                             60   ”
31. Paul Lemmenhoffer   21   ”
32. Johann Simon Müller   18   ”
33. Susannah Holtzer   48   ”
34. Anna Maria Rieser   25   ”

In the year 1738

35. Maria Pichler   30   ”

B. CHILDREN

In the year 1734

1. Magdalena Huber   15   ”

In the year 1735

2. Hans Huber   10   ”
3. Marg. Schoppacher   9 weeks
4. Maria Huber   8 years
5. Thomas Gschwandel   2 hours
6. Georg Schweiger   a few hours
7. Maria Schoppacher   2 years

8. Maria Eischberger,
9. Cathar. Eischberger
            died soon after baptism
10. Agatha Steiner   2 weeks
11. Ruprecht Rottenberger   10 days
12. Wolfgang Rottenberger   13 days

In the year 1736

13. Joh. Jac. Schmidt   2 years
14. Margar. Steiner   a few hours
15. Matthias Steiner   1 day
16. Anna Cath. Ossenecker
                             10 weeks
17. Johann Riedelsperger   7 weeks
18. Cathar. Arnsdorf   9 weeks
19. Adam Lemmenhofer   9 months
20. Cathar. Gronau   10 weeks

In the year 1737

21. Joh. Georg Lemmenhofer
                            2 months
22. Anna Elisabeth Ernst   6 months
23. Margar. Cronberger   4 days
24. Maria Cronberger   6 weeks
25. Joh. Jac. Schmidt   1 & 1/4 years
26. Maria Cathar. Arnsdorf   1 day
27. Maria Schweiger   3 days

In the year 1738

28. Peter Gruber   5 days
29. Maria Steiner   3 days
30. Maria Flörel   18 weeks

Appendix IV

An Accot of Servants paid for by the Trustees for establishing the Colony of Georgia in America to Capt. William Thomson.[4]

Whole Heads	*under whole heads*				
M.	W.	B.	G.		

Delivered to Mr. Thomas Christie the Recorder Two Servants in discharge of those assigned him by the Trustees letter the 11th of August 1738, and 3²/₃ heads more returned by him to the Trustees.

vizt. Heads

M.	W.	B.	G.		
1	1	1	3	John Kreamp a Fisherman aged 35. Sophia his Wife aged 40. Catherina his Daughter aged 10. Maria Magdalena his Daughter aged 7. John Ulrick his Son aged 4 and Anna Margaretta his Daughter aged 2. In all 6 persons.	$3^2/_3$
1				Adam Stroup a Weaver aged 37.	1
1				John George Holland a Taylor aged 22.	1
					$5^2/_3$

Delivered to Mr. Mathews who married Mr. Musgrove's Widow Interpreter to the Indians as a Recompence in lieu of her Indian Servant killed in the Disputes with Mr. Watson.   vizt. Heads

| 1 | | | | Abraham Taylor[5] a Taylor aged 20. | 1 |

Delivered to Andrew Duche the Potter to be paid for to the Trustees by him.   vizt.

| 2 | | | | Christopher Shantz[6] aged 21 and William his Brother aged 16.   Heads | 2 |

Delivered to Mr. Henry Parker the first Bailiff at Savannah to be accompted as part of Payment of his present Salary.

vizt. Heads

| 0 | 1 | | | Margaret Volthoward[7] aged 19. | 1 |

Delivered the Reverend Mr. Bolzius at Ebenezer in Discharge of 16.2.6 Balance in

M.	W.	B.	G.	

the Trustees hands for the Saltzburghers and the Residue to be received from the several Persons themselves by Mr. Bolzius to be applied with the Trustees Consent for the Benefit of the Saltzburghers at Ebenezer.   vizt. Heads

M.	W.	B.	G.		
1	1	1		Solomon Adde a Shoemaker aged 30. Margaret his Wife aged 32 and John his Son aged 3.	2$^1/_3$
0	1			Barbara Volthoward aged 14.	1
0	2		1	Magdalen Gephart aged 19. Elizabeth Gephart aged 14 and Eva Gephart aged 10.	2$^1/_2$
0	2			Catherina Henrick[8] aged 20 and Margarett Henrick aged 15.	2
1	2			Peter Henrick aged 48. Juliana his Wife aged 54 and Eve Barbara his Daughter aged 22.	3
0	1			Kunegunda Knowart Widow aged 54.	1

11$^5/_6$

Delivered Mr. John Fallowfield the second Bailiff at Savannah to be accompted as part of Payment of his present Salary.
                                                          vizt. Heads

M.	W.	B.	G.		
1	1			Simon Guring a Farmer aged 32 and Anna Maria his Wife aged 30.	2
1	1			Hans Michael Wuller aged 36 and Anna Maria his Wife aged 36.	2

4

Delivered Noble Jones to be paid for to the Trustees by his Bond for the same.   vizt.

M.	W.	B.	G.		
2	1	1		Leonard Muller a Farmer aged 41. Eve his Wife aged 40 Hans Michael his Son aged 13 and Hans Bernard his Son aged 6.	3$^1/_3$

3$^1/_3$

Delivered the late Mr. John West, whereof one was returned to the Trustees, and the other becomes an Increase to the Colony.
                                                          vizt. Heads

M.	W.	B.	G.		
1	1			John Clements Wagenerak aged 48 and Catherina his Wife aged 23.	2

2

Delivered Mr. Mouse at Skidoway as an Encouragement to him for remaining on that Island.   vizt.

M.	W.	B.	G.		
1				John Smith[9] a Baker aged 44.	1

1

M.	W.	B.	G.			
				Delivered Mr. Perkins to be accompted as part of Payment of his present Salary as a Magistrate at Frederica vizt. Heads		
2	0	0	1	Jacob Rooff a Farmer aged 48, Jacob his Son aged 21 and Margaretta his Daughter aged 7.	2¹/₂	2¹/₂
				Delivered Thomas Walker at Frederica to be paid for to the Trustees by his Bond for the same. vizt.		
0	1	0	0	Elizabeth Cluer aged 33.	1	1
				Delivered Andrew Walset[10] to be paid for to the Trustees by his Bond for the same. vizt. Heads		
1	0	1	1	John Frederick Bineker aged 35. Christiana his Daughter aged 10 and John Urich[11] his Son aged 7.	2	2
				Settled upon Village Bluff at St. Simons to be paid for to the Trustees by the Peoples Bonds for the same. Vizt. Heads		
1	3	2	0	Widow Victor aged 36. Anna her Daughter aged 20. Annalis her Daughter aged 16. Peter her Son aged 17. Jacob her Son aged 10 and Sule her Son aged 7.	5	
2	1	1		Andrew Volthoward a Farmer aged 49. Anna his Wife aged 41. Tobias his Son aged 12 and Hans George his Son aged 9.	3¹/₂	
0	1	2	1	Widow Shanbacher[12] aged 36. Hans Michael her Son aged 8. Hans George her Son aged 7 and Magdalena her Daughter aged 3.	2¹/₃	
0	1			Widow Clements aged 35.	1	
1	2	2		Philip Gephart a Farmer aged 45. Martha his Wife aged 43. Maria Catherina his Daughter aged 17. Philip his Son aged 6 & Hans George his Son aged under 2.	3¹/₃	
0	1	2	2	Widow Derick aged 26. Elizabeth her Daughter aged 8. Malchier her Son aged 7. Jacob her Son aged 5 and Margeretta her Daughter aged 1.	2¹/₃	
1	2	1		Christopher Kensler a Farmer aged 43. Agnes Christiana his Wife aged 39. Anna Margaretta his Daughter aged 12 & Bastian his Son aged 3.	3¹/₃	

M. W. B. G.				
2 2 1 1				

{ Jacob Ichinger a Farmer aged 48. Catherina his Wife aged 52. Sophia his
Daughter aged 18. Hans Michael his Son
aged 14. Annalis his Daughter aged 9
and Jacob his Son aged 5. $4^5/_6$
                                                        $25^2/_3$

Delivered Mr. Mackintosh Moore to be Ac-
compted as part of Payment of his present
Salary as Overseer of the Trust Servants at
Darien.   vizt.

1
───
25 29 15 10   Joseph Upsha[13] aged 16.   1
                                                              ───
                                                               1
Persons
      In all 79 Persons making 64 heads   64 Heads

They arrived in
Georgia, the 7
Oct. 1738

An Accot of Servants paid for by the Trustees for establishing
the Colony of Georgia to Captain William Thomson.[4]

Delivered to Mr. Habersham to be employed in cultivating Lands for Religious
Uses at Savannah.   vizt. Heads

2 2   { Christian Kreamer a Farmer aged 49.
            Clara his Wife aged 43. Anna Maria his
            Daughter aged 14 and Christopher his
            Son aged 12.   4

3 2   1 { John Adam Miller a Taylor aged 48.
            Christiana his Wife aged 30. Veronica his
            Daughter aged 16. Philip his Son aged
            14. John Nicholas his Son aged 12 and
            Mary Catherina his Daughter aged 10. $5^1/_2$

1 1   { Christopher Bender a Taylor aged 46.
            and Elizabeth Bender his Neice aged 24.   2

1   And Blaiz Huber a Carpenter aged 28.   1
────   ────
7 5 0 1 $12^1/_2$
                                                        $12^1/_2$

Delivered at Savannah to be employed in
Cultivating Trust Lands at Fort Argyll
cleared by Captain Mackpherson's Rang-
ers.   vizt. Heads

3 2 3 2 { John Slechterman[14] a Cooper aged 50.
            Anne Barbara his Wife aged 40. Mar-
            garetta Barbara his Daughter aged 19.
            Joseph Mich. his Son aged 18. John Peter
            his Son aged 16. Julian his Daughter
            aged 11. George Bartholomew his Son
            aged 10. John Lawrence his Son aged 8.
            George Maurice his Son aged 7 and Mar-
            garetta his Daughter aged 4 Months.   7
                                                      ───
                                                       7

M.	W.	B.	G.		

Delivered to the Reverend M[r]. Norris the Trustees Missionary   vizt.

M.	W.	B.	G.	John Leonard a Weaver aged 19.	
1					1
11	7	3	3	Carrd. Over.	$\frac{1}{20^1/_2}$

Delivered to Joseph Fitzwalter to be employed in the Publick Garden under his Care.   vizt. Heads

2 2   { Condrit[15] Heldt a Weaver aged 52. Elizabeth his Wife aged 53. Hans Michael his Son aged 23 and Elizabeth his Daughter aged 17.   4

4

Delivered to the Reverend Mr. Bolzius To be employed as Cowherds to the Saltzburghers.   vizt. Heads

2 1 1   { Michael Sneider[16] a Taylor aged 40. Anna his Wife aged 30. Hans George his Son aged 12 & John his Son aged 6. $3^1/_3$

1 1   { And Frederick Nett a Weaver aged 31 and Elizabeth his Wife aged 36. $\frac{2}{5^1/_3}$

To attend the Orphan Saltzburghers.

1   Catharina Custabader[17] aged 50.   1

To Christopher Ortman the Schoolmaster at Ebenezer.

1 1   { Christian Lewenberger a Weaver aged 32 and Margaretta his Wife aged 35. $\underline{2}$

$8^1/_3$

Delivered to William Stephens Esq. Secretary for the Affairs of the Trust in Georgia.   Heads

1   The Widow Bishoffen aged 39. $\underline{1}$

1

Delivered for cultivating Lands for Religious Uses in the Southern part of Georgia, if not before provided, otherwise to be employed in cultivating Trust Lands at Frederica.   vizt. Heads

2 2 3   { John Peter Shantze[18] a Gardener aged 42. Anna Maria his Wife aged 41. Anna Magdalena his Daughter aged 18. Hans Adam his Son aged 12. Charles his Son aged 7. Andreas his Son aged 4 and Philip his Son aged 2. $5^1/_6$

3 1 1   { Hans George Picklie a Shoemaker aged 43. Agnes his Wife aged 40. John his Son aged 17. Thomas his Son aged 13 and Jacob his Son aged 8. $4^1/_2$

M.	W.	B.	G.
2	1	0	1

{ And John Ragnous a Carpenter aged 34. Margaretta his Wife aged 36. John his Son aged 12 and Anna Maria his Daughter aged 8.

$3^1/_2$

| 24 | 18 | 8 | 4 |

$13^1/_6$

54 Persons

47 Heads

Appendix V

In the year 1739 the inhabitants of Ebenezer harvested the following under divine blessing.[19]

	Indian or Welsh corn, bushels	Beans or Indian peas, bushels	Potatoes or sweet roots, bushels	Rice, bushels
Ortmann	71	27	6	24
Rauner	69	13½		10½
Bruckner	23	2	5	11
Ernst	18	22	24	23
Schmidt	62½		22	30
Krause	80	4½	10	8
Kornberger	64		28	15
Simon Reiter	86	16	20	15
Peter Reiter[20]	75	1		19½
Leitner	40			8
Helffenstein	22			8
Bacher	121	20	26	20
Kogler	46	10		30
Lemmenhofer	41	17	30	30
Ruprecht Steiner	119	39	42	16
Simon Steiner	89	12	15	45
Gschwandel	111	29	9	24
Brandner	98	18	38	10
Paul Zittrauer	30	8	18	30
Ruprecht Zittrauer	22½	1	2	5
Hans Maurer	25	21	25	18
Gabriel Maurer	70	10	24	13
Müller	78	4	50	30
Pichler	58	6	50	15
Arnsdorf	10	13	28	
Spielbigler	48		7	7
Pletter	46	2½	13	14

Zettler	6			
Zübli	22	5	11	
Schweiger	71	16	61	11
Gruber	99	25	28	11
Hössler	33	1	5	1½
Ott	36	2½	32	5½
Rottenberger[21]	48	15	30	14
Grimmiger	30	4		
Lackner	95	1	10	8
Zimmermann	82	2	20	9
Eischberger	48	17	28	9
Leimberger	47	16	8	
Burgsteiner	38¼	4	32	15
Michael Riesser	75	13	24	36
Hernberger	2½			
Zant	50	8	22	
Barthol. Riesser	130	13	22	23
Miss Maurer	2			
Riedelsberger	56	15½	13	3
Landfelder	55	12	12	12
Nett	3		12	
Hans Flörl	58	2	13	20
C. Flörl	42	1	13	18
Orphanage	190	46	220	50
Total (bushels)	2,982¼	495½	1,120	717
In quarts	95,448	15,856		
In pounds	190,896	31,712		

In addition to this we both (especially I, because I had the industrious Peter Heinrich, who died before the harvest) had some increase in corn, beans, rice, and sweet potatoes, which, however, is not calculated in the above total. N.B. An English bushel contains 32 quarts, the quart being reckoned as 2 pounds of corn or beans.

Notes

INTRODUCTION

1. George F. Jones, ed., *Henry Newman's Salzburger Letterbooks*, Wormsloe Foundation Publications, No. 10 (Athens, Ga.: University of Georgia Press, 1968).

2. Samuel Urlsperger, ed., *Ausführliche Nachricht von den Saltzburgischen Emigranten* . . . (Halle, 1735 ff.).

3. Franckesche Stiftung—Missionsarchiv Abtheilung 5A. Universitäts- und Landesbibliothek Sachsen-Anhalt, Halle, D.D.R.

4. Jaroslav Pelikan, ed., *Luther's Works* (St. Louis: Concordia Publishing House, 1963), vol. 26, pp. 4 ff. Boltzius read an English translation of this treatise on 25 October 1738 (George F. Jones and Renate Wilson, eds., *Detailed Reports on the Salzburger Emigrants Who Settled in America, 1738*, vol. V [Athens: University of Georgia Press, 1980], p. 252).

5. See entries for 19 July, 11–12 August, 6 October. In his letter of 17 February 1738 to the Trustees' accountant Harman Verelst, Thomas Jones claimed that Causton had taken this linen on his own private account and had sold most of it (Allen D. Candler, ed., *The Colonial Records of the State of Georgia* XXII, pt. II, 82). Nevertheless, on 12 January 1741, at Boltzius' and Gronau's repeated request, the Trustees agreed to pay Norris and Drewett, Schlatter's London correspondents, £17 17s 1d (*ibid.*, II, 354).

6. Typical is an extract of a letter from Urlsperger to Ziegenhagen, which was forwarded to one of the Trustees, James Vernon, dated 15 September 1738 (Candler, ed., *Col. Rec. Ga.* XXII, pt. II, 250). See also p. 159; vol. XXII, pt. I, 109; vol. II, pt. I, 114.

7. See Candler, ed., *Col. Rec. Ga.* V, 181, and XXX, 40, 74, 76. The Captain's name was written Harramond, Haermond, Haeramond, etc. An extract of Sanftleben's travelogue appeared in Urlsperger, ed., *Ausführliche Nachricht, Vierte Continuation*, pp. 2292–2306.

8. This interesting petition, dated 13 March and signed by the entire community, is published in Candler, ed., *Col. Rec. Ga.* III, 428–31. A German version of this letter appears in Urlsperger, ed., *Ausführliche Nachricht, Dritte Continuation*, pp. 2062–65; see also the letter of 25 November 1738, *ibid.*, 2047–53.

9. Boltzius' house was still standing and functioning when Heinrich Melchior Mühlenberg revisited Ebenezer in 1774 (*The Journals of Henry Melchior Mühlenberg*, vol. II, trans. Theodore Tappert and John Doberstein [Philadelphia: Mühlenberg Press, 1945], p. 653).

10. He and Baron von Reck talked with "Moors" on 19 May 1735. The account was submitted by von Reck, but it is clear that Boltzius shared his views (George F. Jones, ed., *Detailed Reports on the Salzburger Emigrants Who Settled in America, 1733–1734*, vol. I [Athens: University of Georgia Press, 1968], p. 117).

11. Henri François Chifelle. Although he could scarcely speak German, it would seem that his name was originally German Swiss, since he had a kinsman named Tschiffeli (Candler, ed., *Col. Rec. Ga.* XXXI, 40). Tschiffeli could easily become Chifelle, but not vice-versa. Chifelle was a worldly man who acquired many land grants. See Henry A. M. Smith, "Purrysburgh," *South Carolina Historical and Genealogical Magazine* 10 (1909): 212, 213, 217, 218. Nevertheless, the Trustees awarded him £20 for his good work among the Savannah Germans (Candler, ed., *Col. Rec. Ga.* XXIV, 31–32).

12. Mr. John Fallowfield, who had come over at his own expense, was appointed second bailiff on 20 June 1739, just before striking the servant (Candler, ed., *Col. Rec. Ga.* V, 192).

13. At a meeting of the Trustees on 28 November 1739 it was reported that, on 18 June 1739, £30 sterling had been given for Gronau's house (Candler, ed., *Col. Rec. Ga.* II, 309; V, 127).

14. Benjamin Martyn, secretary of the Trustees, had written on 1 May 1735 to Samuel Eveleigh that "the Germans are a sober, strong, and laborious people" (Candler, ed., *Col. Rec. Ga.* XXIX, 122). See also Oglethorpe's letter of 29 December 1739 (*ibid.*, XXII, 293).

15. Candler, ed., *Col. Rec. Ga.* V, 107.

16. *Ibid.*, 195.

JANUARY

1. This is one of the many German-speaking people who passed through Georgia without leaving any official records. Since he did not come over on the charity and did not take up land, he appears on no official documents.

2. Being Swedish, Falk had probably learned Low German of the Lübeck variety, that being the lingua franca of most of Scandinavia.

3. Boltzius is quoting Psalms 68:20. In the Luther version it is "Wir haben einen Gott, der da hilft, und den Herrn Herrn, der vom Tode errettet." The King James version has "He that is a God is a God of Salvation; and unto God the Lord belong the issues from death."

4. For names of girls, see February, note 14.

5. Boltzius is, of course, speaking figuratively and alluding to the parable about the merchant and the pearl in Matthew 13:45–46.

6. Thomas Causton had been replaced by Thomas Jones.

7. Matthias Zettler. This lad prospered, became prominent, and left a large progeny. A Mathias Zettler was appointed "Commissioner and Surveyor of Roads" on 11 April 1768 (Candler, ed., *Col. Rec. Ga.* XIX, Pt. I, 58).

8. Obviously with Reck, who is left unnamed because of his bad reputation. This Reck was probably the Jacob Reck who was granted fifty acres in Purysburg on 16 September 1768 (Henry A. M. Smith, "Purrysburgh," *South Carolina Historical and Genealogical Magazine* 10 [1909]:212).

9. These families seem to have been the Helds and the Gebhards.

10. *Ob mir wol eben nicht viel kund worden.* Since Boltzius' meaning is not clear, there may be a typographical error.

11. The Catholic and Lutheran Bibles number the commandments differently from the English Bible, lumping the first two as number one and dividing the tenth into two. Therefore this is the fourth commandment according to the English system.

12. Possibly Jacob Schartner.

FEBRUARY

1. See Candler, ed., *Col. Rec. Ga.* XXII, pt. II, 290–92, for Oglethorpe's original disposition of these servants.

2. It is to be remembered that in the Savannah River delta the word "French" usually designated French Swiss, that being the dominant element in Purysburg.

3. Andrew Duchee.

4. The "stones" appear to have been lumps of clay worn round by the action of the current.

5. Boltzius uses the word *Ziegelsteine*, which usually means tiles (from Latin *tegulum*), but he surely means bricks.

6. See January, note 11.

7. Boltzius uses the term *fremde Sünden* (Latin *peccata aliena*), the sins of encouraging or conniving at sin.

8. "In twofold respect."

9. Not Proverbs 30:10, but 30:20. Boltzius is doubtless quoting from memory.

10. Muggitzer (written Meiggitzer on petition of 25 November 1738) had probably acquired a functional use of English while working, much to Boltzius' chagrin, for Causton at Thunderbolt in 1737 (see Jones and Wilson, eds., *Detailed Reports on the Salzburger Emigrants Who Settled in America, 1737*, vol. IV [Athens: University of Georgia Press, 1976], pp. 78, 146). Riedelsperger, the first Salzburger to desert, caused Boltzius much anguish during 1737. See index to *op. cit.* He later wrote from a place 100 miles from Philadelphia, where he had settled.

11. The Held family (see entry for 17 August). The manager is Kalcher.

12. According to the minutes of the Trustees' meeting of 11 July 1739, "Two Heads (of indentured servants) were given to the Salzburgh School Master" (Candler, ed., *Col. Rec. Ga.* II, 293). The Earl of Egmont's list in Appendix IV gives their names as Christian Lewenberger, a weaver aged 32, and his wife Margaretta, aged 35.

13. Boltzius had previously related this marital difficulty, but without betraying identities. The older son, Johann Jacob, had done well in school at Ebenezer. See George F. Jones, ed., *Detailed Reports on the Salzburger Emigrants Who Settled in America, 1734–1735*, vol. II (Athens: University of Georgia Press, 1969), p. 166.

14. Harmon Verelst, the Trustees' accountant, later listed them as "Solomon Adde a Shoemaker aged 30, Margaret His wife aged 32, and John his Son aged 3, Barbara Waldhaver aged 14, Magdalen Gephart aged 19, Elizabeth Gephart aged 14, Eva Gephart aged 10, Catharina Henrick aged 20, Margaretta Henrick aged 15, Peter Henrick aged 48, Juliana his Wife aged 54, Eva Barbara his Daughter aged 22, Kunegunda Knowart aged 54." Verelst's letter, written to Boltzius on 11 June 1740, was granting him as much of the £82 15s 8d as had been paid, or would be paid, by them or their sponsors for their passage (Candler, ed., *Col. Rec. Ga.* XXX, 30). It is not known whether Barbara Waldhaver (written Volthoward on the Earl of Egmont's manuscript list of Capt. Thomson's passengers in Appendix IV) was related to the other "Volthowards" among Capt. Thomson's passengers or to the later Walthours, who played such a role in Ebenezer. The name Henrick should be Heinrich, and Kunegunda Knowart was actually Catherina Kustobader. According to Boltzius's letter of 29 December 1740 to Verelst, Juliana Henrick had died in Savannah upon arrival (Candler, ed., *Col. Rec. Ga.* XXII, pt. II, 464).

15. See this petition, with the Earl of Egmont's rebuttal, in C. L. Ver Steeg, ed., *"A True and Historical Narrative of the Colony of Georgia" with comments by the Earl of Egmont* (Athens: University of Georgia Press, 1960).

16. This Capt. Robert Williams had given seeds to Boltzius on 27 September 1736 (George F. Jones, and Marie Hahn, eds., *Detailed Reports on the Salzburger Emigrants Who Settled in America, 1736*, vol. III [Athens: University of Georgia Press, 1972], p. 217). The petition was purportedly written by Patrick Tailfer, Hugh Anderson, and David Douglas; but it may have indeed been instigated by Williams, who was Tailfer's brother-in-law, since he had much to gain from it.

17. Ambrosius and Johann Jacob Zuebli.

18. David Zuebli, father of Johann Joachim Zubly, subsequent leader of the dissenters in Georgia and representative at the Continental Congress.

19. While a Pietist could justify God's destroying a blasphemer, it must have been difficult to justify His drowning of the younger brother and sister too.

20. Boltzius is alluding to Jeremiah 21:9, which Luther renders as "er . . . soll sein Leben als eine Ausbeute behalten."

21. "Potatoes" always refers to sweet potatoes, Irish potatoes being *Erdäpfel.*

22. This was Hans Krusy, his son was Adrian (Urlsperger, ed., *Ausführliche Nachricht, Achte Continuation*, pp. 902, 906).

MARCH

1. Our fifth commandment. See January, note 11.

2. Hymns are identified, when possible, in Appendix I.

3. For Boltzius, "temptation" (*Anfechtung*) nearly always means the temptation to doubt the mercy of Jesus.

4. She is apparently alluding to the annual memorial and thanksgiving service each March 12th, the anniversary of the Salzburgers' landing in Georgia. This year, strangely enough, Boltzius celebrated it on 3 March.

5. See January, note 11.

6. Col. William Stephens, the Trustees' secretary in Georgia, reported this sad event similarly on 1 March 1739 (Candler, ed., *Col. Rec. Ga.* IV, 292–93).

FRIDAY. A German Servant who was committed to the Log-House, was found dead there this Morning; which may need a little Explanation here, of some Circumstances attending it. The Man had once been a Servant under Mr. Causton, with whom he voluntary indented, on Condition of Mr. Causton's paying for his and his Family's Passage, rather than make himself liable to be sold by the Captain, to one whom he could not expect so good Usage from. The Fellow nevertheless left Mr. Causton's Service, without his Leave, or any just Cause, as his Master says (which is not material here) and in several Months could never be persuaded by fair Means to return to Ockstead; but liked better to nest in an old-deserted Hut in the Out-Part of the Town, as some others of his Countrymen did; and these having Arms, were some of the Folks particularly aimed at in the late Order of Court against Servants carrying Arms; by which it was visible these disorderly People lived; and under Pretence of shooting Deer, frequently destroyed other Mens Property in Cattle, &c. neither were any Threats available to deter them from these Practices. This Fellow happened to be espied Yesterday with a Gun on his Shoulder, in the Street openly, by his Master, who was walking at that Time in Company with Mr. Parker, our first Magistrate, and they both called him to come to them; but he walked off, without taking any Notice of one or the other (the certain Index of that incurable Stubbornness which generally prevails among them). Mr. Parker, therefore, sent the Constable Mr. Fallowfield, to follow him, and take his Arms away; pursuant to which he went, taking one or two with him to assist; but the Fellow resisting and struggling, and by clubbing his Piece, attempting to knock down any of them who stood most in Opposition, some Blows passed, and he was carried before the Magistrate, who committed him for resisting the Constable, &c. Upon his Death the Coroner's Inquest sat on the Body, and examined several Witnesses who saw what passed; as also an able Surgeon was called, to give his Opinion touching the Blows he received, which it seems were given by the Constable with the Handle of a small Whip, so that no Sort of Mark appeared, either on the Head or Body, of any Wound which might occasion his Death; and the Posture the Body lay in, when found dead, being flat on his Face, and a great Effusion by Vomiting also appeared, it was judged a Suffocation; and the Jury's Verdict was Accidental Death.

Capt. Thomson, who brought the "good Germans" to Georgia, mentioned a "Mr. Fallowfield, Naval Officer, a man of good Sence, and industrious" (Phillipps Collection, Egmont Manuscripts, University of Georgia Library, Athens, Ga. Vol. 14, 209, p. 211 for 5 May 1739). On 24 November 1739 the son of William Stephens wrote to the Trustees that the bailiff "had no Reason to strike the German who died, because Several People were at hand, who the law directed him to command to his Assistance, in Case the man had not been obedt." (*ibid.*, vol. 14, 210, p. 109).

7. The "first transport" refers to Capt. Hewett's shipload.

8. One hand washes the other. See entry for 13 March.

9. This would suggest that Urlsperger saw fit to delete some unhappy event.

10. See entry for 6 March 1739.

11. See February, note 12.

12. See January, note 11.

13. Chinkapins (chiquapins), a kind of dwarf chestnut.
14. For a contemporary account of the Stono Uprising, see Candler, ed., *Col. Rec. Ga.* XXII, pt. II, 233–36.
15. See the contemporary English translation, with names of signers, in Candler, ed., *Col. Rec. Ga.* III, 428–31. This was published many times, with varying degrees of abridgement, for propaganda purposes. Boltzius failed to mention that he wrote a letter the next day to Verelst, which is included in Candler, ed., *Col. Rec. Ga.* XXII, pt. II, 118–22; it is a good illustration of Boltzius' command of English and indicates the many temporal responsibilities he had assumed.
16. Isaac Bradford. See April, note 11.
17. Very clearly Johann Christ. See entry for 9 March.
18. A large dugout. Boltzius wrote *Petti-Auger*, his understanding of the Spanish word *petiagua*, a folk etymological corruption of a Carib word.
19. If they drank that much on St. Patrick's Day, it is hard to imagine how much they would have drunk on St. Andrew's Day.
20. Boltzius did not know that many of the Highlanders, like those at Darien, could not speak English. Concerning the Scots who sailed with the Salzburgers on the Judith in September 1741, the Earl of Egmont wrote on 15 September 1742, "43 Highlanders, two of whom speak English" (Candler, ed., *Col. Rec. Ga.* V, 549). In a letter of 23 August 1735 to Nicholas Spence of the Society for Promoting Christian Knowledge in the Highlands of Scotland, Verelst asked the Society to recommend a "Godly minister for the Highlanders in Georgia, since they speak no English" (Candler, ed., *Col. Rec. Ga.* XXIX, 155).
21. This was John McLeod (MacLeod, MacCleod, McCloud, MackCloud, etc.) of New Inverness, who received a grant of 300 acres on 23 January 1739 (Candler, ed., *Col. Rec. Ga.* XXXIII, 71 ff.).
22. Surely the widow Schweighofer.
23. Zant recovered from this affliction, for the very next year he was accepted for military service. On 9 December 1756 a Solomon Zaut (sic) received a grant of 52 acres (Candler, ed., *Col. Rec. Ga.* VII, 455).
24. Boltzius calls this *Dominica Oculi*.
25. *In gesetzlicher Unruhe*; in anxiety to achieve salvation through good works, instead of through faith.
26. Wild boars are now found in the vicinity of Ebenezer, descended from strayed domestic pigs (razorback hogs) and wild boars recently imported from the Black Forest.

APRIL

1. Boltzius calls it *Dominica Laetare*.
2. Peter Heinrich (see February, note 14), who was 48 upon his arrival.
3. Martin Herzog.
4. An allusion to Revelations 2:6.
5. Apparently the widow Arnsdorf, for whom the Salzburgers had built a house.
6. Johann Arndt, *Paradis-Gärtlein*, probably the edition bound with his *Wahres Christentum*, which was published by A. H. Francke at the Halle Orphanage in 1735.
7. Johann Habermann, either *Christliche Gebätlein auff alle Tage in der Wochen . . . alten stettin* (1660), or *Tägliche Morgen- und Abendgebete* (Leipzig, 1672).
8. *Güldenes Schatz-Kästlein der Kinder Gottes* (Halle 17??), devotional tract by Carl Heinrich Bogatzky.
9. Typical of Boltzius' prefigurations (*Vorbilder*), i.e. persons or events in the Old Testament that prefigure or signify those in the New.
10. "Des sel. Prof. Francken Sendschreiben von Christus," unidentified devotional tract by A. H. Francke.
11. On 8 May 1739, Col. Stephens entered in his journal that "Isaac Bradford, that notorious Thief, who had lately committed so many Villanies here," had been ap-

prehended in Charleston and returned to jail in Savannah. On 3 June he added that Bradford had escaped (Candler, ed., *Col. Rec. Ga.* IV, 333, 348). On 23 August he reported to the Trustees that "Isaac Bradford a notorious theif was seized & committed to jayl in Carolina" (Candler, ed., *Col. Rec. Ga.*, V, 221).

12. This sounds contradictory and suggests that he must make bowel actions, but elsewhere he uses *Motion* to mean a stroll, as in the entry for 6 September.

13. Persimmons (*diospyros virginiana*).

14. Again we see the influence of Gottfried Wilhelm Leibniz's theodicy.

MAY

1. See April, note 8.

2. Missionaries from Halle were sent to Malabar, Tranquebar, and elsewhere in India. See *Der königlichen dänischen Missionarien aus Ost-Indien eingesandte ausführliche Berichten* (Halle, 1735).

3. Surely Benjamin Sheftal, the advocate of the Georgia Germans. By this time Boltzius had despaired of converting this obstinate man and must have chortled at his difficulty. The woman may have blamed the child on Sheftal as the only German in town financially able to support it.

4. On 27 June 1739 a Rev. Mr. Vallois donated eight guineas to buy "twelve Dozen New Testaments and two Dozen of Arnot's true Christianity and a large Number of spelling Books and short Catechisms" for the use of the Palatine servants (Candler, ed., *Col. Rec. Ga.* I, 351.

5. "Die kleinen Sonntags-Predigten des sel. Prof. Franckens," no doubt August Hermann Francke, *Kurtze Sonn- und Fest-Tags-Predigten* (Halle, 1718).

6. On 30 May 1739 the Trustees ordered "the Children of six years old and upwards of such servants, to be employ'd as the Overseer shall direct; And the maintenance of them for Provisions and Cloathing; to be paid by the Week after the rate of four Pence a day each, One with Another But those Children of such Servants under six Years old are to be maintain'd by the Parents out of their Allowances" (Candler, ed., *Col. Rec. Ga.* II, 277).

7. Unless denoted as the "late Prof. Francke," the reference is to the son, Gotthilf August, not the father, August Hermann.

8. The Orphanage (*Waysenhaus*), a part of the Francke Foundation (*Franckesche Stiftungen*), was the model for that in Ebenezer and, indirectly, for the one at Bethesda. Both Boltzius and Gronau had taught at the Orphanage school.

9. The bulk of the Salzburger exiles had gone to East Prussia, mostly to the vicinity of Gumbinnen.

10. On 20 December 1738 the Trustees had resolved "That a Sum not exceeding One hundred pounds be applied for sending over to Georgia the said Trades Men and Unmarried Women."

11. Raccoons. On the next page Boltzius identifies the animal correctly, but the Halle typesetter printed "Rackous."

12. It is surprising that Boltzius mentions large starlings, since it was usually little rice-birds or bobolinks (*dolinchonyx oryzivorous*) that did the damage.

13. It was two years before the Salzburgers began to plow. In 1745 they received a hogshead containing twenty plowshares (Candler, ed., *Col. Rec. Ga.* XXXI, 44).

14. This herdsman must have been Held, who had a son old enough to guard cattle. Father and son, along with John Robinson, enlisted to fight the Spaniards. See Boltzius' letter to Oglethorpe in entry for 16 April 1740 in Urlsperger, ed., *Ausführliche Nachricht, Sechste Continuation*, pp. 458–59.

15. The King James version unites these two commandments in number 10. See January, note 11.

16. Boltzius is referring to the Moravian or Herrnhuter missionaries Georg Schulius

and Peter Böhler. See Adelaide Fries, *The Moravians in Georgia* (Winston-Salem, 1906), pp. 209–13.

17. One of the *Sammlung auserlesener Materien zum Bau des Reiches Gottes* (Leipzig, 1731 ff.).

18. "Readings, lessons."

19. In 1727 Boltzius had visited Pastor Daniel Gottlieb Mäderjan of Thommendorf in the district of Bunzlau in Silesia, who ministered to many Protestant refugees from Habsburg territories. See Hermann Winde, *Die Frühgeschichte der lutherischen Kirche in Georgia* (dissertation), Halle, 1960 (unpublished), pp. 158–59.

20. In the 18th century the name "Ebenezer" was translated both as "the stone of help" and also as "the Lord has helped so far."

21. "The reason is at hand," or "The reason is evident."

22. This is the first time that Boltzius has admitted that Kieffer owned slaves. To the younger Kieffer's credit, we may say that he was truly concerned for their souls, as is indicated by an entry in the Ebenezer church records of 1756: "Mary, a negro girl, was born on Theobald Kieffer's plantation, December 14, and baptized in his home the following day" (A. G. Voigt, trans., and C. A. Linn, ed., *Ebenezer Record Book* [Savannah, 1929], p. 3). The son's piety is also revealed in his letter of 27 June 1750 to Professor Francke, which is reproduced in the *Georgia Historical Quarterly* 42 (1978): 50–57.

23. This disorderly man must have been forgiven and accepted again in Ebenezer after serving the Trustees for less than three years; for on 18 March 1742 he wrote a letter to Privy Counselor Georgii from Ebenezer thanking him for a benefaction in which he had shared (Urlsperger, ed., *Ausführliche Nachricht, Achte Continuation*, p. 1227). On 23 December 1744: "Solomon Addie and ffrederic Nett applied to the Board (Pres. and Assistants) for Allowance given to all servants who had faithfully served their time" (Candler, ed., *Col. Rec. Ga.* VI, 89). Nett remained and served out his time at Ebenezer, as is indicated in the minutes that follow for 10 December 1746:

"Frederick Nett formerly a Servant, but now an Inhabitant at Ebenezer, petitioning this Board for a Cow, Calf &c, as had formerly been given to the Trusts Servants; It appears to Us that the said Nett was not at any Time a Servant to the Trustees, but had faithfully served four Years in Ebenezer, and as he falls under the same Denomination with a great Number of others The Board could not comply with his Request without bringing a heavy Charge on the Trust, as They will find by a Minute of the twelvth Day of October 1743, to which this Board have as yet had no Answer" (*ibid.*, 163).

24. Up to this time "Mr." Jones always refers to Thomas Jones, Causton's successor as storekeeper, since the class-conscious Boltzius did not dignify the surveyor Noble Jones with a title until later, after he had held offices of trust.

25. There were three English boys at Ebenezer. On 16 October 1734 the Trustees had read an indenture binding "Henry Bishop of the Charity School in St. Dunstan in the West End Labourer as Servant to the Trustees for seven years in order to be as-sign'd over to Mr. Bolzius" (Candler, ed., *Col. Rec. Ga.* II, 74). For this he was given free passage and one year's maintenance on 9 October of the same year (*ibid.*, 72). On 5 May, John Robinson was sent as a servant to Gronau and Nicholas Carpenter as an "Under servant" to Mr. Bolzius (*ibid.*, 99; see also p. 101). According to a letter from Bishop to his parents dated 26 August 1735, the other two boys were "sad reprobate boys" who could "neither write nor read" (*ibid.*, XXI, 66). By 1739 Bishop was complet-ing his indenture, according to the entry for 27 September. The herdsman in question, John Robinson, left the following year with the Helds to fight against the Spaniards (see May, note 14).

26. Raccoons. See entry for 10 May.

27. Probably Reck, the shoemaker from Purysburg, who was constantly being re-pelled from Holy Communion and expelled from Ebenezer, only to be readmitted as indispensable. Perhaps he returned this time after hearing of Adde's dismissal.

28. "In case of necessity."

29. George Whitefield.

30. This letter has appeared in the *Georgia Historical Quarterly* 42 (1978):50–57.

31. Surely Whitefield's friend, John Wesley.

32. On 2 August 1742 Harman Verelst, the Trustees' accountant, wrote to Boltzius to advise him that the Trustees recognized this debt of £169 3*s* due to the Salzburgers for the bounty of one shilling per bushel of corn and beans raised in 1739.

33. "Defense."

34. "Small states grow by agreement," or "Small things prosper with concord."

JUNE

1. The German word *Hure*, cognate with Latin *cara* (dear one), originally meant sweetheart and did not necessarily imply meretriciousness. In Salzburg a peasant boy could sing *Hurenlieder* (lovesongs) to his sweetheart. Boltzius' English contemporaries could also use the word "whore" without mercenary connotations. For Boltzius, all non-marital sex was sinful, be it for pleasure or profit.

2. The Sunday after Ascension.

3. It is annoying that Urlsperger has deleted such names. Here the city is probably Charleston and the author either Whitefield or Wesley.

4. See May, note 14.

5. *Eigene Gerechtigkeit* (work-righteousness), justification through one's own merits.

6. Wild rice (*zizania aquatica*).

7. See the quote in Introduction taken from Luther's preface to the Galatians.

8. See April, note 8.

9. This is an error. Jeremiah goes only to 50:34.

10. The "oldest" here means the older of the two at Ebenezer. Boltzius regularly uses the superlative when distinguishing between two things. The oldest Zuebli was David, in Purysburg. Urlsperger shows his usual inconsistency in leaving the name Zuebli here but suppressing it on 16 June.

11. See April, note 11. If this was Bradford, he seems to have been in a hurry to return to Ebenezer.

12. Johann Jacob Zuebli.

13. Their brother David.

14. Christian Friedrich Richter, *Erbauliche Betrachtungen vom Ursprung und Adel der Seelen*, etc. (Halle, 1718).

15. Boltzius means that they put their trust in their good works and show no poverty of the spirit.

16. George Whitefield. On 27 December 1738 the Trustees had "Seal'd a Commission to the Revd Mr George Whitefield to collect Benefactions in general, but which when Collected are particularly to be applied for erecting an Orphan House in Georgia, and building a Place of Worship for the Salzburgers at Ebenezer" (Candler, ed., *Col. Rec. Ga.* I, 333). Before leaving England in June 1739, Whitefield had collected £76 for the Salzburgers (*ibid.*, XXX, 231–32).

17. Johann Anastasius Freylinghausen, *Ordnung des Heyls, nebst einem Verzeichnis der wichtigsten Kern-Sprüche*, etc. (Halle: Waisenhaus, 1724). The "Golden ABC" must have been appended to it.

18. "Teachers of divinity."

19. At the Trustees' meeting on 28 February 1739 it had been agreed that £30 be sent for building Gronau's house and £40 be sent to Boltzius for maintaining the widows and orphans (Candler, ed., *Col. Rec. Ga.* V, 127).

20. It is surprising that there is no mention of James Vernon's benefaction of £20, which was sent on 21 February (Candler, ed., *Col. Rec. Ga.* I, 32).

21. George Whitefield.

22. See Jones and Wilson, eds., *Detailed Reports*, vol. V, 254, entry for 28 October 1738.

23. Typical Pietist rhetoric. Cf. title of Friedrich Eberhard Collin's *Das gewaltige Eindringen ins Reich Gottes* (Frankfurt, 1722).

24. Johann Caspar Ulich.

25. See March, note 18.

26. All references to a *Frau von* refer to Frau von Hasslin (Heslin, etc.), the wife of "Mons. le Banquier de Hoslin," who, according to Urlsperger's letter of 3 November 1739, sent 400,000 florins to Berlin for the Salzburger emigrants, which must have been the payments subsequently collected for their properties (Candler, ed., *Col. Rec. Ga.* XXII, pt. II, 261).

27. An ointment made in Augsburg by Johann Caspar Schauer.

28. See April, note 8.

29. See April, note 9.

JULY

1. This was Capt. Haermond of the Charles (see Candler, ed., *Col. Rec. Ga.* V, 181); see also Introduction, note 7.

2. He did so. An extract appears in Urlsperger, ed., *Ausführliche Nachricht, Vierte Continuation,* pp. 2292–306.

3. This is Psalms 145:19.

4. Boltzius is speaking metaphorically. We are not supposed to take these Pietistic images literally. A crawling dog illustrates *Demutsstellung*, or the attitude of humility. The idea of cooing, derived from amorous literature, signifies divine love, as in the anonymous devotional tractate *Girrendes Täublein, die Gebundene Seufzerlein eines mit Gott verbundenen Hertzen* (Leipzig, 1731).

5. Pomesin?

6. The Halle typesetter wrote *Ihnen* (you), but the context calls for *ihnen* (them).

7. Oglethorpe was eventually refunded. On 6 January 1742 the Trustees resolved "That the Sum of forty Pounds be allowed to Mr Boltzius for building his House at Ebenezer in consideration that the said House shall remain for the Minister for the time being as was the Condition of allowing forty Pounds before to Mr Gronau" (Candler, ed., *Col. Rec. Ga.* II, 379–86).

8. Freestone peaches.

9. Clingstone peaches.

10. An extract from the Bible, to be read during a sermon.

11. See Introduction, note 9.

12. *Er hat alles wohl bedacht, und alles, alles recht gemacht, gebt unserm Gott die Ehre,* allusion to a hymn by Gustav von Mengden. See entry for 6 April and Appendix I under "*Gott hat alles.*"

13. See Boltzius' account of the confrontation in his letter of 19 July in Candler, ed., *Col. Rec. Ga.* XXII, pt. II, 180–83.

14. According to Egmont's list in Appendix IV, these were Christian Lewenberger and Margaretta, his wife.

15. "According to the rigor of the law."

16. See Oglethorpe's letter to Boltzius of 3 November 1739 in Candler, ed., *Col. Rec. Ga.* XXII, pt. II, 338.

17. Unfortunately, there was considerable truth in this impertinent lie.

18. Boltzius must be referring to Thomas Jones and the storehouse in Savannah.

19. This letter, dated 19 July, is published in Candler, ed., *Col. Rec. Ga.* XXII, pt. II, 180–83.

20. The fifth commandment, English style. See January, note 11.

21. Despite the context, "they" refers to the Salzburgers, not to the wicked people of Old Ebenezer.

22. The governor of St. Augustine, who kept himself remarkably well informed about the situation in South Carolina and Georgia, made frequent references to intel-

ligence gathered by spies. See *Letters of Montiano, Siege of St. Augustine* (Savannah, Ga., 1909), in Collections of the Georgia Historical Society VII.

23. This fever-stone has not yet been identified. It was probably a spleen swollen by malaria.

24. These men had been missionaries to the Negroes. See Adelaide L. Fries, *The Moravians in Georgia* (Winston-Salem, 1906), pp. 209–13.

25. Probably Benjamin Sheftal.

AUGUST

1. Charles Pury, son of Jean Pury, founder of Purysburg.

2. This policy of "fencing out" survived until recently in those parts of Georgia where land was cheaper than fences. It was the duty of a landowner to protect his land by fencing it against roaming cattle, not the duty of the cattle owner to "fence in" his cattle.

3. "In one's own cause."

4. "Testimony of poverty." This probably refers to poverty of the spirit.

5. This was one of the contributions (*Beyträge*) in the collection (*Sammlung*) mentioned in May, note 17.

6. See note 5 above.

7. The schoolmaster was James Habersham, a staunch supporter of the Salzburgers all his life. The merchant was probably Francis Harris, who later became Habersham's business partner.

8. Held. See entry for 17 August and also December, note 7.

9. See Introduction, note 5.

10. *Schein und Kraft des Christenthums*, allusion to 2 Timothy 3:5, which the King James version renders as "form of godliness" and "power thereof."

11. See April, note 8.

12. See August, note 5.

13. See March, note 18.

14. Anton Wilhelm Boehme, exemplary Pietist at Halle.

15. This was probably Hugh Bryan, who supplied most of the cattle for the Salzburgers. On 8 June 1736 Thomas Causton wrote that Oglethorpe had paid Bryan for delivering his cattle and rice (Candler, ed., *Col. Rec. Ga.* XXI, 168). This document confirms the conjecture in the index of Jones, ed., *Detailed Reports*, vol. II, 249. Hugh was a brother of Jonathan, a pious friend of the Salzburgers (Urlsperger, ed., *Ausführliche Nachricht, Achte Continuation*, pp. 1083, 2087).

16. See April, note 8.

17. The French were avenging a defeat which is vividly told in Candler, ed., *Col. Rec. Ga.*, XXI, 176–78, 203–5.

18. The story of the ransomed Frenchman is told in Candler, ed., *Col. Rec. Ga.*, XXI, 266–68. See also 277–78.

19. Hebrews 13:17. Luther has "Gehorchet euren Lehrern und folget ihnen," which is more favorable to Boltzius than the English translation "Obey them who have rule over you, and submit yourselves."

20. Egmont's list of Thomson's passengers (Appendix IV) lists Eve Barbara, aged 22; Catherina, aged 20; and Margarett, aged 15. He does not list Anna Maria, Boltzius' maid. See entry for 30 October.

SEPTEMBER

1. Boltzius means Old Ebenezer. See entry for 13 September.

2. See August, note 10.

3. Unidentified devotional tract, unless Boltzius is thinking of Stephan Praetorius,

Geistliche Schatzkammer der Gläubigen, in welcher die Lehre vom wahren Glauben, Gerechtigkeit, Seligkeit, Majestät, Herrlichkeit, christlichem Leben, und heilsamen Creutz der Kinder Gottes, etc. (Lüneburg, 1699).

4. The widows Schweighofer, Helfenstein, and Arnsdorf were the only widows with a *Häuflein* of children. This appears to be Arnsdorf.

5. Obviously Mrs. Schweighofer.

6. Held. See May, note 14.

7. Mrs. Schweighofer again.

8. "Great deeds of God."

9. Many of these brands and markings can be found in the Cattle Brand Book in the Georgia State Archives.

10. Ruth 3 : 7 does not say that Boas praised the Lord. This addition must have been made by Boltzius or his Pietist predecessors.

11. August Hermann Francke, *Vom rechten Wesen des Christenthums*, devotional treatise.

12. Allusion to the rich man and Lazarus in Luke 16 : 19.

13. Boltzius writes *dies* (this), but he is surely referring to the previously mentioned frame of mind, which was negative.

14. See May, note 9.

15. *Durchkommen*, a Pietist expression meaning "to break through," or "to become assured of God's mercy."

16. "Concerning lapse into sin."

17. For a vivid account of the Stono Uprising, see Candler, ed., *Col. Rec. Ga.* XXII, pt. II, 232–36.

18. This was Anna Maria Bischoff. See Urlsperger, ed., *Ausfürliche Nachricht, Siebente Continuation*, p. 513. Boltzius does not mention that he has personal need of her. See entry for 22 November.

19. Oglethorpe's success with the Indians is well told by Kenneth Coleman, *Colonial Georgia: A History* (New York: Chas. Scribner's Sons, 1976), pp. 82–83; and his return from Coweta is told in an anonymous letter in Candler, ed., *Col. Rec. Ga.* XXII, pt. II, 214–15.

20. Purysburg was the only place from which the Salzburgers had fetched brides. This may be Mrs. Georg Schweiger, née Unselt.

21. See April, note 8.

22. While she still thought that salvation could be won through good works alone.

23. This is one of the many references to the debt to the merchant, Schlatter, in St. Gall. See October, note 9.

24. This was the sum finally granted. See May, note 32.

25. Pichler must have conceded in this point, for he remained in Ebenezer and achieved importance. On 31 May 1748 the Trustees appointed him constable with an allowance of £5 per year and entrusted him with arms and musters (Candler, ed., *Col. Rec. Ga.* XXXI, 210).

26. Anna Maria Heinrich. See entry for 30 October.

27. By now Bischof (Henry Bishop) had become a Salzburger!

28. On 20 June 1739 the Trustees obtained special permission for Capt. Thomson's *Two Brothers* to sail despite the embargo (Candler, ed., *Col. Rec. Ga.* XXXIII, 30).

29. "The law of vengeance."

OCTOBER

1. "Ancient sayings." Boltzius probably means Biblical passages.

2. "Secondary causes."

3. Johann Ludwig Hartmann, *Pastorale Evangelicum, seu Instructio plenior ministrorum verbi*, etc. (Nürnberg 1697). The "B" was probably an error for "D" (i.e., Dr.), as also below in the case of Spener.

4. Phillip Jacob Spener, *Consilia Latina*.

5. Juliana Ortmann was the only woman whose husband came from London.

6. *Äusserliche Ehrbarkeit, bürgerliche Gerechtigkeit*, worldly virtues which are sins in Pietist eyes.

7. This informative letter, dated 5 October, is published in Candler, ed., *Col. Rec. Ga.* XXII, pt. II, 219–22.

8. No doubt Reck of Purysburg, the only available shoemaker.

9. See September, note 23. This letter was answered on 29 March 1740 by Verelst, who stated that the Trustees would pay Norris and Drewett £71 17s 1d as soon as Thomas Jones certified that the linen was used for the good of the colony (Candler, ed., *Col. Rec. Ga.* XXX, 231).

10. James Habersham, who wanted them for work on the Bethesda Orphanage. See entry for 17 November.

11. *Elend*. This word originally meant "exile," then, in religious parlance, "alienation from God," or "state of sin."

12. See June, note 26.

13. "Cursory reading of the New Testament."

14. See June, note 26.

15. Boltzius is citing Luther's translation of Isaiah 66:2, "Ich sehe aber an den Elenden und der zerbrochenes Geistes ist," which the King James version renders as "To this man will I look, even to him that is poor and of a contrite spirit."

16. This must be an error for "verbatim."

17. We are not told why Sanftleben's sister was asocial. Perhaps Ebenezer was not what her brother had promised, and she had still found no husband in that favorable matrimonial market.

18. The superscription of Psalms 146 in Luther's translation is "Die ewige Treue Gottes."

19. Sometimes Urlsperger suppresses Mrs. Gruber's name and sometimes he does not.

20. Apparently a hymn.

21. *Haus-Tafel* or *Tabula Oeconomica*, a devotional book by Martin Luther. See Kurt Aland, *Hilfsbuch zum Lutherstudium* (Witten, 1970).

22. "The kindling up of a dormant fire, stirring, reviving."

23. "A praying spectator."

24. A good example of the Lutheran work ethic.

25. Johann Friedrich Frisch, *Neu klingende Harfe Davids oder Erklärung der Psalmen* (Stuttgart 17??).

26. "Die Pareneses des sel. Herrn Prof. Franckens über die Epistel an den Titum und an die Ebräer," a theological work by A. G. Francke.

27. See October, note 9.

28. Oglethorpe complied on 3 November 1739 (Candler, ed., *Col. Rec. Ga.* XXIII, pt. II, 338).

29. This large stone now graces Wright Square just in front of Christ Church.

30. Boltzius means all the islands along the coast as far south as the St. Johns.

31. These were the Schlechtermanns. The oldest sons, Joseph Michael and Johann Peter were 18 and 16 years old respectively. See Appendix IV.

32. "Useless weight of earth."

33. Boltzius did not mean to be tactless, nor was he implying that Miss Lackner was a sinner. He merely meant that her physical condition well illustrated the ugliness of sin. We still say "as ugly as sin," even though sin often appears very lovely.

34. She was one of those who arrived with the shoemaker Adde. It is surprising that Verelst does not give her name and that Boltzius says she has served "almost a year" (see February, note 14).

35. The signatures to this letter, dated 26 October, are given in Appendix II.

36. Boltzius is alluding to the previous shoemakers, Reck and Adde, both of whom had to be expelled because of bad behavior.

NOVEMBER

1. Usually written Floerel. It is remarkable that he is given the title "Mr." (*Herr*), which Boltzius seldom gives the Salzburgers. Perhaps Floerel is now being groomed as future schoolmaster.

2. See October, note 28. The result of this letter was Johann Ulrich Driessler.

3. Here he takes "Ebenezer" to mean "So far the Lord hath helped us." See May, note 20, and entry for 7 November.

4. See June, note 26.

5. See note 3 above.

6. It is easy to see why Urlsperger has suppressed the name Johann Christ, but not why he has suppressed that of the Kalchers.

7. See October, note 21.

8. "Thou shalt not steal." The Sixth Commandment according to English reckoning. See January, note 11.

9. A copy of the letter from Oglethorpe to Boltzius, dated 3 November 1739, is in Candler, ed., *Col. Rec. Ga.* XXII, pt. II, 338.

10. Barker was dismissed soon afterwards because of the testimony of his German servants.

11. See June, note 26.

12. For James Habersham. See entry for 10 October.

13. See Hugh Rose's report in Candler, ed., *Col. Rec. Ga.* II, 444. His failure and recalcitrance somewhat exonerate the previous surveyor, Noble Jones.

14. *Ein dauerhafter s. h. Schweine-Stall.* The *s. h.* is unexplained; Might it possibly mean *Scheiss Haus*?

15. See June, note 23.

16. East Prussia, where most of the Salzburger exiles went, lay outside the Holy Roman Empire, for which reason the Elector of Brandenburg, although only a margrave in the Empire, could be "King of Prussia."

17. It was no coincidence that Oglethorpe had sent the Salzburgers a trained midwife. See entry for 22 September.

18. It is possible that the name Gotthilf also honored Gotthilf August Francke, the "Reverend Father" of the Georgia Salzburgers.

19. See entry for 17 November.

20. Boltzius was not convincing when he said that the Salzburgers would not consider the land their own. He should have argued that Abercorn Creek, as it was called in English, was a creek and not a river.

21. Samuel Wragg seems to have profited from his traffic in indentured Germans, because on 11 May 1737 the Trustees had resolved "That the Trustees will give to Mr. Wragg six Guineas Sterling per Head for Eighty foreign Servants to be delivered in Georgia from Rotterdam provided None be under twelve Years of Age or above Forty" (Candler, ed., *Col. Rec. Ga.* II, 198). The Trustees ordered that £200 be paid him on 12 April 1738 when the servants reached Tybee (*ibid.*, 229). He was part owner of the *London Merchant* (*ibid.*, 126). "Lambton" was probably Richard Lambton, who died in 1768; see *South Carolia Historical and Genealogical Magazine* 28 (1927):220.

22. Despite their barbarity, Oglethorpe hired far more Indians than the Spaniards did. He too described the murders on 16 November but failed to mention that the Spaniards were Indians (Candler, ed., *Col. Rec. Ga.* XXII, pt. II, 266).

23. Once subdued by Boltzius, Pichler became docile and won his favor, like the lost sheep that is worth a hundred who have not strayed. In due time he was appointed captain of the rangers, and later constable.

24. *Corpus Evangelicorum*, a Protestant caucus at the diet of Regensburg.

DECEMBER

1. "Contrition, remorse."

2. Magdalena Gebhard. See entry for 10 December.

3. The "younger" Zoberbiller must have been Bartholomäus (as opposed to the old father who died in Purysburg), rather than the son Sebastian, since the person in question is apparently a minister of the gospel. Bartholomäus later became the leader of the established church in Georgia.

4. This was Captain and Judge Lindner (Urlsperger, ed., *Ausführliche Nachricht, Achte Continuation*, p. 1060).

5. This would appear to be Johann Schwarzwaelder, progenitor of many Blackwelders.

6. Elisabeth Held. See entry for 11 December.

7. The father's name was Philip Gephart, a farmer aged 45, whose wife Martha was 43 (see Appendix IV).

8. Egmont's list gives the father's name as Condrit, which must be an error for Conried or Konrad. He was a weaver, aged 52, and his wife Elisabeth was 53, the son Hans Michael was 23, and the daughter Elisabeth was 17. The ages given are for 1738 (see Appendix IV).

9. The entries for 12–14 December have been deleted, perhaps because they related the sin atoned for on 16 December.

10. Mrs. Pichler.

11. See August, note 19.

12. "The divine market-place," here perhaps humorous for "church."

13. It is hard to see why Urlsperger suppressed Mrs. Kalcher's name this time.

14. Boltzius is not concerned with her virginity, he is merely alluding to the wise virgins of Matthew 25.

15. See February, note 7.

16. Regrettably the surviving records go back only to 1756. See May, note 22.

17. In the 18th century "perverted" (*verkehrt*) meant "turned from God," the opposite of "converted."

18. Boltzius is inconsistent. If it was really so hard just to accompany the surveyor, then the surveyor should not have been blamed for his failure.

19. "Glory to God alone."

APPENDIXES

1. Urlsperger, *Ausführliche Nachricht, Fünfte Continuation*, pp. 2587–89.

2. Grimmiger.

3. Urlsperger, *Ausführliche Nachricht, Vierte Continuation*, pp. 2307–12.

4. University of Georgia Libraries, MSS Collection, Egmont Papers, Additional, items 2 & 3.

5. Surely Schneider.

6. Possibly these were independent sons of John Peter Shantze, below.

7. Waldhauer.

8. Heinrich.

9. Surely Johann Schmidt.

10. "Walset is a good planter, has a large Family, came at his own Expense from Germany." Oglethorpe to the Trustees, 29 December 1739, in Candler, ed., *Col. Rec. Ga.* XXII, pt. II, 292. Walset may be an error for the common German name Walser.

11. Ulrich. A popular name among the Swiss and South Germans.

12. Probably Schönbacher, written according to Swabian phonology.

13. This name does not appear to be German; if it is, then it must be very corrupted.

14. Schlechtermann. Survivors of this unfortunate family wrote their names as Slechterman, Sletterman, Sleighterman, Slittman, etc.

15. Probably Conried.

16. Possibly Michael Schneider.

17. This woman seems to have been the reality behind the name "Kunegunda Knowart."

18. This must be the "Shatz" who served as foreman for the Germans at St. Simons, even though he knew "not one word of English." See Candler, ed., *Col. Rec. Ga.* V, 283; also XXII, pt. II, 353.

19. Urlsperger, *Ausführliche Nachricht, Sechste Continuation*, pp. 359–66.

20. Urlsperger has erroneously given the name as "Seiter," instead of Reiter.

21. Urlsperger has "Sottenberger."

Index

Note: For a listing of Salzburgers and other inhabitants of Ebenezer, including indentured servants, during the years 1734–38, *see* pp. 325–28, 329–30, 333.